Caesarea Maritima gold coin hoard excavated by JECM in 1993.

THE JOINT EXPEDITION TO

CAESAREA MARITIMA

EXCAVATION REPORTS

EDITORS FOR THE SERIES

ROBERT J. BULL
OLIN J. STORVICK

American Schools of Oriental Research

The Joint Expedition to Caesarea Maritima
Excavation Reports

Joseph A. Greene, ASOR Editor

Robert J. Bull
Olin J. Storvick, Series Editors

Volume VI
The Coins and the Hellenistic, Roman and Byzantine Economy of Palestine

By
Jane DeRose Evans
With a Preface by Robert J. Bull

The Coins and the Hellenistic, Roman and Byzantine Economy of Palestine

By

Jane DeRose Evans

with a Preface by Robert J. Bull

THE AMERICAN SCHOOLS OF ORIENTAL RESEARCH • BOSTON, MA

THE COINS AND THE HELLENISTIC, ROMAN AND BYZANTINE ECONOMY OF PALESTINE

By

Jane DeRose Evans
With a Preface by Robert J. Bull

ISBN 0-89757-074-X

Library of Congress Cataloging-in-Publication Data

Evans, Jane DeRose, 1956-
The coins and the Hellenistic, Roman, and Byzantine economy of Palestine / by Jane DeRose Evans ; with a preface by Robert J. Bull.
p. cm. -- (The joint expedition to Caesarea Maritima excavation reports ; v. 6)
Includes bibliographical references and index.
ISBN 0-89757-074-X (alk. paper)
1. Coins, Ancient--Palestine. 2. Coins, Greek--Palestine. 3. Coins, Roman--Palestine. 4. Coins, Byzantine--Palestine. 5. Caesarea (Israel)--Antiquities. 6. Excavations (Archaeology)--Israel--Caesarea. 7. Palestine--Antiquities. 8. Palestine--History--70-638. 9. Palestine--Economic conditions. I. Title.

CJ1375.E93 2006
933--dc22

2006021666

Printed in the United States of America on acid-free paper

For
JAMES F. DEROSE

Father
Friend
and Mentor

Cover design by Carlson Bull.

The coin on the cover is the reverse of a coin minted in Caesarea Maritima between 161 and 180, with an obverse of the empress Faustina. The reverse depicts a turetted Tyche, dressed in a short chiton and sword, standing left, with her right foot on a prow. In her right hand she holds the bust of an emperor and in the left a flagless vexillum; below to her left is the upper body of Sebastos, the harbor. The inscription reads:
COL(onia) PRIM(a) FL(avia) AVG(usta) CAESAREA.
The coin is shown at approximately twice life size.

Frontispiece: Caesarea Maritima gold hoard,
as photographed in Caesarea Maritima.
Photograph by Dr. Vivian Bull,
digitally enhanced by Carlson Bull.

Contents

Preface

In the summer of 1971, the Joint Expedition to Caesarea Maritima (JECM) began archaeological excavation in the dune sand that has for centuries covered the remains of the city of Caesarea, the former port and capital of Palestine. The Expedition was endorsed by the American Schools of Oriental Research, licensed by Dr. Avraham Biran, Director of the Department of Antiquities of the State of Israel, and was directed by Professor Robert J. Bull of Drew University. A workforce of volunteers, primarily faculty and students from twenty-four American and Canadian universities, seminaries and colleges, began what was to become a long-term effort to recover the stratigraphic history of Caesarea, to gather evidence of the street plan of the city, and to probe the course of Caesarea's Herodian Wall. This inquiry continued for twelve full excavation sessions between 1971 and 1987 and for limited periods of work in the summers of 1990, 1992, 1993, and 1995. During that time, JECM undertook excavation in 115 Areas, the majority of which were located between the shoreline of the Mediterranean Sea and the semicircular curve of the Herodian (Roman) city wall. Approximately 2000 volunteers and staff served with JECM: as members of excavation teams at Caesarea, as members of support teams from the Drew Institute for Archaeological Research (DIAR), or as technical and advisory personnel sent from several of the academic institutions associated with JECM.

Before attempting to excavate in the sands that cover much of ruined Caesarea, JECM undertook a surface survey of the central sand-covered areas within the limits of Caesarea's Roman city wall. The survey yielded a few broken, battered, and corroded artifacts, among which were twenty-nine corroded coins and coin fragments. All metal objects recovered in the survey evidenced some degree of corrosive damage, but the copper coins were, by far, the most severely damaged. All copper and copper-alloy coins found were encased in a dark green residue composed mostly of copper oxide, copper carbonate, and copper silicate, a combination and condition traditionally referred to as weathering products. Such products occur when copper is immersed over time in sea water or in wet sea sand. The amount of residue found on the coins varied in thickness from a coating that was less than half the thickness of the flan of the coin to an accumulation of residue that was approximately twice the thickness of the original coin.

The removal of residue from the coins for the purpose of identifying them proved to be a delicate and difficult procedure. The use of a sharp edge to scrape residue from the surface of a coin or the use of a soft metal brush to abrade the residue (however gently) ran the danger of damaging the faint features retained on a coin's surface. As a precautionary measure, JECM's survey coins were cleaned by immersing them in a very mild acid solution, then drenching them in clean water and, in turn, vigorously rubbing them with a soft dry cloth. Unfortunately, when all of the survey coins had been cleaned by this slow and somewhat awkward process, it was discovered that none of the retrieved coins retained sufficient surface detail to allow them to be accurately identified.

At Caesarea, sand blown about by the light winds of summer was a minor inconvenience for the excavator. But the storm-driven winds of winter (or of several winters) blew quantities of sand across the remains of Caesarea, altering the patterns of the ever-shifting dune sands and piling up ridges of drift-sand that on occasion lay athwart proposed digging-areas and had to be cleared away. In such cases, a bulldozer was used to remove (as carefully as possible) the realigned dune sand. JECM very seldom used bulldozers, because of their cost, but more importantly, because of the damage they did to the excavation area below the sand or the debris that was being removed.

The Joint Expedition found it almost impossible to maintain stratigraphic control in the sand of a standing sand dune and only temporary control, at best, in most damp or wet sands. Two or three days of hot Mediterranean sun changed moist or wet sand into dry, loose sand and thereby set up conditions that could lead to balk collapse. It became, therefore, general practice for JECM to clear excavation areas of loose sand and then undertake stratigraphic excavation in the lower compacted sands or in the deeper earth and rubble layers that covered much of the structural remains of the city. Few coins were found in the overburden of sand and, if found, their condition was similar to that of the coins recovered in the early surface survey. It was in the deeper layers of compacted sand (frequently moist) and in the darker earth layers encountered beneath the compacted sand that the majority of the excavated coins were recovered.

It was the original intention of the Joint Expedition to dig a series of excavation squares along a north–south line that would be extended from the North Gate of Caesarea's Herodian city wall to the centrally located remains of the Temple to Roma and Augustus and beyond, to the probable location of the South Gate of the Herodian city wall. It was assumed that such a line of excavation squares would follow the course of the *cardo maximus,* the major north–south street of Roman Caesarea. It was probable that the *cardo maximus* itself was a part of the *Via Maris,* the major north–south Roman land route between Egypt and Asia Minor. The Joint Expedition also laid out a second series of excavation squares in such a manner that the line of squares ran perpendicular to the *cardo maximus* at its mid-point and proximate to the remains of the Temple of Roma and Augustus. The second line of excavation squares extended from the point of its intersection with the *cardo maximus* eastwards across the remains of the city to the arc of the Herodian city wall.

The purposed extended excavation plan was not fully realized by the end of the dig in 1987, but a considerable portion of it was completed. Work in the 115 excavation squares yielded considerable new evidence of the orthogonal street plan of the city and the relationship of street organization to the harbor. The wall of Herod that encompassed the city of Caesarea in a somewhat flattened semicircle was centered on the Temple to Roma and Augustus and was traced, partly uncovered, and dated. The course of the *cardo maximus* between the North Gate and the South Gate in the Herodian city wall was determined and put on plan. The sequence of excavated balks, that is, the sides of the excavated squares, laid out in line, presented the stratigraphy of the city as it extended from its center to the limits of the Herodian city. As a result of this method of artifact retrieval, pottery and coins were gathered from across the length and breadth of the city and not just from one zone or quarter of the city.

From the beginning of stratigraphic excavation at Caesarea in 1971, JECM recovered large numbers of copper and copper-alloy coins, the majority of which were covered with a heavy corrosive coating, as noted above. JECM was unable to obtain (or afford) a resident numismatist who could oversee the cleaning, registration, and dating of the coins at the site. As a result, JECM found itself without enough help to tend the coins as they appeared. Members of the JECM staff and student volunteers were called out of the field in order to help with the coin cleaning. One of the first persons to help with the coins was Peter Lampinen, a student at Drew University and a member of the Drew University Excavation Team. Peter took the lead in organizing the coin cleaning effort and very quickly demonstrated his ability, not only in the cleaning of coins, but also his ability to identify and date them. Aware of Peter's demonstrated ability, the Director of the Excavation invited Peter to join the JECM staff. He accepted the offer and for more than two decades Peter Lampinen served as numismatist for the Joint Expedition to Caesarea Maritima. Whenever JECM went into the field at Caesarea, a coin lab was set up for Peter Lampinen's use. He, like all staff members of JECM, could expect no salary, but was given the full use of an office and small lab at the Drew Institute for Archaeological Research, located on the campus of Drew University. There, Peter worked diligently, full time when he could, part time when he wanted to. He did an excellent job over the course of more than twenty years, during which time he cleaned, recorded, and dated, with few exceptions, the coins contained in this volume. It was under Peter Lampinen's patient and persistent leadership that a new order of numismatic cleaning, identification and care came into being in the field at Caesarea and in the coin lab at Drew University. Not the least of Peter's accomplishments was his use and development of chemical and electrolytic processes that could handle twenty to thirty coins at one time. Meticulous in the care and dating of coins, Peter was somewhat disinclined to write about the excavated coins from Caesarea in semi-annual or annual reports, in spite of repeated invitations to him to do so.

It was well known in numismatic circles that Peter Lampinen had cleaned and dated almost all of the coins excavated by JECM at Caesarea and had worked on their history in the lab at the Drew Institute for Archaeological Research and elsewhere for almost two decades. So it was, based on Peter's long and creative service with JECM, that the Director of the Joint Expedition to Caesarea asked Peter if he would prepare for publication the proposed JECM coin report, Volume VI in the series of final reports. Much to JECM's surprise and sorrow, Peter Lampinen said that he could not write the volume. Repeated requests and efforts to have him reconsider were of no avail. Professor Bull, therefore, asked Peter to turn in the Caesarea coins, his prepared notes and photographic material on the coins. This Peter did, and both coins and notes were deposited in the coin safe at the Drew Institute for Archaeological Research. In a last word to Peter, Professor Bull thanked him for the enormous amount of time and effort he had given to the Joint Expedition and told him that JECM would acknowledge his long service in Volume VI, when that volume was written and published.

With Peter Lampinen's decision not to write the coin volume, the Director of JECM was left with a major problem. He had to find a person with archaeological experience and a working knowledge of Hellenistic, Roman, and Byzantine coinage. A search was begun and through the help of members of ASOR and others, Dr. Jane DeRose Evans of Temple University was recommended to JECM as a person who could undertake the difficult job of marshaling the Hellenistic, Roman, and Byzantine coinage of Caesarea Maritima and setting that coinage in the economic context of the Palestine of its day. Professor Bull contacted Dr. Evans and told her the story of the Caesarea Maritima coins and of our need to acknowledge Peter Lampinen's long work on them. He further assured Dr. Evans that if she completed Caesarea's first coin volume and the manuscript passed ASOR's critical peer review, her name would appear as author. After some consultation with family and friends, Dr. Evans told JECM that she could and would write the manuscript for Volume VI. When Dr. Jane Evans accepted the challenge of writing the coin volume, the Caesarea corpus of coins along with Peter Lampinen's notes were put in her care. Within two years she had written the full manuscript for JECM's Volume VI, "The Coins and the Hellenistic, Roman and Byzantine Economy of Palestine."

A difficulty arose, however, when Dr. Evans reported that there were no photographic negatives or prints of the Caesarea coins in the mass of coin material that Peter Lampinen had turned over to JECM, and which was subsequently turned over to her. Early in his work on the Caesarea coins, Peter Lampinen, while working in his lab at the Drew Institute for Archaeological Research asked that JECM have the Caesarea coins photographed by a professional photographer. JECM did so, and as a result Peter would present quality photographs of the coins to members of JECM and others who were writing reports or giving lectures. But when Dr. Evans needed photographs for her research and publication the Caesarea coin negatives could not be found. The only solution to the problem was to re-photograph the Caesarea coin corpus, or short of that, re-photograph those coins that Dr. Evans deemed necessary for the completion of the volume.

In the summer of 1992, a small JECM team of volunteers from Concordia College, under the leadership of Professor Olin Storvick of Concordia College, accepted the invitation of Dr. Avner Raban and Professor Kenneth Holum, Co-directors of The Combined Caesarea Expedition (CCE) to return to Field G and complete unfinished work in that Field. Professor Olin Storvick, as JECM Field Supervisor, and his team were able to clear, clean and draw the deteriorating balks in Field G, but were unable to examine much of the stone structure that was proximate and probably related to the peristyle building partially uncovered by JECM in 1987.

In 1993, a JECM team of seven students, again under the supervision of Professor Storvick of Concordia College, returned to Field G with the expectation of gaining a clearer understanding of the peristyle complex and the nature of the structures located to the west of it. Excavating in Area 25 of Field G, the JECM team uncovered a blue and white patterned mosaic floor that was generally in bad shape with open spaces appearing through the *tesserae*. The damage to the mosaic floor appeared to have been caused by the impact of heavy stone fall. Some loose mosaic *tesserae* were cleared away, but in order to preserve as much of the mosaic as possible, a probe of the stratigraphy under an open section of the mosaic floor was examined. In a pit, dug prior to the laying of the mosaic floor, there was found a portion of the upper half of a Roman grinding mill of a type called *mulos onikos*. The mill stone, made of basalt, had lost some of its features, but had retained the socket or opening, located in the upper section of the mill, that formed the holder into which a wooden bar or small timber would have been inserted. Traditionally, a donkey would have been hitched to the timber and constrained to follow a circular course around the mill, causing the upper stone to turn and grind grain poured in the top opening of the mill.

It was a student of Professor Storvick's G25 team who, while excavating earth from around the broken mill, discovered the opening or socket in the upper mill stone. Attempting to retrieve a sample of the earth contained in the socket, he put his hand into the opening and, upon withdrawing it, found his hand full of gold coins. A total of 99 gold *solidi* were found in the mill socket. The mill opening had served as a "safe" for the coins and had helped preserve them in their pristine or near pristine condition. The 99 gold *solidi* in the hoard all date from the last half of the fourth century C.E., and represent the largest stratigraphically defined gold hoard ever found in Israel.

Professor Storvick and his team decided that they would keep silent about the hoard until it was registered, recorded, and turned over to the Department of Antiquities. Professor Storvick and Professor Bull carried the fortune in gold to their room in the Excavation Headquarters. They then tried to contact Dr. Avner Raban, only to find that he was out of the country on a lecture tour. Efforts to find Professor Holum also failed. Professors Storvick and Bull then took the hoard of 99 gold coins to Peter Lampinen, who had become numismatist for CCE and who was working in the Excavation Headquarters. They asked Peter if he would date and record the 99 *solidi* in order to have Aaron Levin, the CCE photographer, photograph the coins in color and in black and white. Peter began at once and did his usual excellent work dating and recording the coins. Professor Storvick and Professor Bull, the next day, helped Aaron Levin set up his lights and cameras in the only place available, namely, the dorm room where the coins were kept. Aaron Levin worked through the late afternoon and into the early evening completing both a color and black and white record of the 99 *solidi*.

Professors Storvick and Bull had resolved to get the coins, as soon as they were dated, registered, and photographed, into the hands of the Department of Antiquities in Jerusalem. Before they began that journey, however, they were informed that Dr. Joseph Patrich, a representative of the Department of Antiquities, was in Caesarea and could receive the coins. A place of meeting was agreed upon and Dr. Patrich and several members of CCE, JECM, and others crowded into the dorm room of Professors Storvick and Bull in the Headquarters Building to witness the transfer of the 99 *solidi* from JECM to Dr. Patrich. The 99 coins were displayed on a table in the dorm room along with the basalt "safe" in which they were found. Dr. Patrich was invited to count and/or examine the coins, but thought it not necessary. He did sign a receipt of acceptance on behalf of the Department of Antiquities for the 99 *solidi* and took with him both the coins and the basalt "safe." A short time later, Dr. Patrich displayed the coins and the "safe" to the archaeological communities and others at Caesarea, and at the same time Professor Olin Storvick was asked to recount the story of their discovery.

Since the discovery of the gold hoard occurred at the very end of the 1993 session, and the JECM team had drawn the Field G balks and read the 1993 pottery, the end of JECM's field work at Caesarea was at hand. The drawings were finished on site in 1995. At the last moment, however, a message arrived from *The Biblical Archaeologist*, requesting of JECM a short article about the excavation of the 99 gold *solidi* with pictures of the find site and pictures of the coins. Professors Storvick and Bull opted to write the article jointly. They sought pictures of the location, Field G Area 25, where the coins were found from the expedition photographer, Aaron Levin, and pictures of the coins from the expedition numismatist, Peter Lampinen. Peter said that the color photographs of the *solidi* had not been developed and that he had only a few black and white prints of the coins available. Professors Storvick and Bull took with them black and white photographs of the site and coins and lamented the fact that no color photographs of the gold hoard would be available for the first publication of the coin discovery. Another message from *The Biblical Archaeologist* stated that they had space for a single good color photograph of the gold hoard coins. Dr. Vivian A. Bull had taken a good color photograph of the 99 coins shown piled together when they were first displayed publicly at Caesarea and she offered that photograph for our use. So it was that an article, "The Gold Coin Hoard at Caesarea" was published in *The Biblical Archaeologist* (vol. 56 [1933], pp. 116–120), with black and white photographs of the site and single coins, but with a single full color photograph of the piled 99 gold *solidi* displayed on the back cover of the last issue of *The Biblical Archaeologist.*

After the 1993 archaeological session was over, the JECM team returned to the United States and began again the arduous task of writing and preparing final reports for publication. Because the discovery of the 99 *solidi* gold hoard had created considerable interest in numismatic and archaeological circles, Professor Bull asked Professor Kenneth Holum, Co-director with Dr. Avner Raban of the Combined Caesarea Expeditions, for copies of the color photographs of the 99 gold *solidi.* Repeated requests were then made over the course of several years by JECM for color photographic copies of the 99 *solidi.* In the interim, Peter Lampinen was able to publish the entire corpus of coins in black and white along with his excellent notes in *The Journal of Roman Archaeology* (Supp. Series 35. Caesarea Papers II, pp. 368–388). Professor Bull renewed his request for color photographs of the 99 gold *solidi.* Professor Holum, Co-Director of CCE, informed JECM that no copies of the colored slides of the gold *solidi* had been made and that the making of copies was expensive, but it could be done. Professor Bull replied that JECM would gladly pay for color copies of the gold coins, and did so with the generous support of a donor. Thus it was in 2003, that JECM was able to buy full color slides of the gold *solidi* that it had dug up in Caesarea almost a decade before and to begin preparation of them for publication.

As first steps toward publication, Camper Bull, a son of the Director of the Expedition, scanned the obverse and the reverse of all 99 color images of the gold *solidi,* thereby producing 198 digitized depictions of the coins. Professor Storvick and Professor Bull initially examined the scanned images of the coins at the diameter of the original *solidus,* but discovered that when a digitized image of a *solidus* was enlarged twenty times, the fine detail of the coin, the inscriptions, and the symbols came into clear view. In a few cases, it could be seen that certain details on the surface of the coin (obverse or reverse) had been overlooked or not recorded when the coins were first identified. As a result of close examination of the enlarged images of the *solidi,* they were able to contribute a short list of corrections and omissions to the earlier definitions of the 99 gold *solidi* excavated at Caesarea. In another step toward publication, Carlson Bull, son of the Director, undertook design and layout of the 198 color images of the coins.

This very brief review of the history of the coins excavated by JECM at Caesarea would not be complete without expressing our sincere appreciation to the hundreds of volunteers and staff who excavated thousands of coins at Caesarea over the course of years and then cleaned, registered and helped date them in order to prepare the coins for publication.

This preface must necessarily contain a sincere word of thanks to Professor Jane DeRose Evans of Temple University for her willingness to marshal the mass of material represented in this volume and to mold it all into a manuscript worthy of publication by ASOR

Many other individuals and organizations contributed to the completion of this work: ASOR Publications, including successive chairs of the ASOR Committee on Publications, the Directors of ASOR Publications, past and present, the present and former Editors of the ASOR Archaeological Reports Series, and the anonymous reviewers of this manuscript; Olin J. Storvick, Member, JECM Publication Committee; Concordia College; Drew University; Temple University and The Department of Antiquities of the State of Israel; Carlson Bull, for digitizing photos, and Susanne Wilhelm, who set up a beautiful manuscript.

Robert J. Bull,

Director,

Joint Expedition to Caesarea Maritima

Acknowledgements

When Dr. Robert J. Bull contacted me to ask if I would be interested in analyzing the coins from the Joint Expedition to Caesarea Maritima, I had no idea how interesting the project would be. I am much indebted to him for his confidence in me and his support during the writing. Warm thanks are also due to Dr. Olin J. Storvick, for his careful readings of the manuscript and his thoughtful discussions with me about Caesarea and the JECM work there. I am grateful for Peter Lampinen's hard work of cleaning and preliminary identification of the coins, and drawing up the field inventories. I have seen all but 130 or so of the excavation coins and can attest to his accurate eye, especially on coins so badly treated by the wind, waves, and sand of Caesarea. Beth Peckman made the photographs of the coins, and the late Andrea Powers digitized them and helped me recover after my computer and back-up diskettes were stolen from my office.

Several scholars have been kind enough to review my work and so point me in directions I would not have otherwise taken, or saved me from missteps: R. Bland, T. V. Buttrey, W. Hahn, and the anonymous readers of the manuscript. W. E. Metcalf discussed problems with me and provided a close reading of the entire manuscript at an early stage; his judgment was especially appreciated because of his work on the coins excavated from Carthage. The remaining errors are, of course, mine alone.

Temple University supplied a study leave to allow me to work on the manuscript; I also received a grant from Temple to cover the costs of the photography. Dr. Bull was kind enough to cover the expenses of recovering the lost manuscript and digitize the photos.

July 2003

List of Figures

List of Tables

Abbreviations

AASOR	*Annual of the American Schools of Oriental Research*
ACNAC	*Ancient Coins in North American Collections*, New York, NY: American Numismatic Society
ADAJ	*Annual of the Department of Antiquities, Jordan*
AJC	Meshorer 1982
AJN	*American Journal of Numismatics*
ANSMN	*American Numismatic Society Museum Notes*
Ant	Josephus, *Antiquities*
BA	*Biblical Archaeologist*
BASOR	*Bulletin of the American Schools of Oriental Research*
BMC	*British Museum Catalogue*
Carthage 1975	Buttrey 1976
Carthage 1978	W. Metcalf 1982
CH	*Royal Numismatic Society, Coin Hoards*
CNP	*Corpus Nummorum Palaestinensium*
de mort. pers.	Lactantius, *De Mortibus Persecutorum*
DOC I	Bellinger 1966
DOC II	Grierson 1967
ESI	*Excavations and Surveys in Israel* (English-language version of *Hadashot Arkhe'ologiyot*)
GIC	Howgego 1985
HA	Procopius, *Historia Anecdota*
HE	Eusebius, *Historia Ecclesiastica*
IEJ	*Israel Exploration Journal*
INJ	*Israel Numismatic Journal*
JRA	*Journal of Roman Archaeology*
JRS	*Journal of Roman Studies*
JW	Josephus, *Jewish War*
LA	*Liber annuus (Studium Biblicum Franciscanum)*
LRBC	Carson, Hill and Kent 1965

Mart. Pal.	Eusebius, *On the Martyrs of Palestine*
MIB	Hahn 1973–1981
NC	*Numismatic Chronicle*
NH	Pliny, *Natural History*
NumCirc	*Numismatic Circular*
PEQ	*Palestine Exploration Quarterly*
POxy	*Oxyrhynchus Papyri*
RIC 1	Sutherland 1984 (*Roman Imperial Coinage,* vol. 1)
RIC 2	Mattingly and Sydenham 1926 (*Roman Imperial Coinage,* vol. 2)
RIC 3	Mattingly and Sydenham 1930 (*Roman Imperial Coinage,* vol. 3)
RIC 4.2	Mattingly, Sydenham and Sutherland 1936 (*Roman Imperial Coinage,* vol. 4 part 2)
RIC 4.3	Mattingly, Sydenham and Sutherland 1949 (*Roman Imperial Coinage,* vol. 4 part 3)
RIC 5.1	Webb 1927 (*Roman Imperial Coinage,* vol. 5 part 1)
RIC 5.2	Webb 1933 (*Roman Imperial Coinage,* vol. 5 part 2)
RIC 6	Sutherland 1973 (*Roman Imperial Coinage,* vol. 6)
RIC 7	Bruun 1966 (*Roman Imperial Coinage,* vol. 7)
RIC 8	Kent 1981 (*Roman Imperial Coinage,* vol. 8)
RIC 9	Pearce 1933 (*Roman Imperial Coinage,* vol. 9)
RIC 10	Kent 1994 (*Roman Imperial Coinage,* vol. 10)
RIN	*Rivista Italiana di Numismatica*
RPC 1	Burnett, Amandry and Ripollès 1992 (*Roman Provincial Coinage* I)
RPC 2	Burnett, Amandry and Carradice 1999 (*Roman Provincial Coinage* II)
SNR	*Schweizerische Numismatische Rundschau*
TJC	Meshorer 2001

INTRODUCTION

The army of Mu'awiya, frustrated by the fortification walls built by Byzantine emperors to protect the city of Caesarea Maritima, finally took the city by stealth, in the year we reckon 640 or 641 C.E. It seems that Caesarea was not destroyed by the invaders – it was far too large a city and the Muslim army was too small to wreak much havoc. But the city began a slide into obscurity, as people left and buildings and neighborhoods were abandoned. Roman and Byzantine Caesarea became a quarry for the Muslim builders, or raw materials for fertilizer and mortar. Yet in some ways, life returned to normal, with Muslim rulers minting familiar-looking coins, soldiers stationed on watchtowers on the coast, and worship resuming on the site, though the churches of the Byzantine culture were replaced with a mosque.

The Byzantines, eager to have this port on the coast, returned to Caesarea in 685 and sacked the city, but were not allowed to stay long, as Caliph 'Abd al-Malik retook the town in 690. Such was the pattern of life in Caesarea for another three hundred years, it seems, though life still was bounded by the strong fortification walls, centered on the mosque built on the site of the great Temple to Rome and Augustus, and fed and watered possibly by the Roman aqueducts (more certainly by the new cisterns and wells) and farms reestablished outside the walls. Industry flourished, and so did tourism, encouraged by the Fatimid rulers, of Christians coming to the Holy Land.

Christian visitors of another sort arrived north of Caesarea in 1099 with Godfrey of Bouillon. They were the army of the First Crusade, intent on recovering Jerusalem from "infidel" hands. Caesarea was briefly spared by treaties, but fell to the army lead by William Embriaco. The mosque was converted into a church honoring St. Peter, and the Crusaders rescued a cup from the mosque that they valued as the Holy Grail. But the Crusader kingdom only lasted until 1187, when Saladin's lieutenants seized the city and razed its fortifications. The city changed hands several times over the course of the next generation, and was largely uninhabited.

St. Louis, as Louis IX of France came to be called, is said to have personally helped lay the stones of the still impressive Crusader fortification walls in 1251–1252, yet the days of the Crusaders in Caesarea were numbered. Surrounded and overwhelmed by stone-throwing artillery, the Frankish defenders of the citadel were allowed to leave the city forever in 1265 by the Muslim sultan Baybar. In the next generation, the Muslim rulers destroyed much of the Crusader fortress, to prevent Crusaders from obtaining a strong point if they decided to invade. The sands from the six hundred years of abandonment still blanket every trench opened by modern archaeologists.

Much of this history of Caesarea is known to us from military chronicles and even poetry – and from the archaeological work, which began in the 1950s. It is the earlier periods, as illuminated by the coins from the Joint Expeditions to Caesarea Maritima, that are the focus of this study.

The earliest phase of the settlement on the site that became Caesarea is controversial. Some scholars suggest that Strato's Tower, mentioned in an Egyptian document (P. Cairo Zeno 59004) as a settlement with an anchorage or even a harbor, was the forerunner of the Herodian city. This settlement was named after the ruler of Sidon, and thus was a Phoenician city. If our information is correct, then the settlement began in the fourth century B.C.E., when Strato ruled Sidon. Strato may have been interested in the site, for it had long been known as a convenient harbor for ships plying the coast. This same Egyptian document records the arrival of Zeno to Strato's Tower in 259 B.C.E., during his mission for Ptolemy II Philadelphus to inspect the pharaoh's holdings in the area. The extent and type of settlement that existed in the Hellenistic period is highly controversial as well, but it is clear that the harbor was in use. During the chaos of the second half of the third and the second century B.C.E., a local tyrant named Zoilus ruled Strato's Tower. He was thrown out by the Hasmonaean general and king Alexander Yannai (Jannaeus) in 103 B.C.E., after which the city remained part of the Jewish state.

The city that was renamed Caesarea (we have added the appellation Maritima to distinguish it from other Caesareas) blossomed in the Herodian period. Herod the Great (r. 40–4 B.C.E.) decided to build a city and harbor worthy of a king. Josephus (*JW* 3.408–15 and *Ant* 15.331–41) tells us that between 22 and 10 B.C.E. Herod began construction of a huge harbor, a palace, a Temple to Rome and Augustus, a marketplace, an amphitheater, a theater, and perhaps a wall (which was not mentioned by Josephus) all arranged – in good Hellenistic fashion – on a grid plan. The city housed a mixed population of Greek-speaking pagans and Jews, veterans of Herod's army and Samaritan farmers.

After Herod's death, the city was ruled briefly by Herod's son as *ethnarch*, or subject king, and, for a longer time, by procurators, Roman officials appointed by the emperor. The procurators (or governors) probably spent much of their term housed in the palace of Herod, and stationed troops in the city. They increased the Roman aspect of the city by building more temples to the pagan gods or emperors, and introduced Latin inscriptions (most famously, the inscription put up by Pontius Pilate that was reused in the theater, but also on coins). It was from the harbor at Caesarea that Paul began his final journey to Rome, after being held in the governor's palace for slightly less than two years. The Revolt of 66–70 C.E. began with the massacre of Jews by pagans in Caesarea, and the port functioned as an important military and resupply base throughout the war. Vespasian also left from the city to press his case to be appointed emperor in Rome.

The city's loyalty was rewarded by Vespasian and his son Titus by promoting the city to the rank of colony. Some inhabitants of the city thus became citizens with voting rights and were released from the poll tax; their security and economic future were established by the veterans who were settled in the fields outside the city. Caesarea essentially became a non-Jewish city, another city of the Roman Empire in the East. As such, the emperor Hadrian paid for the refurbishing and extension of the aqueducts, which surely fed those essentials for an urbanized Roman: fountains and baths, and possibly funded the hippodrome. Yet like the rest of the Empire, Caesarea fell on hard times in the third century, even if the city became a central location for influential early Christian teachers and writers like Origen and Eusebius. Since the governor still lived in Caesarea, it seems that the Christians in the city suffered severely during the persecutions of the mid-third to early-fourth centuries.

Yet the persecutions stopped and the economy recovered with the acceptance of Christianity by the emperor Constantine. Imperial money flowed into the region as the emperor and his family took an interest in the Holy Land. It seems that the population of Caesarea swelled, and fourth- and fifth-century building phases are found everywhere on the site. Some were richly appointed buildings, graced with mosaics and peristyles; the streets were newly repaved. But gone were the theaters and the amphitheater, relics of forms of entertainment that were no longer amusing; the temples to the pagan gods also disappeared, and were in some cases replaced with Christian churches. Although the fourth- and fifth-century phase of the building on the site of the Temple of Rome and Augustus remains controversial, certainly by the seventh century a large church, possibly in honor of the martyr Procopius, ruled the heights above the harbor.

The state of the harbor during the fourth and fifth centuries is also a problem that is still in the process of resolution, bringing modern geomorphological techniques to bear on the question. Procopius of Gaza tells us that in 502 the Emperor Anastasius repaired the harbor to once again allow ships to dock in Caesarea. But scholars have suggested that the region was prospering, or that the harbor was unusable long before Anastasius' time. Certainly, Caesarea remained the seat of civil authority for the region and retained a strong voice in ecclesiastical authority as well. The bishop who ruled Caesarea was the highest ranked bishop in all of Palestine, surpassing even the bishop of Jerusalem, until the mid-fifth century, when that city toppled Caesarea from its lofty perch. But her library of Christian writers remained pre-eminent, and was used by St.

Jerome and Procopius of Caesarea. Caesarea was also the seat of important Jewish scholarship, though there certainly was not a large number of Jews living in the city during the fourth through sixth centuries.

New imperial policies instituted by Justinian (527–565) imposed penalties on Jews and Samaritans. These policies came upon tensions already rife within the community, and the Samaritans revolted three times in the space of seventy years (484, 529/30, and 555). The last uprising was the most severe: all of Caesarea's churches were burnt, the governor was murdered, and the palace was plundered. When Justinian re-established control, he massacred or enslaved the Samaritan inhabitants of the area. This was the city that Mu'awiya conquered, a city already torn by religious strife, but rich with possibility.

The Joint Expeditions to Caesarea Maritima conducted excavations at the site over the course of seventeen years, from 1971–87, with study seasons in 1977, 1981, 1985, and 1986. Although most of the excavation awaits final publication, Robert J. Bull and a large team have already made preliminary results of their findings available to the archaeological community: Bull and Toombs 1972; Bull and Toombs 1973; Bull 1973; Bull 1974; Bull 1975; Humphrey 1975; Toombs 1978; Wiemkin and Holum 1981; Bull 1982; Bull, Krentz and Storvick 1986; Humphrey 1986: 477–91; Bull, Krentz, Storvick, and Spiro 1990; Vann 1992; Bull, Krentz, Storvick and Spiro 1994; and Lehman and Holum 2000. I owe a debt to Olin Storvick for rounding out the information (pers. comm.). For general histories of the city, the reader should consult Levine 1975a and 1975b; Foerster 1975; Bull 1982; Holum, Hohlfelder, Bull, and Raban 1988; Holum 1989; and Holum and Raban in Raban and Holum 1996.

The earliest areas opened by the JECM excavations were Fields A and B, to understand the network of Late Roman/Byzantine streets first uncovered by S. Yeivin in 1951 (see Fig. 1). Field C was also begun, to understand the area first probed by A. Negev, who found a large Late Roman building south of the Crusader city. In 1972, the excavators conducted probes of the large sewer (SP, for "sewer project"), whose three-foot-tall outlet is visible on the northern beach of Caesarea; the excavators suggested it was in use from the Roman into the Muslim period. Two smaller sewers were also explored and were dated to 330–614 C.E. The archaeologists found very few Roman remains, though they did find substantial fills that they attributed to Herodian building activity. They surmised that the later builders had largely removed the Roman structures to build anew. For the excavators, the Byzantine period begins in 330 C.E.; in this volume I use the term Late Roman for the period between 324 and 491 C.E., in keeping with the term used by numismatists. The end of the Byzantine period at Caesarea comes in 640/1. The reader should note this terminology, for it may cause confusion when switching between numismatic and archaeological texts.

The work in Field B uncovered a ramped road, at the top of which was a mosaic-paved court (where, it was later determined, the Tyche statue found in 1971 was originally erected), the remains of water pipes probably for fountains, and small shops off the mosaic court. This court was parallel in orientation and design to the paved court found by Yeivin, which was called, after later excavation in the Field, the "Byzantine Esplanade." In Field A, the impressive road that came out of Field B became an ordinary paved street, which led to an industrial area. The Late Roman building in Field C was an elaborate affair, paved with mosaics, with benches built along the walls; it was likely a civic building. This building phase was designated stratum 6, 330–614 C.E. (the "Main Byzantine" phase). Later use of the buildings in Fields A, B, and C showed that they were adapted for domestic use by being subdivided, and hearths, ovens and cisterns inserted (stratum 3, the Arab stratum), dated between 640/1 and the Crusader era. The stratum below this, stratum 4, showed evidence of burning. This the excavators attributed to the destruction of Caesarea in 640/1, dating stratum 4 to the period between 614 and 640/1. More recent work suggests that the destruction layer that was dated to ca. 614 (the brief Persian occupation) did not extend through the site, but that the site remained largely intact through the seventh century; so stratum 4, the destruction layer, was limited to the 640/1 campaign. The period just preceding it was designated stratum 5 (the "Final Byzantine" stratum), and dated 614–640/1. Thus, the sequence reads: main building phase between 330 and 614 (stratum 6); the era just preceding the destruction (stratum 5), 614—640/1; the destruction layer (stratum 4) in 640/1; subdivision into smaller, domestic units (stratum 3); the Crusader (stratum 2) and modern levels (stratum 1).

Work in 1973 uncovered more Roman/Late Roman buildings in Field C, including a third-century portico (the "Honorific Portico or Esplanade," also called the "U-shaped Building;" this stratum was designated stratum 7, or "Roman," and was dated from 10 B.C.E. to 330 C.E.). The portico was paved with marble slabs and furbished with honorary columns naming procurators; at least some were topped with sculptures, in a good Roman tradition. Underneath the Roman/Late Roman buildings a series of barrel-vaulted structures were discovered. They seem to have originally consisted of perhaps as many as one hundred vaults, one side of which fronted onto a street running parallel to the coast. The vaults were used for varying purposes over a long time. Vault 1 was in use at least by the mid-first century C.E., judging from the amphorae found inside; the excavators decided that the building was probably originally built in Herod's day for storage for the ships coming into the harbor. This vault proved to be especially interesting, since it was converted into a Mithraeum by the insertion of benches along the wall, painted decorations alluding to the rituals of the cult, and a sculpted medallion depicting Mithras slaying the bull.

In 1974, the excavators returned to the courts and streets of Field B to recover fragments and the base of the Tyche statue, and to the colonnade that was centered in the court. The paving was lifted and discovered to date to the sixth century; a further probe uncovered late third- to early fourth-century material. In Field C, work continued on the "Archive Building" (also known as the "Byzantine Public Record Building," now the "Imperial Revenue Building") and the vault complex. Three layers of mosaics were found in the Archive Building, dating from the late fifth or early sixth century, the fourth or fifth century, and possibly the third or fourth century. A sixth(?)-century bath, decorated with mosaic floors, was discovered in front of Vault 1. Further work inside Vault 1 suggested that the Mithraeum found in 1973 was the second phase of a Mithraeum here; the original phase dated to the second century, with a refurbishing in the late third century. Trenches were opened in the hippodrome, which prompted a readjustment of the dimensions of this structure. The date of its original construction is somewhat unclear, but can be put roughly between 150–300 C.E.; its floor was refurbished twice after the original construction, probably sometime in the fourth century, and the circus was abandoned and demolished in the early- to mid-sixth century C.E. The site was then used for small buildings until at least 640/1. The horse races mentioned by Josephus are now thought to have taken place in the amphitheatral hippo-stadium found on the modern beach by later excavations (Porath 1995).

Attention turned to the problematic dating of the eastern half of the high aqueduct. In 1975, Probe PA failed to find construction trenches, frustrating those who believed the aqueduct was built by Herod. Another probe (PB) in Field E sought to clarify the date and use of the "edificio Christiano" excavated by the Italian team in the 1960s. Later work in this area confirmed that the building was a villa dating to 550–640/1; no coins were found in the probe. Probes were also undertaken in Field C to clarify the street grid (PC, PW, west of Field C), as was Probe S (PS), which was placed in front of the vaults. Probe ST was placed in Field G to determine the date of the round towers; no coins were found in this probe.

In 1976, trenches along the wall in Field G revealed the foundation courses and trenches of Herod's city wall, about one third of a mile north of the harbor (beyond which the city expanded in the third through fifth centuries). Yet most of the work in Field G in 1978 concentrated on finding the occupation layers outside the wall. Continuing excavations in this area found pottery dated to 10 B.C.E.–100 C.E., but produced no structures, except for the substantial fortification wall, which excavators suggested belonged to the Herodian phase of the city. The domestic structures explored dated to 100–200 C.E.; they were somewhat reworked between 200 and 330 C.E. and again 330–450 C.E.

The area east of the Archive Building in Field C revealed a stylobate that bounded one side of an eighteen-foot-wide mosaic paving, which had three layers that were contemporary to those inside the Archive Building. A matching stylobate was discovered eighteen feet away, across a paved street, showing this to be a colonnaded street, a form very familiar in eastern cities. The *cardo* or north–south street (now not considered the Cardo Maximus, as first proposed, but called Cardo I West) debouched at the Herodian theater; it is dated to the fourth century, at the earliest, but is now thought to follow the Roman *cardo*, since the grid plan is aligned with the Herodian vaulted warehouses. The same year, the sewer system beneath the street was explored, and again appeared to date later than the Herodian city.

Fields K, M, and L were opened in the 1979 season, south of Field C. The trenches were placed along the Cardo I West and the intersections of the *decumani*. The excavations revealed that the sixth-century streets were a modification, as well as a rebuilding, of the Late Roman streets (dated by the excavators to ca. 200–330

C.E.); the buildings along the streets were interpreted as commercial or industrial in nature. Sewer outlets in Fields K and L were also explored. The "urban renewal" project was dated to about 525–550; it appears that the quarter was abandoned after the Muslim occupation of 640/1.

In 1980, work concentrated on Fields C and G, along the line of the street excavated in Field A in 1976. Further work was also done in the hippodrome and helped to date the wall, which later enclosed the structure, to the fourth or early fifth century. In Field C, excavators uncovered what they suggested was a *bouleuterion,* dated to the Roman period (10 B.C.E.–330 C.E.), and a small section of a Roman *cardo.* The Roman phase is difficult to find because of massive Late Roman/Early Byzantine (330–550 C.E.) rebuilding. The vaulted warehouses were retained intact, but the *bouleuterion*(?) was turned into a public fountain, and the "Honorific Portico" or U-shaped building was rebuilt as another type of public construction. Yet another phase of rebuilding, this one dated to 550–640/1 destroyed the earlier two phases; it was suggested that a large *agora* or *forum* replaced the buildings here. A potter's shop was inserted into another area of Field C. The streets in Field G also attested to a phase of reworking between 450–550 C.E., leading to a major renovation of the area between 550 and 640/1.

The excavators sought to understand the original street plan by opening new areas in Fields B, C, and G, and opening Field N in 1982. Work was also undertaken to draw the synagogue(s) excavated by Avi-Yonah in the 1960s; this was Field O (since no excavation was done, there are no coins from this Field). Work in Field B concentrated on the Islamic industrial buildings. Roman (10 B.C.E.–330 C.E.) occupation was again uncovered in Field C, but it was not clear whether the phase was Herodian or later. The later phases (330–640/1) were also much disturbed by Abbasid and Fatimid–Seljuk phases, and the Field's use as a cemetery between 900 and 1900. Most of the structures in Field G dated to 550–640/1, including the construction of the street.

Understanding the Islamic industrial quarter in Field B was one of the goals of the 1984 work. Exploration in the vaults of Field C suggested that although the original phases were Herodian, the vaults had been restored or rebuilt several times, possibly because of earthquake damage, or reuse in another function (some vaults were frescoed, one had been turned into a Mithraeum). The substantial destruction layer that overlay the Field was dated to the Muslim conquest of 640/1. Efforts in Field G confirmed a fourth-century phase for at least one of the streets, though the remains again showed a major building phase dating to 550–640/1, which was greatly disturbed by robbers' trenches associated with the Early Islamic period (640–900). A small probe to clarify the phases of the Synagogue in Field O was undertaken, and dated the structures to ca. 100–200 and 550–640.

Three more seasons of work concentrated on problems in Fields C and G (1987), and later G alone (1992 and 1993), the last resulting in the spectacular gold hoard discovered within a house. Thus, the coins can give us insight into a city that was settled for over a thousand years, through various cultures and rulers, and still remains a "jewel on the sea."

Chapter 1
Coins from the Excavations

Just over 8,000 coins were found in the Joint Expeditions to Caesarea Maritima excavations, of which about 2,700 were datable to some degree to the years 350 B.C.E. to about 640 C.E. In addition, 129 Arabic, 15 Crusader, 70 blanks, and approximately 5100 "nils," or coins that were completely unrecoverable were noted in the inventories. Of all the coins I studied, almost all were bronzes; one was silver and two were gold (**50**, **899**, **2215**; see also Appendix 1 on the gold hoard). My study concerns the coins from the last three centuries B.C.E. through the seventh century C.E.[1]

Coins from Caesarea have attracted attention as a corpus and as excavation finds. Much information was collected by Kadman *CNP* v.2, who discussed the mint, types, denominations and chronology, and Hamburger 1956, who addressed the likely minting of *minima* in Caesarea in the second century. More specific problems were discussed by myself (1993) and Lampinen 1999a and 1999b, Levine 1972, and Hamburger 1970. Excavation reports from Hohlfelder 1994, Hohlfelder 1992, Hohlfelder 1985, Hohlfelder 1984, Hohlfelder 1981, Lampinen 1992, Ariel 1986, and Frova 1966 give varying amounts of detail to the finds. This is the first accounting of the Hellenistic, Roman and Byzantine coins from the JECM excavations, and an attempt to put these coins into a context – what they mean about the city of Caesarea and the region of Palestine (Figs. 1–3).[2]

Coins of the Third and Second Centuries B.C.E.

The date and place of the establishment of a settlement on the coast are controversial. Strato's Tower is at least active by the third century B.C.E.; ancient authors place the anchorage near Dora. If Strato was the ruler of Sidon, then the settlement should date to the fourth century B.C.E.[3] There is yet little evidence for the earliest phase of occupation on the site; only one coin (no. **1**) can be dated 350–320, a bronze from Cyme, Aeolis. Several might date to the early third century, but cannot be placed here with any security, as the types continue to be minted through the second century as well, except for the coin from Antioch probably minted for Antiochus I (280–261; nos. **2**, **8**, **383–86**). These coins come from all different Fields, except for three from A.1 (the Field is broken into squares called Areas, which are designated by numbers), but the loci are very different here, too; they were found mixed in the fill with Roman imperial period coins. Field A is a domestic quarter (Fig. 1; see also Fig. 4).

As we move into the second century, the number of coins begins to grow, though the coins were mostly minted in the first half of the century. These are bronzes from Antioch and Tyre, mostly of the Seleucid kings (**9–18**, **40–49**, **387–97**). A smaller group survives, which was issued in Ake-Ptolemais under Antiochus IV (175–164 B.C.E.). The coins are particularly easy to identify, even given their worn state, by their serrated edges (**29–36**); the *dilepta* show Antiochus IV radiate on the obverse and a standing female figure with a scepter on the reverse (cf. **14–17**). Second century coins were found primarily in Field G, the domestic quarter that was excavated to early levels, judging by the Hellenistic pottery found (though no structures are securely dated to the Hellenistic period). Locus 121 in G.8 had three earlier second century coins and no later coins (see Index

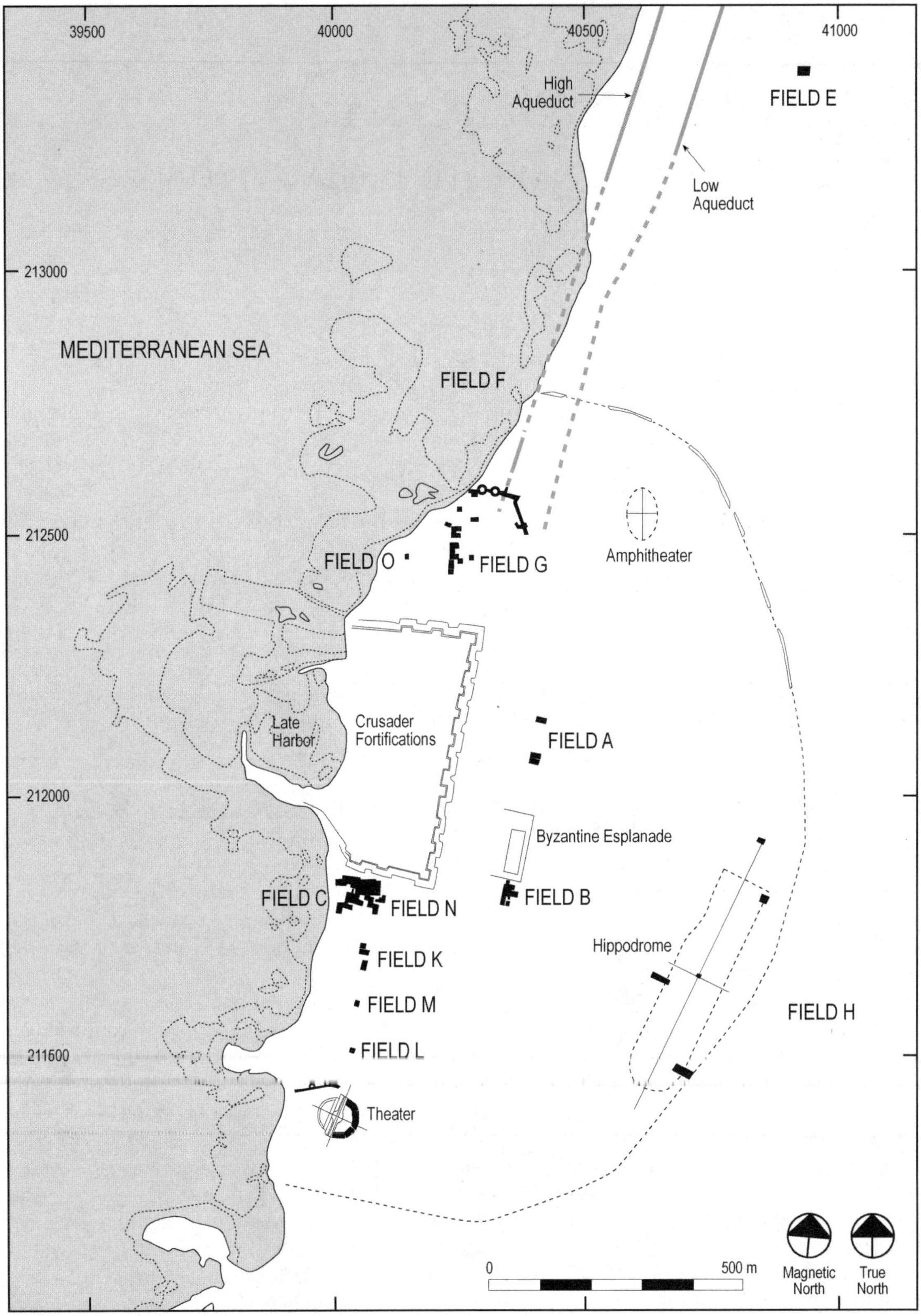

Fig. 1 *Caesarea Maritima. Field locations.*

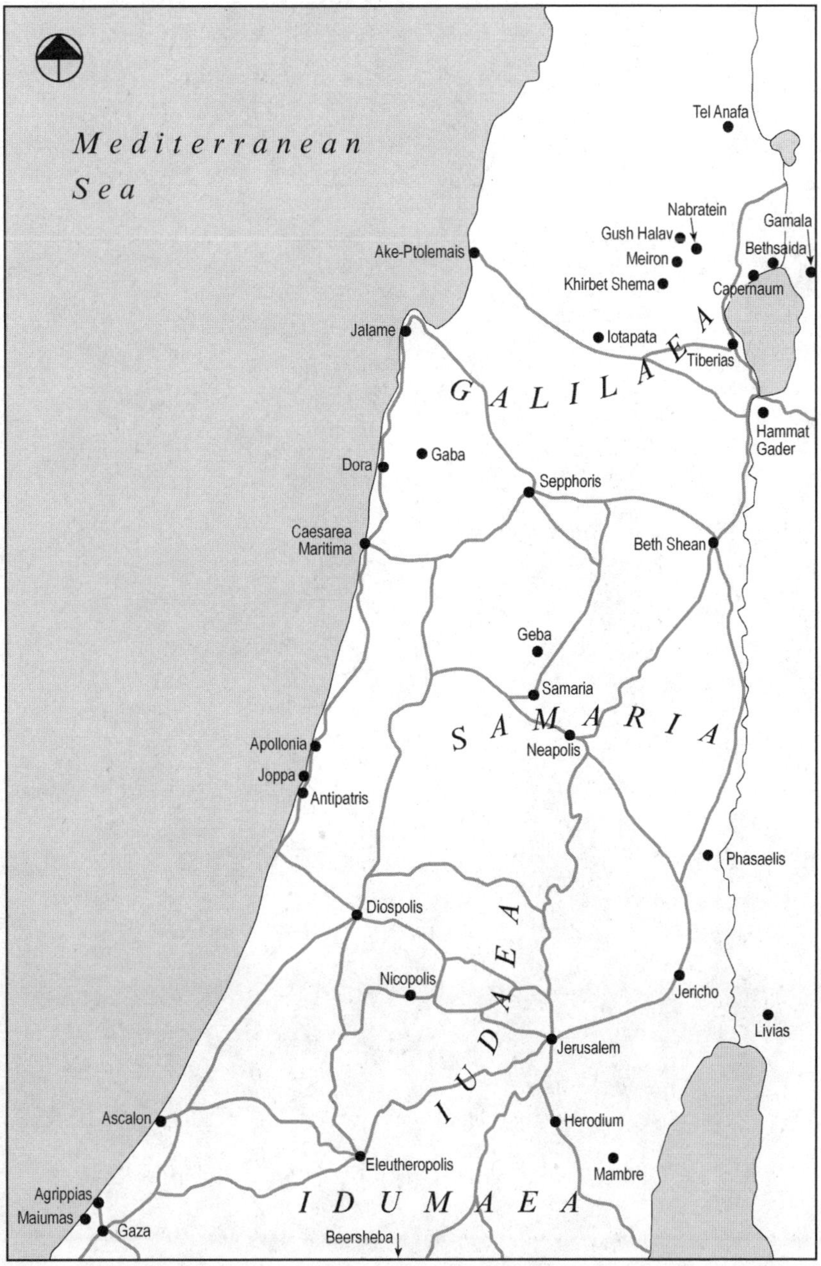

Fig. 2 *Comparative Sites and Road Systems in the Roman Era.*

of Loci); Locus 119 in the same square presented seven Seleucid (and no later) coins. The rest of the second century coins from the site were mixed with coins from later dates, or found as singletons, in Fields A, C (the commercial quarter) and G (Fig. 4). Ptolemaic-Seleucid coins comprise two percent of the coins in Field A, but twelve percent in Field G, the only two fields where these early coins appear.

The Revolt of the Maccabees (166–161 B.C.E.) seems to have interrupted commercial life in Caesarea, for the next group of coins found dates to the very end of the second century. Probably the earlier bronzes are so well worn because the area was without a functioning mint for two generations. There are only five stray coins from 150–100 B.C.E. (**7**, **18–20**, **50**) including one silver *tetradrachm* from Tyre dating to the reign of Antiochus VII (138–129). Silver *tetradrachms* were commonly used as currency in second-century Palestine,

Fig. 3 *Asia Minor, Egypt and the Near East.*

and even much later.[4] Coins of 150–100 B.C.E. were found only in several areas of Field G, though one locus stands out. G.8 Locus 119 had seven Seleucid coins, ranging from 222 to 122 B.C.E. These are probably not a hoard, as wear on them is quite different, but help to date the layer to at least the second century B.C.E. (**15, 19, 31, 34, 40, 48, 393**).

First Century B.C.E.

The Hasmonaean mint opened in Jerusalem by the beginning of the first century B.C.E., and the last Hasmonaean coins were minted in 37 B.C.E.[5] Three, possibly six, coins of Alexander Yannai were found; they were probably minted in Jerusalem, and date to 103–76 (**187–92**). Considering that the coins of Yannai are the most common Hasmonaean coins found on sites,[6] the numbers at Caesarea are very low. Only one other small bronze from this era was found (**68**).

The coins of the Hasmonaeans show aniconic types – anchors, stars, or wheels; they range in size from 12 to 14 mm and weigh between 0.5 and 1.15 grams; Meshorer records Yannai's coins to weigh mostly between 1 and 2 grams, with an average of 1.8 grams.[7]

Coins minted between 100 and 30 B.C.E. are not common at all in Caesarea, implying that the Seleucid bronzes were still pressed into use. Interestingly, Josephus calls Caesarea *kamnousan*, or 'worn out' at this period.[8] Coins from this period were found as singles, scattered in loci in A.4 and G.9 (both domestic quarters), and in the area of the vaults by the harbor (C.16). The other loci show an impressive range of coins in the same strata, to the Roman imperial period (A.1), Byzantine (A.1, G.18), and even post-640 C.E. phases (G.18). In Figure 4, Hasmonaean and other first century B.C.E. coins make up only one percent of the finds in Field A, and Blakely suggested that Field G was abandoned for the first three quarters of the first century B.C.E.; yet coins dating after 164 B.C.E. and before the third century C.E. are rare throughout the city.[9] Thus, the coin evidence can contribute little to this argument.

Caesarea was to be Herod's showplace and he built the city between 22 and 10/9 B.C.E. All of the Herodian coins from the excavation were the double *cornucopiae* and *caduceus*/anchor *prutot* (**193–208**). Herod kept aniconic types – even using some symbols used by Hasmonaean minters, as a concession to powerful political forces in Judaea, but inserted his name, "[coins] of King Herod" or simply "King Herod," in Greek. The winged *caduceus* and the double *cornucopiae* should be read as ancient symbols of prosperity; the anchor is a symbol of naval power.[10] Sizes of the coins range from 11 to 17 mm; weights are again low, ranging from 0.47 to 1.92 grams, contrary to coins in collections, which range from 1.75 to 2.75 grams.[11] Only two other coins from the Augustan period were found, one from Berytus (**26**) and one from Sidon (**39**), both small bronzes comparable in size to the Herodian bronzes.

Most of the coins from this period still come from Field G, the only area where Hellenistic pottery was found in any amount. Yet most of the Herodian coins from Field G are singletons. Three come from Field A; two of the loci have large numbers of coins in them, ranging in date from the second century B.C.E. to the Late Roman period. There are also strays from L.1 and C.28; Field L is the quarter straddling Cardo I West and Decumanus V, a later commercial/industrial area. C is the area of the vaulted warehouses first built by Herod.

There has been some disagreement as to when the mint at Caesarea opened, resulting in two schools of thought. The view of the majority of numismatists is that only after the First Revolt was the mint transferred permanently from Jerusalem to Caesarea. Other numismatists have argued for an earlier opening date. Meshorer sees the mint opening in the reign of Claudius, when large bronzes with a bust of Claudius and an anchor were minted for Agrippa I (37–44 C.E.).[12] Levine argues that the maritime symbols on the coins of Herod and his successor Archelaus show that the small bronzes were minted in Caesarea, as prows, anchors and rudders are only otherwise used as types by port cities. The Hellenizing types also point to Caesarea, as such symbols would be offensive to the Jewish population of Jerusalem. Sutherland suggested that the procurators wished to have the mint in the same city as the government center.[13] The percentages of survival

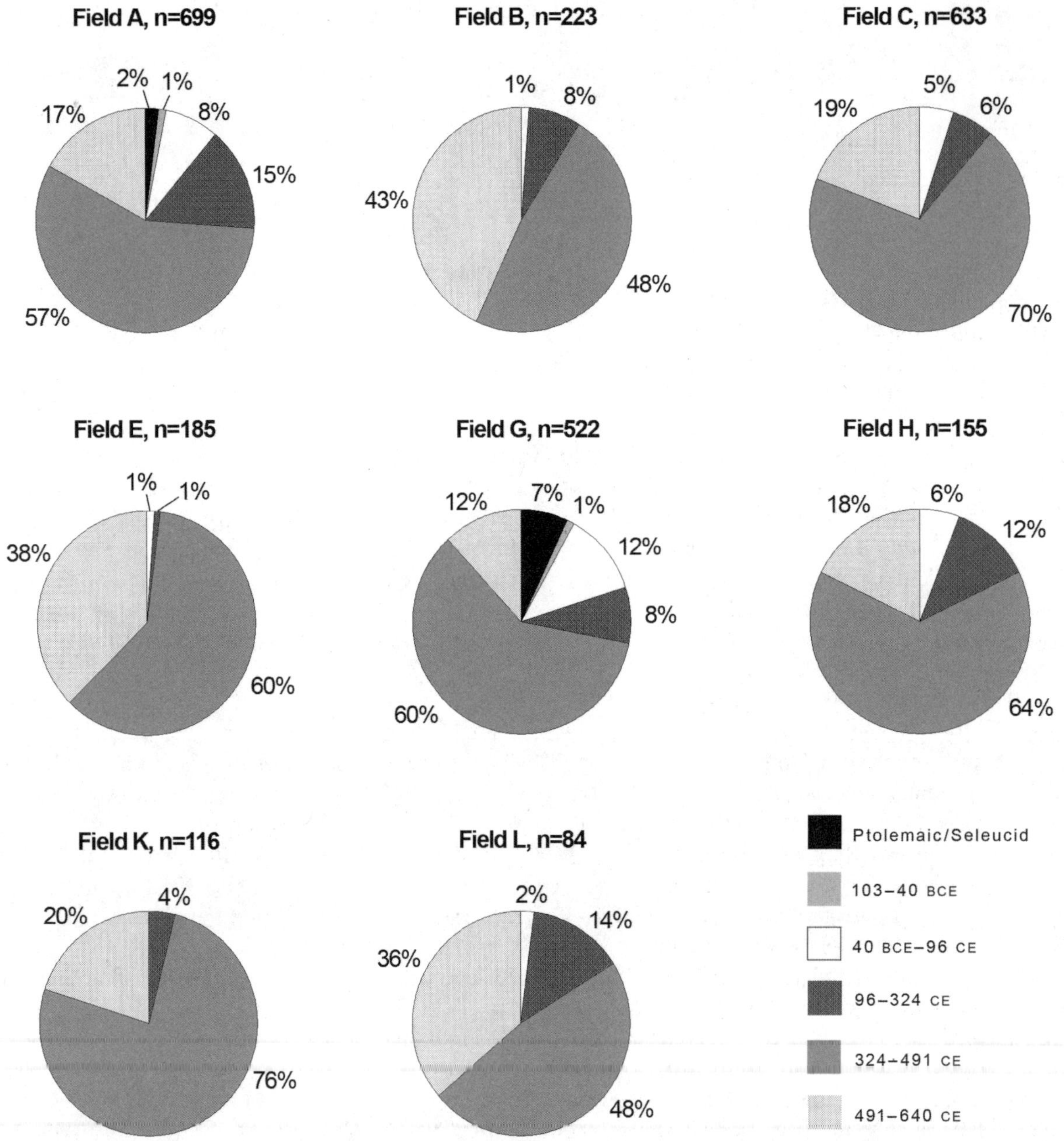

Fig. 4 *Percentages of coins by era, as found in each Field. Totals do not include coins from probes PA, PC, PS, PW, SP and from Field N, as these numbers are too few to make a significant graph. Also not included are coins from unknown loci (designated Field X in original inventory).*

favor the retention of the mint in Jerusalem, as many more Herodian coins were found there than in Caesarea, though the picture may change as more Herodian levels are reached in Caesarea. In fact, the sheer number of specimens found at a particular site may be entirely meaningless, based on accidents of survival and recovery, so other arguments may be more meaningful. Ariel and Carradice cite stylistic parallels between the coins of the procurators and the Hasmonaeans and the continuance of the aniconic types to show that the mint remained in Jerusalem even during the procuratorial period. Yet stylistic evidence may not be much help if the mint personnel were transferred to the new mint (as Carradice himself admits). The evidence from the Caesarea excavations is equivocal, as there were twenty-three types minted by the procurators and Agrippa I; nineteen of the types were found in Jerusalem, and seventeen in Caesarea. Similarly, ninety-nine percent of the first-century C.E. coins found in Jerusalem were procuratorial, compared to ninety-two percent from Caesarea. However, based on the change of flan and design types, I believe the mint in Caesarea opened with the larger bronzes minted by Agrippa I under Nero, featuring the Tyche of Caesarea on the reverse (as no. **83**). No *prutot* were minted in Caesarea; the mint opened in earnest after the First Revolt.[14]

Coins of the Hasmonaean rulers, Herod and the procurators are made with flat, irregularly shaped flans, often showing how the flans were cut from a band of bronze; the Hasmonaeans used open molds, with the flans connected by strips of bronze, which were then cut away.[15] Because of their relative thinness, several of those found are fragmentary.

FIRST CENTURY C.E.

Coins of Herod's son, Archelaus, minted between 4 B.C.E. and 6 C.E. are plentiful; of seven types assigned to his reign, four were found (**209–39**). Not surprisingly, only one coin of Herod's other son Philip was found (**72**); none of Herod's third son Antipas were found.

Archelaus retained the Hellenizing flavor of Herod's types, emphasizing maritime symbols, such as the anchor, prow, and galley.[16] One coin has as a type a bunch of grapes (perhaps a Jewish symbol, though certainly known in the Greek world as well) coupled with a crested helmet, surely a Greek type. Archelaus placed his political title of *Ethnarch* (in Greek) on his coins. Some of the legends have retrograde letters or entire inscriptions, showing the relative shoddiness of production. Flan diameters range from 11 to 18 mm; weights are low, from 0.38 to 2.36 grams.[17]

Agrippa I minted the first coins that can be certainly placed in the Caesarea mint, since they bear the inscription (in Greek), "Caesarea the city near the harbor Sebastos."[18] The reverse type is a Tyche resting her hand on a rudder and holding a palm branch; she is shown as a conventional Greek goddess, with a long *peplos*, but without a mural crown, which would typically identify a Tyche – only the inscription on the coin identifies her. Tyche continued to be a favorite type through the first century, but she took a different form on later coins. Agrippa's head is featured on the obverse, accompanied by his name and titles in Greek, including "Philocaesar", or "friend of Caesar." None of these coins were found in the excavations. Stylistically, Agrippa's large bronzes are very different from the small *prutot* also minted during his reign. Coupled with the new subject matter, these coins make a very different impression from all the small bronzes minted since the first century B.C.E., and are stylistically closer to the products coming out of the mint at Paneas during Agrippa's reign.

Small bronzes, in the style of the Hasmonaean/Herodian coins were also minted by Agrippa I, from the mint in Jerusalem (**287–310**). These show a canopy (an ancient reference to kingship) and three ears of barley or wheat.[19] The flans range in size from 12–19 mm and 0.71 to 2.61 grams in weight, varying as widely as the Herodian coins. Agrippa's (and Philip's) large and small bronzes (and the later procuratorial coins) almost entirely drove out any foreign bronzes. Between 14 and 69 C.E., possibly six foreign coins were found (**4–6**, Commagene?; **21–22**, SC bronzes from Antioch, dating to the first century; **355**, from Nabataea), though they come from more distant mints than in previous centuries. Again, most of the coins from this time period were found in isolation in their loci, in Fields A, B, C, G, and H. The coins from the hippodrome (Field H) especially were often mixed with Late Roman bronzes dating 300 or more years later, but this occurs in Field G as well. The hippodrome was not yet built, so the coins are in a later context. One interesting deposit comes from A.1 Locus 143, where there were thirteen coins dating to 54–59 C.E.; while two other coins were Seleucid, thirteen of the remaining coins were from the Early Imperial period (one other dated to the third century C.E.). This may point to an accumulation or agglutination of Early Imperial coins, especially of the Neronian-Flavian periods.

After the death of Agrippa I, the province was governed by procurators. Flan diameters of the procurators' coins range from 12 to 21 mm and weights from 1.13 to 2.81 grams. The *prutot* of the procurators, surely minted in Jerusalem, follow the Hasmonaean/Herodian coins in minting technique as well as iconography and flan size. The procurators retained aniconic types, adopting old types, as palm trees, or Herodian types like the palm branch or double *cornucopiae* and *caduceus*. The types normally include a regnal date (as in common in eastern coinage), and the emperor's name in Greek. As Meshorer points out, the types of Pilate were not especially sensitive to the subject Jewish population, as he used Roman religious symbols, the *lituus* and *simpulum*, though he did refrain from putting the head of the emperor on the coins.[20] The procurators of Augustus (Coponius and Ambibulus) both struck coins with an ear of barley and a palm tree, differentiated only by the date. Fourteen were found on the site (**240–53**), almost all coming from the domestic quarter G and the industrial/commercial quarter A, in strata that included much earlier Hellenistic coins or Late Roman coins; one comes from Field C.

Gratus and Pilate are heavily represented, with thirty-three coins (**254–86**), mostly found in Fields G and A (where procuratorial coins were found with much earlier and much later coins), and some from the commercial center C (where almost all were isolated in their strata). One stray comes from Field B and two were found in the fill from the hippodrome (Field H). Coins from the hippodrome (H.3–6) were associated with first century C.E. pottery; the site may have been used in Herod the Great's day for spectacles. Recent excavations along the shore have produced a definite first century C.E. hippodrome-like structure.[21]

Hamburger argued that the legate C. Umidius Durmius struck coins at Caesarea in 52 C.E.[22] None of his rare coins were found in the excavations; the obverses have the head of Claudius with the Latin inscription CLAVDIVS CAESAR AVG PM TR P IMP PP (Pontifex Maximus, holding tribunician power, Imperator, Father of his Country), and the reverse of an anchor or rudder, with no discernible inscription. If Hamburger is correct, this would be the first use of Latin on coins of Caesarea; the inscription is also somewhat unusual in following so closely Roman terminology and dating by listing the emperor's current offices. The Latin legends are puzzling, especially since Caesarea was not yet a Roman colony. The provenances of coins may be the deciding factor in the allocation of the coins to the mint.[23] Stylistically, the coins resemble those minted in Paneas; if they were minted in Caesarea, it could be that the two cities shared dies or engravers.

Agrippa II (37–44 C.E.) mostly confined his activity to the mint at Paneas; yet the mint at Caesarea also produced large bronzes (22–25 mm) in Nero's name, with his portrait on the obverse, which survive in more numbers than the Agrippa/Tyche bronzes. The reverse shows a Tyche with a short tunic, baldric, spear, and mural crown, more closely approximating the image of Roma. That she is Tyche (though listed in the *RPC* simply as a male), and not another personification, can be seen by her mural crown; yet she is distinct from the Tyche on coins from the mint at Paneas (and all earlier Tyches), which continue the Greek goddess figure, in some cases wearing a high *polos*-type hat. On the coins of Caesarea, she extends her hand to hold a bust, perhaps that of the emperor, since one countermark is carefully placed across the face of the bust (**85**). The inscription is repeated from the earlier coin; a few examples of this coin were found at the site (**83–87**). Flans range in size from 19–23 mm, and the coins are quite worn, showing weights ranging from 5.84 to 10.72 grams.

After the end of the reign of Agrippa II, governance by a procurator was re-established and lasted 22 years until the beginnings of the First Revolt in 66 C.E. Not every procurator coined, but some procurators turned out large numbers of small bronze coins, which served to replace many city coins in the latter part of the first century B.C.E. and the first half of the first century C.E. Only one coin from outside of the Caesarea and Jerusalem mints was found dating to this era, a coin from Ake-Ptolemais (**37**).

The small *prutot* issued by the procurator Antonius Felix (52–60 C.E.) keep the old eastern types of palm branches or a palm tree, with large inscriptions on the obverse, in Greek, of Claudius' and his wife Agrippina's name. The Claudian and Neronian coins were mostly found in Fields A and G; unless they were the only coins found in their strata, most were found mixed with much later coins. The three exceptions were A.1 Locus 149, A.2 Locus 074, and C.8 Locus 040, all of which consisted only of Early Imperial coins. Unfortunately for archaeologists, the sewers must have been cleaned regularly, for only one coin from this era was found in the excavations (Field SP, or "Sewer Project").

The First Revolt began after Gentile inhabitants of Caesarea massacred Jews living in the city; we would not expect to find coins of the First Revolt in Caesarea, but two strays are recorded (**347–48**) from issues that were widely distributed.[24]

The mint of Caesarea opened in earnest after the Revolt; it operated almost continuously until 253 C.E., and had a large output especially during the reign of Severus Alexander (222–235 C.E.). The minting place for the "Judaea Capta" types of the Flavian emperors has recently been called into question. The types were sharp reminders of Judaea's defeat: a Nike to symbolize the Roman victory, or a personification of the province grieving under a trophy of captured Judaean arms, types not usually minted within the defeated province.[25] Under Vespasian and Titus the legends continued to be written in Greek (e.g. ΙΟΥΔΑΙΑΣ ΕΑΛΩΚVΙΑΣ or "Judaea Capta"), but under Domitian, Caesarea's new rank of colony was proudly advertised in Latin, as more appropriate to a Roman colony: COL(onia) (prima) FLA(via) AVG(usta) CAES(area). The designs of the coins are well-executed, with heads or figures that fill the obverse or reverse fields, and neat lettering. The style is similar to the products of the Paneas mint; Carradice also notes similarities to the products of the mint at Antioch, and he suggests a transfer of mint personnel for his Group 2, minted in 84 and later. Carradice lists three denominations struck during the reign of Domitian; he categorizes them as 16–18 grams, 10–12 grams, and 5 grams.[26] The excavation coins tend to fall into lower weight categories, mostly because of the worn condition of the coins. Unlike the previous period, the Flavian period sees the introduction of coins from many mints, probably due to the movement of troops and people in connection with the Revolt and in the period immediately following. Coins from Antioch (**23**), Kanata (**25**), Paneas (**73–78**) and Ascalon (**352**) are found with coins of Jerusalem (**347–48**) and Caesarea (**88–95**, cf. **398–99**). The coins were found primarily in Field A; other Flavian period coins were found in G, PA (a probe at the side of the high aqueduct), and C. In Figure 4, first century B.C.E. through first century C.E. coins make up one to twelve percent of the coins in all Fields except K, where they are entirely missing.

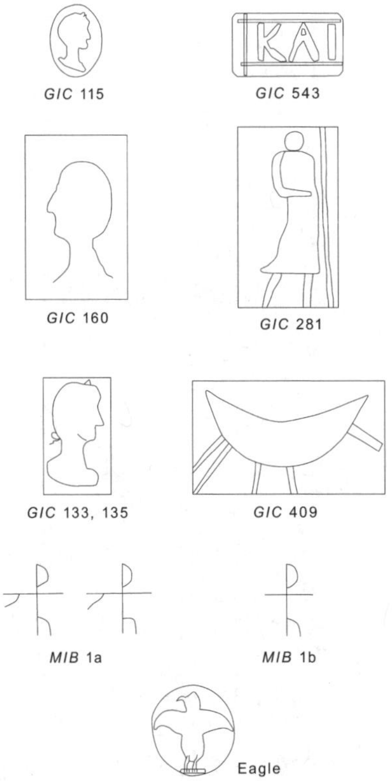

Fig. 5 *Countermarks on coins found at Caesarea.*

Nineteen of the imperial coins were countermarked (Fig. 5 and Table 1). Countermarking is a process of placing a small stamp on the obverse or reverse of a coin. The stamp can be epigraphical or figural. Almost all of the Early Imperial countermarks on the coins at Caesarea consisted of a male bust right, in a rectangular punch. Ten are probably *GIC* no. 133; the countermark is a laureate male head right, in a rectangular punch. Howgego found this countermark only on Flavian coins; the excavation coins greatly increase the known number of this countermark. The countermarking thus may have been done in the mint at Caesarea. Most of the countermarked coins are extremely worn, testifying to long use, even if the countermark is quite clear. The countermarking could have been done during the reign of Nerva (96–98 C.E.), when the mint was not producing any coins. The well-worn coins may not simply have been Flavian issues, but earlier issues that had circulated in Palestine for a long time.

Versions of *GIC* no. 133 are evident, too. Three examples of *GIC* no. 135 appear: one alone; one in combination with *GIC* no. 281, a figure holding a staff, in a rectangular punch; and one in combination with *GIC* no. 409(?), a galley in a rectangular punch, 4 by 5 mm, found on Flavian coins. The galley countermark is the

Table 1. Countermarks on coins found at Caesarea.

Catalog No.	Types	Mint	Plate
Coins of the Imperial Period			
GIC 115 (male head r. in circular punch, 4.5 mm); **GIC 543** (KAI, 8 × 5 mm) and an unidentified male head r. (5 mm), all on reverse			
85	Nero/Tyche holding bust	Caesarea	
GIC 133 (laureate male head r., 6.5 × 5 mm), all found on the obverse			
91	Domitian/Nike	Caesarea	Pl. 1
94	Domitian/uncertain	Caesarea?	Pl. 1
155	uncertain/uncertain	Caesarea?	
156	head r (Domitian?)/uncertain	Caesarea?	
157	head r/uncertain	Caesarea?	Pl. 1
158	uncertain/uncertain	Caesarea?	
159	uncertain/uncertain	Caesarea?	
160	uncertain/uncertain	Caesarea?	
161	Domitian?/uncertain	Caesarea?	Pl. 1
162	head r./uncertain	Caesarea?	Pl. 1
GIC 135 (laureate male head r., 4.5 × 3.5 mm), on obverse			
399	Domitian/uncertain	uncertain	Pl. 2
GIC 135 found in conjunction with **GIC 409**? (galley 4 × 5 mm), on obverse			
163	uncertain/uncertain	Caesarea?	
GIC 135; **GIC 281** (figure with staff, 4.5–5 × 3–4 mm), on obverse			
93	Domitian/Judaea capta	Caesarea	Pl. 1
Male head right, 10 × 7 mm, obverse			
4	Tiberius/double cornucopiae	Commagene	Pl. 1
Male head right, in rectangular stamp, 6 × 4 mm, on obverse			
92	Domitian/Nike	Caesarea	
Uncertain type, rectangular stamp, 8 × 6 mm, on obverse over face of emperor			
398	Domitian/uncertain	Caesarea?	Pl. 2
Athena? head right in circular stamp, 5 mm			
87	Nero?/Tyche?	Caesarea?	
Standing female left? in circular stamp, 5 mm			
114	Diadumenianus/Serapis	Caesarea	
Heraclian countermarks			
MIB 1a			
2220 on reverse	Justin/M	Constantinople	
2448 on reverse	Maurice/K	Thessalonica	
2452 on reverse	Maurice/M	Constantinople	
2455 on obverse	Maurice/M	Constantinople	
2456 on reverse	Maurice/M	Constantinople	
2460 on reverse	Maurice/M	Constantinople	
2461 on reverse	Maurice/M	Constantinople	
2462 on reverse	Maurice/M	Constantinople	Pl. 3
2463 on obverse	Maurice/M	Constantinople	
2467 on obverse	Maurice/M	Nicomedia	Pl. 3
2474 on reverse	Maurice/M	Antioch	
2622 on reverse	Heraclius/M	Constantinople	
2623 on reverse	Heraclius/M	Constantinople	
2629 on reverse	Heraclius/M	Constantinople	Pl. 4

Table 1. (continued) Countermarks on coins found at Caesarea.

Catalog No.	Types	Mint	Plate
2643 on reverse	Heraclius/M	Constantinople	
2645 on reverse	Heraclius/M	Constantinople	Pl. 4
2647 on reverse	Heraclius/M	Constantinople	Pl. 4
2669 (multiple times)	Heraclius/M	Constantinople	
2674 on reverse	Heraclius/M	Nicomedia	Pl. 4
2676 on reverse	Heraclius/M	Cyzicus	
2713 on obverse	Heraclius/M?	uncertain	
Philips and Goodwin 1997 no.12, probably from Hama, Heraclius class A follis, Constantinople			
probably **MIB 1a**			
2672 on obverse	Heraclius/M	Nicomedia	Pl. 4
MIB 1b			
2652 on reverse	Heraclius/lambda	Constantinople	
2654 on reverse	Heraclius/lambda	Constantinople	
2665 on reverse	Heraclius/K	Constantinople	Pl. 4
2666 on reverse	Heraclius/M	Constantinople	
Barkay in Hirschfeld 1997 nos. 70 and 99, from Hammat Gader, Heraclian folles, Constantinople			
MIB 1b twice, on reverse			
2642	Heraclius/M	Constantinople	
2667	Heraclius/M	Constantinople, with third mark of uncertain type	
MIB 1a in conjunction with **MIB 1b**, on reverse			
2207	Anastasius/M	Constantinople	
2620	Heraclius/K	Thessalonica	Pl. 4
2646 (1b 2 times)	Heraclius/M	Constantinople	
2651	Heraclius/M	Constantinople	Pl. 4
Monogram of uncertain type, second indistinguishable, on reverse			
2644	Heraclius/M	Constantinople	
Eagle in circular stamp, on reverses			
2218	Justin/M	Constantinople	Pl. 2
2360	Justinian/M	Antioch	
2363	Justinian/M	Antioch	Pl. 3
2394	Justin or Justinian/M	Constantinople	Pl. 3

emblem of the Legio X Fretensis, and was probably applied in Palestine early in the reign of Domitian.[27] It is normally found in conjunction with *GIC* 135. The 281 mark can now be clearly seen to be female; it is not clear where and when the 281 countermark was applied. Since the 135 mark is a variant of the 133 mark (135 has a smaller punch, and it is not clear if the head is laureate), it is likely that the countermark too dates to the reign of Nerva, and perhaps can be attributed to the Caesarea mint.[28] Two versions of the head and probably the uncertain rectangular types should also be attributed to this period and the Caesarea mint.

One coin of Nero was countermarked three times, with the letters KAI (*GIC* no. 543) applied in 68/69 C.E. and twice with the mark *GIC* no. 115 (a laureate? head in a circular punch of about 4 mm). The latter is often found in combination with the KAI punch, and may date to approximately the same time. Howgego noted that the KAI mark may have been used before the city was granted colonial status, when the inscriptions on the coins from the Caesarea mint shifted to Latin; the marking may have occurred in Caesarea itself.[29] The third countermark, an unidentified bust right in a rectangular punch, was placed over the bust in Tyche's hand.

Second Century c.e.

Though the mint at Caesarea operated until 253 c.e., with no coins minted between 96–98 c.e. and again 235–244 c.e., finds from the mint are not especially numerous on the site. The coin types of second-century bronzes minted in Caesarea continued to advertise her connections to Rome. Under Trajan, the mint produced reverses that depicted the emperor sacrificing in front of an altar (**96**); Hadrianic reverses found on the site had Apollo standing at an altar and a bust of Serapis, an Egyptian god, who was also pictured on coins of Diospolis, Neapolis, Aelia Capitolina and Eleutheropolis, from the time of Antoninus Pius. Serapis continued to be used throughout the second and into the third century on coins from Caesarea.[30] Minute coins were probably minted in Caesarea in the second century, possibly during the reign of Trajan; these have no inscriptions, a barely discernible emperor's head on the obverse, and an animal on the reverse.[31] Although Hamburger reported finding many of these coins on the site, comparatively few were recovered in the excavations, and almost all of these were recovered in Field A. Several explanations come to mind. Different techniques of excavation could have been employed, for example, such as more use of sieving. Or, second century levels may not have been exposed in the excavations, and the coins that survive are from mixed fills. Hamburger suggested that many of the *minima* he found were in the dunes along the shore.[32] One coin from the Dora mint has not been reported in other collections. The obverse shows the head of Trajan, laureate, with the inscription AVTOKP KAIC NEP TRAIANC CEB ΓΕΡΜ ΔΑΚ (that is, celebrating his victories in the provinces of Germania and Dacia). The reverse has the Greek-style Tyche standing on a galley, holding a legionary standard and *cornucopiae*; only part of the inscription is legible, but it reads ΔΑΦΝΑ..C..NL.., ΔΟΡ? (**70**; pl. 1). The combination of the reverse and obverse is unique, and the reverse is a variation of the Tyches known from the mint at Antioch.[33]

Klimosky postulated a system of denominations for the second century that seems too complicated; yet in Asia Minor the denominations began to settle into a regular pattern under Hadrian.[34] For the Caesarea coins, we can perhaps distinguish a pattern in the types, weights, and flan sizes. The small denomination was marked with an animal reverse; either the diameters and weights were allowed to fluctuate or the coins began to be minted around 15 mm in diameter and weighing up to 4 grams, and sinking to 8–12 mm and 1.5–2 grams (**100–110**). The middle denomination measures between 18 and 22 mm, and weighs 6 to 9 grams; from the first half of the century, the reverses consist of the emperor pouring a libation (*CNP* reverse type 23), or Apollo pouring a libation (*CNP* reverse type 29, here **98–99**). The former type has been previously noted for the larger denomination, and now can be seen as having been used for the middle denomination as well (**96**). After 161, the preferred reverse is Serapis, though other reverses may also be of this denomination. The types of the heaviest denomination vary quite a bit; we would expect the types to vary more for these special issues, which measure between 22 and 25 mm, or even larger (**97**, **111–12**). Very few of the heaviest coins were lost by their owners, to be found in the excavations of Caesarea, though the largest issues very often appear in collections.

No coins of the Bar Kochba Revolt were found in Caesarea; the farthest west the coins have been found is Nicopolis (Emmaeus).[35] After the rebellion, the number of coins increased markedly, with a special concentration in Trajan's and Hadrian's reign; most are small *minimi*, which accounts for their loss. Levine's calculations of the number of types used per year shows a corresponding increase in the second century (Table 2).[36] Gitler noted an almost complete cessation of coining in Palestine in the second half of the second century c.e., especially between 166/7–175/6, possibly due to recession and the plague.[37] As the number of mints represented in the city grew in the Flavian period, the number of mints represented by second century coins increased tremendously: Gaba (**3**); Tyre (**54–58**); Dora (**69–71**); Sepphoris (**79–81**); Gaza (**354**); small bronzes from Alexandria (**357–69**); and Rome (**434–38**; see also **400–422**). Most second century coins were found in Field A.1, with fewer in A.2, A.3, Fields B, C (where all were singletons in their strata), G, H (but only one example), L and N (one example from a small field).

Table 2. Reverse types per year from the Caesarea mint, 81–253 C.E (after Hamburger 1956, Kadman 1957, Levine 1975b, and Meshorer 2001).

Emperor	No. of types	Types/ Year	No. of reverses in JECM coins
Domitian	8	0.5	1
Trajan/Hadrian	15	2.7	7
Antoninus	5	0.2	0
Marcus Aurelius	14	0.7	1
Verus	6	0.8	1?
Commodus	5	0.4	0
Septimius Severus	3	0.2	0
Caracalla	8	1.0	0
Macrinus/Diadumenianus	6	6.0	1
Elagabalus	7	1.8	1
Severus Alexander	21	1.6	1
Philip	15	3.0	3
Trajan Decius	75	25.0	3
Trebonius Gallus	33	16.5	0

Third Century C.E.

The number of coins found steadily increases in the third century; it may be that the mint increased production due to the costs associated with Septimius Severus' visit to Caesarea in 199–200 C.E. and Caracalla's visit c.215 (see Chapter 2).[38] The number of coins found especially increases after c.220, with the large issues of Severus Alexander, perhaps minted for his campaigns against the Persians.

Levine has attempted to judge the output of the mint, and thus the economic prosperity of the region, by noting a rise in the number of types used for each emperor (Table 2). The methodology of extracting the number of coins minted from the number of dies made has recently been called into question.[39] Although I will show that the number of coin types made per emperor has little bearing on the problem of defining the economy, I think we can say that in general terms, the more types made (and the more dies cut), the more coins were likely produced from the mint. Interestingly, the number of types known, but not represented in the excavation coins, is high for all periods. The number of types per year is less than the numbers in the second century; this only shows a lack of invention in the mint, as the number of coins per year increases from the reign of Diadumenianus (217–218) through Severus Alexander (222–235; **113–40**) but especially in the reign of Trajan Decius (249–251; **144–49**), when an enormous number of types are also created.[40] This outpouring is not reflected in any of the other mints of ancient Palestine.[41]

The types remain quite conservative; Tyche (e.g., **146–47**) and Serapis are common. New to the period are eagles and wreaths with inscriptions boasting SPQR (The Senate and the Roman People) and METROPOLIS ALEXAND (the city of Alexander, the new rank of Caesarea), though types like these are found earlier in the east (**126–39**). The suggested three denominations are hard to find in the excavation coins. The middle denomination may be distinguished by three reverses: a bust of Tyche, Tyche inside of a temple, and the head of Serapis. The middle denomination ranges between 17 and 23 mm, 4 to 10 grams (e.g., **113**, **118**, **146**, **151**). The eagle or eagles and wreath are found on slightly smaller coins (15–20 mm, 2.25–3.75 grams), possibly a smaller denomination (**138–39**). Larger coins have more varied types; some, such as Dionysos on a panther (**142**), appear in other cities (Nysa, Aurelius, Aelia Capitolina and Raphia).[42]

There are a couple of interesting coins from the period 235–253 C.E.; one has on the obverse a bust of Otacilia, right, with the inscription OTAC SEVERA AVG. The reverse was previously known only for Philip I and Herennius Etruscus, an eagle supporting a wreath with a bust of Tyche and the inscription SC... within (**141**, pl. 1). A rare type of Philip II, listed in the American University in Beirut Collection (no. 556 var.) shows the fragmentary inscription ... AVG MET... around a seated Minerva handing a *victoriola* to Philip II (**143**, pl. 1).[43] Yet another coin of Philip II has the reverse of Dionysus riding a panther with the inscription COL PRI FL AVG FC CAES, a reverse previously not associated with Philip II, though it did appear on coins of Philip I (*BMC Palestine* p. 29 nos. 138–39; here **142**).

An *æs* coin from Tyre, dated 253–268, shows a type that combines a reverse known to be used with Gallienus, with an obverse not normally paired with the empress Salonina (with the obverse *BMC Palestine* p. 295 nos. 494–99); the reverse shows Astarte in a hexastyle temple (*BMC Palestine* p. 291 nos. 467–77; here **62**, pl. 1). An *antoninianus* of Claudius Gothicus, from Antioch, shows a combination not listed in the *RIC*, but recorded by Alföldi (here **456**, pl. 2).[44] And an *antoninianus* from Cyzicus has the reverse CONCORDIA MILITVM paired with a new obverse: a radiate, draped bust of Maximian, IMP C M AV MAXIMIANVS AVG (**476**).

The coins come from a large number of mints, as we would expect as local mints in the east begin to be shut down: Britain (**481**), Rome (**439–43**), Siscia? (**465**), Cyzicus (**470–71**, **476**), Heracleia (**474–75**), "Asia" (**445–50**), Antioch (**451**, **453–60**, **463–64**, **466–68**, **477**), Tripolis (**461**, **469**), Berytus (**27–28**), Ake-Ptolemais (**38**), Tyre (**59–67**), Gadara (**82**), Neapolis (**186**), Jerusalem (**349–51**), Bostra (**356**), and Alexandria (**373**, **472**, **478**).

Wide distribution is the norm for the period between 200–253 C.E., in Fields A, B, E, and G; the commercial sectors C.8, 11–12 (vault 1, the Mithraeum), C.16 (vault 4, which had in Locus 045 a large concentration of coins dating between 200 and 225), C.25 (vault 12), C.21 (a fill for a later street), C.23 (Cardo I West, though the excavators found the lack of remains from the period 200–330 in the Cardo puzzling);[45] C.30 (the intersection of Decumanus II and Cardo II West); C.3, 27, 42, and K.1–2, L.1. Coins were also found in the hippodrome (H), in a fill belonging to the fourth century structure.[46] Between 253–324 C.E., most of these areas are still represented, including Fields A, B, E, and G; Field C.8 (vault 1), C.26 (vaults 2 and 11), C.17 and 25 (vault 12), C.29 (Cardo I West) and C.10; the southern commercial sectors K, and L; and the hippodrome (H). In Figure 4, the coins of the second and third centuries comprise one to fifteen percent of all the coins in any given Field.

FOURTH THROUGH FIFTH CENTURIES C.E.

The fourth century is well represented in the finds, even though numismatists believe there was a recall in 354. For the period 324/326–348 C.E., the excavation coins show a progressive reduction in weight, from about 2 to 0.5 grams, with the median falling just under 1.5 grams. The GLORIA EXERCITVS (2 soldiers, 1 standard) reverse was much more common than other reverses minted during this period. There are many FEL TEMP REPARATIO (falling horseman) reverses from the excavations, fewer of the larger (AE2) denomination, and more of the smaller (AE3). The excavation coins range from 1.3 to 2.4 grams, with the mode at 1.7–1.8 and a secondary mode at 2–2.1 grams. The smaller denomination (or module), with a new reverse, SPES REIPVBLICE, falls between 0.8 and 2.3 grams, with the mode between 1.4 and 1.6 grams. All of the official mints of the empire are represented in the finds, from Lyon to Constantinople to Alexandria; there is even a stray from Axum (**374**). By far, most coins come from the mint of Antioch.

Only one denomination is given to the period 364–379 C.E., at about 2.5 grams, with the reverse types GLORIA ROMANORVM and SECVRITAS REIPVBLICAE.[47] Many coins of this period have been found at Caesarea. The coins at Caesarea from the period after 378/9 to about 400 are of the smallest denomination, and are quite common, as they were easily lost and not worth much trouble to retrieve. The small VOTA and victory reverses were especially well represented, and come from almost every mint of the empire; these often weigh less than a gram. One *solidus* was recovered (**899**). It was the same emperor, type, and mint as the most common coin in the gold hoard (see Appendix 1), and was the only coin found in its locus, vault 4 in C.16.

Small fifth-century coins are once again well represented at Caesarea. These coins are crudely made; only one denomination was minted, in increasingly fewer mints. The most common reverses are the monograms of the emperor's name; most are under 10 mm in diameter and weigh less than a gram. Also serving as the everyday change in Caesarea in this period are coins from Axum (**375–82**) and the Vandalic mint in Carthage (**1777–1881**).

The most common Vandalic type is the palm tree reverse. Hahn attributed these small bronzes to the reign of Maurice, saying that they copy a type of a rare *pentanummium*; he dated the series to 596–601.[48] W. Metcalf, who published many of the excavated coins of Carthage, noted that the type must have been minted around the reign of Justinian, due to the composition of hoards and the deposit in a cistern in Carthage, though he admitted that fifth- and sixth-century *nummia* have no real fixed points for dating.[49] Hohlfelder noted that the palm tree type was an old one in the east. He suggested that the coins were minted in Antioch.[50] Asolati has recently strongly favored a mint in Carthage, due to the numbers found at Carthage and the few from published excavations in the east.[51] He has also argued for a date of 530–534, based on hoard and stratigraphic evidence from Athens and Corinth.[52] Unfortunately, the one coin that was found in a sealed context in Caesarea comes from a later context, and so can provide no information as to the date of issue. However, Locus 071 in E.4 consists largely of late fifth- through early sixth-century coins, including seven Vandalic and three Justinianic *nummia*.

Late Roman coins are found in every part of the excavation, though not necessarily from every area: they come from Fields A, B, E, and G. They comprise between forty-eight and seventy percent of all the coins found in each Field (Fig. 4). In A.1 Locus 097 there was a peculiarly large group of coins dating from 310–314. The economic and political center was well represented by C.2–4, 8, 10, 11 (vault 1 and the Cardo in front of it), C.17, 22, 25 (vaults 3 and 12), C.16 (vault 4), C.9 (vaults 4 and 5), C.28 (vaults 8, 9, 10); vaults 3–10 are now believed to have been (re)constructed in the period between 330 and 640 C.E., possibly after earthquake damage.[53] C.13, 23, 24, and 30 were part of Decumanus II; in square 30 the road intersected with Cardo I West, which continues in C.29. Cardo II West and Decumanus II are represented in C.36; Cardo I West and Structure 1 in C.5; fill in C.19, 20 and 21 comes from later building projects and the (re?) building of a street; other squares with coins of this period in Field C are 14, 15, 22, 25–27, 42. C.14 Locus 032 was interesting in having a large group of coins in it that dated to 346–378, perhaps an agglutination; forty-one coins were found in C.21 Locus 159, dating 445–518 (though the Locus also includes a Justinianic coin). Late Roman coins also come from the commercial sections K.1–3 and L.1. K.3 Locus 009 is a sealed layer, with coins in two groups, dating 346–361 and 445–522. Coins from the later levels of the hippodrome were found in H.2–6.

BYZANTINE PERIOD: SIXTH AND SEVENTH CENTURIES

It is scarcely an exaggeration to say that Byzantine coins were found in every excavated square, comprising twelve to forty-three percent of the coins found in each Field (Fig. 4): the domestic quarters A.1–4, B.1–9, G.3, 5 (a peristyle house), G.17 (a street dating to the Byzantine period), G.18 (reuse of Late Roman walls), G.7–10, 19–21, 23; and the Byzantine villa (E). All of the areas of C are represented (the commercial district, including the Archive Building, the Bath, streets and their colonnades, Structure 1 and an apsidal building, water installations), the commercial quarters K.1–4, and the horrea in L.1; the sewers, PW.1; and the Byzantine city wall in H.

Only one silver coin, a *tremissis* of Justin I, was found (**2215**). It was found in the domestic quarter G, a singleton in its locus. The finds from the reign of Anastasius are much like the previous century – few large pieces, but plenty of small *nummia*; only one comes from Nicomedia (**2213**), and all the rest from Constantinople. Constantinople continued to be the primary source of coins throughout the Byzantine period, replacing Antioch, although the numbers are somewhat skewed by the large presence of *nummia* minted at Constantinople in the excavated coins. It is not until c.600 that small coins from Alexandria replace the small bronzes from Constantinople. Larger denominations show more of a mix of mints, including Antioch, Cyzicus, Nicomedia, and Thessalonica. D.M. Metcalf argued that *folles* from eastern sites are normally supplied by the mint at Constantinople. However, he goes on to argue that for the reigns of Anastasius through Justin I, the *officinae* (or workshops) have limited circulations. He specifically says coins of *officina* A are "commonly found in Palestine," and may even have been minted specifically for consignment to Palestine.[54] No coins of Constantinople's *officina* A were found in the excavations.

Anastasius's coinage has been divided into three phases by Metcalf (with modifications by Bellinger): pre-reform *folles* of approximately 9 grams (though a high tolerance of variation is noted);[55] reformed *folles* of c.18 grams, and large-flan coins of approximately the same weight. Bellinger's system makes the first two phases not divided by weight, but flan size (though the two phases have overlapping measurements to some degree).[56] Metcalf's pre-reform *folles* were minted sparingly, or were withdrawn from circulation at least in Asia Minor, though he expected more to appear in Palestine, where they would have been used to pay the troops.[57] Two *folles* (**2198**, **2202**) and four half-*folles* (**2199–2201**, **2203**) seem to fall into Metcalf's pre-reform category, and Bellinger's first two phases. None combine small flans and heavy weights. And though the mints at Antioch, Cyzicus and Thessalonica were opened to strike large *folles*, Metcalf notes that coins from these mints "are very scarce at the present day, and there is no reason to think that they were ever at all plentiful, relative to the quantities struck at Constantinople."[58] His conclusion is confirmed by the excavation coins.

D.M. Metcalf has noted how common *folles* of Justin and Sophia are in Palestine;[59] from the published reports, it is difficult to gauge how common they are, though Caesarea seems to have many more than any other site. These were primarily from the mint at Constantinople (**2216–24**), though they are joined by a group from Nicomedia (**2232–34**) and one from Antioch (**2238**). Small bronzes replace the monogram coins of Anastasius, especially the *pentanummia* from Constantinople (**2225–30**) and Nicomedia (**2236–37**).

Justinian I (527–567) provided small change through a mint argued to have been placed in Carthage. Great numbers of these coins appear in the finds (**2250–2335**), attesting to their utility. In 539 Justinian reformed the coins to increase their weight. Numismatists have noticed that the lighter coins did not disappear from hoards, leading them to assume that the call-in of the lighter coins was perfunctory, especially in provinces without a functioning mint.[60] Indeed, while the small change from this period overwhelms the number of *folles*, the latter do appear in the finds, from the mints of Constantinople and Antioch (**2337–45**, **2357–63**, **2365–66**, cf. **2384–92**). The coins show approximately the same spread and mean as the earlier coins in terms of weight. No coins from 539 through the end of the reign of Justinian were found in the JECM excavations, though two were recorded by Levine 1986, confirming D.M. Metcalf's suspicion that the reformed coins did not penetrate into Palestine.[61] Thus the very worn condition of early sixth-century coins can be attributed to long use; several coins from the reigns of Anastasius and Justin I were still in circulation, to be countermarked in the time of Heraclius or even later (**2207**, **2218**, **2220–21**, **2360**, **2363**, **2394–95**).[62]

The number of coins continues to rise through the sixth century, with the mints at Constantinople and Antioch most heavily represented. This trend reverses for the reign of Phocas (602–610 C.E.), save the *dodecanummia* from Alexandria, if all of these can be attributed to his reign (**2504–90**). Coins from the mint of Alexandria deserve a special note. Few coins from this mint are represented through the reign of Maurice; all consist of *dodecanummia*, with the I+B reverse type, many of which appear in the excavated coins. As the die cutters for the series were rather inept and often seem illiterate, it is difficult to distinguish "official" coins from "copies"; the series may have been copied elsewhere in the East to provide for an intense need for small change.[63] Hahn divided the official coins from the copies by the inscription; on copies, the obverse has some letters meant to be Justin's or Justinian's name, and the coins weigh between 1.5 and 2.5 grams.[64] In practice, some very good portraits have inscriptions limited to the letters "OIO", and weights even below 1 gram. Unfortunately, these very common coins have not been adequately sorted out.

From the histogram (Fig. 6), the weight distribution of the earlier *dodecanummia* (Justin I–Justinian I) falls around 3 grams, the coins of Tiberius II and Maurice around 2–2.25 grams, and those attributed to Phocas peak between 1.25–2.25 grams, with a fairly substantial representation under 1 gram (though these are generally of the cruder style). Heraclius restored the weight, with 2 examples weighing 6 grams (**2678–79**) and striking the next lower denomination, the *hexanummium*, on earlier *dodecanummia* (**2683–84**, **2690–91**, **2693**, **2697–98**, **2707**).

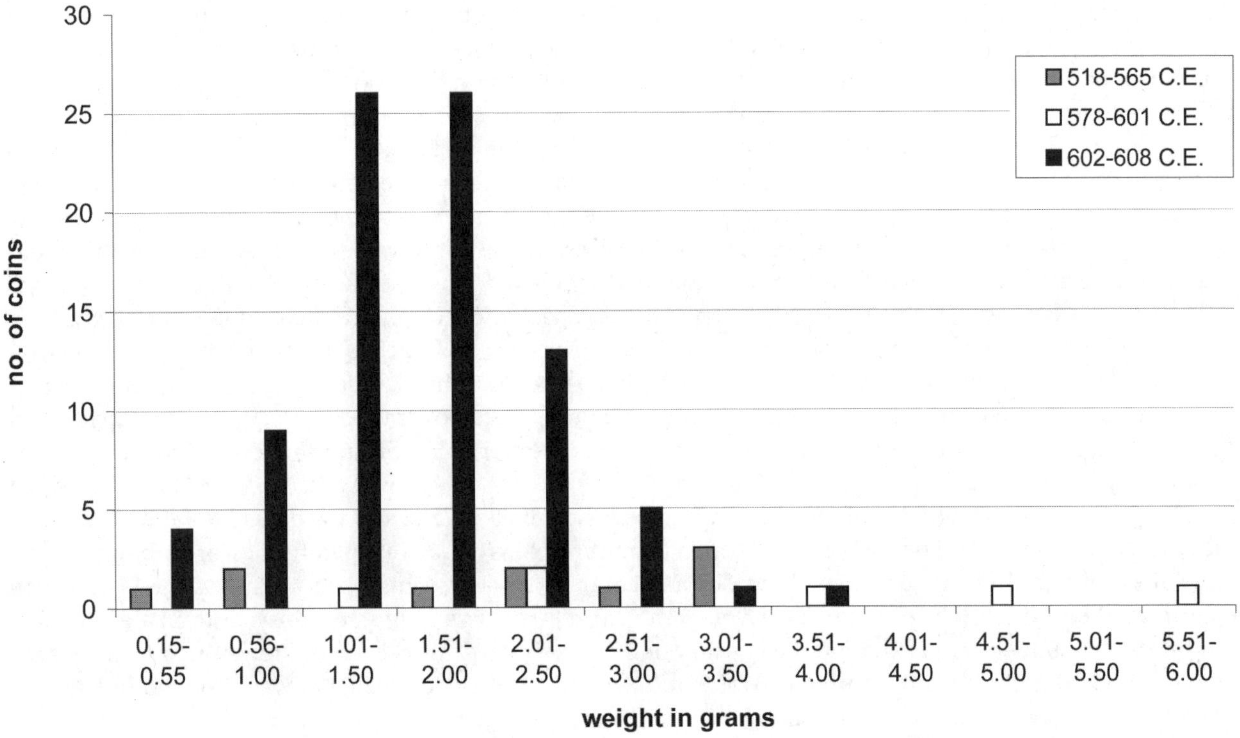

Fig. 6 *Weight of* dodecanummia *from JECM coins.*

With Heraclius, the *folles* show a wider weight distribution, partly because of the use of older coins for overstriking. But in general, there is a continued loss of weight through his reign, with the latest *folles* weighing between 4 and 7 grams. The phenomenon of the reuse of older coins, overstruck with Heraclian types, is not confined to the site nor the region, but is a general fact of Heraclian coinage. While small change is obtained from the mint at Alexandria, most of the *folles*, three-quarter *folles*, and half-*folles* were minted in Constantinople.

W. Metcalf proposed that declining numbers of post-year 6 (616 C.E.) copper coins of Heraclius in the Myers, Tell Bisa, and Coele Syria hoards reflect the closing of the mints in Cyzicus and Nicomedia, and a probable slowdown in minting at Constantinople, due to the siege of the city by the Persian army. The numbers of copper coins in Syria from the early years of Heraclius' reign and prior emperors were also swelled by the Byzantine army moving through the area.[65] Qedar suggested that quasi-official coins, imitating Byzantine types, were struck locally to supply coin.[66] This relative lack of later coins is also apparent in coins excavated from Caesarea. Of ninety coins found, forty-two can be attributed to the years 610–616 C.E., and only forty-one to the next twenty-four years of his reign. Very few coins of Heraclius are found from the period 616–628 C.E. and again from 634–640/1 C.E., when the Persian army controlled or was besieging Caesarea.

The Byzantine coins are heavily countermarked, proving previous speculation that countermarking probably occurred in Syria, Lebanon, or Palestine (Fig. 5 and Table 1). Hahn lists two varieties, his 1b, the ⳩ form and 1a, the ⳩ form, both of which occur on *folles* of Tiberius II, Maurice, and Heraclius' year 20/21 *folles*.[67] His type 2 countermark was not found on any of the coins excavated at Caesarea.

Of the Byzantine coins found at Caesarea, thirty-four carry the Heraclian countermarks noted above. Ten coins from the excavation bear Hahn's type 1b; all are placed on the reverses of coins, in punches varying between 8 and 9 mm. Although half of the examples are *folles*, the group includes three half-*folles* and two three-quarter *folles*. All of the coins punched only with the type 1b countermark were minted during the reign of Heraclius, specifically the years 629–640. In fact, all but two date to 629–631; the two exceptions are a coin dating to 632/3 and one to 634–640. The countermarks are placed on coins already overstruck, can be placed twice or possibly even three times on the reverse, and are sometimes found in conjunction with the type 1a countermark. I have argued that this is a coherent group, placed on the coins around 634; some coins were struck, overstruck and countermarked within a 6-year span.[68]

Hahn's type 1a countermark consists of the letters Hrc conjoined; it can be formed as  (with a large punch, from 9–10 mm), or less commonly formed , with a slightly smaller punch of 7 mm. Almost all type 1a countermarks are found on *folles*; twenty-six (possibly twenty-seven) were found in the excavations. The countermarks are found five times on the obverses of coins, the rest on reverses. Interestingly, on one coin of Maurice, where the countermark is placed on the reverse, his face has been defaced with chisel cuts (**2452**). This group shows a wider chronological sweep of coins. The earliest coin with this countermark is a *follis* of Anastasius, but more common are *folles* of Maurice and early *folles* of Heraclius, the latest being the same coin that provided the terminus for the type 1b countermark. The countermark is sometimes found with the type 1b countermark. Three crucial coins have both countermarks placed over the Heraclian types, which can be dated between 619/20 and 630–641. I have argued that this countermark was in use around 630, being superseded by type 1b in 634.[69]

The countermarks should probably be connected to the Persian Wars, and the dates mesh nicely with the independent evidence of the coin types. Although Byzantine coins were quite plentiful prior to the siege, very few coins are found in the succeeding decades in Caesarea. Thus it seems likely to me that the coins were countermarked possibly beginning as early as 627/8, to reassert Byzantine authority in the Palestine area; the process continued in 634, though the number of countermarked coins becomes fewer, in a futile gesture to assert the strength of the Byzantine ruler. I would argue that the countermarks were applied in Palestine – probably Caesarea, since so many countermarked coins appear here.

A much rarer type of countermark appears on four coins from Caesarea, an eagle with upraised wings and a pellet between the wings, in a circular punch, 8 mm in diameter (Fig. 5 and Table 1).[70] All are placed at approximately the same place on the reverses of *folles*, obscuring the *officinae*, but carefully avoiding disfiguring the M or mintmark. The four examples are all early sixth-century *folles*, from the reign of Justin I, the combined reign of Justin I and Justinian, and Justinian alone. In all cases, the coins are worn and the countermarks are fresh.

Only six other examples of this countermark are known, two of which were found in the excavation at Nag Hammadi in Egypt; one was said to have been obtained in Egypt.[71] All of these examples are also found on the reverses of *folles* and the *folles* are again dated to the early sixth century, none post-dating the reign of Justinian. Bendall, who first published the countermark, suggested that it was applied not long after the last coin had been minted, that is, around 540, and that the countermark was applied in Egypt and had some "local significance."[72]

Hahn connected the eagle to a rare three-*nummi* type, minted in Alexandria, suggesting even that the coins and the countermarks were made with the same die. He dated the countermark to the Heraclian period, partly because this is the period when countermarks were first applied, and partly because the eagle motif would have been copied from the consular scepter on coins of Tiberius II, Maurice and Phocas (though no such coins circulated in Egypt), and was common on seventh-century lead seals. He suggested a date early in Heraclius' reign, between 613–617 C.E., for the countermarking, and argued that it was done in Alexandria.[73] As noted previously, coins from Alexandria became common in Caesarea in the reign of Phocas. But it is precisely coins of 613–618, especially *hexanummia*, that appear in the excavations from the mint of Alexandria, perhaps confirming Hahn's argument.

It is possible that the few *fals*, or imitation Byzantine coins made on small flans with crude obverses and reverses mimicking Byzantine types, found at Caesarea date to the period after 640; otherwise, coins from the era immediately after 640 are few.[74] With the Muslim occupation of Caesarea, we pass beyond the scope of this study.

Chapter 2
Comparison of Caesarea to other Sites

The huge majority of coins found in any excavation are bronze, just as in Caesarea.[1] Lists of excavation coins are dutifully published by numismatists, but it has been left to archaeologists/numismatists in Britain and Germany to theorize what these coins can tell us about the site. It is this theory that seeks to answer what light excavated bronze coins shed on the ancient economy or trade. What Richard Reece and John Casey, in particular, have tried to establish is a "normal" profile of a site, based on the bronze coins found there.[2] These profiles are then used to find "normal" villas, towns, forts and cities; the sites that do not follow these profiles then must be explained in terms of the historical use of the site. There is simply not enough detailed information yet to do this in terms of Judaea, but I will attempt to define "normal" for the larger cities in the east, beginning with Caesarea, Jerusalem, and Samaria, and including Pella, Pergamon, Antioch, Sardis, Hama, and Gerasa. Deviations from the norm may show periods of isolation, a dip in the local economy, or a local population loss.

Numismatists have been trying to use the bronze coins to explain aspects of the site for many years. The first, and basic, tabulation is to find the percentage of coins of different periods from each site, to see if the profiles match (Figs. 7–10).[3] This has proved of limited use in extracting information from the excavated coins, as the method is primitive and depends on too-broad categories of coins. We are also dependent on having a large number of sites that were continuously occupied. For a discussion of the strengths and weaknesses of this and other methods, see Appendix 2.

In Chapter One (see Table 2, p. 19) I briefly described the effort to count the number of different types that come from the mint as an indicator of mint productivity. It is thought that the more coins that were produced from a mint, the more prosperous the region was. The methodology of extracting numbers of coins minted from given known types, by equations that calculate the average number of coins struck from each die, has recently been shown to be built on a series of assumptions that are not statistically valid.[4] Even if they were, we most often do not know why a particular mint issued coins, nor why a city chose a large or small issue of coins.[5] I make reference to the number of coin types minted per year in the argument in this chapter, but show that the numbers have little bearing on the state of the economy. Other factors must be used to reconstruct the state of the economy.

The third methodology, finding the Annual Average Coin Loss, attempts to refine the commonly used methodology of listing the coins found and dividing them by the number of regnal years of the emperor. The result is given in a table that lists the percentages of coins that belong to the emperor Augustus, Tiberius, Caligula (etc.) or divides the reigns into reasonable segments of time (e.g., 340–348 c.e.). Casey presented his refinement by means of histograms and introduced the idea of standardizing the amounts of coin, so that we can compare sites with large numbers of coins to sites with few coins, and the coins from long reigns to the coins from short reigns, in order better to understand the general trend of coin loss. His equation divides the number of coins from a certain emperor by the length of his reign to find the number of coins lost per regnal year, and then multiplies that result by 1000 divided by the total number of coins found on the site.[6]

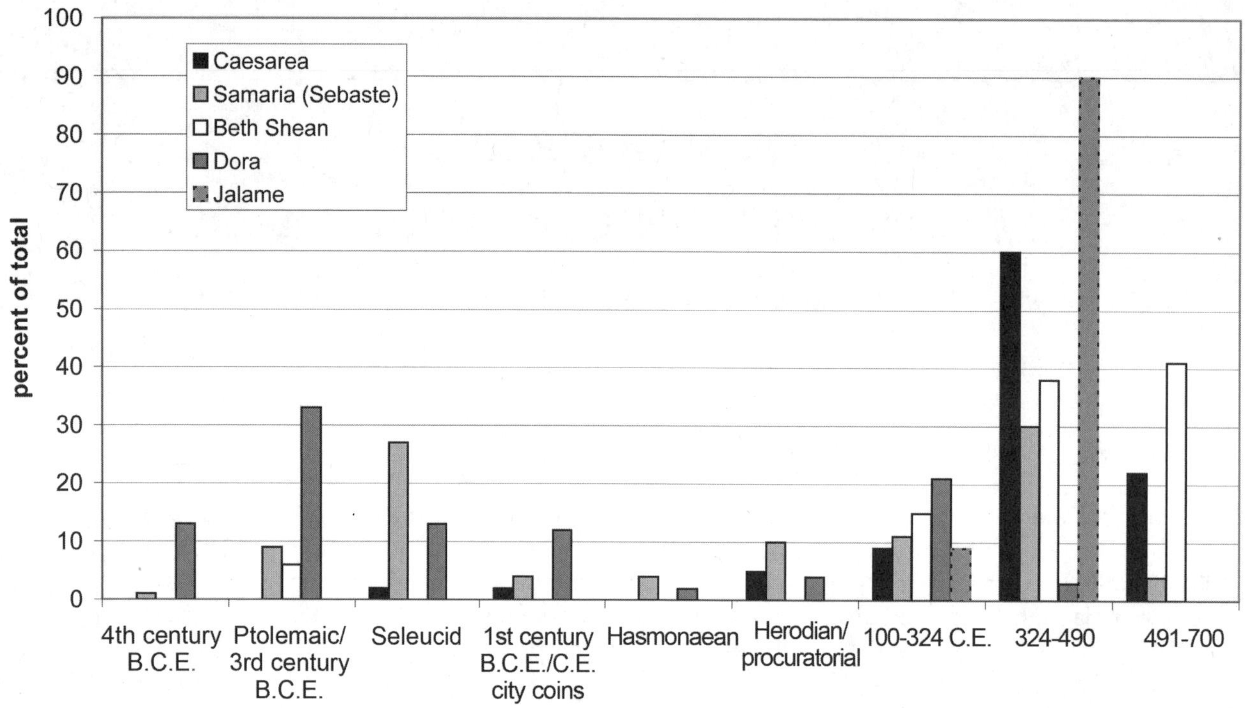

Fig. 7 *Percentages of excavated coins of Regional Comparative Cohort: Samaria and Phoenicia.*

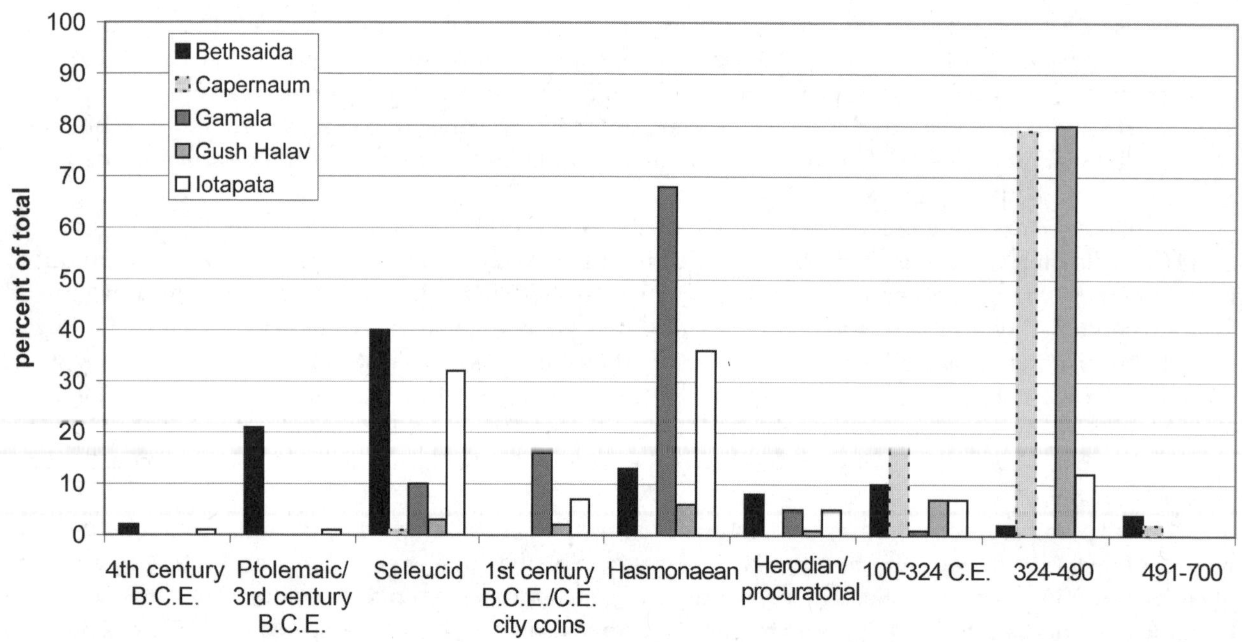

Fig. 8 *Percentages of excavated coins of Regional Comparative Cohort: Galilee and the Decapolis, part 1.*

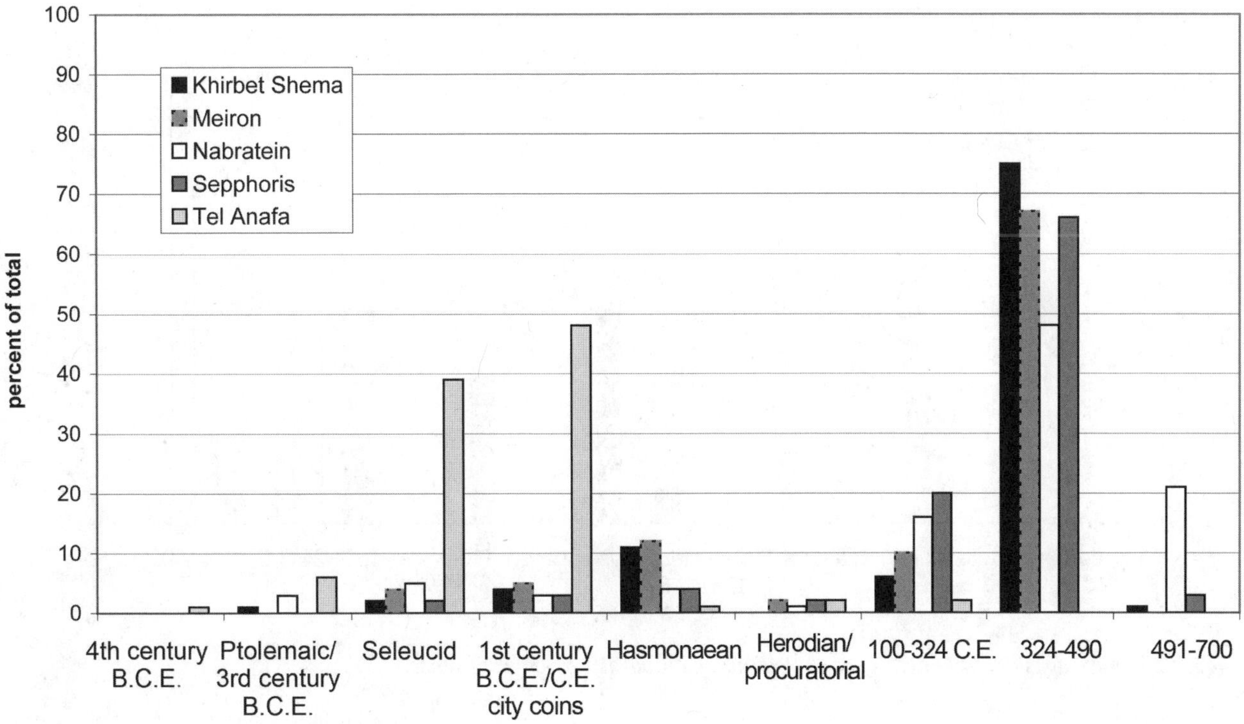

Fig. 9 *Percentages of excavated coins of Regional Comparative Cohort: Galilee and the Decapolis, part 2.*

This methodology is used for Romano-British, Italian, and German sites, but as far as I know, has never been applied to a site in the east.[7]

The results for Caesarea are shown in Figure 11 and Table 3. For instance, in the issue period for the reign of Herod the Great (40–4 B.C.E.), sixteen coins were found. Thus 16 divided by 43 is 0.37, which is multiplied by 1000/2734 (the site total) for a result of 0.14. The vertical axis shows the annual rate of loss out of every 1000 coins found on the site; the horizontal axis smoothes out the differences between short and long periods of issue. The numbers can only be used as a comparison among sites, since we do not know how many coins were produced each issue period. Nor can the equation take into account how long the coin remained in circulation before being lost. And the results cannot be used to simply track a rise or fall in the prosperity of the city.[8] More coins recovered per issue period may only mean that a single coin has become of less worth, and is less likely to be retrieved by the person who lost the coin, as much as it may mean that there was more coin in circulation, and thus more were dropped on the ground as more transactions took place. Thus, it is an incomplete analysis, and only used to wring some information from the scattered finds. We need another method to ascertain that the variations in the numbers are not just random variations.

That method is the Chi-Square Test, the "goodness-of-fit" test, the results of which are in Figure 12 and Table 4.[9] For a discussion of the aim and limitations of the Chi-Square Test, and how I derived the "normal" profile, see Appendix 2. The Chi-Square Test must use broader parameters for the time periods than is possible in the Average Annual Coin Loss test. It is also of limited use, since we do not know the number of coins produced during that time period. And since few of the Judaean sites have coins reported from all the time periods that Caesarea has, this is where I depend on other large cities in the east to build the "normal" profile. However, the Chi-Square Test does reinforce the findings of the Average Annual Coin Loss calculation, and more importantly, it shows that the variations in the coin numbers are not insignificant, but are something we need to explain.

But the economy cannot be reconstructed simply by looking at the number of bronze coins lost at a particular site. In order to reconstruct the economy of ancient Palestine, we must look at the coins in conjunction

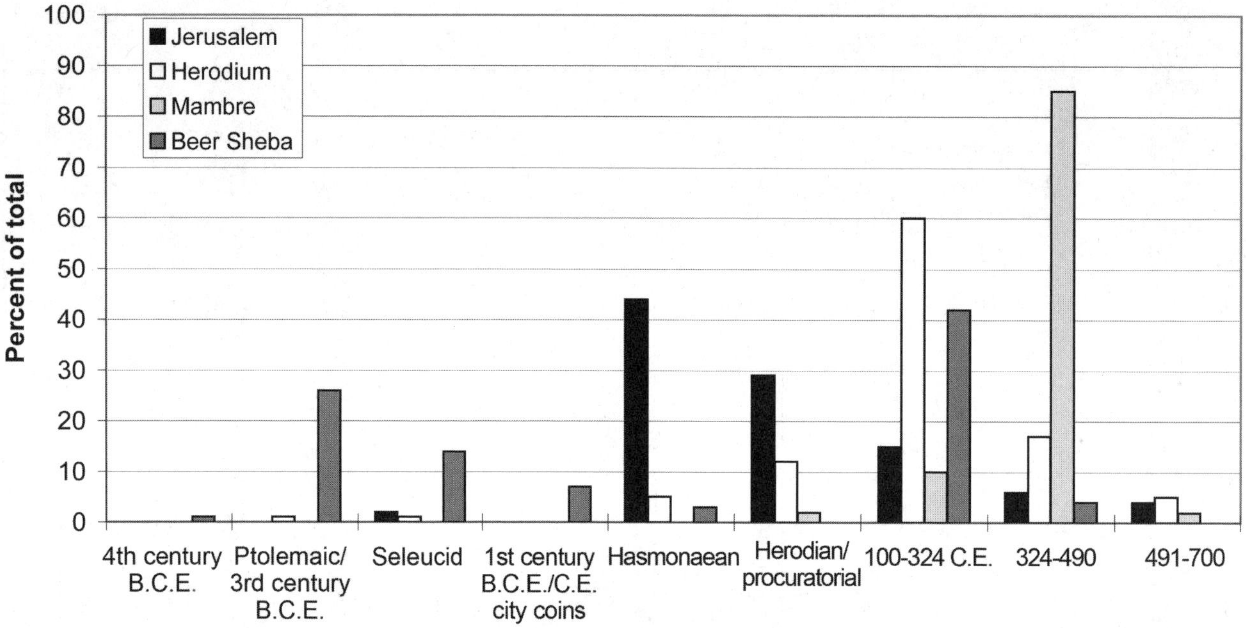

Fig. 10 Percentages of excavated coins of Regional Comparative Cohort: Judaea.

with other indicators of the economy. For although coins are a primary indicator of the economy of a region, they cannot stand alone.[10] The coins can be used in conjunction with other indicators in order to accumulate a picture of the regional economy over a broad span of time. These other indicators include literary sources, inscriptions, and material culture.

Material culture, as noted in archaeological finds, tells us the quality and quantity of goods found on the site. For instance, the best preserved—imported pottery—implies income, which can be used for luxury items, either the pottery itself or the goods found in the pots. Building programs (which can be attested in inscriptions, dated by strata or noted in the literary sources) imply the injection of funds into the local economy, normally by the government, but also by local patrons, and a consequent drop in unemployment. Certain events (which again are noted in literary sources or inscriptions) might inject money into the local economy, as funds from abroad or locally were redistributed to skilled and unskilled workers, from innkeepers and foodsellers to masons and hod carriers. Athletic games and visits by emperors might temporarily bring outside money into the area. Literary sources, although they must be used with caution, may also provide hints to the economy of the region.[11] And although the issue is still somewhat controversial, I agree with those who think that the permanent stationing of legions in Palestine would be a help, not a hindrance, to the local economy, as soldiers bought local goods and paid for them by money issued by the Roman government.

It used to be thought that soldiers were an economic liability, as each province had to pay for the soldiers housed in it, but since the 1940s, British scholars in particular have revised this theory, arguing that the more prosperous provinces were obliged to contribute to the maintenance of the forces in the less prosperous provinces.[12] Millar attempted to estimate the cost of housing a legion, and decided that for Syria, at least, the equation was a wash—the legionaries pumped as much money into the local economy as was spent to maintain them. That is, Rome did not make a profit, but neither was the legion a burden on the province.[13] During the period c.70–120 C.E. (and possibly even later), Safrai has pointed out that 25,000 auxiliaries and two legions were stationed in Judaea, a far greater proportion of troops to civilian population than in any other province; the number is eight percent of all the troops in the Roman army. The general tax rate set by the emperor was not, as far as we know, prorated by the number of troops housed in the province, but was the same for every province. The burden of supporting those troops would have been unbearable, and though we hear the inevitable complaints about taxes, we do not hear of this specific complaint. Even if Hopkins' tax rates of

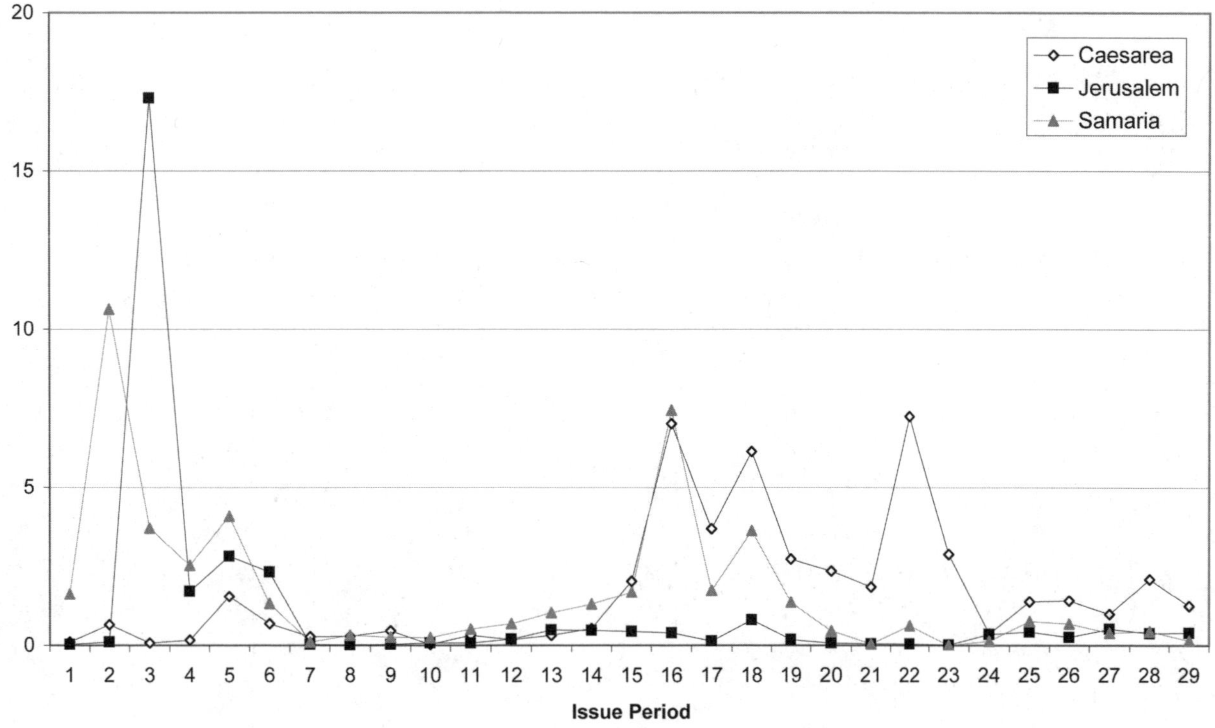

Fig. 11 Annual Average Coin Loss (coins/1000).

ten percent of the Gross National Product of the province are applied (which may be too low, Safrai argues), Judaea makes up only one percent of the Empire, and it is thus highly unlikely that the province could have raised much more than one percent of the total tax income of the Empire. If we accept Hopkins' suggested rate of payment to the troops, then over sixteen percent of the GNP of the Roman Empire must have been earmarked to support the troops in Judaea alone. Yet not all of the wages the troops earned went into their pockets. They had to pay for their own food, clothing, and weapons. These purchases were made locally, some of which may have been derived from the taxes delivered in kind from the Judaeans (that is, the government accepted food as a form of taxes, and then turned around and sold it to the legionaries). Thus, taxes from provinces where no troops were stationed (e.g., Gaul) were used to support the troops in the provinces that were relatively poor but with large troop concentrations (e.g., Britain and Judaea).[14] Hopkins argues that the immediate consequence of legions in the province was the monetization of the local economy, increased trade contacts, increased employment for people who clothed and fed legionaries, as well as bankers and shippers, and a high level of urbanization.[15]

Coins may be good indicators of inflation, trade routes, or circulation patterns. That is why it is crucial that excavations publish their coins. To begin with Caesarea itself, the coins from the Italian, Israeli, and harbor excavations (which did not find the earlier levels of the city), published in list form, confirm the overall statistics of the finds from JECM (Table 5). In researching sites in the ancient Palestine area to compare to Caesarea, I was able to use the excavation reports of only two other sites in Samaria, two from Phoenicia, and four from Judaea; most of my comparative material comes from the small cities of Galilee and the Decapolis (see map of comparative sites, Fig. 2). Only Jerusalem and Samaria were comparable, in terms of inhabitation periods and the amount of urbanization, for the Annual Average Coin Loss test. Information from the sites in Judaea and Samaria is less clear than from sites in the upper Galilee, due to the age in which the excavations took place and incomplete recording of the finds; I suspect that the fourth- and fifth-century bronzes, especially, are under-represented in all reports except the most recent.[16] Comparison sites were difficult, as no well published site in Palestine truly parallels Caesarea, and there are only a limited number of large cities in Palestine.

Table 3. Average Annual Coin Loss (coins/1000): Caesarea, Jerusalem, Samaria.

				CAESAREA		JERUSALEM		SAMARIA	
PERIOD	DYNASTY	YEARS	NO.YEARS	COINS	AACL	COINS [E]	AACL	COINS	AACL
1	Antiochus III	222–187	35	9	0.10	6	0.03	42	1.63
2	Antiochus IV	175–164	11	18	0.65	7	0.10	86	10.63
3	Hasmonaean/city	103–40	37	7	0.08	4265	17.29	101	3.71
4	Herodian	40–4	43	18	0.17	492	1.71	80	2.53
5	Archelaus	4 B.C.E. –6 C.E.	8	31	1.55	151	2.83	24	4.08
6	Procurators/Agrippa I	6–69	62	107	0.69	958	2.32	60	1.32
7	Flavian	69–96	27	19	0.28	5	0.03	2	0.10
8	Nerva-Trajan	96–117	21	15	0.29	1	0.01	5	0.32
9	Hadrian [A]	117–138	21	24	0.46	4	0.03	4	0.26
10	Antonine	138–192	54	4	0.03	30	0.08	10	0.25
11	Severan	193–256	63	51	0.32	34	0.08	24	0.52
12	Third Century II	256–270	26	12	0.18	33	0.19	13	0.68
13	Third Century III	270–300	30	24	0.32	97	0.48	23	1.04
14	Fourth Century I	300–324	24	32	0.53	75	0.47	23	1.30
15	Constantinian [B]	324–346	21	107	2.04	61	0.44	26	1.68
16	Fourth Century III	346–363	17	298	7.01	45	0.40	93	7.44
17	Fourth Century IV	364–378	14	129	3.69	12	0.13	18	1.75
18	Valentinian II [C]	378–383	6	92	6.13	43	0.81	16	3.63
19	Theodosius I	378--395	18	123	2.73	22	0.18	18	1.36
20	Arcadius/Honorius	395–425	30	177	2.36	16	0.08	10	0.45
21	Theodosius II/ Valentinian III	425–450	25	116	1.86	7	0.04	1	0.05
22	Fifth Century I [D]	450–474	24	435	7.25	7	0.04	11	0.62
23	Fifth Century II	475–498	23	166	2.89	2	0.01	0	0
24	Anastasius, reformed	498–518	20	18	0.36	46	0.35	2	0.14
25	Justin and joint reign	518–527	9	31	1.38	25	0.42	5	0.76
26	Justinian	527–565	38	134	1.41	65	0.26	19	0.68
27	Justin II/Tiberius II	565–582	17	42	0.99	59	0.52	5	0.40
28	Maurice/Phocas	582–610	28	146	2.09	70	0.38	9	0.44
29	Heraclius	610–640	30	93	1.24	79	0.39	3	0.15
	TOTAL			**2478**		**6717**		**733**	

NOTES: All coins were put into the latest period possible, if there was a question of the date of the ruler on the coin. Excludes coins from periods not on the chart (about 100), and from periods too long to fit into the chart (e.g. Vandalic), about 150.
[A] Totals include all Trajan/Hadrian coins. [B] Totals include all unidentified fourth century coins. [C] Valentinian II, Theodosius I, Honorius and Arcadius are each given ¼ of the coins that could not be differentiated among the four rulers. [D] Includes ¾ of uncertain monograms and ½ of the unidentified fifth–sixth century coins; the remainder are placed in Fifth Century II.
[E] Totals do not include Gitler 1996, due to the difference in data collection.

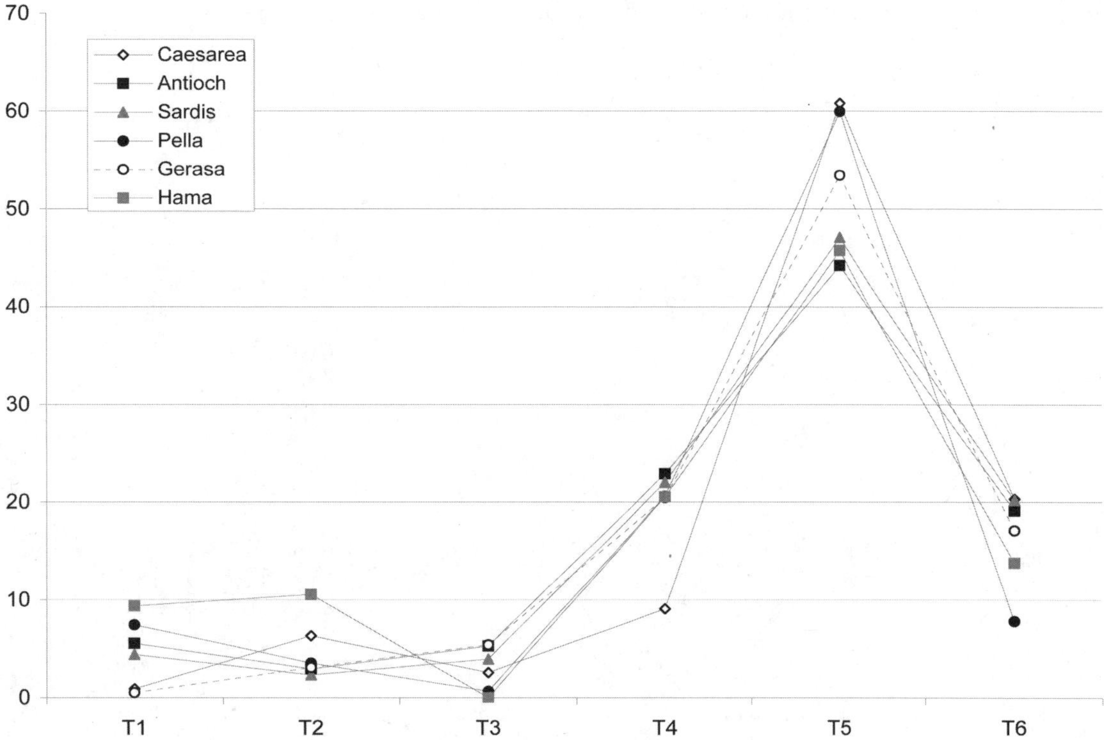

Fig. 12 Chi-Square Test: "normal" eastern cities, percentage of coins from time period.

Samaria would be the best parallel to Caesarea, since it was another city heavily subsidized by Herod and it retained its importance into the Late Roman period; yet the early excavation reports are incomplete. Information is also limited for Beth Shean; the Galilean sites are better published, but the sites are either small towns or the excavations are very limited. Jerusalem is the next obvious parallel, but the coin finds reflect certain aspects of Jewish life that were simply not found for Caesarea, especially the large number of "foreign" visitors, who would need to change money while in the city attending to their religious duties. That, coupled with the devastation and consequent depopulation by the Romans in 70 and 132–135 C.E. (especially the latter) means that the numismatic record is not a good parallel after c.130 C.E. Hence, for mint parallels in the Late Roman and Byzantine periods I looked farther away, to the well published site of Sardis. And for the Chi-Square Test I looked for a pattern that could be broadly applied, and so incorporated the results of cities from Asia Minor, Syria and the Decapolis. As more excavations are published, the patterns I have proposed will have to be reworked or at least refined.

Fourth and Third Centuries B.C.E.

After Alexander's conquest in 332, Palestine was given to Laomedon as a satrapy, yet it became an area of conflict in 320, the first of the so-called Five Syrian Wars, when Laomedon was forced to relinquish control to Ptolemy I (323–282 B.C.E.). All of the sites in the regional comparative cohort agree that very few coins circulated before the reign of Ptolemy I;[17] the outlier is Dora (Figs. 7–10). Dora was an important harbor in Phoenicia in the fifth through first centuries B.C.E., losing its importance when Herod constructed the harbor at Caesarea.[18] One reflection of the increasing importance of Caesarea can be seen in the declining percentages of coins found at Dora in the centuries succeeding the first century B.C.E.

Table 4. Chi-Square Test. Frequency of period by city: "Normal" eastern cities.

Frequency Chi-Square Percent Row Percent Cell Percent	CAESAREA	ANTIOCH	SARDIS	PELLA	GERASA	HAMA	TOTAL
T1	24	697	242	78	6	32	1079
	79.26	22.13	0.62	17.69	59.49	16.55	
222–100	0.10	3.00	1.04	0.34	0.03	0.14	4.64
B.C.E.	2.22	64.60	22.43	7.23	0.56	2.97	
	0.91	5.54	4.41	7.44	0.52	9.38	
T2	167	371	128	37	36	36	775
	70.85	5.50	16.46	0.12	0.20	53.43	
c.103 B.C.E.	0.72	1.60	0.55	0.16	0.15	0.15	3.33
–69 C.E.	21.55	47.87	16.52	4.77	4.65	4.65	
	6.32	2.95	2.33	3.53	3.09	10.56	
T3	68	664	217	7	63	0	1019
	19.69	23.20	2.28	33.02	2.83	14.94	
69–192 C.E.	0.29	2.85	0.93	0.03	0.27	0	4.38
	6.67	65.16	21.30	0.69	6.18	0	
	2.57	5.28	3.95	0.67	5.41	0	
T4	240	2878	1208	216	238	70	4850
	175.45	24.94	3.54	0.03	0.09	0.02	
193–346 C.E.	1.03	12.37	5.19	0.93	1.02	0.30	20.85
	4.95	59.34	24.91	4.45	4.91	1.44	
	9.08	22.88	22.01	20.59	20.45	20.53	
T5	1606	5561	2585	629	622	156	11159
	90.34	36.98	0.87	31.42	7.24	0.35	
347–498 C.E.	6.90	23.91	11.11	2.70	2.67	0.67	47.98
	14.39	49.83	23.17	5.64	5.57	1.40	
	60.79	44.22	47.10	59.96	53.44	45.75	
T6	537	2405	1108	82	199	47	4378
	3.17	0.61	5.45	67.50	1.84	4.60	
498–640 C.E.	2.31	10.34	4.76	0.35	0.86	0.20	18.82
	12.27	54.93	25.31	1.87	4.55	1.07	
	20.33	19.12	20.19	7.82	17.10	13.78	
Total	2642	12576	5488	1049	1164	341	23260
	11.36	54.07	23.59	4.51	5.00	1.47	100.00

Table 5. Non-JECM excavation coins from Caesarea (from Frova 1966, Hohlfelder 1985, Ariel 1986, Lampinen 1992 and Hohlfelder 1994).

PERIOD	1966	1985	1986	1992	1994
4th century B.C.E.	–	–	–	2	–
Ptolemaic	–	–	2	3	–
Seleucid	–	–	–	–	–
Hasmonaean	–	–	–	–	–
1st century B.C.E-1st century C.E.	–	1	3	–	1
Palestinian-Roman procuratorial	–	–	6	7	–
100–200 C.E., Imperial and colonial	–	–	4	4	–
200–256 C.E., Colonial	–	–	5	–	4
200–324 C.E., Imperial	–	–	2	–	9
325–491 C.E.	19	8	21	62	40
491–640 C.E.	8	12	206	39	26

The problem of the date of the foundation of Strato's Tower, the settlement upon which Herod built his city named for Caesar Augustus, cannot be solved by the study of the coins of the site alone. While there is one possible fourth-century B.C.E. coin and two Ptolemaic coins of uncertain date, these coins could have been brought to the site at any point after their date of minting. They do not necessarily point to a settlement in the fourth century on the site of the later city, even if the literary sources seem to suggest this date and location for the town. The lack of any Hellenistic structures has also stymied the quest for the city.[19]

Palestine changed hands five times between 320 and 201, alternating between Seleucid and Ptolemaic control. Although the various rulers established garrisons and built shipyards, the civil chaos and military campaigns must have had a negative effect on the economy. Yet during this time, Ptolemy I opened a mint in Judaea, joining the mints at Alexandria and Damascus.[20] The sites rich in Ptolemaic coins are Bethsaida (Galilee), Dora, and to a lesser extent Samaria (in the province of Samaria) and Beer Sheba (Judaea, Figs. 7–10). Samaria may have more coins than other cities, in part because Alexander settled Macedonian veterans here; the Macedonian general Ptolemy may have felt that this city, at least, was fairly secure. The city may also have been the largest in Palestine, and remained so until the Maccabean Revolt.[21]

The reign of Ptolemy II (285–246 B.C.E.) was relatively uneventful for Palestine, allowing Ptolemy to open the mints at Sidon, Tyre, and Ake-Ptolemais, as well as those at Joppa and Gaza, all of which struck substantial issues until the end of the Third Syrian War or the War of Laodice (242/1 B.C.E.).[22] The silver hoard from Beth Shean has at least one coin from all these mints, and one from Cyprus as well.[23] As Mørkholm has pointed out, we expect that silver pieces will be found farther from the mints than bronze pieces; bronzes are normally minted for very local needs.[24] No other site reports more than one Ptolemaic silver piece, though it should be noted that several in the regional comparative cohort were not yet settled, including Nabratein, Hammat Gader, Meiron, and Khirbet Shema. Other towns have few remains from this period: Capernaum, Gush Halav, Beer Sheba, and perhaps Sepphoris are either not settled or have few remains from this period.[25] The bronzes of Ptolemy II are better represented at Tel Anafa, Bethsaida, Dora, and Samaria. At Samaria, the predominant mint is Tyre, even though Ake-Ptolemais is the closer mint.[26] Even stranger, the bronze coins reported from Tel Anafa all come from the mint at Alexandria.[27] Unfortunately, only one Ptolemaic coin from Tyre could be identified (**43**, cf. **376–77**, possibly also from Tyre). The relative lack of Ptolemaic coins at Caesarea may simply be due to the fact that the Hellenistic settlement has not yet been identified, yet it is suspicious that with the exception of the functioning port of Dora, the sites with Ptolemaic coins are all in the interior, on the north–south roads. Gaza was the mercantile center of the province, and most trade passed through the Idumaeans.[28] All these factors point to the importance of inland, not coastal trade.

Most sites in the regional comparative cohort display a complete lack of coins minted between 250 and 220 B.C.E., with the result that many early third-century coins continued to be used throughout the century and are too worn to identify.[29] Palestine does not seem to have been involved in the Third Syrian War between Ptolemy III and Seleucus II, beginning in 246. It does seem clear that the entire region suffered from the lack of new coins introduced into the economy, though it is not clear if this is due to an economic slowdown or a surplus of coins minted by Ptolemy II.

It is not until the Fourth Syrian War (219–217 B.C.E.) between Ptolemy IV and Antiochus III that the fighting came to Palestine. Strato's Tower was captured by Antiochus III in 218, but was regained by the Ptolemies when Antiochus was thrown out of Palestine at the Battle of Raphia in 217. He returned in 201 to conquer Phoenicia and Palestine. It may have been that when Antiochus paid his troops, he re-introduced coins into the economy of Palestine, for all of the sites that had no coins minted in the years 250–222 B.C.E. exhibit coins minted under the authority of Antiochus III; the coins certainly point to the change in rulers, as few Ptolemaic coins are found in Israel that date to after the reign of Ptolemy III.[30] Ariel suggested that the coins of Antiochus III were plentiful in Jerusalem in part because Antiochus came to the city.[31]

Coins of Antiochus III (229–187 B.C.E.) form the first recognizable group in the Caesarea finds, from the mints of Tyre and Antioch; Antioch is the mint that supplied all of the coins at Samaria.[32] The sites in Galilee tended to obtain their coins from Tyre, though Antioch is represented in small numbers.[33] Because the mint at Tyre struck far fewer issues than did the large and important city of Antioch, it is not entirely surprising to find many coins from this more distant mint in Palestine.

SECOND AND FIRST CENTURIES B.C.E.

Ptolemy V (204–180 B.C.E.) initiated the Fifth Syrian War. Control of Palestine changed several times during the war, with accompanying devastation to cities and harbors, but the area remained Seleucid after the conclusion of the war. Strato's Tower remained in Seleucid hands after 198 B.C.E. The author of II Maccabees (3:1–3) informs us that the reign of Seleucus IV (187–175 B.C.E.) was a period of peace and prosperity, with the country ruled by Onias III as High Priest, yet few coins from Seleucus' reign are reported from Caesarea, Samaria, Jerusalem, or the Galilean sites.[34] Perhaps we should rely on other historical sources to argue that the economy was depressed, for Seleucus looted the Temple treasury and may have imposed a heavy tax on Palestine, in part to help pay a heavy tribute to the Romans after the defeat of his father Antiochus III in 191–190.[35] The area was not wanting in mints, as Antioch, Tyre, and Ake-Ptolemais stuck coins for Seleucus.

The next group of coins in Caesarea dates to the reign of Antiochus IV (175–164 B.C.E.), and consists of coins from the mint at Ake-Ptolemais. Caesarea, Sepphoris, Samaria, and possibly Jerusalem are the only cities that show this change in mint supply, as Beer Sheba and the sites farther to the north continued to use coins from Tyre.[36] The number of coins and the change in mint probably reflect military preparations and operations of Antiochus, who razed Jerusalem and seized the Temple treasury in order to secure his rear and provide funds for his campaign against the Parthians.[37] The Annual Average Coin Loss for this issue period is dramatically low in Jerusalem, especially when compared to Samaria (Fig. 11 and Table 3, issue period 2). Antiochus also allowed several municipal mints to strike coins in Phoenicia and Palestine (the so-called autonomous issues): Tripolis, Byblus, Berytus, Sidon, and Ascalon, supplementing the mints at Antioch, Tyre, and Ake-Ptolemais. For the most part, these municipal mints struck small issues that are not well represented in any excavation. Seleucid issues make up a huge percentage of all the coins found on the sites of Tel Anafa and Bethsaida, and to a lesser extent Samaria; smaller, though significant proportions are found in Dora (since it is still an important harbor) and Beer Sheba (Figs. 7–10).

The Maccabean Revolt (166–161 B.C.E.) was the direct offspring of Antiochus' policies in Palestine. The successes of the sons of Mattathias led to the establishment of a kingdom in Israel, headed by the Hasmonaeans. Strato's Tower was ruled by an independent despot, Zoilus, until Alexander Yannai caused his downfall. The upheavals in the civic life of Palestine—including damage to coastal cities and desertion of rural sites—are reflected in the lack of coinage from Strato's Tower after 164; the cities and towns to the north, much farther removed from the fighting, do not share this lack of coin. The Galilean sites[38] show the northern extent of Hasmonaean influence; the sites around the Sea of Galilee have a great many Hasmonaean coins, especially compared to the Phoenician autonomous bronzes or Seleucid issues we would expect (Figs. 7–10); Tel Anafa, far to the north, still relied on coins from the mint at Tyre (with a few from Antioch and Sidon). In Tel Anafa, there were one hundred fifty-three city/Seleucid coins, which can be dated definitely to this era, in contrast to only three Hasmonaean coins. The town seems to have been abandoned c.75 B.C.E. and not reoccupied until the early first century C.E.[39] In Gamala, over four hundred city/Seleucid coins can definitely be attributed to the time of the Hasmonaean rule, yet almost four thousand Hasmonaean coins. The city coins come especially from Tyre, and to a lesser extent from Sidon and Antioch. Khirbet Shema was possibly being used as a staging area for the troops, as no habitation from the early period was found. In Samaria, the coin of choice continued to be the autonomous city coins and Seleucid issues, and to a much lesser extent, Hasmonaean bronzes.[40] Just as in Samaria, Hasmonaean coins are not common in Strato's Tower, perhaps reflecting the destruction of the city by the Hasmonaeans or their demotion of the city from the status of *polis*.[41] Instead, the population used coins of the Seleucid kings, but their well-worn condition shows how long they were pressed into service; as with the other sites in Samaria and Galilee, the city coins come primarily from Tyre and Antioch. The greatest concentration of Hasmonaean coins comes from Jerusalem, site of the Hasmonaean mint (Figs. 7–10).[42]

After fighting with his southern neighbors the Nabataeans, whose capital city was Petra, Yannai established formal trade relations with them. Some sites (especially Beer Sheba) show a number of Nabataean coins that were used through the first century.[43] Strato's Tower was too far west to have any Nabataean coins penetrate, although a few sherds of Nabataean pottery have been found. Under Herod, relations deteriorated, and very few Nabataean coins are found in any site in Palestine; one stray arrived in Caesarea after Herod's death.

The Annual Average Coin Loss (Fig 11 and Table 3) for the end of the third through the second centuries B.C.E. (issue periods 1–2) shows that Caesarea lags far behind Samaria in terms of percentage of coins recovered from the sites. Samaria peaks with Antiochus IV, with the strongest numbers it will ever have. For the Hasmonaean period (issue period 3), Caesarea again lags far behind Samaria, and especially Jerusalem, which reaches its peak in terms of percentages of recovered coins in the Hasmonaean period. When the comparison is extended to other cities, in the Chi-Square Test (Fig. 12 and Table 4), the norm for the period 222–100 B.C.E. (T1) in the "normal eastern city" is a number less than ten percent. This means that less than ten percent of total number of coins found in the "normal eastern cities" could be dated to this time period. Interestingly, all the cities I tested (Caesarea, Jerusalem, Samaria, Pella, Hama, Gerasa, Antioch, Pergamon, and Sardis) fell within norm for this time period (see Appendix 2). For the Late Hellenistic era, the number of mints and movement of people and goods worked together to mean that large and small urban centers had access to small change at about the same rate, whether or not the city had a mint to provide such small change.

Herod and the Procurators (22 B.C.E. to 68 C.E.)

With the foundation of Caesarea by Herod sometime between 22 and 10/9 B.C.E., and his lavish building program, it is no surprise to find an increasing number of coins in Caesarea, as the city became the economic and later the political center of the province. In addition to building the port, the Temple to Rome and Augustus, sewers and streets, the theater and amphitheater, warehouses, and a palace,

Herod instituted quinqennial games, which would bring money and tourists to the city every five years. Herod attempted to strengthen the trade routes of his empire by building projects in the cities of Samaria, Jerusalem, Caesarea Paneas, Beer Sheba, Agrippias (Anthedon), Sepphoris, Gaba, Phasaelis, Antipatris, Mambre, and the fortresses of Masada, Jericho, and Herodium, among others. Capernaum and Nabratein may have been founded in this period, Tel Anafa was reoccupied, though it was a much smaller town than the Hellenistic settlement.[44] Scholars are just beginning to assess the economic benefits of the commissioning of so many public works.[45]

Herod built the harbor in Caesarea to attract international trade, a trade which is made evident in the types of amphorae found in the vaults along the harbor. Goods from North Africa, Italy, the Aegean, the Spanish peninsula, and Palestine were housed in these structures.[46] The coins do not come from as far afield. However, this simply means that the coins are functioning more locally, as they do everywhere else in the Roman world at this time.[47] Because the Romans struck coins on one weight standard in the west, and allowed the local cities of the east to continue manufacturing the kinds of coins they were used to striking (almost always on a different weight standard), coins from the west rarely circulated in the east, nor were coins taken from eastern cities to be spent in the west. Further, cities in the east could strike on very different weight standards, even if the cities were not separated by much physical distance. Such coins would have to be changed (at a profit to the moneychanger) to the local currency in the city where they were spent. Hence, the first century B.C.E. city coins found in Caesarea are from the local cities of Berytus and Sidon; even so, the Herodian bronzes seem to have driven out almost all the city bronzes from use in Caesarea (Figs. 7–10). The same situation prevails at Samaria, Caesarea's "sister" city, but not at Jerusalem, where the influx of Jewish pilgrims brought foreign coins to the city. Although Mambre does not yet show the high numbers of foreign coins it did later, more often than not Mambre's coin profile resembled Jerusalem's, because it was one of the most important inland trading cities in Palestine (Figs. 7–10).[48] All of the other sites, except Samaria, have few Herodian coins; Galilee especially seems outside of the area of circulation of Herodian coins, and the population used coins from Tyre, Sidon, and Nabataea instead.[49] We will see in the sixth century C.E. another period when building projects, population increase, and imported pottery point to a period of economic prosperity, which is not reflected in the volume of excavated coins. Nevertheless, we should see the period as a prosperous one in Caesarea at least.

After Herod died in 4 B.C.E., Augustus divided his kingdom among his three sons; Caesarea, Samaria and Judaea were given to Archelaus. The Roman generals jockeyed to obtain Herod's treasury: Sabinus and Quinctilius Varus' troops were joined by cavalry, auxiliary troops, and troops of Aretas IV of Nabataea. Presumably all but one legion left after Archelaus returned from Rome with instructions concerning the settlement.[50] When Archelaus was deposed in 6 C.E., Augustus placed a procurator in charge of the province, annexing Syria and calling the whole Judaea. The legion stationed in Palestine remained in Jerusalem, joined by auxiliary units (which had been Herod's troops).[51] The rule of the procurators was interrupted by the short reign of Agrippa I (41–44 C.E.). The capital was Caesarea; the first procurator who lived in the city was Pontius Pilate. Along with the civil administration came troops; the influx of new people to Caesarea would have been a source of income to the local population.

Pilate was not the only procurator to have to deal with civil disturbances in Caesarea; yet it was also in Caesarea that Agrippa celebrated Claudius' triumph in Rome, an occasion when tourist money must have flowed into the coffers of Caesarea's merchants, cut short when Agrippa himself died during the ceremonies. Another source of income for the citizens would have been in the provisioning of the soldiers (possibly as many as three thousand) stationed here.[52] That the soldiers contributed to the economic well-being of the citizens of Caesarea is borne out by a story in our ancient sources that the people of Caesarea were able to raise eight talents (a huge sum) to bribe the procurator Florus.[53]

Was the rest of the province as wealthy as the individuals of Caesarea? Again, this is a subject of controversy, which is not yet resolved. After the census was completed in 6 C.E., the province began to pay tribute to Rome, a tax that replaced the tax paid to Herod. The tax was onerous enough that in 17 C.E., Syria and Judaea appealed the amount imposed on the provinces. Josephus also recorded that the amount was crushing. It is not certain whether the tax was paid in coin or kind, nor is there any record of the Roman reaction to the appeal.[54] The Romans left it to private businessmen to collect the taxes they imposed on Palestine. This situation was not unique to Palestine, and many provinces complained of the rapaciousness of these tax collectors. One scholar has lately argued that the taxes themselves were not onerous, but in combination with the corruption, inefficiency in collection, and the lack of giving back to the province any public works to offset the amount collected made the tax burden too heavy. The result was a depression in the era of the procurators,[55] though this depression may not have extended to Caesarea, buffered as it was by the harbor and the army.[56]

Not surprisingly, coins of the rival rulers Antipas and Philip did not come into Caesarea; procuratorial coins are plentiful. The few city coins that survive from Caesarea in the first half of the first century are from the mints of Paneas, Berytus, Nabataea, and coins from the mint of Commagene, far to the north. Syon suggested that such coins were brought into Palestine with troops supplied by Antiochus IV of Commagene to Vespasian during the First Revolt.[57] As Carradice pointed out, Antiochean coins with the SC reverse are probably found in Judaea because the troops used them; they are often countermarked (though no countermarked coins were found in the JECM excavations of Caesarea) with the mark of the Legio X Fretensis and were not minted after 83.[58]

Samaria is unusual in reporting few coins from this era from mints other than procuratorial mints. Jerusalem shows a wider range of mints, including Lyon, Rome, and Antioch, as well as the more local mints of Tyre, Ake-Ptolemais, Ascalon, and Aradus.[59] Again, we would expect this in Jerusalem because of the high rates of visitors. Procuratorial coins rarely penetrated Galilee, though not many coins of Antipas are recorded either. In fact, coins of the first half of the first century C.E. are not well represented in the Galilean sites (Figs. 7–10); for Sepphoris, the lack is explained by the events after the death of Herod, when the citizens were sold off as slaves, and Antipas changed the head of the province to Tiberias.[60] Gamala records the largest number of procuratorial and city coins, yet only thirty-seven procuratorial coins were found there, compared to many times that number of Phoenician and Palestinian coins of the first century B.C.E. to first half of the first century C.E. Syon argued that the procuratorial coins show the strong ties between Gamala and Jerusalem. Meiron has nineteen coins from the same time period, mostly coins of Herod, but also of Antipas, Philip, and Agrippa I, and four procuratorial ones. Tel Anafa only has coins from Paneas (Caesarea Philippi), after which the coin finds basically end. Hence, the sites in Samaria and Judaea (save Jerusalem) seem locked into the local economy, while the Galilean sites traded with cities to their north. More work will have to be done to assess the economy of the first five decades of Roman rule in Palestine.

The Annual Average Coin Loss result in Caesarea (Fig. 11 and Table 3, issue periods 4–6) shows a rise from the result for the Herodian period, with a strong "bump" with the coins from Archelaus, while the numbers remain fairly consistent in Jerusalem, falling dramatically from the Hasmonaean high, but retaining numbers close to Caesarea's "bump." Samaria's numbers are high during Herod's and Archelaus' reigns, but begin to fall off during the time of the procurators, since military and civilian functions were concentrated in Caesarea and Jerusalem. The Chi-Square Test (Fig 12 and Table 4) for normal eastern cities shows the period from 103 B.C.E. to 69 C.E. (T2) to be a period of loss of fewer coins, compared to the total number of coins in the sample. The cities of the Near East have far less divergence than the cities of ancient Palestine; the Jerusalem totals (because of the huge numbers of Hasmonaean coin reported) here effectively throw it out of the norm.

The First Revolt through the Third Century C.E.

The prelude to the First Revolt occurred between the Greeks and Jews in Caesarea, when the synagogue was desecrated; in the fighting that followed, the Greeks massacred the Jews in Caesarea. Vespasian made Caesarea his headquarters while he overran the country; Titus subsequently used the city as his own headquarters. Many troops arrived to put down the revolt: Agrippa sent cavalry, Cestius the Legio XII Fulminata (along with other troops), Sohaemus of Emesa sent archers. In all, the Romans had well over five legions in the province when Vespasian fought, many of whom entered the province through the harbor at

Caesarea.[61] It was Caesarea that saw the largest celebrations when Titus destroyed Jerusalem, for he brought back his Jewish prisoners to make them participants in his gladiatorial games in the amphitheater. Caesarea became the capital of Palestine, a role she played until 375 C.E., and she was called "Colonia Prima Flavia Augusta Caesarea." Vespasian is said to have erected an Odeion (a covered theater) over the site of Caesarea's synagogue with some of the spoils of the Jews.[62]

Coins of the second half of the first century C.E. are not especially common, even with all the troop movements and supplies being brought into the harbor at Caesarea. Besides the Odeion of Vespasian (not yet identified), and the Caesarea–Beth Shean road (built by the Tenth Legion in 69, according to inscriptions found along the road), little building on the site is known from the period 66–135 C.E., except for the U-shaped building built over the Mithraeum.[63]

This situation is reflected in all of the cities in the cohort, with the exception of Jerusalem—that is, few, if any, building projects can be identified from this era and few coins were found in the excavations; Hayes pointed to the lack of imported pottery in Palestine between 70 and 250.[64] In addition, the country was severely depopulated, in part because of the numbers of Jews sold into slavery after the Revolt; Caesarea and Samaria may have avoided depopulation because of veteran colonies that were established in both cities after the Revolt (Pliny *NH* 5.69), even if Samaria was severely damaged in the fighting. Neapolis (Shechem) and Legio seem to have expanded in this period, since they housed soldiers.[65] Yet Dora, Geba, Apollonia, Bethsaida (Julias), and Livias show destruction layers or a severe decline dating to the time of the Revolt. Additionally, the poll tax was instituted in the province, funneling money that once paid for the upkeep of the Temple in Jerusalem back to Rome. Thus most of Palestine seems to have suffered a sharp downswing in its economy immediately after the First Revolt.[66]

Caesarea may have been insulated from the worst effects of the depression, due to the troops and the holding of games in the city. Yet if, as Raban argues, the harbor was already in disrepair in the late first century C.E., the economy may have functioned on a much more local level.[67] In terms of Annual Average Coin Loss (Fig. 11 and Table 3), Caesarea's total for the Flavian period (issue period 7) is about half that of the previous, procuratorial total, implying a certain lack of coin in the city. The circulation of the Judaea Capta reverses from the Caesarea mint is very limited. In Jerusalem, coins of the First Revolt are more common than elsewhere (since the main mint was here), along with an array of city coins.[68] But the Average Annual Coin Loss falls dramatically in the Flavian period, as it does in Samaria. Lack of coins, in this case, mirrors the lack of building projects, loss of population, lack of imported pottery, and extreme wear on the first century C.E. coins. All the evidence points to a continuing province-wide depression through the second half of the first, and the first quarter of the second century C.E.

The ancient sources rarely mention Caesarea after the period of the First Revolt; similarly, modern scholars tend to lose interest in the province after the Bar Kochba Revolt. The *opinio communis* is that "Palestine was in low economic water" due to the disruption in farming, breakdown of trade and industry, confiscation of Jewish land, monetary fines paid to the Romans, and depopulation.[69] There are some dissenting voices, although the issue has never been seriously argued.[70]

The sequence of events leading up to the Bar Kochba Revolt is not clear, but it appears that a visit by Hadrian, a plan to settle Gentile colonists in the province, and a proposed ban on circumcision led to the uprising. At least four legions and various other troops took part in the suppression of the Revolt.[71] The bulk of the fighting occurred in Judaea and, to a lesser extent, in Samaria. Galilee was relatively untouched. When the population was exiled from Jerusalem, many people made their way to the hills of Galilee, as well as farther east. The populations of Sepphoris, Joppa, and Tiberias surged. Large estates were broken up; some of the land may have reverted fairly quickly into Jewish hands, though certainly not on the pre-135 scale.[72] The taxes imposed by the Romans may in part simply mirror the rise in taxes all over the empire that accompanied the slowly rising pace of inflation.[73] Rules for the Sabbath year, which imply that landowners had enough foodstuffs accumulated to last them through the fallow year, remained in effect until the economic crises of the third century.[74]

Other, more general, comments in the ancient sources imply prosperity that returned with peace in the second century. Caesarea and her sister cities were called the "lands of life," and prices of services and goods in the city were proverbially high.[75] Coins dating from the 100–130s C.E. are more common than the period between 70 and 100; many are very small bronzes. The number of types per year, for most of the High and Late Imperial period, follows the pattern set by the mint under Domitian, with one or fewer reverse types introduced per year (Table 2). Only during the reigns of Trajan and Hadrian (combined) does this ratio almost triple, mostly due to the minting of small bronze coins.

Some of the possible reasons for the upswing in the economy are troop movements associated with the Bar Kochba Revolt and building projects associated with Hadrian (117–138 C.E.) and his visit to the province in 130; Caesarea in particular was singled out for special treatment. After the Bar Kochba Revolt, Caesarea became the capital of Syria-Palestina and its governor commanded two legions, some of which must have been housed at Caesarea.[76] That the games continued to be held in Caesarea is seen by inscriptions as far away as Aphrodisias and Laodicea.[77] Specific projects known to have been undertaken in Caesarea were the Hadrianeum, the hippodrome, the repair or building of the aqueducts, and the Honorific Portico (identified by Patrich as part of the praetorium).[78] Scholars have argued that the harbor was in disrepair in the second century, though more recent analysis of the sediments and microscopic life in the harbor suggests a gradual filling accompanied by steady use of the harbor through the third century.[79] Certainly the site (and most of Palestine) is lacking in imported pottery from the first two centuries C.E.[80] Similar building projects were undertaken in Beth Shean, Sepphoris, Samaria, and Jerusalem (though the city was depopulated and did not recover economically). Hence, the economy of Palestine, outside of the city of Jerusalem, recovered soon after the Bar Kochba Revolt.

How long this prosperity lasted is in dispute. Marcus Aurelius visited the province in 175/6, yet the number of building projects known drops in the Antonine period. Most scholars believe that the economy of the entire Roman Empire was suffering from inflation and depression. In Caesarea, imported pottery is still scarce, as is the number of coins found in the Caesarea excavations. Most of the mints in Palestine and the Decapolis shut down, especially between 166/7 and 175/6. This phenomenon, leading to an increasing homogenization of the types and denominations, occurred in the eastern Empire as a whole. The Antonine Period returns to the level of mint originality, in terms of reverse types produced, of the Domitianic era. The coins of Jerusalem are more inventive, and more reverse types per year are seen there, possibly in part due to its reopening under Hadrian.[81] In terms of mints represented at each site, Meiron has approximately the same mints as Caesarea, that is, coins from Philadelphia, Gadara, Antiochia ad Hippum, Sepphoris, Tiberias, Dora, Aelia Capitolina, Caesarea itself, Ascalon, Gaza, Alexandria (small bronzes) and Rome. Capernaum has coins from Tyre, Dora, Aelia Capitolina, Sepphoris (Diocaesarea), Tiberias, and Beth Shean (Nyssa-Scythopolis); that is, nothing from outside of Phoenicia and Palestine; Samaria shows a slightly greater range (Aelia Capitolina, Ascalon, Caesarea, Gaba, Neapolis, Petra, Antioch, Alexandria, and Rome). Those mints are matched at Sepphoris (Antioch, Sidon, Tyre, Ake-Ptolemais, Caesarea, Samaria-Sebaste, Petra, Bostra, and Rome).[82]

It has been thought that part of the economic malaise during the Antonine period was due to depopulation and a plague.[83] Caesarea's mint was exempt from the shut-down, but surprisingly Caesarea did not become a major supplier of coins to the province, except to Jerusalem, as all of the cities in the cohort report the majority of their city coins from other mints of the second century. In the regional comparative cohort, the large cities (except Jerusalem) report increased numbers of coins in the second century, rising further in the third century, just as in Caesarea. Yet this rise is incremental in the overall statistics of coins lost at each site. Some of this rise in the Annual Average Coin Loss (Fig. 11 and Table 3, issue periods 9–10) can be explained by inflation, for as inflation grows, each coin is worth less; the loser will not try as hard to recover lost coins. In the Chi-Square Test (Fig. 12 and Table 4), the profile for T3 (69–192 C.E.) shows all of the normal eastern cities clustering around three to five percent. Again, no city rises higher than five percent, but most are quite low (less than one percent). Thus, the literary sources, lack of building projects, lack of imported goods from this period, as well as the weakening in the numbers of coins from the Annual Average Coin Loss and the Chi-Square Test combine to argue that the economy of Caesarea, and likely the province, at least stagnated, if not worsened in the late second century.

It has been suggested that the increasing number of reverse types (implying an increase in minting activity) during the third century can be attributed to visits from the emperors Septimius Severus (193–211 C.E.)

and Caracalla (211–217 C.E.), Severus Alexander's (222–235 C.E.) campaigns against the Persians, and building projects. Several cities were newly founded in Palestine, including Eleutheropolis, Nicopolis (Emmaeus), and Diospolis (Lod), implying a recovery in population.[84] Building projects in the cities of the regional comparative cohort increase in the Severan period as well: Beth Shean obtained a theater and amphitheater, Beer Sheba a legionary camp,[85] Samaria new walls, refurbished colonnaded streets and a rebuilt Augusteum, and the synagogue at Nabratein was built.[86] The road system was largely rebuilt, especially in the north.[87] The Mishnaic and Talmudic sources describe life in second and third century Palestine as "a place of cheapness where there is plenty to eat."[88] Both the building projects and the literary sources agree that Palestine was prospering in the Severan era; the range of mints found in the excavation coins argue that Palestine was engaging in lively commerce with her neighbors. For instance, Samaria, which was granted colonial status by Septimius Severus, reports more coins from the next-nearest mint, Neapolis, in the third century than Caesarea, along with coins from Caesarea, its own mint (Samaria), Aelia Capitolina, Tyre, Caesarea in Cappadocia, and two coins from Rome. Likewise, Sepphoris tends to be supplied by the mint at Ake-Ptolemais, and Mambre by Aelia Capitolina, Eleutheropolis, and Neapolis. In Galilee, Meiron reports an increased number of Severan coins from the mints of Caphyae (Arcadia), Philomelium (Phrygia), Carrhae and Rhesena (Mesopotamia), Raphanea (Syria), Antioch, Orthosia (Phoenicia), Sidon, Tripolis, Tyre, Ake-Ptolemais, Caesarea, Bostra, and Petra. And Capernaum reports coins from Tiberias, Beth Shean (Nyssa-Scythopolis), Paneas, Caesarea, Ake-Ptolemais, Tyre, Tripolis, Damascus, Gadara, Gaza, and Bostra.

The numbers of reverse types per year jumps markedly in the Severan period and especially afterwards. The reverses from Elagabalus' (218–222 C.E.) and Severus Alexander's reigns double the average from the Antonine period (Table 2). Yet that number is highly conservative compared to the types created for Trajan Decius (249–251 C.E.) and Trebonius Gallus (251–253 C.E.). This picture varies in Jerusalem, where the reverses under Elagabalus number almost seven times as many as those from Caesarea, with a large drop-off for Severus Alexander (when the Caesarea mint produced more types). And while the number of types from the Jerusalem mint under Trajan Decius is considerable, almost six times as many types were produced at the Caesarea mint. One could argue that the more tenuous the hold on the throne, the more effort is put into creating new coin types (while the workmanship normally becomes more shoddy). Yet it may simply be that, as mints are closed in the early to mid-third century, die cutters moved to new cities for work and stimulated the invention of new types. The reasons why mints began to close in the third century are not entirely clear. Most often numismatists suggest an Empire-wide economic failure, combined with military setbacks and growing inflation; all these factors combined to make the government consolidate control of the local mints.[89]

When the local Palestinian and Phoenician mints closed down, cities had to look farther afield for coins; thus there is a rise in the number of mints attested, beginning in the second century. Imperial minting efforts concentrated on the production of debased silver coins, the *antoninianus*, across the whole Empire. But none of the cities show coins from the mint at Rome, testifying to the increasing isolation of the cities in the third century from the mints in the west.[90]

The introduction of the *antoninianus* around 215 C.E. (but not produced regularly until 238) seems at first to have little impact on the excavation coins. Made with a small amount of silver mixed in the copper, perhaps at first these coins were too valuable to lose. But by the second half of the third century, they begin turning up as regularly as bronze coins, which they replaced. Hence, each coin was worth less and the person who dropped it made less of an effort to recover it. In the course of the third century, *antoniniani* grew less and less fine, as inflation drove the government to issue more debased coins.

The reasons for the greatly increased rate of inflation are still being debated, but the introduction of debased silver coinage accelerated the rise in prices, which had remained fairly steady during the first two centuries of the Empire. For instance, the base pay of soldiers changed little in the two centuries between the reign of Augustus and that of Marcus Aurelius; it was Septimius Severus and Caracalla who increased the base pay of legionaries. The rise in base pay is reflected in the rise in grain prices, as far as we can reconstruct them.[91]

The Annual Average Coin Loss numbers (Fig. 11 and Table 3) show an uptick for Caesarea and Samaria (and a slight downturn for Jerusalem in the Severan period, issue period 11); this slight upswing, combined with the building projects, city foundations, and literary evidence, shows that the period was a prosperous one in the region, even if the rate of inflation continued to grow.[92] However, the years immediately following the death of Severus Alexander tell a very different story. There is no new construction in the cities of Palestine between 230 and 280. Taxes rose, and the emperors imposed more of them, as taxes in kind or as imposed labor, negating the need to pay the taxes with the increasingly worthless coins. They also instituted the "crown tax," payable in silver or gold as a "voluntary" tax upon the emperor's accession or after a particularly significant military victory. The tax soon became an obligatory tax, paid every fourth year. Combined with the extortion of crooked tax collectors, taxes became overwhelmingly burdensome, and the rabbinical sources complain of poverty, lack of food and the loss of the upper class, many of whom fled to more prosperous provinces.[93] The huge increase in the number of reverse types minted per year cannot be attributed to prosperity, but, as I have suggested, may refer to movement of die cutters or imperial propaganda needs. The Average Annual Coin Loss continues to rise for Caesarea and Samaria, even while Jerusalem continues to sink (Fig. 11 and Table 3, issue period 12). In this case, the rise in the numbers may be linked to increasing inflation and the lack of worth of the individual coin.

The emperor Aurelian attempted to stem the flood of rising prices and falling currency by reforming the coinage. In an attempt to regularize production, Aurelian (270–275 c.e.) established mints at Ticinum, Siscia, Serdica, and Cyzicus, which joined the older mints at Lyon, Rome, Antioch, Tripolis, and Alexandria (possibly also Byzantium) to produce his reformed coins (see map of mints, Fig. 13). These mints coined gold and debased silver (the *aureliani* or *radiates*), but rarely, if ever, bronze. Unfortunately, our picture of the circulation of coins from c.270–294 is confused; places where we expect *aureliani* to show up instead show barbarous imitations or coins from competing emperors, and Caesarea is no exception. While there are coins of Aurelian from the imperial mints (especially Antioch, and to a much lesser extent Tripolis), one coin minted in Britain actually found its way to Caesarea (no. **481**).[94] Caesarea is the only city with such a coin: Sepphoris and Meiron have coins from Siscia and Antioch for this period, the coins in Jerusalem and Mambre come almost exclusively from Antioch (Cyzicus being the next-highest provider of coin), those in Samaria come from no other mint besides Antioch. If the harbor was still in use, it may explain the "foreign" coins brought into Caesarea; the rest of the province shows a more local pattern of mints upon which they draw, as the economy contracted.

Diocletian tried, in several ways, to restore prosperity to the Roman Empire. Inflation was still rising at a ruinous rate. Diocletian tried to combat the problem by freezing prices in his Edict, but his attempt was futile, as merchants simply responded by withdrawing goods from the market (Lactantius *de mort. pers.* 7.6).

Between 293 and 296 c.e. Diocletian reformed the coinage, opening new mints and standardizing the reverses. Diocletian's reforms released the coinage for wide distribution, as there was no longer an eastern and western standard. Of Diocletian's ten (the mints striking for Aurelian), later expanded to fifteen mints (adding Nicomedia, Heracleia, Sirmium, Thessalonica, and Carthage), only the mints of Cyzicus, Antioch, and Alexandria are recorded from Caesarea until c.310. The Annual Average Coin Loss (Fig. 11 and Table 3, issue period 14) remains fairly constant; it has been suggested that the coin supply of the area should have been affected by the removal from circulation, around 300 c.e., of older coinage, recalled to be struck on the new weight standards and to a new fineness. We would expect the coins from the period just before 300 to be the most heavily affected by this recall, but the numbers do not sustain this theory. Only eastern mints were recorded at Sepphoris, Meiron and Capernaum, only coins from the mint of Antioch at Samaria; eastern mints and strays from Trier are recorded at Jerusalem and Mambre. Jalame has one coin from Rome, the rest are from eastern mints. Thus, while in theory the standardization of the coin types and denominations meant that coins from the west could circulate in the east, there is little evidence that they did in Palestine, at least at the beginning of the reform.

Caesarea's harbor was almost certainly in decline after the third century.[95] The governor no longer lived in Caesarea, and the legion stationed in the province probably moved to the *limes*. Yet the visits of Diocletian and Maximinus must have pumped money into the local economy, especially for the shows put on in honor of Maximinus' birthday, and the spate of temple building and reconstruction to which Eusebius refers.[96] For the first time since the first century c.e., imported pottery began to arrive in the province. The non-local amphorae from the excavations identified by Blakely are tentatively identified as coming from Spain or North Africa and possibly the Aegean during the third century; fine wares identified by Magness include wares from North

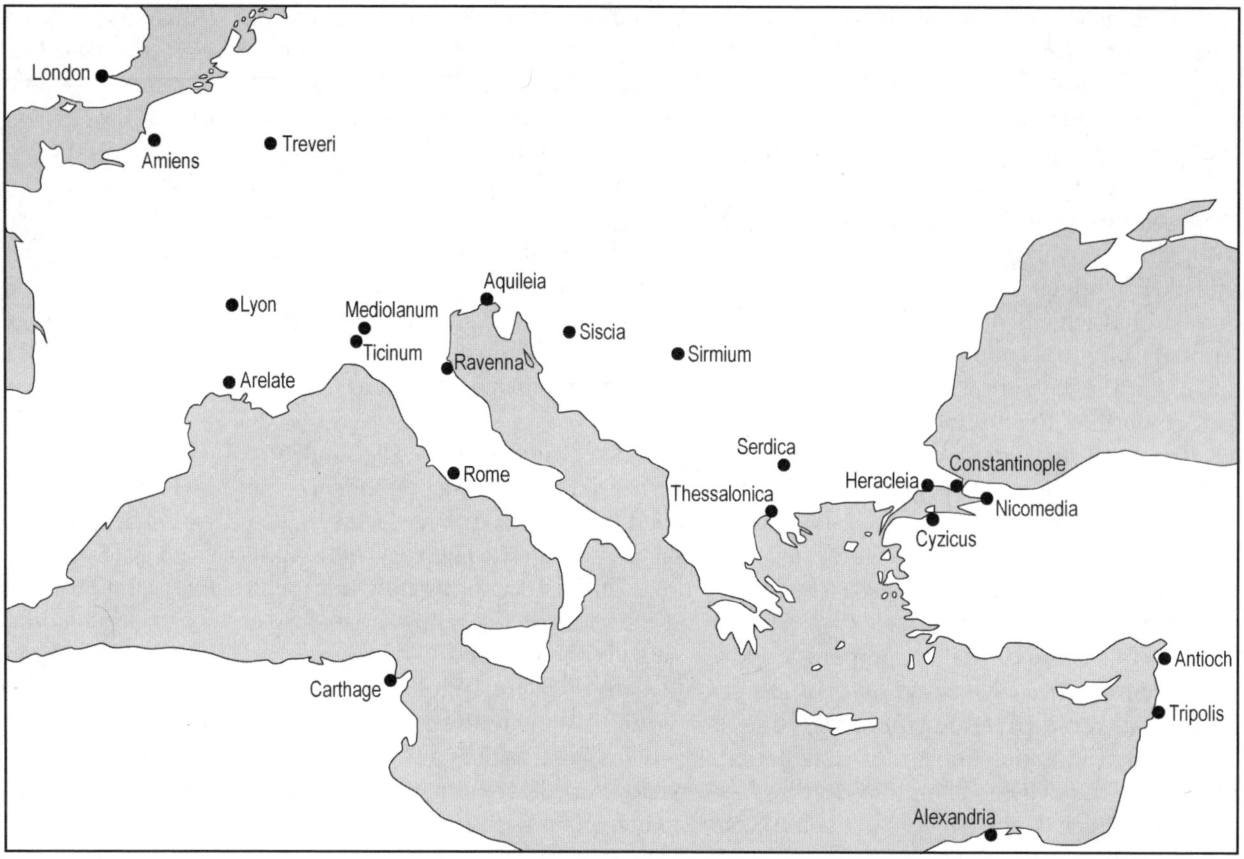

Fig. 13 *Map of Roman mints, 275–498 C.E.*

Africa and Cyprus.[97] Yet the western provinces were no longer producing amphorae to ship their wares, and we just may not have the barrels or other containers of perishable materials as evidence for western trade.

Under Diocletian, Palestine was urbanized as never before: Legio was formally granted the title of a *polis* (under the new name Maximianoupolis); building projects were undertaken at Dora, Geba, Apollonia, Azoterus Paralios, Maiumas Gaza; Bethulia, Helenoupolis, and many more sites were newly settled, making Palestine one of the most urbanized provinces in the Empire.[98] The emperor Galerius even resided for periods in Caesarea between 305 and 311. Levine has seen the period as the apex of Caesarea, since it was the time of the greatest territory and power of city.[99] We can perhaps see the literary sources, growth of population, and imported pottery as indications that the economy of Palestine was not doing badly, even if inflation was taking a toll on prices of goods at the very end of the third century.

LATE ROMAN (FOURTH AND FIFTH CENTURIES C.E.)

With the reign of Constantine, we enter into a period when Caesarea, indeed all of Palestine, benefited greatly from imperial attention and money. Though soldiers were no longer stationed near the large cities of the province, the loss of income from them was more than compensated by the arrival of pilgrims to the Holy Land.[100] In the regional comparative cohort, Dora may have been in ruins, Beer Sheba seems to have been abandoned, the authorities in Sepphoris had to put down a revolt (in 351) and rebuild the city after the earthquake in 363. No coins were found in Nabratein after 350, suggesting that the site was abandoned then for almost 150 years; Meiron was also at least partially abandoned. But the rest of the province shows that a number of building projects were undertaken between c.300 and 350. The colonnaded street in Beth Shean dates to the mid-fourth century.[101] Constantine built the Church of the Holy Sepulchre in Jerusalem, a church on the Mount of Olives, in Bethlehem, and in Mambre, and visited the province himself.[102] The *Comes* Joseph, a friend of Constantine's, built churches in Tiberias, Sepphoris, Capernaum, and Nazareth.[103]

The picture in Caesarea is similar to the rest of the province. From the size of the city enclosed by the walls, there was no drop in population in the fourth century. In fact, a new enclosure wall encompassed the growing number of houses. Other building projects include the repair of the high-level aqueduct, the building of the low-level aqueduct, and possibly the first phase of the Archive Building, also known as the Imperial Revenue Building.[104] The pottery on the site is predominately local, and transport amphorae are found in abundance. These amphorae are made in Palestine; rare ones come from the west, slightly more from the Aegean. Lamps were imported from Cyprus on occasion, but most were made locally.

From c.310–350, coins in Caesarea come from Arles, Lyon, a large group from Rome, Ticinum, Aquileia, and all the imperial eastern mints, of which Antioch is the biggest supplier; a generation after Diocletian's reforms of the coinage, the effects are finally seen on the supply of coin (Fig. 14).[105] In Jerusalem and Capernaum there are several coins from western mints and all of the eastern mints are recorded as well. Mambre has a similar profile (but including a coin from London): Antioch and Alexandria supply the largest number of coins. Mambre is unusual in that it was an important market town; the largest extent of the town dates to the first half of the fourth century.[106] Samaria, as well, mostly shows coins from Antioch, but there are also coins from the western mints. In Galilee and at Jalame all of the eastern mints are again represented, but the number of coins from the western mints is small (though again, a stray from London appears in Capernaum). The major mint suppliers to the region, then, were Cyzicus, Antioch and Alexandria. The latter two remained constant suppliers of coin to Palestine through the Byzantine period.

The Annual Average Coin Loss in issue period 16 (346–363) for Caesarea shows a remarkable jump upwards (Fig. 11 and Table 3); a similar increase is seen in Samaria, while the numbers for Jerusalem dip slightly, even if we would not expect such a finding, given the number of building projects undertaken in Jerusalem. All of the normal eastern cities show a rise for the period 193–324 in the Chi-Square Test (Fig. 12 and Table 4), though not as dramatic a climb as for the following period. Thus, the period seems to have been a prosperous one, due to all the building projects in the region, but coupled with high inflation that shows up in the Average Annual Coin Loss rate.

Emperors tried to harness inflation by reforming the coinage. The dates of the monetary reforms of the fourth century are difficult to ascertain. What is certain is that the emperors tried from time to time to restore the fineness and weight of the coins, only to reduce both. A new set of denominations was instituted in the reform of 348, with the reverses reading FEL TEMP REPARATIO (aptly translated as "Happy Days are Here Again"), though the weight and fineness of the individual coin dropped through the entire period of minting until about 383. Numismatists have suggested that the heavier coins were recalled in 354 for remelting and restriking since the heavier coins are missing from hoards, but at least in Capernaum, Sepphoris, Caesarea, and Samaria there are numerous coins from the period before 354, suggesting that if there were official recalls, they did not effectively remove earlier coins from circulation.

At Caesarea and Samaria, the Annual Average Coin Loss rate drops precipitously after 363 (Fig. 11 and Table 3, issue periods 17–19), rising somewhat under Valentinian II (issue period 18); this is not because the coinage was returned to fineness or was heavier.[107] In fact, the value of each individual coin became less as we move from 346 to 395. Instead, Caesarea seems demonetised and people must have depended on the earlier small change for their everyday transactions. Most coins still came from the mint at Antioch, though Constantinople became a major supplier; there is still a scattering of coins from the west (Fig. 15).[108] The profile is similar to Jerusalem and Capernaum (where the number of western coins begins to decline) and Sepphoris; Samaria has twice as many coins from Constantinople as Antioch. Jalame has almost as many coins from Constantinople as Antioch. At Mambre, Thessalonica is best represented. Meiron has coins from

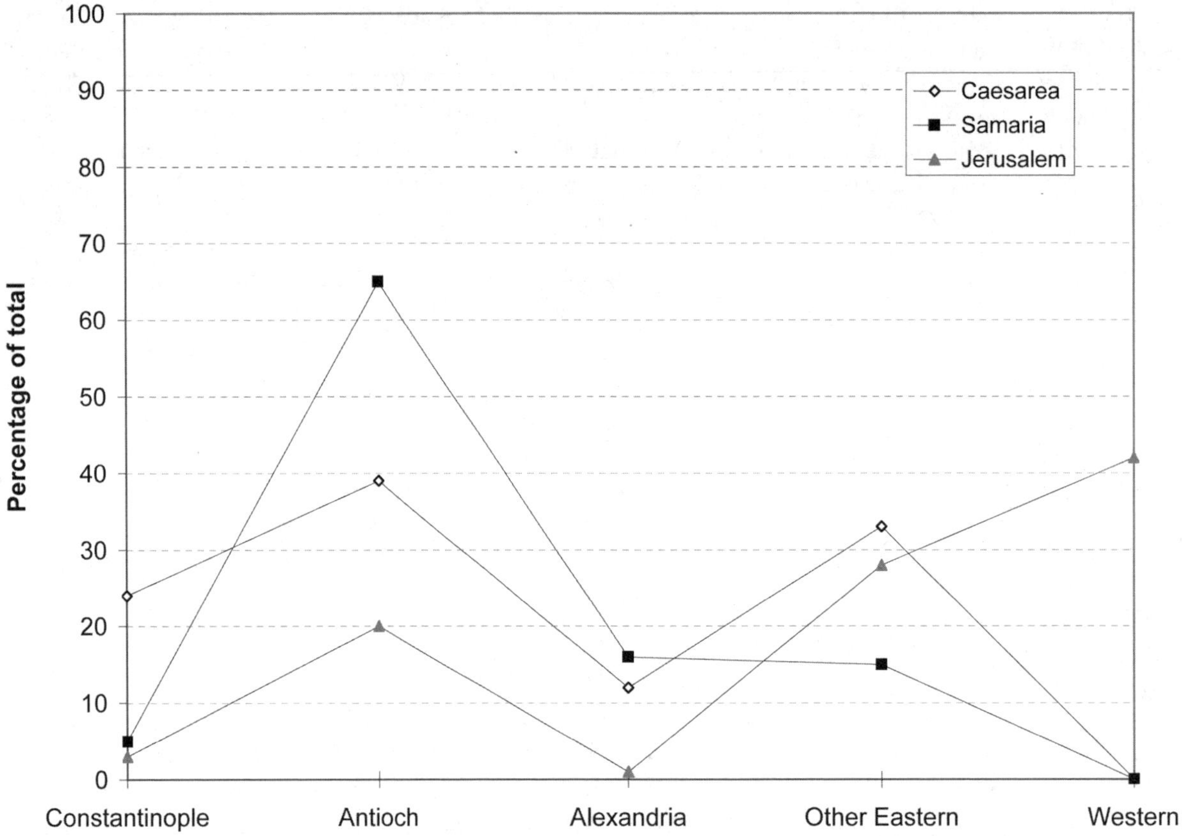

Fig. 14 Mint origin: Coins of Constantine.

Constantinople, Antioch, Cyzicus, and Alexandria in almost equal numbers, and very few from western mints. Gush Halav has few from Constantinople, but most come from Antioch.

Between 350 and 400, there was little, if any, building in Caesarea or the cohort cities.[109] Samaria was in decline, Sepphoris and Meiron were severely damaged in the earthquake of 363. However, this is the period when the glass factory at Jalame was established; it seems to have gone out of business by the end of the fourth century.[110] Hammat Gader was entering into its prosperous phase. Thus, except for pockets of very local prosperity, the region enters into a period of decline with continuing inflation. The high numbers in the Annual Average Rate of Loss for the period 346–395 (Fig. 11 and Table 3, issue periods 16–19) surely shows the increasing inflation and the declining worth of individual coins.

The economy of the region, and indeed the whole Empire, continued to struggle with rising inflation and falling fineness of the coins in the whole of the fifth century. The mint system was simplified, with the number of mints dropping to nine, and far fewer under Zeno (474–491 C.E.). Most of the coins from this period are small (less than one gram) bronzes with reverses of a Victory holding a wreath; the larger denominations ceased being made after 425. Such was the state of the coinage until the reforms of Anastasius in 498 C.E. The Annual Average Coin Loss (Fig. 11 and Table 3, issue periods 20–23) from Caesarea dropped precipitously, although the rate rises (very rapidly in Caesarea) in the third quarter of the century, probably due to the small size of the coins. It should be noted that the numbers may even be artificially low due in part to problems of identification. Many excavation coins minted between 383 and 498 may simply be listed as "Late Roman, types obliterated," or excavation methods, such as sieving, may not have been used, leading to non-recovery of these small coins. The Chi-Square values for the normal eastern cities (Fig. 12 and Table 4) show a steep rise for the period 347–498 (T5); almost all of this rise is surely due to the fourth and second half of the fifth century coins that are so common in sites in Palestine. It is not surprising that the numbers also rise in all of

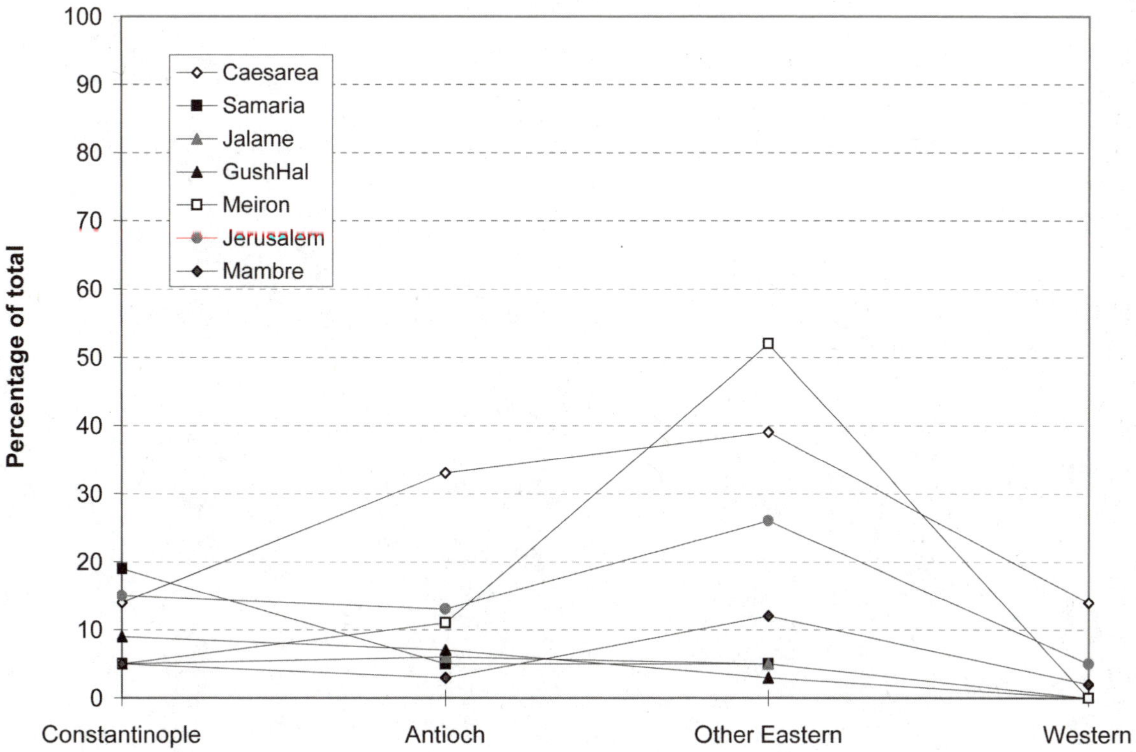

Fig. 15 Mint origin: 348–383 C.E.

the cities in the East, as the entire Empire is using one system of coinage, and all the cities are laboring under heavy inflation.[111]

There were not many building projects in this era in the cohort cities;[112] only Jerusalem was enriched by building programs instituted by Eudocia, wife of Theodosius II, when she visited the city (402—450 C.E.). It has recently been argued that many building projects must have taken place in Sepphoris after 363, but the evidence seems to be mostly private houses. Caesarea was damaged in the Samaritan uprising in 484, and possibly in the earthquakes of 447 and 502, even if there is little evidence of rebuilding after these events. The Herodian temple to Rome and Augustus was dismantled in the fifth century, to be replaced by another building of uncertain use, and then by an octagonal church in the late fifth century; the synagogue was rebuilt; and the Byzantine wall is now dated to the fifth century. Imported pottery, especially Cypriot and Late Roman C, becomes more common after the middle of the century.[113]

Caesarea sees a great shift in terms of the mints supplying the coins in the fifth century (Fig. 16). The supply from Constantinople drops to about half of what it had been, while Antiochean coins are almost entirely missing. Western coins are fewer, and those numbers are replaced with the Vandalic coins that appear on the site. These percentages are somewhat uncertain, as there were so many coins of uncertain mint; more than half could be placed in an uncertain eastern mint, though I could not exactly identify which.[114] The regional cohort had few coins from this period from which the mints were identified. The period is largely missing from reports of Samaria (though more recent reports list more of the small coins of this century probably missing from earlier reports), Beth Shean, Sepphoris, Capernaum, Meiron, and Gush Halav. The excavation lists at Jerusalem and Mambre have a few from this century. The inhabitation at Jalame seems to have been sparse, and most mintmarks were recorded as illegible.

It is notable that the Sardis excavation did not record any of the small Vandalic bronzes; it may be that trade with North Africa was confined to the coast of Palestine, and these coins will not be found inland nor any farther north. Hahn has already noted that during the fifth and sixth centuries small bronzes are widely

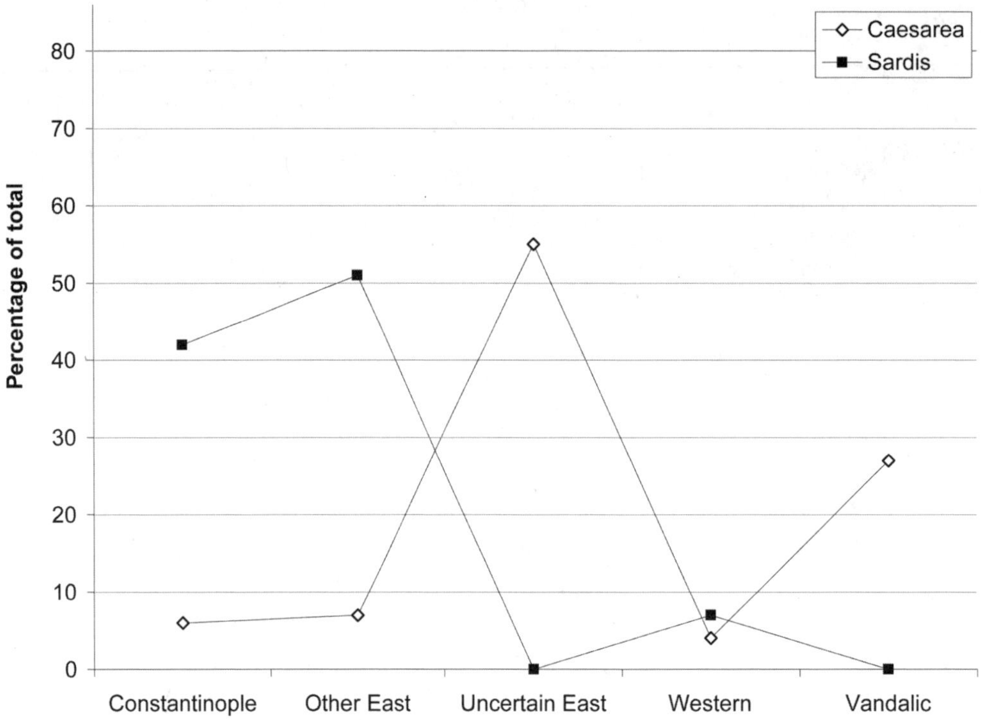

Fig. 16 Mint origin: Coins of the Fifth Century.

circulated, and so coins from Carthage and even Axumite, Ostrogothic, and imperial issues from Rome and Ravenna came east (the specific issues were discussed in Chapter 1). The wide circulation does not necessarily point to trading contacts, he says, but it does point out the area was starved for small bronze coins.[115] Yet evidence of trade between Caesarea and North Africa includes African Red Slip Ware of the late fifth and early sixth century, the period when the Vandalic coins were minted.[116] Interestingly, this is the period where Palestinian pottery at Carthage is most abundant, strengthening the evidence of lively trade between Carthage and Caesarea.[117] The physical evidence from the harbor is contradictory, with one team seeing the harbor as closed in the fifth century, and the second team seeing the harbor in use through the later fifth century.[118]

The fifth century is certainly one of increasing inflation, political and economic hardships, and it may be that, outside of the largest cities, the economy was functioning in a non-monetary manner, yet the few building projects in Caesarea lead me to suggest that the fifth century was not as bleak in Caesarea as once thought.

Byzantine (491 to 640 c.e.)

The region of Palestine shows good evidence of an economic boom in the Byzantine period, especially the sixth century c.e. Various historical reasons have been given as to why Palestine was so prosperous, such as the relative peace in the area before the Persian incursions and the development of trade routes by the Byzantine emperors. Christian wealth in the form of building programs and private investments became a major source of income for people in the province.[119] At Caesarea (which remained the provincial capital), sixth-century projects include the fortress in the southwestern quarter of the city, refurbishment of the water supply and street paving, the Byzantine Esplanade, a basilica paid for by Flavius Euelpidius and Elias (taking over at least part of the Hadrianeum). Many of the buildings in Field C (the area of the Archive Building), and warehouses in KK[120] show evidence of rebuilding. In Field E, a villa of this date was found, and there was much evidence that domestic housing and streets in Field G were refurbished. It is reported that Anastasius paid for the dredging of the harbor.[121] Goods were imported in amphorae from the Aegean, Egypt, and Gaza; fine wares were brought in from Cyprus, Egypt and North Africa.[122]

In the regional cohort, the story is much the same, especially for the larger cities. Recent excavations in Sepphoris point to several fifth- or sixth-century building projects in the city, especially the refurbishment of the streets and a church, funded by the Bishop Eutropius. Two synagogues also date to the fifth and sixth centuries. The refurbishment of a basilica by Procopius, the building of another by Silvanus and Sallustius, and rebuilding of the city wall all date to this period.[123] The sixth-century building projects in Beth Shean include refurbishment of the city wall, and the building of the northern portico to the gymnasium and the bath-house for lepers.[124] Justinian, especially, funded several building projects in Jerusalem, including completion of the Nea Church of the Theotokos and the building of a hospital.

The region's prosperity is only rarely reflected in the excavated coins, another period where the economy is not reflected simply by the number of coins found on the site. At Samaria, Byzantine coins were "unexpectedly rare,"[125] possibly due to the shift in habitation sites,[126] and coins are not abundant at Mambre, Sepphoris, Capernaum, Gush Halav (possibly abandoned in the mid-sixth century), Khirbet Shema, and Nabratein (though the synagogue was rebuilt).[127] Only Beth Shean shows a large percentage of coins.

After the twin disasters of the runaway inflation and constant debasement of the coinage, the emperor Anastasius took steps to reform the system in 498, as noted in Chapter 1. The imperial mint at Antioch opened during Anastasius' reign, but though this was the closest mint to Caesarea, it supplied very few coins which can be firmly placed in his reign.[128] Constantinople supplied almost all of the coins found at Caesarea (Fig. 17). The same mint attributions and ratios are found at Samaria and Jerusalem. Jerusalem has a smaller number of Byzantine coins, only half of the specimens per year that Caesarea has, and while most of the coins come from the mint at Constantinople (via the port at Caesarea?), slightly more are reported from Antioch. The Annual Average Coin Loss for issue period 24 (Fig. 11 and Table 3) overall shows a huge decline for Caesarea from the Late Roman highs.

The higher numbers of the Annual Average Coin Loss in the years just after the reign of Anastasius are due to the small *nummia* minted in Carthage during the reigns of Justin I (518—527) and Justinian (527—565), and *pentanummia* from the eastern mints, which are probably under-counted in some excavations (Fig. 11 and Table 3, issue periods 25 and 26). The small coins are not reported from any other excavation in Palestine. Caesarea, by contrast, shows a huge drop in the percentages of coins from Constantinople, in part due to the large number of small coins minted in Carthage during the reign of Justinian (Fig. 18). Constantinople is a secondary supplier of coin, with small numbers from Nicomedia, Thessalonica, and Cyzicus ("Other Eastern" in Fig. 18), Antioch and Alexandria. The coins from Sardis show almost a mirror-inverted profile compared to Caesarea. While most of the coins from Sardis came from the mint at Constantinople, and one quarter of the coins from the mints at Nicomedia, Thessalonica, and Cyzicus, hardly any come from Carthage, and none from Alexandria.

As noted in Chapter 1, there must have been an interruption in coin supply between 539 and 565, the post-reform coinage of Justinian. Sepphoris, Samaria, and Caesarea show this lack of coin; no *folles* dating between 542 and 566 were identified at these sites.[129] The greater appearance of coins from the eastern mints in the period after 565 in Sepphoris and Caesarea does not appear in coins from Jerusalem nor in hoards from Palestine. Since we do have coins from Carthage that were minted under Justinian, and since there is evidence of eastern pottery in Carthage at this date, it is likely that the Vandalic coins entered Caesarea during the Justinianic period, even if eastern pottery seems to be absent.

When Palestine's prosperity began to end is problematic; some scholars believe the economy began to decline after the reign of Justinian, in part due to the lessening number of coins from the Jerusalem excavations and in hoards, in part due to evidence from the entire Byzantine Empire.[130] We have seen again and again how coin numbers rarely reflect the actual state of the economy, so we need to look at other factors. In Palestine the Samaritans rose in revolt three times (484, 529/30, and 555). The settlement at Gush Halav was abandoned after an earthquake in 551. In 614, the Persian army invaded Palestine and captured Caesarea, which remained in Persian hands until 627/8, when Heraclius drove the Persians out of Syria. The city finally fell to the Muslims in 640 or 641.[131]

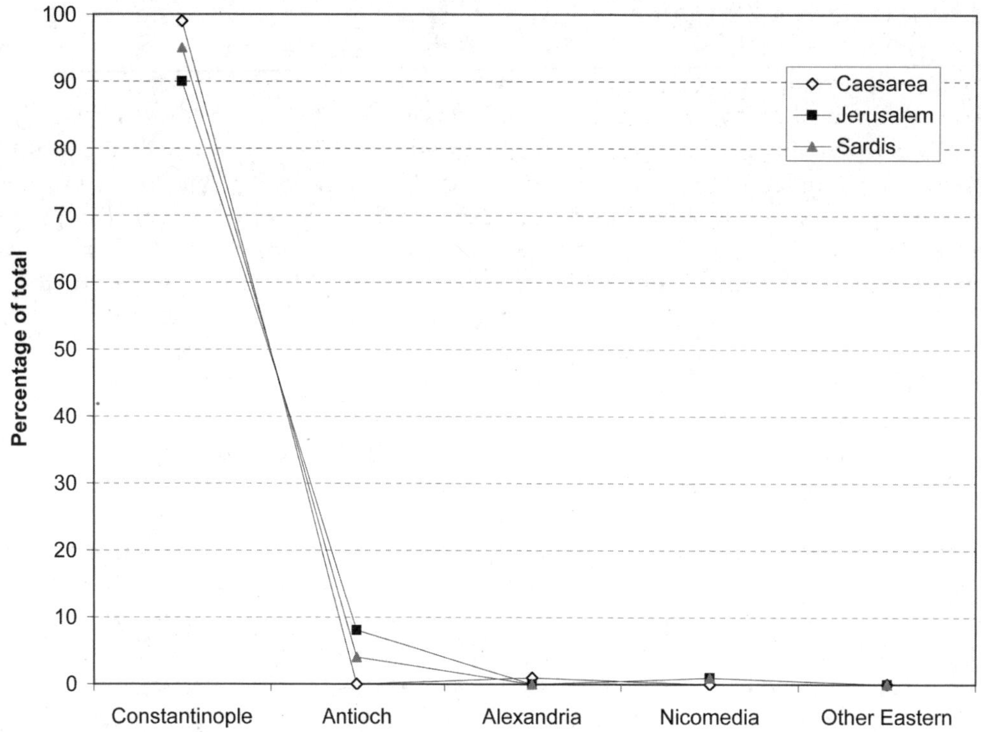

Fig. 17 *Mint origin: Coins of Anastasius.*

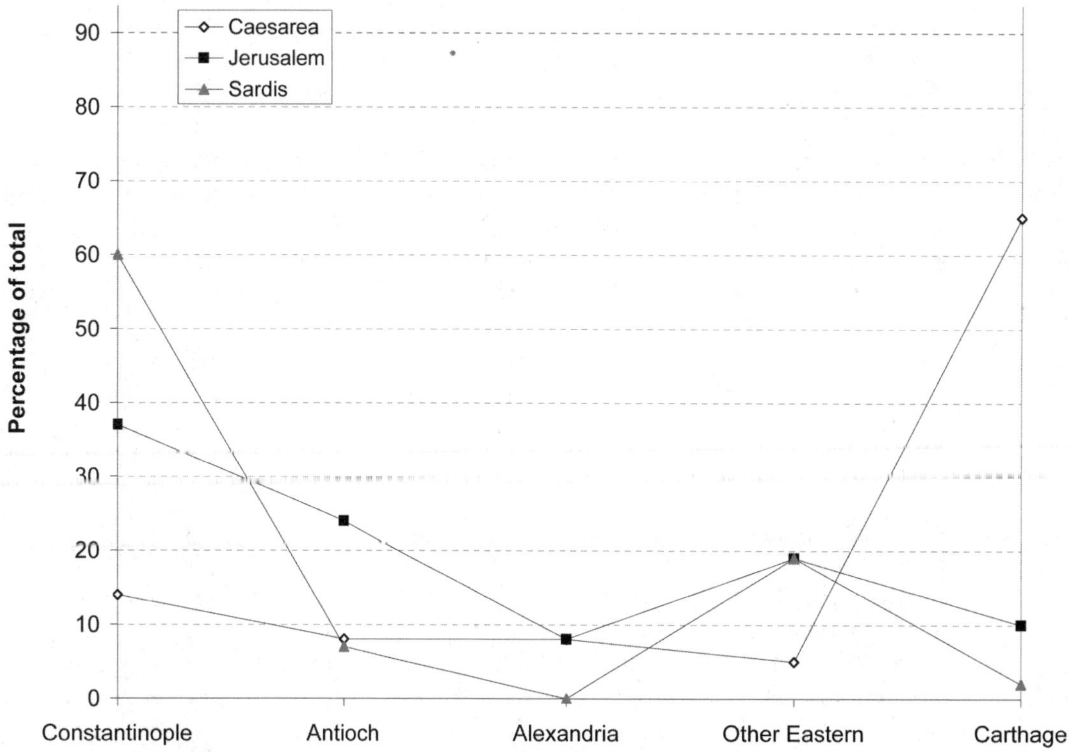

Fig. 18 *Mint origin: Coins of Justinian.*

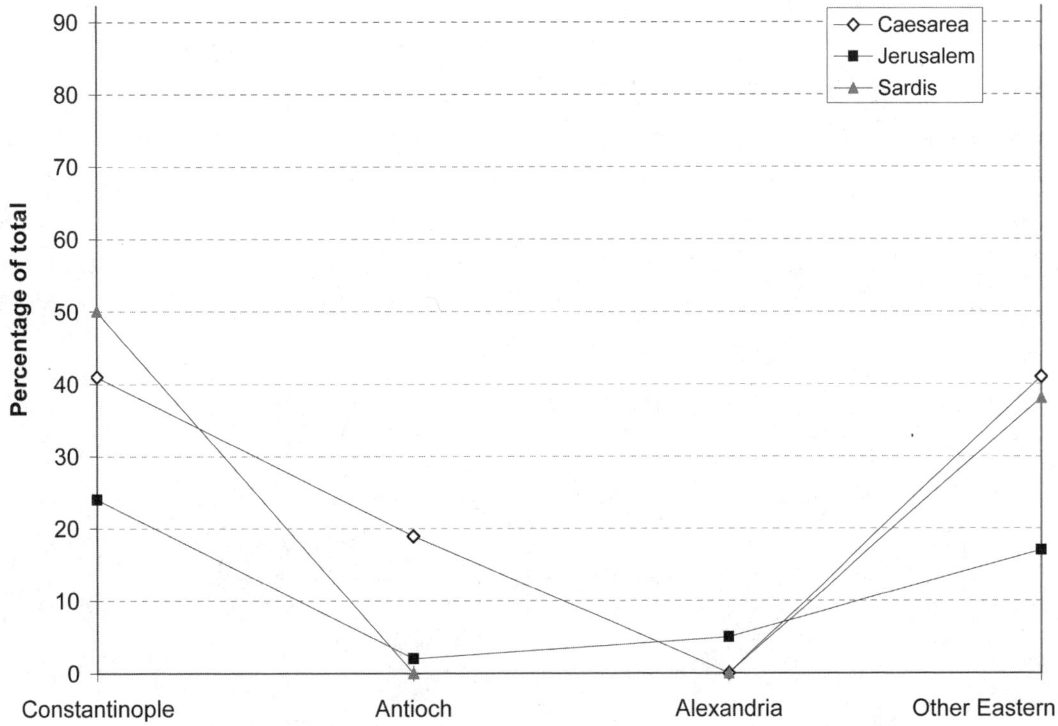

Fig. 19 *Mint origin: Coins of Justin II.*

The number of early to mid-sixth century building projects suggests a continuing prosperity at least in Caesarea itself. It is notable that the Annual Average Coin Loss for issue period 27 (Fig. 11 and Table 3) drops for Caesarea, though it remains steady for Jerusalem and Samaria. In the reign of Justin II (565–578), Constantinople returns as the main mint of origin, due to the lack of small coins from Carthage (Fig. 19). Other Eastern mints are Thessalonica, Nicomedia and Cyzicus. During the reign of Maurice, the percentages of mint origins in Jerusalem and Caesarea are similar to those found during the reign of Justin II (Fig. 20), as the Average Annual Coin Loss (Fig. 11 and Table 3, issue period 28) shows an increase from the previous period, at least in Caesarea.[132]

Large coins of Phocas (602–610) are poorly represented in the Caesarea finds, but the numbers of *dodecanummia* coins actually raise the number of specimens per year, and skews the mint percentages to favor Alexandria to an overwhelming degree (Fig. 21). Such coins may be underrepresented in the Jerusalem reports, though many coins of Alexandria are reported from his reign. The Antioch mint closed in 611, never to be reopened by the Byzantine emperors.[133]

Heraclian coins are particularly easy to identify, mostly because of the number of overstrikes, resulting in thin, curved flans. The percentages of supplying mints (based on the overstriking, not the original coin) are surprisingly similar in Caesarea and Jerusalem (Fig. 22). The Annual Average Coin Loss (Fig. 11 and Table 3, issue period 29) shows a decrease from the reigns of Maurice and Phocas in Caesarea and Samaria. As has already been noted in Chapter 1, the declining numbers of post-year-six bronze coins of Heraclius reflect the closing of two mints, and a probable slowdown at Constantinople. It should be noted that no "local imitations" can be found that are dated to these years. There are few Heraclian coins from the years 634–640/1; instead, as I have argued, around 630–634 earlier coins were countermarked and released for use.[134] Since Byzantine Syria and Palestine had been without a mint since 611, there may have been a pressing need for Heraclius to get money to his troops as fast as possible, hence he set up a temporary mint in Caesarea to reaffirm the authenticity of his coins. I ignored the countermarked coins when setting up the 'n' values for each graph, since the coins may well have been circulating in Caesarea before being countermarked there. However, if we

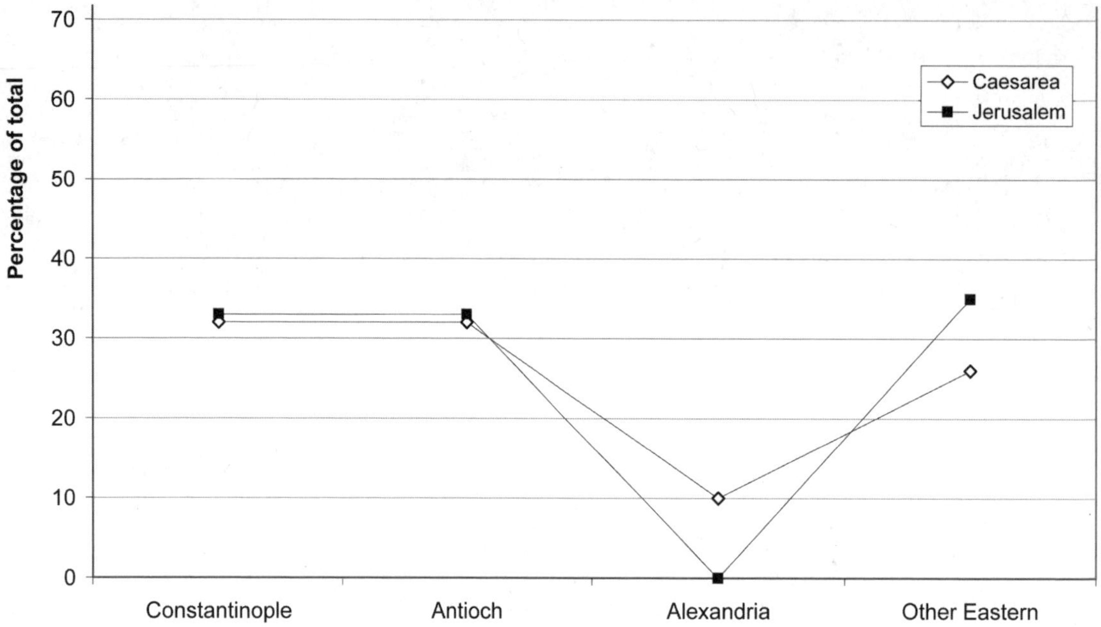

Fig. 20 Mint origin: Coins of Maurice.

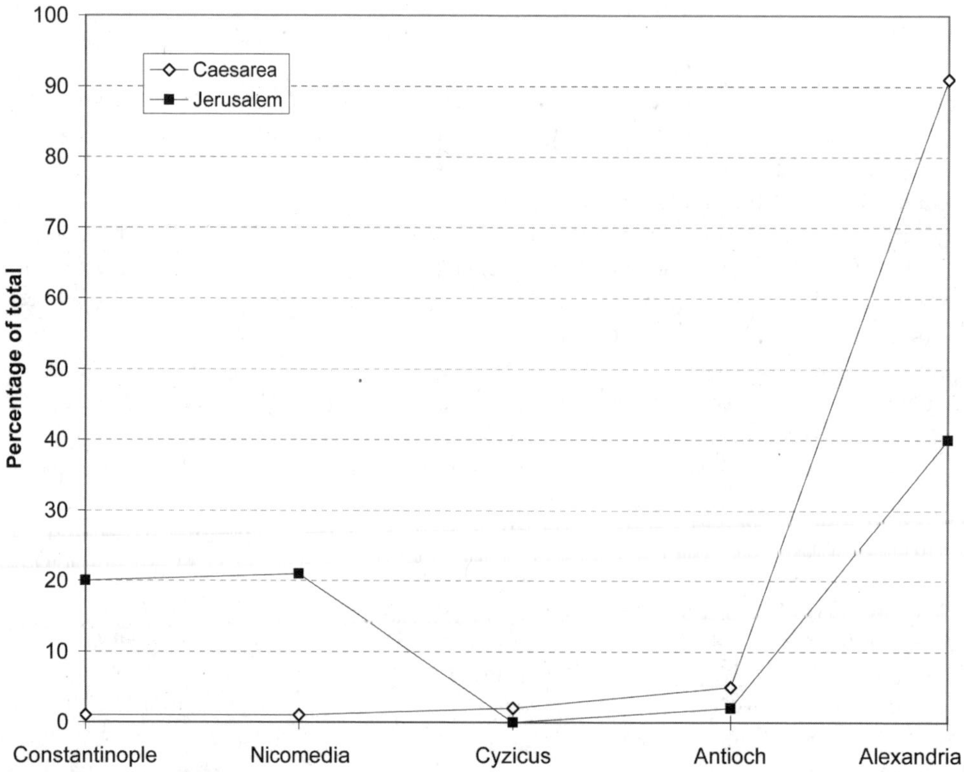

Fig. 21 Mint origin: Coins of Phocas.

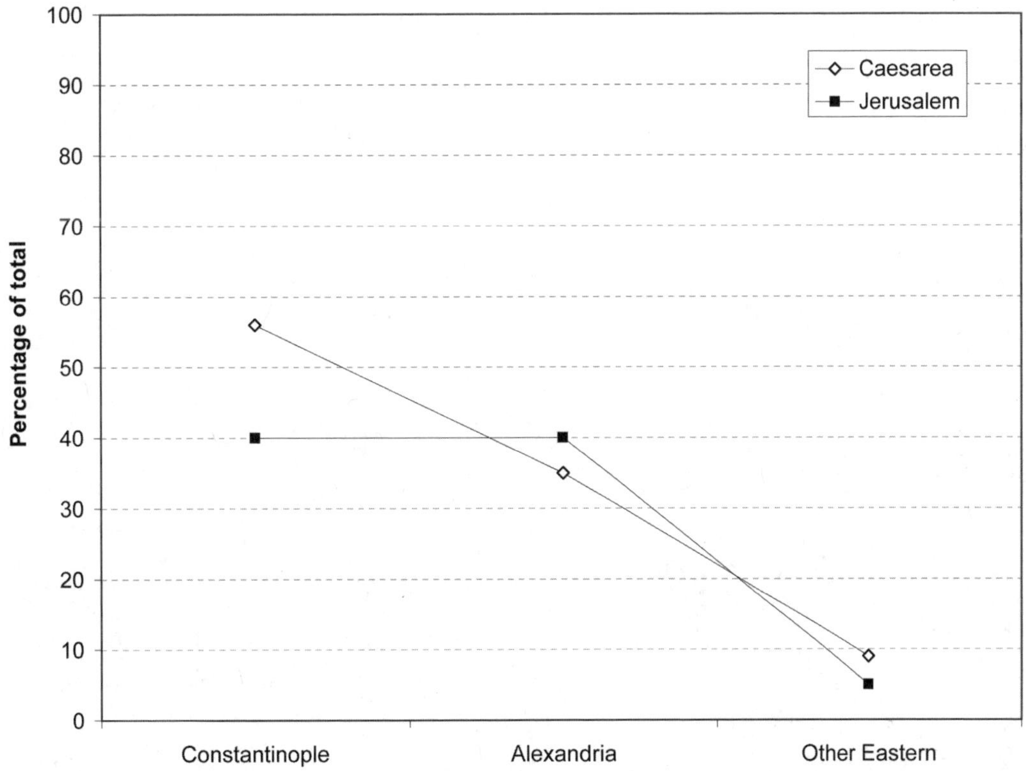

Fig. 22 *Mint origin: Coins of Heraclius.*

add the countermarked coins to the Annual Average Coin Loss chart, then numbers for the Heraclian period increase dramatically. Thus, the numismatic record alone testifies to the increasing chaos in the region during the reign of Heraclius, as overstruck and countermarked coins were repeatedly pressed into service as indicators of the re-establishment of an imperial authority that could not afford to issue new coins.

The Chi-Square Test encompassed all of the Byzantine period, and shows a consistency of results across the eastern cities (see Fig. 24 and Table 10; period T6). All of the normal eastern cities (Pergamon and Jerusalem are exceptions to the norm again) decline in percentages from the Late Roman highs to a level that averages just under twenty percent. Caesarea, Antioch, Gerasa, and Sardis all fall very close to this number. Most of the decline occurs after the reign of Justinian, but numismatically, at least, the cities of Palestine are not much represented in the Byzantine Period.

Some later Byzantine and Arab-Byzantine coins were found in the excavations, though the population at Caesarea seems to have been greatly reduced and few, if any, building projects were undertaken. The Arab-Byzantine imitations can be identified by their wide deviation from Byzantine weight standards and flan sizes, the clumsy style of lettering (often with pseudo-epigraphical inscriptions), and misinterpretations of Byzantine clothing styles. Their dating is still controversial, but the local mints seem to be Beth Shean and Damascus.[135] Very few of the official Byzantine coins that post-date Heraclius are found on any site, including Caesarea. The entire area seems to have been cut off from the rest of the Mediterranean.

Thus, with the evidence from the JECM excavations of Caesarea joining the publications of excavations from Judaea, Samaria, and Galilee, we may be able to start piecing together the economy and trade of Palestine. It is by combining the numismatic with archaeological, epigraphic, and historical sources that we form a better picture of ancient Palestine, and the finds from Caesarea are the first step on a long road.

Appendix 1
The Gold Hoard of Caesarea

Excavation by a JECM team from Concordia College, supervised by Olin Storvick, uncovered the spectacular hoard of 99 gold coins featured on the frontispiece. The hoard, which was cleaned, cataloged, and published by Peter Lampinen,[1] mostly consists of coins from the reigns of Valens and Valentinian I (364–375 C.E.), and from the mint at Antioch. It was closed in 395, the date of the last coins in the hoard.

Gold began to be struck regularly around 300 C.E., when the coin was called the *solidus*. Each coin weighed about 4.5 grams, but steadily began to drop after c.309 and to be debased by the addition of silver. Around 365, the coins were again reformed, or brought up to the previous standard of purity. The last debased *solidi* issued were the RESTITVTOR REIPVBLICAE reverses; the reformed coins carried a reverse legend of VICTORIA AVGG. Both debased and pure coins were hoarded indiscriminately, not just at Caesarea.

The emperors Valentinian I and Valens increased the amount of gold in circulation. Several means were tried: increasing production of the gold mines; collection of some taxes in gold only; and, to counteract the substitution of plated coins for pure gold coins, requiring that all tax payments in gold coin were to be melted down in the Imperial Treasury in Constantinople (to test the result for fineness) and to be re-struck into new gold *solidi*.[2] Because of the reminting, there are few coins that can be dated to the pre-365–368 reform, as seen in the Caesarea hoard. As with most other gold hoards of this period, the gold remained in circulation only for a short time; thus, the coins in the hoard look newly minted.[3] Gold was increasingly minted in the fourth century, peaking in the middle of the century.[4]

The emperors marked the reformed gold pieces with the letters OB. The letters stand for *obryza* or *obryziacum aurum*, "refined gold." Eighteen coins (nos. **82–99**) carry this designation, dating 383 and after, all from the Constantinople, Thessalonika, or Mediolanum mint. Other letters and marks on the coins establish the *officina*, or workshop, that the coins came from in particular mints. At their heights, some mints have ten *officinae* producing simultaneously, including that of Antioch during the reign of Valentinian I.

Occasions for the Government to Obtain Coins

Every five years or at an imperial accession, a "contribution" of gold and silver was imposed upon the cities of the Empire; the tax was to be collected by the decurions in the form of gold coins. The tax is called the *collatio lustralis* and was possibly used to cover the costs of distributions of coin to the soldiers and citizens at these occasions. Senators also paid at this time in the form of an "offertory," the *oblatio senatoria*. Although the amount was supposed to be voluntary, we assume that senators and decurions were told the approximate amount the treasury would expect from them; on the *decennalia* (10-year anniversary of his reign) of Valentinian II, the prefect of Rome was told that the city should volunteer 1600 pounds of gold (115,200 *solidi*), though Valentinian was assured this was an unusually high contribution. In the west, this tax was paid in gold coin; in the Code of Theodosius (395 C.E.), the tax was made annual.[5] Senators also paid the *gleba senatoria* for the privilege of belonging to the senate: this tax was also levied in gold. Three rates are known: 1 (72 *solidi*), 1/2 (36 *solidi*) and 1/4 (18 *solidi*) pounds of gold, depending on the amount of land owned. In 393, Theodosius I created a fourth class of senators who only had to pay seven *solidi*; interestingly, this tax was a tax on the senator's property, and the government continued to demand payment of the owner of the land even after the land had been sold to a non-senator.[6]

The tax on merchants, shopkeepers, and prostitutes—that is, any person engaged in trade or commerce—was collected every five years (the *aurum coronarium*). Valens and Valentinian decreed that only gold would be accepted in payment, but we have no idea how much the tax was. This tax may also have been used to pay for distributions to soldiers and citizens or the forgiveness of tax arrears.[7]

Less regular was a tax on commutation of army service (the *aurum tironicum*), also payable only in gold. Payment of this tax began c.370. Although the normal rate was only 25–30 *solidi* per man, during the military crises in the reign of Valentinian and Valens the fee rose as high as 80 *solidi*.[8] It should be noted that in the first half of the sixth century, the governor of Caesarea was given 1584 *solidi* (22 pounds) of gold annually to pay his staff; the Caesarea hoard represents about 1.4 Roman pounds.

The amount of gold in the hoard argues that the building was not an administrative center – there are too few pieces in the hoard to allow for the hoard to be an annual contribution of the town, nor to allow for a hoard of pay that was never distributed. On the other hand, such a hoard would have taken a soldier or citizen between fifteen and twenty years to accumulate, a range which agrees with the dates of the coins in the hoard.

In addition to the payment of salaries in gold coin, which became increasingly common after 300, coins were given out at several occasions: the birthday of the emperor; imperial accessions; and quinqennial celebrations, to name the best known examples. Most of our information about the distribution of coin at anniversaries comes from the most frequent recipients, the soldiers. Although the exact amounts of these *donatives*, as they are called, is not known, a hint can be found in Procopius, *HA* 2A, where the amount is reduced before the sixth century to five *solidi* (and one pound of silver) for each soldier.[9] Civilians also received coins on special celebration days; these handouts were called *largitiones*. While emperors certainly gave away precious objects other than coin, ivory consular diptychs showing *largitiones* do show bags of coins ready to be distributed.[10] There did exist occasions for the distribution of coins during the period of the Caesarea hoard: Valens and Valentinian I came to office in 364, and would have celebrated their quinqennial celebrations in 369 and 374. And note that the Valens and Valentinian I coins are round numbers (40 and 30, respectively) in the Caesarea hoard, increasing the probability that the coins were obtained by *donatives* or *largitiones*.

We can begin to assess the wealth of the hoarder by noting prices and taxes of the period. Although records from Caesarea do not exist in the way that they do for Egypt, soldiers there were paid in kind (i.e., by government-issued clothing and food) and coin, at the rate of five *solidi* per year (and an unknown amount for clothing) for infantrymen, and nine *solidi* per year for cavalry.[11] From another papyrus, which recorded the will of a centurion or a Roman officer (and hence one of the better-paid soldiers), we see that he left to his heirs gold and bronze coins, yet only twenty percent of the value of his bequest was in gold coin.[12] Some scholars estimate that seventy percent of landowners in fourth-century Egypt held land that was taxed annually less than one *solidus*.[13] Closer to home, a late third or early fourth-century text implies that a *solidus* could pay for two loaves of bread per day for one person for an entire year in Palestine; a slightly later text gives the fair price of a cow as eight *solidi*.[14] Hence, our hoarder must have been a modestly wealthy man.[15]

COMPARISONS TO OTHER GOLD HOARDS IN THE EAST

While publications on gold hoards from the west abound, there are many fewer references to gold hoards found in the eastern Roman provinces, making comparison that much more difficult. The ones that we do find have interesting parallels to the Caesarea hoard; I note here only hoards that cover approximately the same time period as the Caesarea hoard (Tables 6–8).

Table 6. Caesarea *solidus* hoard compared to other eastern hoards: by emperor.

	Caesarea	Karanis	Antioch 1981a	Antioch 1981b	Sidi Bu Said	Yemen
Constantius II	5	1	–	2	3	299
Julian	–	2	–	4	1	2
Jovian	2	–	–	–	1	15
Valentinian I	30	12	14	–	11	–
Valens	40	14	7	13	15	3
Gratian	2	–	–	–	53	–
Valentinian II	4	–	–	–	81	–
Theodosius I	7	–	–	–	155	–
Arcadius	6	–	1	–	69	–
Honorius	3	–	–	–	–	–
Theodosius II	–	–	–	–	–	1

The *solidus* hoard from Karanis, Egypt, consists of twenty-nine coins, dating from the reign of Valentinian I and Valens; approximately the same percentages of mints appear here as in the Caesarea hoard: Antioch is the largest supplier, with sixty-nine percent of the coins, though Nicomedia is the second largest, with seventeen percent.[16] Like the Caesarea hoard, the main reverse type is RESTITVTOR REIPVBLICAE, few of the coins come from the west, and a variety of *officinae* from Antioch is found (though not as many as in the Caesarea hoard).

The Antioch 1981a hoard consisted of more than eighteen *solidi*, but the entire hoard was not recorded before it was dispersed.[17] The hoard closed about a decade before the Caesarea hoard closed, with coins from the reign of Constantius II through Arcadius. Again, the main reverse type was RESTITVTOR REIPVBLICAE, not surprisingly in this hoard, because Antioch was the main mint of this reverse type. Nor is it surprising that the overwhelming number of discernible mint marks show Antioch as the source of the coins; but these do not show as wide a spread of *officinae* as the Caesarea coins do. Fewer details are available for the Antioch 1981b (or Israel?) hoard;[18] closed c.470–480 c.e., it consisted of twenty-four *solidi*, ranging from coins of Constantius II to Zeno. The bulk of the coins (13) come from the reign of Valens. No mints are published.

Most of the coins from the al-Madhariba (Yemen) hoard were from the local minting authority, Aksum (868), but 320 were *solidi* dating from Constantinius II (as Caesar) to Theodosius II. Some western mints were represented, but the large majority of the *solidi* came from the mint at Antioch during the reign of Constantius as Augustus (125), with the second largest group from Nicomedia (78).[19]

The hoard from Qom al Kebir, found sometime before 1923, was closed around 360 c.e.[20] It consisted of about fifty *solidi*, of which twenty-six were recorded before the hoard was bought by the British Museum. These were all coins of Constantius II, with the VOTA reverse, mostly from the mint at Antioch (19 *solidi*).

From Abualanda, Jordan, came a small hoard of seventeen *solidi* dating from Valentinian I to Anastasius; Kent suggests that the four coins of Zeno and the three coins of Anastasius belonged to a separate hoard, as the seven coins of Valentinian I and three of Valens are all the RESTITVTOR REIPVBLICAE reverse type. No mints are recorded.[21]

A different profile comes from the Sidi Bu Said (Barke, Libya) hoard of 390 *solidi*.[22] Coins from Valentinian I to Arcadius are present, but instead of Valens and Valentinian being strongly represented, coins of Theodosius I form the bulk of the hoard. Most of the coins come from the mint of Constantinople; *officina* S is best represented in the hoard, but coins are found from each *officina* in Constantinople. The scholars who studied the

Table 7. Caesarea *solidus* hoard compared to other eastern hoards: by mint.

	CAESAREA	KARANIS	ANTIOCH 1981A	SIDI BU SAID	QOM AL-KEBIR	YEMEN
Trier	–	–	–	21	–	–
Lyon	2	–	–	–	–	1
Arles	–	1	–	–	–	1
Rome	2	1	–	–	1	27
Milan	4	–	–	7	–	–
Aquileia	–	–	–	1	–	–
Siscia	–	–	–	1	1	5
Sirmium	–	–	–	2	–	22
Thessalonica	–	1	–	18	–	9
Cyzicus	1	–	–	1	–	2
Constantinople	20	1	2	312	–	30
Antioch	66	20	9	25	19	143
Total	99	29	12	390	26	320

hoard believe that the owner had traveled widely in the east between 379 and 388, accumulating coins from the *donatives* and quinquennalia of Valentinian II, Theodosius I and Arcadius.

We can thus begin to find points of comparison between the Caesarea hoard and other hoards found in the east. Except for the Qom al Kebir hoard (which we do not know in its entirety) and the al-Madhariba (Yemen) hoard, coins of the first half of the fourth century are not common; the upswings in the Caesarea, Karanis, Antioch 1981a, Antioch 1981b, and Abualanda hoards all come with the reigns of Valentinian I, Valens and Gratian, after Valentinian's reform of the gold coinage. The Sidi Bu Said hoard shows a later bulge, during the reigns of Valentinian II to Theodosius I. Most of the coins from Caesarea, Karanis, and about half the coins from Antioch 1981a are the RESTITVTOR REIPVBLICAE reverse. All of the other hoards consist largely of coins from Antioch (which is the closest *solidi*-producing mint to these areas), except the Sidi Bu Said hoard, which differs from this profile in having most of its coins come from the mint at Constantinople. All of the hoards, except the Yemen hoard and the Sidi Bu Said hoard, show few or no coins from the western mints. Though information on workshops was more difficult to find, Caesarea is unusual in having coins from all ten *officinae* of the mint at Antioch and seven of the eleven marks of *officinae* in Constantinople. Lampinen only noted four coins that shared dies, even given the large number coming from the Antioch mint. That is, there seems to be little systematic collecting of coins from one particular *officina*. Either the coins from different *officinae* were mixed before shipping out, or the collector got them in many stages.

CIRCUMSTANCES OF BURIAL

The excavation uncovered a domestic building in Field G, Area 25. The house was oriented along an east–west axis; although the western half of the house was not excavated, the excavator believes that it fronted on a north–south paved street (Cardo I west). The building was covered with a destruction layer, which was dated to the end of the Byzantine era, and showed no sign of having been re-occupied in

Table 8. Caesarea *solidus* hoard compared to other eastern hoards: by workshop (Antioch and Constantinople only).

	CAESAREA	KARANIS	ANTIOCH 1981A	SIDI BU SAID
ANTIOCH				
Α	7	7	2	1
Β	3	3	–	1
Γ	9	–	1	1
Δ	7	–	–	–
Ε	5	2	5	4
S	8	2	–	7
Ζ	8	–	–	1
Η	9	–	–	3
Θ	4	–	1	2
Ι	4	6	–	4
CONSTANTINOPLE				
Wreath	5	1	–	–
Α	3	–	–	20
Β	2	–	–	7
Γ	–	–	–	28
Δ	–	–	–	22
Ε	–	–	–	18
S	2	–	–	32
Ζ	4	–	–	48
Η	–	–	–	17
Θ	1	–	–	13
Ι	2	–	–	16

the Islamic or Crusader eras (though four cist burials were cut into the remains). The house itself showed several layers of occupation. The basalt grinding stone was found underneath a deteriorated mosaic floor; the layer in which the stone was found had sherds in it dating to the fourth century. The surface of the stone was pierced by dowel holes and a socket hole. The coins were found in the cut made for the socket, within a plaster 'cup' created for the hoard; the excavator reports that the coins were "arranged in rows as if unwrapped from coin wrappers." The pottery of the surface in which the stone was embedded agrees with the date of the coins, meaning that the grindstone was no longer used by the end of the fourth century. The building's location near the north gate of the city probably marks the entire neighborhood as an upper- to middle-class residential section of the city.[23]

Although we cannot ever say why a particular hoard was buried, nor why it was never retrieved, we can assign a closing date to the hoard, based on the latest coin in the hoard, here 395. This year was a watershed of Roman history, as it marks the date of the death of Theodosius I and the accession of his two sons, Arcadius and Honorius. While the coins of Arcadius in the hoard come from Constantinople, the seat of the eastern half of the Empire, two of the coins of Honorius come from Mediolanum (Milan), the area controlled by Honorius who became emperor of the western half of the Empire after his father's death. Thus, none of the accession coinages of Honorius or Arcadius are found in the hoard. Had the owner of the hoard fallen out of favor with the rise of the new regime? Or was the hoard buried before the owner had a chance to retrieve his portion of the *donatives* of 395? Why was the house suddenly abandoned at the very end of the fourth century, especially since there is no historical circumstance to pin this abandonment to, and since the economy of Caesarea seems to have stalled badly only at the end of the fifth century? We are probably looking at a very individual story – a secretive man who hid his accumulated wealth and passed away suddenly without revealing the place of his hoard; in the hoard we have a high "SC," or "sheer cussedness" (the phrase of A. Robertson), factor.[24] But even this idiosyncratic contribution to the numismatic record allows us, in a small way, to build a picture of the ancient economy of Caesarea.

Abbreviated Catalog of the Caesarea Hoard

The corrigenda to the Lampinen 1999a catalog were compiled by Evans, Bull and Storvick. We did not see the graffiti on the coins, as we were unable to see the coins and they were not photographed in a strong enough raking light (Evans only had access to the high-resolution digital images). FN refers to the number assigned in the field.

Constantius II, as Augustus

Lyon before 360 C.E.

1. obv.: FL IVL CONST ANTIVS PF AVG, helmeted and armored bust, facing. rev.: GLORIA REI PVBLICAE, Roma and Constantinople enthroned, holding scepters; between them is a shield inscribed VOT XXX MULT XXXX; mintmark LVG. See Lampinen 1999a: 377 no. 5 (FN 49). Bastien notes that he expected such a coin to surface, in part because of the *argentarii* with legends that parallel this *solidus*, which must have been struck in anticipation of the tricennalia of Constantius' II reign, while Constantius was briefly in Lyon. Three *argentarii* are known of this reverse type, but carrying the mintmark SMLVG (Bastien 1985: 70, 231 no. 227; obverse legend reads FL IVL CONSTAN TIVS PERP AVG).

Nicomedia 340–351 C.E.

2–3. obv.: FL IVL CONSTAN TIVS PERP AVG, one as above, one diademed bust r. rev.: GLORIA REI PVBLICAE, as above, mintmark SMNT. *RIC* 8: 477, 74 (facing bust), 473, 32 (diademed r. bust); Lampinen 1999a: 1–2 (FN 94, 65).

Antioch 355–361 C.E.

4–5. obv.: DN CONSTAN TIVS PF AVG, diademed head r. rev.: GLORIA REI PVBLICAE, Roma and Constantinople enthroned, holding scepters and between them a wreath enclosing VOT XXXX, mintmark ANTZ (no. 4 with Z reversed). *RIC* 8: 526, 172–3; Lampinen 1999a: 3–4 (FN 55, 62).

Jovian

Antioch 363–364 C.E.

6–7. obv.: DN IOVIAN VS PEP AVG, diademed bust r. rev.: SECVRITA S REI PVBLICAE, Roma and Constantinople enthroned, holding scepters and between them a shield inscribed VOT V MUL X, mintmark ANTΔ, ANTE. *RIC* 8: 532, 223; Lampinen 1999a: 6–7 (FN 42, 15).

Valens

Rome 364–367 C.E.

8–9. obv.: DN VALEN S PF AVG, diademed bust r. rev: RESTITVTOR REIPVBLICAE, emperor standing facing with labarum and victory on globe, star in field r. (no. 8), mintmarks SMRQ and •RT palmbranch. *RIC* 9: 117, 2.c.3, 2.c.9; Lampinen 1999a: 9, 10 (FN 92, 34).

Constantinople 367–375 C.E.

10–11. obv.: DN VALENS PF AVG, as above. rev.: RESTITVTOR REIPVBLICAE, as above, except emperor holds standard with cross, mintmark *CONS wreath (2); in coin no.11, the mintmark has been reworked, possibly from dot and palm. *RIC* 9: 217, 25b; Lampinen 1999a: 13, 14 (Lampinen misidentifies the labarum; FN 13, 69).

Nicomedia 364–367 C.E.

12. obv.: DN VALEN S PF AVG, diademed bust r. rev.: as above, except emperor holds a labarum, mintmark SMNΘ. *RIC* 9: 250, 2.c; Lampinen 1999a: 15, who reads the mintmark as SMNB- (FN 31).

Antioch 364–367 C.E.

13–47. obv.: DN VALEN S PF AVG, DN VALENS PF AVG, or DN VALENS PER F AVG, diademed bust r. rev.: as above, some with cross or chi-rho in field and some with standard with cross, mintmarks ANTA•, •ANTA•, *ANTB* (2), ANTΓ• (2), •ANTΓ• (2), ANTΔ, ANTΔ• (worn coin), •ANTΔ•, ANTΔ*, *ANTΔ*, ANTE•, *ANTE* (2), ANTH• (3), ANTH*, ANTZ (3), •ANTZ•, ANTΘ•, ANTΘ*, ANTI•, *ANTI*, ANTS (2), ANTS• (2), •ANTS•, ANTS* (2). *RIC* 9: 272, 2a, 2c, 2d; Lampinen 1999a: 17–18, 20–21, 26–27, 33–38, 40–51, 53–57, 65–70; although the victory on a globe is not always mentioned in Lampinen's catalogue, this must simply be an oversight in some descriptions; nor does he note the standards with a cross. Also note that his coin 51, which he reads as a die originating as a Γ changed to a Θ, Evans reads as originating from the S *officina*. (FN 2, 4, 8, 9, 11–12, 14, 17, 27–30, 33, 35, 37–38, 41, 47, 50–51, 53, 56, 59–61, 66–67, 74, 81, 86–88, 91, 97, 99).

Valentinian I

Mediolanum 364–367 C.E.

48. obv.: DN VALENTINI ANVS PF AVG, diademed bust r. rev.: RESTITVTOR REIPVBLICAE, emperor standing facing with labarum and victory on globe, mintmark MED. *RIC* 9: 75, 2a; Lampinen 1999a: 8 (FN 22).

Constantinople 367–375 C.E.

49–50. obv.: as above. rev.: as above, except emperor holds standard with a cross, mintmark *CONS wreath (2). *RIC* 9: 217, 25a; Lampinen 1999a: 11–12 (Lampinen misidentifies the labarum; FN 73, 77).

Cyzicus 364–367 C.E.

51. obv.: as above. rev.: as above, except the emperor holds a labarum, mintmark *SMKΓ. *RIC* 9: 239, 2b.2; Lampinen 1999a: 16 (FN 85).

Antioch 364–367 C.E.

52–77. obv.: as above. rev.: as above or with emperor holding a standard with a cross, some with cross or chi-rho in field, mintmark ANTA, ANTA•, *ANTA* (2), ANTB, ANTΓ•, ANTΓ* (2), *ANTΓ* (2), ANTΔ, ANTE*, ANTH, ANTH*, *ANTH* (3), ANTZ, •ANTZ•, ANTΘ* (2), ANTI (broken reverse die), ANTI*, ANTS (3). *RIC* 9: 272, 2a, 2b; Lampinen 1999a: 19, 22–25, 28–32, 39, 52, 58–64, 71–77 (note: Lampinen 75 is missing, but should have two stars; although the victory on a globe is not always mentioned in Lampinen's catalogue, this must simply be an oversight in some of the descriptions; sometimes the labarum is misidentified (FN 1, 3, 10, 16, 18, 20–21, 26, 36, 40, 44–46, 48, 52, 57, 63–64, 70, 72, 76, 79, 82, 84, 89, 98)

Gratian

Constantinople 367–375 C.E.

78. obv.: DN GRATIA NVS PF AVG diademed bust r. rev.: PRINCIPIVM IVVENTVTIS nimbate emperor standing facing, holding spear and globe, mintmark *CONS wreath. *RIC* 9: 217, 24; Lampinen 1999a: 78 (FN 80).

Antioch 367–375 C.E.

79. obv.: as above. rev.: as above, mintmark ANTA. *RIC* 9: 277, 19 and note; Lampinen 1999a: 79 (FN 43).

Valentinian II

Lyon 388–392 C.E.

80. obv.: DN VALENTINI ANVS PF AVG, diademed bust r. rev.: VICTOR IA AVGG, two nimbate emperors enthroned, holding a globe; between them is a Victory (above) and a palm branch (below); mintmark LD COM. *RIC* 9: 50, 38a; Lampinen 1999a: 81 (although the nimbus is not mentioned in Lampinen's catalogue, this must simply be an error in description; FN 75).

Mediolanum 383–394 C.E.

81. obv.: as above. rev.: as above, mintmark MD COM. *RIC* 9: 78, 8a.2 or 80, 20a; Lampinen 1999a: 80 (FN 71).

Constantinople 383–388 C.E.

82–83. obv.: as above. rev.: CONCORDI A AVGGG, Constantinople enthroned (throne decorated with lion heads), holding globe and scepter, mintmark Z CONOB, S CONOB. *RIC* 9: 230, 67a.2 (pearl diademed) and b.2 (rosette diademed); Lampinen 1999a: 84–85 (Lampinen does not consistently mention the scepter in his descriptions, but it is present on all coins of this type; FN 5, 96).

Theodosius I

Thessalonica 388–393 C.E.

84. obv.: DN THEODO SIVS PF AVG, diademed bust r. rev.: as above, mintmark COMOB. *RIC* 9: 188, 64b; Lampinen 1999a: 82 (where he does not find the *RIC* entry; FN 32).

Constantinople 378–383 C.E.

85. obv.: as above. rev.: as above, except CONCOR DIA AVGGG, mintmark CONOB. *RIC* 9: 223, 44c; Lampinen 1999a: 83 (FN 24).

86. obv.: as above. rev.: CONCORDI A AVGGG, Constantinople enthroned (throne decorated with lion heads), holding scepter and shield inscribed VOT V MUL X, mintmark B CONOB. *RIC* 9: 224, 47b.2; Lampinen 1999a: 88 (FN 25).

383–388 C.E.

87–88. obv.: as above. rev.: CONCORDI A AVGGG, Constantinople enthroned (throne not decorated), holding scepter and shield inscribed VOT V MUL X, mintmark A CONOB, Θ CONOB. *RIC* 9: 231, 70a (neither *officina* is listed in *RIC* with pearl diadem); Lampinen 1999a: 91, 92 (FN 6, 54).

89–90. obv.: as above. rev.: as above, but holding shield inscribed VOT X MULT XV, mintmark A CONOB. *RIC* 9: 231, 71a.1; Lampinen 1999a: 95, 96 (FN 68, 90).

Arcadius

Constantinople 378–383 C.E.

91–92. obv.: DN ARCADI VS PF AVG diademed bust r. rev.: CONCORDI A AVGGG, Constantinople enthroned (throne decorated with lion heads), holding globe and scepter, mintmark E CONOB, I CONOB. *RIC* 9: 224, 46f.1 (I *officina* not listed in *RIC* with pearl diadem); Lampinen 1999a: 89, 90 (FN 95, 58).

383–388 C.E.

93. obv.: as above (small bust). rev.: as above, mintmark Z CONOB (Z reversed). *RIC* 9: 230, 67c (*officina* not listed in *RIC*); Lampinen 1999a: 86 (FN 19).

94. obv.: as above. rev.: as above, mintmark I CONOB. *RIC* 9: 230, 67c.5; Lampinen 1999a: 87 (FN 93).

95–96. obv.: as above. rev.: CONCORDI A AVGGG, Constantinople enthroned (throne not decorated), holding scepter and shield inscribed VOT V MUL X, mintmark A CONOB, Z CONOB (Z reversed). *RIC* 9: 231, 70c.1, c.3; Lampinen 1999a: 93, 94 (the scepter is not mentioned in Lampinen's catalogue, which must be an oversight in description; FN 7, 83).

Honorius

Mediolanum 395–402 C.E.

97–98. obv.: DN HONORI VS PF AVG, diademed bust r. rev.: VICTORI A AVGGG, emperor trampling captive, while holding standard and victory on globe, mintmark MD COMOB. *RIC* 10: 318, 1206; Lampinen 1999a: 97–98 (FN 23, 78).

Constantinople 395–397 C.E.

99. obv.: as above. rev.: as above, mintmark Z SM COMOB (Z reversed). *RIC* 10: 239, 2; Lampinen 1999a: 99 (FN 39).

Appendix 2
The Chi-Square Test

The most common way of summarizing the number of coins found on a site is to list the percentage of coins found per empire (e.g., Ptolemaic, Seleucid, etc.). This basic tabulation is used all over the Mediterranean basin, though not every numismatist chooses to tabulate his results this way from every excavation. Numismatists interested in statistical analysis of excavation coins began using the coins per regnal year, or coins per annum as a way of measuring within these empires the number of coins found, and how that number may compare to the number of years the ruler reigned. For two examples within the regional cohort, see Crowfoot *et al.* 1957: 45 and Buttrey *et al.* 1981: 122.

In an effort to refine the method and to enable numismatists to utilize the results from small excavations as well as large ones, Casey and Reece developed the Annual Average Coin Loss equation. In its barest outline, the formula is:

$$\frac{\text{Coins of Reign}}{\text{Years of Reign}} \times \frac{1000}{\text{Site Total}} = \text{AACL}$$

Note that the "Years of Reign" can be arbitrarily set by the numismatist, but in practice they correspond to the reigns of the emperors. Most numismatists stop here, after producing a histogram or line graph of the results. Reece (1998) has refined the method by making the largest city-sample (in his case, the coins from Richborough) the norm against which he measures other cities or districts. The extremes are averaged to produce the mid-point for each period. The result gives the normal profile. He can then calculate the standard deviation of a value from this norm (which is called the null line). Reece points out that we still need to ascertain the normal deviation from the null line and explain these deviations. Some of the deviations can be explained by the use and occupational phases of a site, but the numismatist should be more concerned with the middle values (according to Reece) and not the extremes. While the AACL is now an accepted form of argument, not many scholars have followed the refinements proposed by Reece. I chose a different method to see if the Annual Average Coin Loss results have any validity.

The Chi-Square Test was developed in 1900 by Karl Pearson in order to test whether the numbers of things in each category are there due to random chance or not; it has been used especially by those interested in social statistics. In a two-way table, the Chi-Square value indicates whether there is a significant relationship between the row and column variables, as opposed to the variables being independent. A standard deviation is less helpful, for we first have to establish a norm and then find the deviation from it. The Chi-Square test helps us to establish that norm.

The numbers I gathered from the excavation reports of Antioch, Caesarea, Gerasa, Hama, Jerusalem, Pella, Pergamon, Samaria, and Sardis enabled me to test the relationship between the time period (the row variable) and the city (the column variable), based on the number of coins discovered at the sites. In a perfect world, we would compare the frequencies to the numbers of coins that were produced annually from all the mints of the eastern half of the Roman Empire, but, as we have already seen, that number cannot be ascertained.

We must remember that the Chi-Square Test has limitations built into it, since it is based upon the amount of information we possess. However, every archaeologist and numismatist knows about limitations in his or her material. Such are the joys and frustrations of figuring out the puzzle that is the ancient world.

The equation for the Chi-Square Test is $$x^2 = \sum_{i=1}^{r} \sum_{j=1}^{k} (Oij - Eij)^2 / Eij$$

where *Oij* is the observed value of cases categorized in row *i* of column *j*. *Eij* is the number of cases expected under H_0 (the Null Hypothesis) to be categorized in row *i* of column *j*. The double sum indicates that the sum is to be done over all of the *r* rows and the *k* columns (that is, over all the cells). The values of x^2 will have $(r-1)$ by $(k-1)$ degrees of freedom (df), where *r* is the number of rows, and *k* is the number of columns in the table. The expected frequency for each cell (*Eij*) is calculated by multiplying the marginal row and marginal column total that is common to a cell, and dividing that product by the total number of cases (N), or the grand total.

Note that the grand total (N) on this test is NOT equal to the number of coins in the catalogue, for the test begins in 222 B.C.E. (the date at which coins start regularly appearing in the comparative cohort) and ends in 640 C.E, when I end the catalogue of coins for Caesarea. The catalogue includes coins that were minted both before and after this date.

In order to explain how I reached the normal eastern city profile, I will explain the chart and results. In Tables 4 (p. 32) and 9–10 (pp. 63, 65) the first line in each box is the frequency, or the number of coins found at the city from that time period. The second line is the chi-square value. The higher the cell chi-square number is, the more the value this city and this time period contribute to the Chi-Square Test. The third line in the box ("percent") shows what the percentage of actual coins in this time period in this city is, as compared to the whole sample. The fourth line ("row percent") notes the percentage of coins within this time period that came from this city, as compared to the cohort. This number is not extremely meaningful, as there are wild divergences among the actual numbers of the cohort cities (e.g., in T1, Gerasa reports only 6 coins, as opposed to 697 from Antioch). Finally, "column percent" lets you view the percentage of coins in that time period that came from the city (e.g., in Table 4, 0.91% of all the coins counted in the Chi-Square Test from Caesarea could be dated between 122 and 100 B.C.E). It can easily be noted, for instance, that T5 (347–498 C.E) holds the largest numbers and percentages of coins from all the cities in the cohort, and, interestingly, that T2 (c.103 B.C.E–C.E 69) follows in second place. The column percent was the number that was used in the graphs.

Without the large numbers of coins from Antioch, this exercise would not be nearly as useful; yet with those numbers we can tell by the cell Chi-Square that even in T3 (69–192 C.E, Table 4) in Hama, where the actual number of coins found ("frequency") is zero, the equation is significant. For this particular instance the Chi-Square test tells us there is a definite, significant relationship between the actual number of coins for a time period and the city.

I am very much indebted to Roslyn Gorin, Assistant Director of Statistical/Research Services, Temple Computer Services, Temple University, for explaining the method and running the program for me.

With the Chi-Square test results, we can begin to find the normal eastern city. The first set of results, with Caesarea, Samaria and Jerusalem only (again, all of the results were shown to be significant) shows that these three cities have little in common (Table 9 and Fig. 23). Jerusalem's highs can be explained by her role as the only Hasmonaean mint (and since these coins practically drove all other small change out of use, the numbers here are very high), and by the number of "foreign" visitors who came to visit the Temple, dropping coins as they exchanged them for other coins or goods. Jerusalem then plunges to the bottom of the chart, due to the two Revolts and subsequent depopulation. Samaria's profile can be explained both by the era when the city was excavated (and the subsequent underreporting of different eras, but especially the Late Roman period), her place in the interior of the province, and the fact that Samaria never minted coins in abundance, nor housed troops or civilian authorities.

Table 9. Chi-square test. Frequency of period by city: Cities in Ancient Palestine.

Frequency Chi-Square Percent Row Percent Cell Percent	CAESAREA	JERUSALEM	SAMARIA	TOTAL
	24	13	511	548
T1	94.473	326.12	3533.80	
	0.23	0.12	4.88	5.24
222–100 B.C.E.	4.38	2.37	93.25	
	0.91	0.19	46.08	
	167	5866	265	6298
T2	1273.10	823.95	242.47	
	1.60	56.04	2.53	60.16
c.103 B.C.E.–69 C.E.	2.65	93.14	4.21	
	6.32	87.33	23.90	
	68	40	21	129
T3	35.58	22.11	3.94	
	0.65	0.38	0.20	1.23
69–192 C.E.	52.71	31.01	16.28	
	2.57	0.60	1.89	
	240	300	86	626
T4	42.56	25.74	5.84	
	2.29	2.87	0.82	5.98
193–346 C.E.	38.34	47.92	13.74	
	9.08	4.47	7.75	
	1606	154	167	1927
T5	2577.60	947.68	6.76	
	15.34	1.47	1.60	18.41
347–498 C.E.	83.34	7.99	8.67	
	60.79	2.29	15.06	
	537	344	59	940
T6	378.74	111.36	16.54	
	5.13	3.29	0.56	8.98
498–640 C.E.	57.13	36.60	6.28	
	20.33	5.12	5.32	
Totals	2642	6717	1109	10468
	25.24	64.17	10.59	100

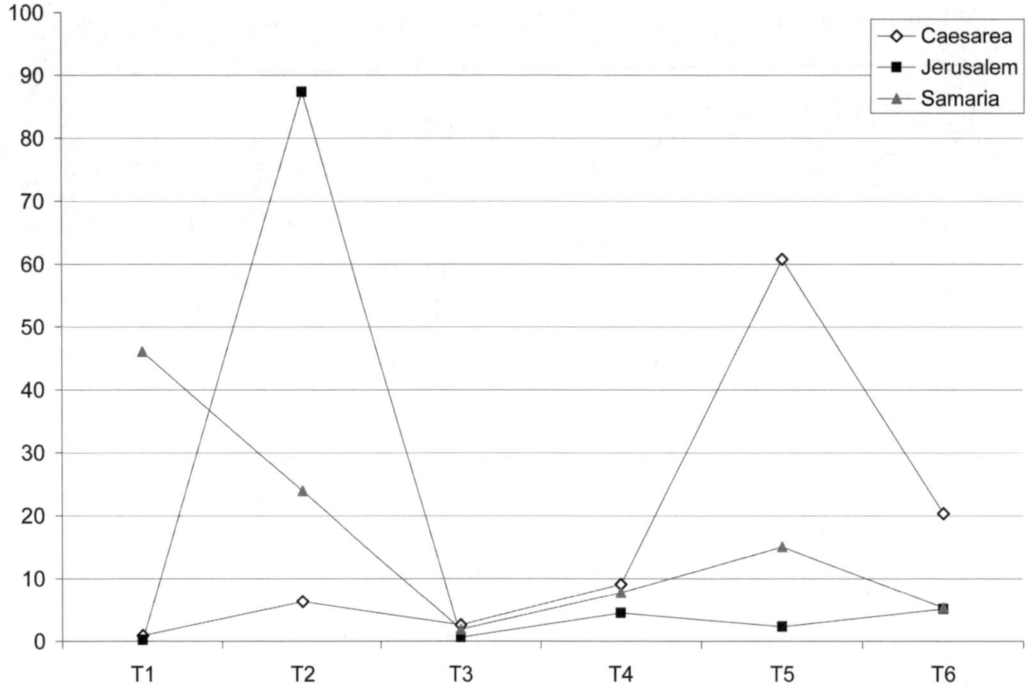

Fig. 23 *Chi-Square Test. Cities of Ancient Palestine, percentage of coins from time period.*

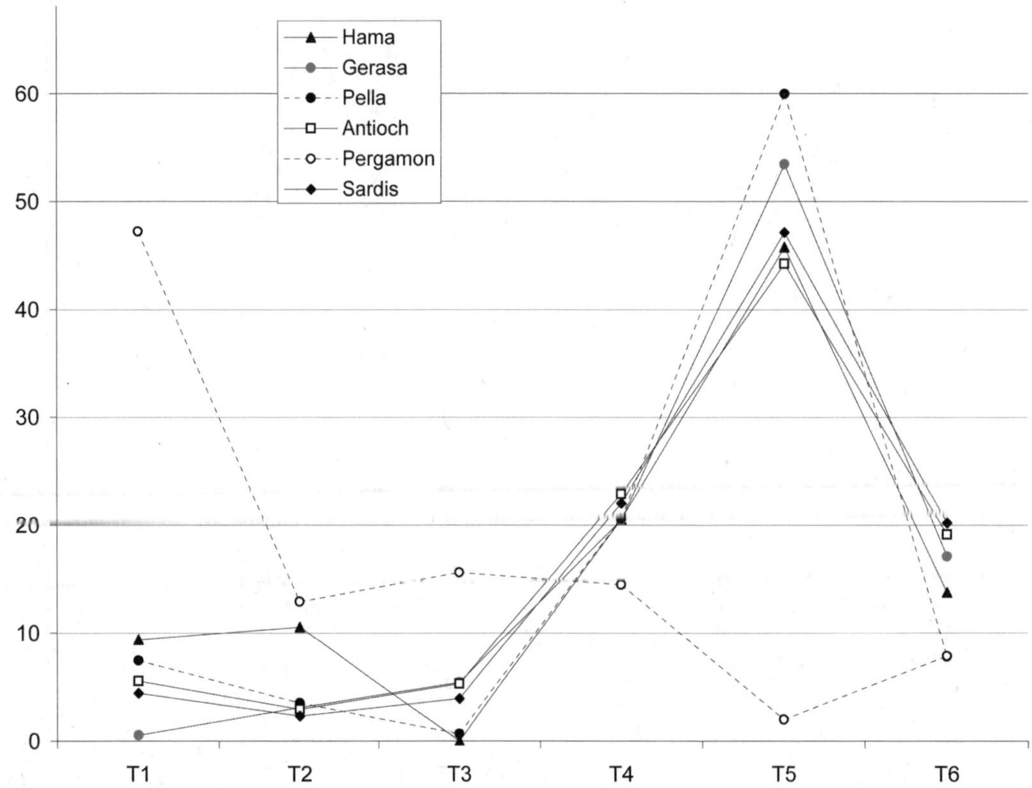

Fig. 24 *Chi-Square Test. Cities of the Near East, percentage of coins from time period.*

Table 10. Chi-square test. Frequency of period by city: Cities of the Ancient Near East, exclusive of Palestine.

Frequency Chi-Square Percent Row Percent Cell Percent	HAMA	GERASA	PELLA	ANTIOCH	PERGAMON	SARDIS	TOTALS
	32	6	78	697	336	242	1391
T1	4.29	64.38	1.34	18.48	1805.90	37.53	
	0.15	0.03	0.37	3.27	1.58	1.13	6.52
222–100 B.C.E.	2.30	0.43	5.61	50.11	24.16	17.40	
	9.38	0.52	7.44	5.54	47.19	4.41	
	36	36	37	371	92	128	700
T2	55	0.13	0.19	4.22	201.60	15.07	
	0.17	0.17	0.17	1.74	0.43	0.60	3.28
c.103 B.C.E.–69 C.E.	5.14	5.14	5.29	53.00	13.14	18.29	
	10.56	3.09	3.53	2.95	12.92	2.33	
	0	63	7	664	111	217	1062
T3	16.98	0.44	39.17	2.29	161.01	11.58	
	0.00	0.30	0.03	3.11	0.52	1.02	4.98
69–192 C.E.	0.00	5.93	0.66	62.52	10.45	20.43	
	0.00	5.41	0.67	5.28	15.59	3.95	
	70	238	216	2878	103	1208	4713
T4	0.38	1.43	1.07	3.55	18.76	0.02	
	0.33	1.12	1.01	13.49	0.48	5.66	23.00
193–346 C.E.	1.49	5.05	4.58	61.07	2.19	25.63	
	20.53	20.45	20.59	22.88	14.47	22.01	
	156	622	629	5561	14	2585	9567
T5	0.06	19.12	53.39	1.12	291.96	6.20	
	0.73	2.92	2.95	26.07	0.07	12.12	44.85
347–498 C.E.	1.63	6.50	6.57	58.13	0.15	27.02	
	45.75	53.44	59.96	44.22	1.97	47.10	
	47	199	82	2405	56	1108	3897
T6	3.76	0.88	62.74	5.02	42.19	11.07	
	0.22	0.93	0.38	11.28	0.26	5.19	18.27
498–640 C.E.	1.21	5.11	2.10	61.71	1.44	28.43	
	13.78	17.10	7.82	19.12	7.87	20.19	
Totals	341	1164	1049	12576	712	5488	21330
	1.60	5.46	4.92	58.96	3.34	25.73	100

Table 11. Chi-square test. Frequency of period by city: all cities in sample.

Frequency Chi-Square Percent Row Percent Cell Percent	CAESAREA	JERUSALEM	SAMARIA	ANTIOCH	GERASA	PELLA	HAMA	PERGAMON	SARDIS	TOTALS
T1	24	13	511	697	6	78	32	336	242	1939
	116.68	384.01	2906.90	6.37	59.49	3.08	6.04	1971.70	25.65	
222–100	0.08	0.04	1.61	2.19	0.02	0.25	0.10	1.06	0.76	6.10
B.C.E.	1.24	0.67	26.35	35.95	0.31	4.02	1.65	17.33	12.48	
	0.91	0.19	46.08	5.54	0.52	7.44	9.38	47.19	4.41	
T2	167	5866	265	371	36	37	36	92	128	6998
	70.85	13024.00	1.80	2075.40	189.23	162.79	20.32	26.71	965.35	
c.103 B.C.E.	0.72	18.45	0.83	1.17	0.11	0.12	0.11	0.29	0.40	22.01
–69 C.E.	21.55	83.82	3.79	5.30	0.51	0.53	0.51	1.31	1.83	
	6.32	87.33	23.90	2.95	3.09	3.53	10.56	12.92	2.33	
T3	68	40	21	664	63	7	0	111	217	1191
	19.69	177.95	10.16	79.05	8.63	26.54	12.77	268.68	0.64	
	0.29	0.13	0.07	2.09	0.20	0.02	0	0.35	0.68	3.75
69–192 C.E.	6.67	3.36	1.76	55.75	5.29	0.59	0	9.32	18.22	
	2.57	0.60	1.89	5.28	5.41	0.67	0	15.59	3.95	
T4	240	300	86	2878	238	216	70	103	1208	5339
	175.45	607.61	54.47	278.20	9.27	9.02	2.84	2.29	89.11	
193–346	1.03	0.94	0.28	9.05	0.75	0.68	0.22	0.32	3.80	16.79
C.E.	4.95	5.62	1.68	53.91	4.46	4.05	1.31	1.93	22.63	
	9.08	4.47	7.75	22.88	20.45	20.59	20.53	14.47	22.01	
T5	1606	154	167	5561	622	629	156	14	2585	11494
	90.40	2129.80	121.43	266.70	96.26	164.59	8.70	230.13	182.24	
347–498	6.90	0.48	0.55	17.49	1.96	1.98	0.49	0.04	8.13	36.15
C.E.	14.39	1.34	1.54	48.38	5.41	5.47	1.36	0.12	22.49	
	60.79	2.29	15.06	44.22	53.44	59.96	45.75	1.97	47.10	
T6	537	344	59	2405	199	82	47	56	1108	4837
	3.17	449.58	76.48	126.53	2.72	37.71	0.46	25.26	89.40	
498–640	2.31	1.08	0.19	7.56	0.63	0.26	0.15	0.18	3.48	15.21
C.E.	12.27	7.11	1.24	49.72	4.11	1.70	0.97	1.16	22.91	
	20.33	5.12	5.32	19.12	17.10	7.82	13.78	7.87	20.19	
Totals	2642	6717	1109	12576	1164	1049	341	712	5488	31798
	11.36	21.12	3.49	39.55	3.66	3.30	1.07	2.24	17.26	100

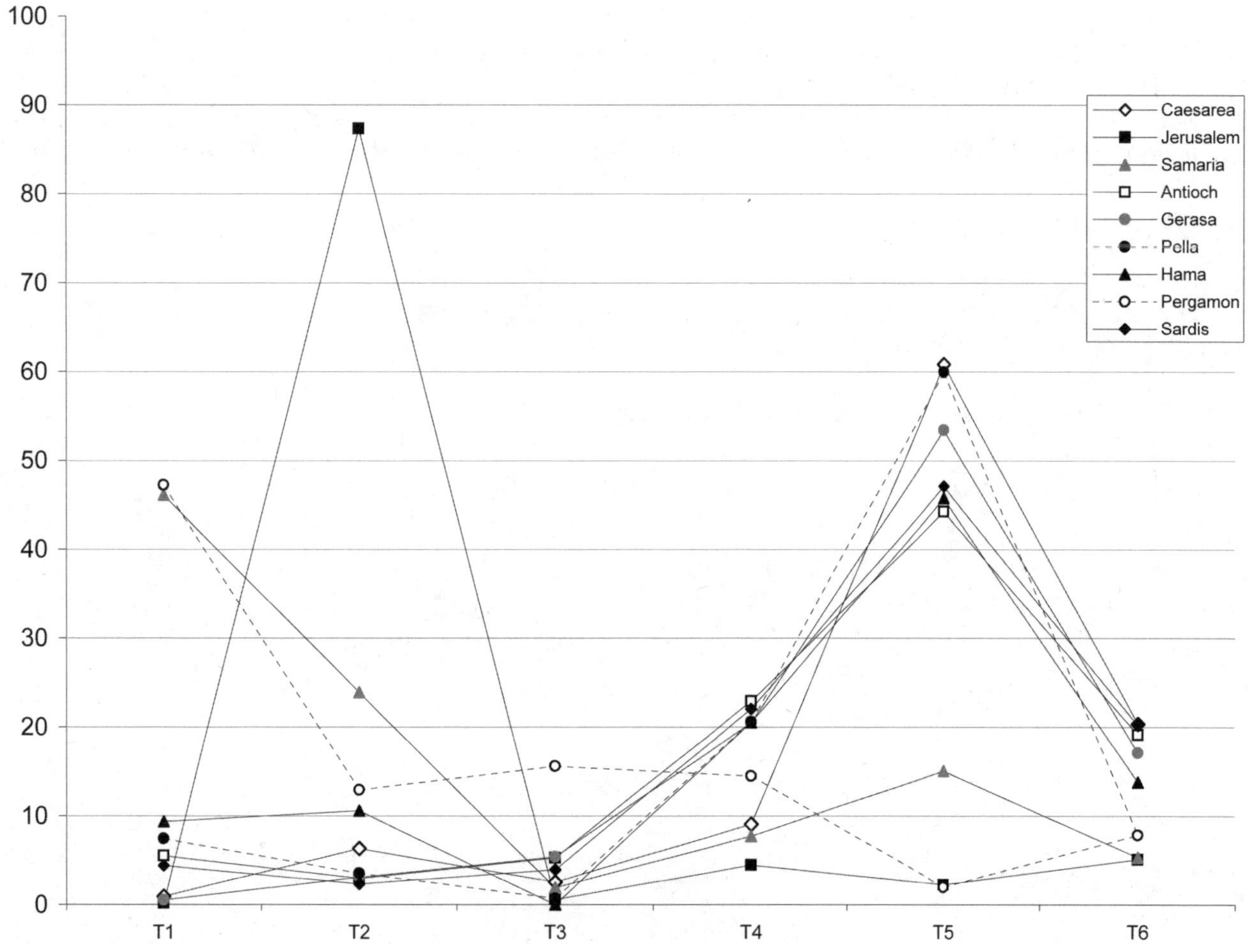

Fig. 25 *Chi-Square Test. All cities in sample, percentage of coins from time period.*

I then ran the test for eastern cities for which I had excavation reports (Table 10 and Fig. 24). These excavation reports ranged in date from the early to the late twentieth century, and so were of varying quality, just as the reports from Jerusalem and Samaria. They ranged from small numbers of coins (Hama, Gerasa, Pergamon, Pella) to large numbers (Antioch and Sardis). Yet except for Pergamon, their profiles were remarkably consistent, although I feel that the T1 and T2 periods (222 B.C.E. to 69 C.E.) are not as settled as periods T3–T6 (69–640 C.E.). Now it was time to compare the graphs of the Palestinian cities to the other eastern cities (Table 11 and Fig. 25).

One immediate conclusion could be seen easily: that Caesarea's profile fit into that of the "normal" eastern city, as shown in Table 4 and Figure 12. Hence, I rejected Pergamon, Jerusalem and Samaria to compile the Chi-Square values for the normal eastern city. Caesarea can be seen to be more closely tied to the large cities of the Roman East, tied by her harbor, and her importance of military and civilian postings. What has not been established is the profile of a normal Palestinian city, perhaps because none can be. Jerusalem is so strongly bound to the events that occurred around the Temple that she cannot be compared to the secular economic powerhouse of Caesarea. Samaria may more closely resemble the numismatic profile of Caesarea, but it will probably need more excavation, or better publications of the excavation coins, to make certain of that.

It is interesting to compare the results of the Chi-Square Test to the Annual Average Coin Loss for Caesarea (Figs. 11–12). Issue periods 1–2 in the Average Annual Coin Loss graph would make up the T1 period in the Chi-Square graph: both show very low numbers for this period, which rise only slightly for issue periods 3–6, or T2 on the Chi-Square graph. The numbers fall again in issue periods 7–10, or T3 on the Chi-Square test. The rise in issue periods 11–15 is mirrored in T4, with the largest peak coming in both T5 and issue periods 16–23. A secondary, and lower, peak is seen in T6, issue periods 24–29. Thus, the Average Annual Coin Loss may be used to give more detail to the overall picture given by the Chi-Square Test.

Notes

Chapter 1

Pp. 7–24

1. For Crusader coins found in the city, see Hohlfelder 1980.
2. Hohlfelder 1984: 265 suggested that some of the bronzes were agglutinations; I have mentioned such instances in this chapter.
3. See, most recently, Stieglitz 1999: 359–60, with earlier bibliography.
4. For a discussion on the use of the Tyrian silver coin and its impact on bronze coinage in Palestine, see *TJC*: 73–78 and Meshorer 1998: 74.
5. See Meshorer 1981 and *idem* 1990/91; McLean 1981; Barag and Qedan 1980.
6. *TJC*: 37.
7. *TJC*: 30, 209; On p.201 Meshorer points out that the average weight for Hasmonaean coins is 1.5–2.5 grams, but the coins range from 0.3 to 5 grams. In Meshorer 1998, he suggested that the anchor on the Hasmonaean coins refers to Yannai's conquest of the coastal cities.
8. *Ant* 15.8.5; thanks to Olin Storvick for reminding me of this.
9. J. Blakely, draft of the report on Field G; see also Holum *et al.* 1988: 53.
10. *TJC*: 64 and Hendin 1990/91. Meshorer suggests a third possibility, that the caduceus was a Jewish symbol, alluding to the bronze serpent raised by Moses (*TJC*: 64, note 23).
11. *TJC*: 71; cf. 72, note 35.
12. Meshorer, in *AJC*: 57–61, 92, 186 and *TJC*: 70, 176, rejects a small bronze of Herod as the first coin minted in Caesarea. Agreeing with the post-First Revolt date for the opening of the mint are *RPC* 1: 678–82; Ariel 1982: 287–89; Carradice 1982/83: 15–16; and Kadman *CNP* 1957: 30, who argued that the "inept lettering" on the coins of Nero pointed to these being the first products of the Caesarea mint. See also Hamburger's theory, below, on the coins of Durmius.
13. Levine 1975b: 18; Sutherland 1967: 90, 100–1, who argues that the transfer of personnel from the Jerusalem mint means that stylistic considerations cannot settle the argument. See also Ariel 1982: 283; Carradice 1982/83: 15.
14. Two different obverses from Agrippa's reign have the head of Claudius, with his titles (in Greek) around the flan. One of the reverses paired with such an obverse shows a distyle temple with three figures sacrificing, and a tiny crouching figure in front. It is not certain which temple this is intended to repre-

sent, though it may be the Temple of Rome and Augustus, which occupied a prominent position by the harbor. Burnett suggested that the temple was the Temple of Jupiter Optimus Maximus in Rome, and is used to describe the treaty between Claudius and Agrippa (Burnett 1987b). Temples appear on coins from Palestine and Phoenicia, but the only other coins which show people sacrificing in the temple were minted for Agrippa I. None of the latter was found in the excavation.

15. For a comment on the method of producing Hasmonaean coins, see *TJC*: 50–51.

16. Meshorer in *TJC*: 79 suggested that the galley refers to Archelaus' trip to Rome to plead his case with Augustus. He also suggested (79–80) the crested helmet is a visual pun on the king's role as "head of the nation."

17. *TJC*: 80 suggested weights of 2 to 2.4 grams.

18. *TJC*: no. 122; *RPC* 1: 4985–86.

19. Meshorer in *TJC*: 96–97 preferred to see the coins of Agrippa I minted between 41 and 44, not just in the sixth year of his reign.

20. *TJC*: 171–72; Meshorer 1998: 91.

21. Humphrey 1986: 480; Porath 1995.

22. Hamburger 1970: 81–83, followed by *TJC*: 178.

23. *RPC* 1: 670.

24. *TJC*: 133–34 (none of the *minima* that Meshorer suggested were struck in Caesarea in this era [p. 183] were found in the excavations); cf. Ariel 1982: 290.

25. Butcher 2000: 203; Levine 1972: 131–32; *TJC*: 190 (reaffirming the Caesarea mint). For a discussion of the iconography, see Barag 1978 and Carradice 1982/83.

26. Carradice 1982/83: 18–19.

27. See also Barag 1967: 117–25.

28. See also *TJC*: 193.

29. See also *TJC*: 191, where Meshorer suggested that the countermarks were applied in the Roman camps so that the coins could function within their localized economy; the marking would date to 81–96.

30. See Levine 1972: 134–40 and *CNP*: 50–76 on the types.

31. Hamburger 1956: 118.

32. Hamburger 1956: 115.

33. This entry corrects the information presented in Evans 1995: 165.

34. Klimosky 1974; see also Buttrey *et al.* 1981: 7; *CNP*: 1957: 39, who divided the coinage into five denominations, based on flan sizes. Kadman suggested that the Tyche only appeared on the small denomination (p. 50).

35. Barag and Qedan 1980.

36. Levine 1972: 135, *idem* 1975b: 50; see also Harl 1996: 106, who noted that across the Empire, minting increased to a peak under the Flavians, with a subsequent drop until an increase in the reign of Hadrian, with a peak in the reign of Caracalla.

37. Gitler 1990/91: 42–45.

38. Levine (1972: 135; 1975b: 50) calculated a drop in the number of types per year and the specimens per year from the second century through the reign of Caracalla.

39. Buttrey 1993.

40. Levine's table matches the rise in specimens per year from the excavations (1972: 135; 1975b: 50). Kadman (*CNP*: 13) noted that the wreath SPQR type was not inspired by any Roman type, and he dated the issue to the beginning of the Parthian war in 231.

41. Levine 1972: 137 explained this increase in coin types by the Roman government's attempt to stem the popularity of Christianity; since Caesarea was one of the major intellectual centers for Christianity in the third century, the emperor concentrated his efforts at the Caesarean mint, striking pagan types for the city.

42. See Klimosky 1974.

43. Baramki 1974.

44. Alföldi 1938: pl. XXIV no. 14; my thanks to R. Bland for this reference.

45. Bull *et al.* 1994: 72.

46. See Humphrey 1986: 480 and fig. 238.

47. Burnett 1987a: 137. The *LRBC* lists a small and large module of the AE3 and the additional reverses of RESTITVTOR REIPVBLICAE and REPARATIO FEL TEMP.

48. *MIB*: 72 and chart, coin no. 134.

49. W. Metcalf 1982: 82 and n. 4.

50. Hohlfelder 1984: 275–76; Wiemken and Holum 1981: 49.

51. Asolati 1994/95: 190–91, though Caesarea can now be taken off the list of cities where no palm tree types occur.

52. Asolati 1994/95: 195–97.

53. Bull *et al.* 1994: 68–69.

54. D. Metcalf 1964: 34–35.

55. D. Metcalf 1969: 87–88, who recorded *folles* under 5.99 and over 12 grams; half-*folles* should weigh about 4.5 grams.

56. Bellenger 1966: 59; the first phase is 24–25 mm, 8.43–9.45 grams, and the second is 23–27 mm, 2.83–9.65 grams.

57. D. Metcalf 1969: 94–99; *idem* 1964: 35–36; see also Hohlfelder 1984: 272.

58. D. Metcalf 1969: 101.

59. D. Metcalf 1961: 137.

60. Grierson 1967b: 290, 296.

61. D. Metcalf 1960: 216; *idem* 1964: 32; see also Grierson 1967b: 291.

62. D. Metcalf 1964: 32 noted that coins of Anastasius were still circulating in 640 (*idem* 1960: 216). Grierson 1967b: 291, 296 suggested that the heavier coins were removed from circulation, though the removal was "perfunctory;" the continual removal of heavier coins occurred through the reign of Heraclius.

63. Phillips 1962: 235 assigns the copying to the reign of Phocas; Ariel (see Levine and Netzer 1986: 138) suggested some were local imitations; see also Hohlfelder 1984: 275.

64. Hahn 1980: 67 n. 78–80.

65. W. Metcalf 1975: 133–35.

66. Qedar 1988/89: 27, 36.

67. *MIB*: 3: 111.

68. Grierson 1967a: 56, *idem* 1982: 121–22; *MIB* 3: 111; Qedar 1988/89: 32; Evans 1993/94: 97–102; Lampinen 1999b concurred with this approximate chronology.

69. Evans 1993/94: 100.

70. Bendall 1976; Evans 1993/94: 100–2.

71. Goehring 1983; Hahn 1978: 181.

72. Bendall 1976.

73. Hahn 1978; see also Goehring 1983.

74. See D. Metcalf 1964: 37; for a discussion of Arabic *fals*, see Bates 1976.

CHAPTER 2

Pp. 25–52

1. Over fifty percent of the items identified as "potentially a coin" could not be read or even placed within a century of their manufacture, were not coins, or disintegrated upon cleaning. This proportion is normal to excavated coins: fifty percent of the coins from the River Liri excavations were illegible and undatable; ten percent of the coin-like objects found in the baths of Hammat Gader were identified (see W. Metcalf 1974: 42–3; Hirschfeld 1997: xi).

2. Reece 1996; Reece 1998; Casey 1986: 51–76.

3. This kind of tabulation is very commonly, though not always, applied to excavation coins: for excavation reports of sites in Israel, see Gitler 1996: 321; Syon 1992/93: 34; C. Meyers *et al.* 1990: 231; Raynor and Meshorer 1988: 83; E. Meyers *et al.* 1979: 50.

4. See Levine 1975b: 50; the ratio of surviving types as an indication of the number of projected coins per issue continues to be a major argument for Duncan-Jones (1994 and 1999); and *contra* Buttrey 1993.

5. For instance Burnett 1987a: 60–61 points out that sometimes coins were issued in advance of or in commemoration of a visit by an emperor; yet few cities actually did so. Most cities strike intermittently, and use only a few dies each time they do strike.

6. Casey 1974: 37–51; Casey 1986: 88–95; Reece 1998. The numismatist is not confined to working with emperor's reigns, but may pick any defined length of time that seems suitable for the evidence. These are called "issue periods."

7. For instance, see Bland and Abdy 2002; Cavada 1994: 263–65; Noeske 1998; Schubert 1986; Schulzki 1989.

8. As Greene 1986: 56 noted.

9. I am indebted to Roslyn Gorin, Manager of Statistical Applications, Academic Services, Temple University for guiding me through this discussion.

10. Duncan-Jones 1994: 169 suggested, based on the coin finds from Pompeii, that bronze coins made up only five to ten percent of the coins in circulation. He does not (nor can he) estimate what percentage of the number of circulating bronze coins were lost on site.

11. See Duncan-Jones 1994: Chap. 3, although he tends to discuss the west more than the east; he uses the same rough categories. For income, he notes civilian and military bonuses (the *congiarium* and *donativum* – both of which are rarely mentioned in the ancient sources), building projects, and imperial gifts and public spending (also unrecoverable). Most of his argument is based on coin hoards.

12. Safrai 1994: 340–41; see e.g., Birley 1981.

13. Millar 1993: 45.

14. Safrai 1994: 339–44; Hopkins 1980, especially 102 and Appendix; Cass. Dio 69.12.2 mentions that troops bought weapons, food and clothing locally in Judaea.

15. Hopkins 1980: 102.

16. Hohlfelder 1984: 266, n. c, suggested that "at least" ninety percent of illegibles are Late Roman/Early Byzantine *minimi*.

17. To find the excavation lists of coins from the sites mentioned in the regional cohort, see the Key to Comparison Sites on p. 79. For quick sketches of the excavations and history of each site in Palestine and the Decapolis, see Stern 1993 and E. Meyers 1997.

18. See Safrai 1994: 23.

19. See Foerster 1975: 9; on the physical site of Strato's Tower, see: Stieglitz 1999; *idem* 1996; *idem* 1993; Raban 1992; Roller 1992; and Arav 1989.

20. Mørkholm 1991: 70.

21. Safrai 1994: 21.

22. Mørkholm 1991: 101.

23. Most of the coins come from the mint at Tyre; see Fitzgerald 1931: 52–56. Because the city was located on an important highway and was surrounded by good arable land, Safrai 1994: 20 considered it to have all the advantages of trade that a coastal city had, hence coins from far-flung mints appear in the finds.

24. Mørkholm 1991: 21.

25. Tzaferis 1989: 139; C. Meyers *et al.* 1990: 232; Aharoni 1973: 1:6; Hirschfeld 1997: 11–12.

26. Barag 1982/83 has commented on this phenomenon, confining his argument to Galilee. He believed the relative lack of Sidonian coins shows that the latter mint struck in small quantities, as compared to the relative abundance of Tyrian silver pieces. Safrai 1994: 302 stressed the limited data available, and (p. 402) that site reports from the Golan show a dependence on Syrian, not Tyrian, silver. The coins should show the trading spheres of each city. Yet see now the evidence from Tel Anafa, which still depended heavily on coins of Tyre. For the data from the sites mentioned in the text as comparative material, see the sources listed in the Key. No mints or rulers are given for the coins from Bethsaida; only five of the sixteen Ptolemaic bronzes from Jerusalem excavations could be identified: three come from Tyre, one from Gaza, and one from Cyprus.

27. Herbert 1994: 242 and Hengel 1974: 43 both pointed to the relative abundance of coins of Ptolemy II, compared to the earlier and later Hellenistic rulers. Coins from Meiron come from Alexandria (3), Tyre (1) and Sidon (1).

28. Hengel 1974: 37.

29. Gamala in Galilee reports two, minted under Antiochus, from the mint at Carrhae; Aharoni 1973 reports two (one a tetradrachm) from Beer Sheba; the same number (but both bronze) come from Jerusalem. Thirteen identifiable coins from the reigns of Ptolemy III and IV were excavated in Samaria; the mints were reported as Tyre and Berytus. Pastor 1996: 39 and Hengel 1974: 44 also noted the decreasing number of coins, from the high point of Ptolemy II, and attributed it to inflation and overtaxation (see also Hengel p. 159).

30. As noted previously by Arav 1989: 136 and Hengel 1974: 44. The Seleucids imposed a poll tax to supplement the previously existing taxes on land, cattle, produce, and the "crown tax," which was used to present gold offerings to the kings; see Avi-Yonah 1975: 203.

31. No mints are recorded specifically for Antiochus' reign.

32. See also Dora, where at least two come from Antioch and one from Apamea.

33. Tel Anafa; Meiron; Gush Halav; Iotapata; Bethsaida (no mints listed); Beer Sheba (mint listed as probably Antioch); Sepphoris (no mints listed); the site may not have been settled this early; Capernaum (mint listed as probably Tripolis); Gamala might not have been settled at this phase, as the first large group of coins found were minted under the authority of Antiochus IV.

34. No coins from the period 187–175 B.C.E. were excavated in Tel Anafa, Gush Halav, Bethsaida, Beer Sheba, Capernaum, Iotapata, Caesarea, Samaria, nor Dora. One was found at Samaria (mint of Ake-Ptolemais) and another from Sepphoris (mint of Antioch). Four were found in Gamala (mints of Tyre and Antioch); Ariel 1982 is not clear if one or thirteen coins were found in Jerusalem from Seleucus' reign. Transport amphora in Caesarea's harbor show close connections to Aegean wine producers, as well as pots from Levantine suppliers (Oleson 1996: 369). This situation changed dramatically in Herod's time.

35. Both II Maccabees 3 and IV Maccabees 4 insist that Seleucus' emptying of the Temple treasury was frustrated by divine intervention. See the political explanation for the story in Maccabees in Schalit 1972: 118–22.

36. In Galilee: Tel Anafa (with coins equally from Tyre and Sidon), Meiron (from Tyre?), Iotapata (almost all from Tyre), and Gamala, where the vast majority of Seleucid coins date to the reign of Antiochus IV and are from the mint of Tyre.

37. See Hengel 1974: 44; Mørkholm 1991: 78 saw the Maccabean Revolt as necessitating a large silver coinage in Tyre, but says the increasing bronze coinage was so that the cities might "take part in the regeneration of his kingdom by giving them greater responsibility" (p. 84).

38. Except Nabratein, which has few coins for this period; see E. Meyers *et al.* 1981: 16. The coins imply that the Hasmonaeans colonized Galilee; see Barag 1992/93.

39. Safrai 1994: 21 noted that "it was as if urban development came to a standstill in spite of the economic growth of that period." Pastor 1996: 76 suggested that Tel Anafa was destroyed by the Hasmonaeans; the excavators prefer to see an abandonment (see Herbert 1993: 122). For Gamala: Syon 1992/93; for the theory of Khirbet Shema, see Stern 1993 (4): 1359–61. The finds at Beer Sheba are too few to argue for or against Hasmonaean influence.

40. Samaritan farms were abandoned in the mid-second century, possibly as a result of increasing tensions between Hasmonaean and Greek cities or because of overtaxation; see Arav 1989: 132–33. In the city of Samaria, the towers were rebuilt in time to briefly withstand the assault of Hyrcanus. However, Josephus (*JW* 1.64–65, 166) tells us the city was razed and then deserted for fifty years.

41. No Hasmonaean coins are reported in other excavations of Caesarea (see Table 5); for the problem of the Hasmonaean relationship with the city, see E. Meyers *et al.* 1973: 10.

42. Ariel 1982: 285–86 argued that so many coins of Yannai were found in Jerusalem because of upheavals, the small denomination, the great number produced for military purposes, and small deposits made in walls and floors, exaggerating the number of Hasmonaean coins in the finds.

43. Also reported at Gamala (Syon 1992/93), Meiron (Raynor and Meshorer 1988), Beth Shean (Janai 1989/90), and Jerusalem (Ariel 1982); for Beer Sheba, see Aharoni 1973.

44. Herbert 1993: 122.

45. See especially Pastor 1996: 107, 112–15, and the symposium papers in Levine 1981. Safrai 1994: 177–78, on the other hand, believed that the Seleucid period was more prosperous than the Herodian. For the argument that Herod overtaxed the people of Palestine, see the sources in Pastor pp. 98–99 and Applebaum 1976: 662–90. Pastor argued that Herod's rate of taxation was equalled by the Roman rate, and was therefore not inordinately heavy. Broshi 1985 argued that agricultural wealth, trade routes, and

contributions to the temple and taxes paid by non-Jews were the bases of the wealth of the provinces in Herod's time.

46. Blakely 1988: 40–41; *idem* 1987: 58–59. The deposits from the harbor agree with the essentials: see Oleson 1996: 369.

47. E.g., Duncan-Jones 1994: 176; trade does not homogenize coinage across the Roman Empire.

48. As Safrai 1994: 256 postulated.

49. Meiron is the exception, as slightly more Herodian than city coins were found. Iotapata has few Herodian coins, but city coins from the Herodian period are even rarer.

50. See Millar 1993: 41–42.

51. Millar 1993: 45.

52. Levine 1975a: 20; from Josephus' numbers (*Ant* 20.8.7).

53. Josephus *JW* 2.287, cf. *Ant* 20.175, 177; see Pastor 1996: 112.

54. Millar 1993: 47-51; Josephus *Ant* 17.2.2.

55. Pastor 1996: 137, 142, 150; even Pilate's project of building the aqueduct in Jerusalem was marred by accusations of extortion and kickbacks.

56. It should be noted that the Annual Average Coin Loss, as seen in Table 3 and Fig. 11, shows a peak for all three sites in the reign of Archelaus.

57. Syon 1992/93: 45, reporting two worn coins from Commagene in Gamala.

58. Carradice 1982/83: 17.

59. Mambre has a few procuratorial coins and one minted under Herod Archelaus.

60. Syon 1992/93: 39. All of the other sites have no coins from this era or so few as to be negligible.

61. Millar 1993: 71–73.

62. See Foerster 1975: 17.

63. Raban *et al.* 1993: 62–63.

64. Although the situation may not be as stark as Hayes proposed, certainly the amount of imported pottery dropped dramatically from the previous period (Hayes 1972: 420). Hayes noted that the picture in Palestine resembles that of Antioch; thus, perhaps the drop in imports is not so much due to the economic condition of Palestine, but a disruption of some kind in the supply.

65. Safrai 1994: 22–23.

66. As already noticed by Crowfoot *et al.* 1957: 43: the reduced number of coins in the late first and second centuries shows the "exhaustion of Palestine as a consequence of the Revolts."

67. Raban 1999: 179–88: a shipwreck of the late 80s / early 90s C.E. shows disrepair, with the primary decay of the harbor possibly due to earthquakes or subsidence of the sea floor.

68. Because Herodium was an outpost of the rebels, there are a number of coins from the First Revolt found in the excavations (forty-four of one hundred and three coins found); the same is true, to a lesser extent, for the coins of the Bar Kochba Revolt (there were eleven). It should be noted that several sites in our cohort were deserted or destroyed by the First Revolt. Samaria was destroyed; Gamala was no longer inhabited, nor Tel Anafa; Bethsaida may have been abandoned around 85 C.E. (Arav and Freund 1995: 61).

69. Smallwood 1976: 476; though she qualified her statement and saw a recovery in the later second century (477, 479). See also Alon 1989.

70. E.g., Avi-Yonah 1984: 28: "The basic economic structure of the nation was sound…"

71. Millar 1993: 107.

72. Smallwood 1976: 477; Avi-Yonah 1984: 21.

73. E.g., Smallwood 1976: 479.

74. Avi-Yonah 1984: 22.

75. Foerster 1975: 18, quoting the Palestinian Talmud, Kila'im IX 32c and Sifre. Deut. Sect. 306: "The parable is told of a man who went to Caesarea and spent 200 *zuz*..."

76. From ca. 120 to the beginning of the fourth century, two legions and auxiliaries (some 25,000 men?) were kept in Palestine; some of Legio X was housed permanently in Caesarea. See Safrai 1994: 339 and Avi-Yonah 1976: 36.

77. Foerster 1975: 18.

78. Patrich 1999: 99–103.

79. For earlier work, see Oleson 1996; Raban 1996 (suggesting the harbor had closed earlier); *idem* 1992; Hohlfelder 1993: 691; and *idem* 1992: 75–78. More recent work on sediments and foraminifera are found in Reinhardt and Patterson 1999, Yule and Barham 1999.

80. Blakely 1988: 39–43, where he noted the decrease in imported amphorae; Oleson 1994: 3–64. Safrai 1994: 208 cited a corresponding increase in the use of imported ceramics in all sites in Palestine beginning only in the mid-third century, as had been noted by Hayes 1972: 420. Oleson 1996: 375–76 suggested that real prosperity never really reached Palestine, as seen in the relative lack of imported pottery. Safrai 1994: 23 saw a decline in the smaller cities, especially after 135.

81. Ariel 1982: 295.

82. See Duncan-Jones 1994: 133, who found the same phenomenon (an increase in the Annual Average Coin Loss and an increase in the number of types used) in the Severan period for the large silver hoard from Reka Devnia.

83. See above, Chapter 1, "Second Century C.E."

84. Bar 2002: 46–51; Safrai 1994: 23.

85. See Humphrey 1995: 235–40.

86. See E. Meyers *et al.* 1981: 6.

87. Smallwood 1976: 494.

88. Quoted by Foerster 1975: 18; since we have seen that the economy was suffering in the second half of the second century, I am more inclined to view this as a statement of third-century Palestine. Bar 2002: 44–46 discusses the sources for the period, and reminds readers that negative comments arise from the sages "living in a land that had undergone a deep crisis in the wake of the destruction of the Temple," and often reflecting the desire to see "signs of distress as a harbinger of [Rome's] fall" (pp. 45–46). Sperber 1998: 117–18 sees the third century as a period of increasing lawlessness, which was exacerbated in the fourth century by armed insurrections.

89. See Carson 1967 and Sperber 1974 for the situation in Palestine.

90. This finding would not surprise Duncan-Jones (1994, Chapter 12), who argued that coins tended to remain in the region where they were minted in the period before the Late Empire; excavation might modify his conclusion. He later suggested (p. 176) that new coins were added into the local mix to replace lost, worn, or hoarded coins.

91. See Harl 1996: 216; Duncan-Jones 1994: 15, 25–28; Sperber 1974: 101–31; Safrai 1994: 26; *contra* Rathbone 1996, who suggested that in Egypt inflation only became a major factor ca. 275 C.E., not earlier.

92. In contrast to the situation in the west, where the economy worsens dramatically in the third century; see Hopkins 1980: 105.

93. King 1980: 147–48; Avi-Yonah 1976: 94–106; Sperber 1974: 141; yet see Bar 2002: 44–46 on the political or religious motivations of these remarks.

94. Duncan-Jones 1994: 106 noted that circulation from each mint is slow, but it occurs only when the army was paid or the emperor traveled.

95. See Yule and Barham 1999; Reinhardt and Patterson 1999; Raban 1996. The last believes the harbor was closed by sandbars in the second or third century. The first four think the harbor was gradually filling in, beginning in the first century C.E., but it was completely closed by ca. 400.

96. *HE* VIII.14.8–9, *Mart. Pal.* 6, 1–2.

97. Blakely 1987: 87–88; also see Magness 1992: 129. Safrai 1994: 24 saw the Diocletianic period as one of hyper-urbanization, as new cities were founded (as noted in surveys) and old cities rebuilt. As discussed below, there is little evidence to support building projects in the regional comparative cohort or Caesarea.

98. Safrai 1994: 24–25, 414; see also Broshi 1985: 421.

99. Levine 1975a: 135–36; *idem* 1975b: 48–50; Safrai 1994: 339.

100. See Holum 1989: 88; Avi-Yonah 1976: 160.

101. I omit reference to the synagogue at Capernaum, which has been variously dated to the late third or late fourth century; see Tsafrir 1995: 150–61.

102. E. Meyers *et al.* 1981: 6; Safrai 1994: 256; Hohlfelder 1981: 47 suggested that the rise in early fourth-century coins was due to the interest of Constantine and his family in the Holy Land, as well as increasing inflation. He traced the decline of prosperity to the second half of the fifth century. Gitler 1996: 320 also notes that Jerusalem has a "significantly lower average compared to other finds from sites in Israel and Transjordan."

103. Avi-Yonah 1976: 168.

104. The wall may date to the fourth or early fifth century century; see Holum 1989: 89. The Archive Building dates to the early fourth century: see Holum 1995: 337. For the aqueducts, see Holum 1989: 90; Olami and Peleg 1977; Humphrey 1975: 9, 14; Negev 1964. For pottery and amphorae, see Oleson 1996: 371; for lamps, see Sussman 1996: 353.

105. On the graph, other Eastern Mints are: Nicomedia, Thessalonica, Heracleia, Cyzicus; Western mints are: Lyon, Rome, Aquileia, and Sirmium.

106. Safrai 1994: 256 suggested that the town was in irretrievable decline by 400 C.E., as part of the general decline of the region.

107. Safrai 1994: 403 noted this phenomenon earlier; yet, he also noted that sites in the Golan have increased numbers of coins after 350.

108. Other Eastern mints are: Thessalonica, Heracleia, Nicomedia, Cyzicus, Siscia, Alexandria; Western mints represented are: Arles, Rome, Aquileia, Sirmium.

109. Except for the synagogue in Caesarea, probably built in the middle of the century; see Bull 1982: 32–33. Carthage finds are also heavily weighted towards the FEL TEMP coins, as well as the small SPES REIPVBLICE; see W. Metcalf 1987: 75.

110. Weinberg 1988: 105–6.

111. Note that Pergamon and Jerusalem are again the exceptions to the norm. Safrai (1994: 405, 414) has argued that the lack of fifth-century coins has been noted in Egypt, the cities of the Transjordan, Syria and Asia Minor, and is, he continues, a mark of a weaker economy and loss of trade volume. See also D.

Metcalf 1969: 11, where a "collapse of confidence" and rapid depreciation of the coins led to the "ruin of petty currency" by the end of the fifth century.

112. For Sepphoris, see Weiss and Netzer 1995 162–76. Khirbet Shema seems to have been abandoned between ca. 425 and 500 (E. Meyers 1983: 61–69).

113. For the synagogue see Bull 1982: 33; for the "Byzantine wall" see Magness 1995: 136–37; for the phases of the temple and church see Holum *et al.* 1999: 12–40; for pottery, see Hayes 1972: 420; Magness 1995. Hohlfelder 1993: 691 found no evidence of building from the period between the mid-fifth century and the reign of Anastasius.

114. Other Eastern mints which were identified include Cyzicus, Nicomedia, Thessalonica, Heracleia and Alexandria. Western mints are confined to Rome and a few from uncertain western mints.

115. Hahn 1980: 65. As a warning, Hahn noted that he could only identify one third of the coins in a hoard he was studying, "though I can claim to have some experience in handling them." I would suggest that many of the unidentified "Late Roman" bronzes could date as late as the seventh century.

116. Magness 1995: 134.

117. Fulford 1984: 258; the pottery levels decline after ca. 575 (pp. 258–61).

118. Reinhardt and Patterson 1999: 259; Yule and Barham 1999: 278.

119. Walmsley 1996; Holum 1989; Avi-Yonah 1958: 40–41.

120. Lehman and Holum 2000: 14.

121. Magness 1995: 136–37; *idem* 1992: 132; Holum *et al.* 1988: 165–99; Bull *et al.* 1986: 38; Hohlfelder 1993: 687 and *idem* 1985: 181. Note that Raban does not think the harbor was dredged by Anastasius (especially Raban 1996). Our evidence for the dredging is literary; Reinhardt and Patterson 1999 and Yule and Barham 1999 see no distinct shift in the sediments nor microfauna to suggest an abrupt change in the late fifth–early sixth century.

122. Magness 1992: 133; Levine and Netzer 1986: 90–121.

123. Weiss and Netzer 1995: 162–76.

124. Di Segni 1995: 312–22. The city was taken by the Muslims in 636 C.E.

125. Reisner 1924: 272.

126. Crowfoot *et al.* 1957: 48.

127. E. Meyers *et al.* 1981: 6.

128. As already noted by D. Metcalf 1969: 132 and Grierson 1967b: 297; he also noted the number of coins from the mint at Nicomedia, and the very few from Cyzicus. Cyzicus plays an even smaller role as supplier in Caesarea than in Jerusalem.

129. Ariel 1986: 142 no.54 records one a *follis* used as jewelry!

130. Hendy 1985: 226, 233 (where the surplus left by Anastasius was "squandered" by Justinian on building projects and military expenses, and one result was the issuing of light-weight *solidi*) and Avi-Yonah 1958: 51. Jones 1964: 301 points out that though Justin complains bitterly about the expenditure of money during Justinian's reign, he appears to have had some money left to pursue his own projects.

131. The idea that the city was destroyed by the Muslims has been challenged by Hohlfelder 1993; Holum 1989: 94 and *idem* 1993: 702; and Levine and Netzer 1986: 179, 184. These scholars prefer to see a long slow decline of the city.

132. Hohlfelder 1984: 275 thought that the number of Maurician coins from Antioch was unique in Caesarea, and attributed them to unrecorded disaster relief or troop movements.

133. The number of *dodecanummia* of Phocas has already been noted in Wiemken and Holum 1981: 47 and n. 48 as the common state of affairs in all of Palestine. It is suggested there that with the closing of the Antioch mint, the coins of Alexandria filled the void, but also point to the opening of trade contacts to the south, as seen in the pottery from Gaza on the site. Hendy 1985: 415–16 and n. 190 noted that current thinking has an operating mint in Jerusalem between 608 and 615, "certainly" minting bronze coins and "probably" gold, using staff from the Antioch mint. He only cites a forthcoming article on the problem.

134. Evans 1993/94. None of the other excavations report their finds in enough detail or have enough Heraclian coins to make a comparison.

135. See D. Metcalf 1964, Awad 1972, and Bates 1976.

Appendix 1

Pp. 53–62

1. Lampinen 1999a: 369–87.
2. Jones 1964 (1): 148, 436, and King 1980: 157.
3. An exception to this rule is the gold hoard from Karanis; see Arce 1987: 181–87. Arce suggests that people were turning their private stores of bullion into coin (hence the increase in *solidi* in the fourth century; in this he follows Kent 1956: 190–93, 203–4), but Valens specifically ordered such bullion confiscated, demanding that the mints work only for the needs of the government, not the private individual. See Jones 1964 (1): 441. For a recent overview of the reforms and policies of the fourth-century emperors, see Harl 1996: 159–75; it should be noted that Harl argues that the reforms of Valentinian I and Valens did not include making all taxes payable only in bullion, nor did they require the re-striking of full-weight *solidi*. For a statement of the policies of the emperors, see Kent 1956: 197–98 and Jones 1964 (1): 439–41, 444–45.
4. Harl 1996: 175 says that the peak of production of gold coins in the Roman world was in the half century between 400 and 450, when tens of millions of *solidi* may have been minted. For a discussion of the OB mark, see Delmaire 1989: 509–17.
5. See especially King 1980: 146–47.
6. Jones 1964 (1): 431; Delmaire 1989: 374–86; King 1980: 146–47.
7. Jones 1964 (1): 430–32; the only amount we know about is the 140 pounds (10,080 *solidi*) collected from Edessa at the opening of the reign of Anastasius; see also Delmaire 1989: 360–67, 387–400; King 1980: 147–48.
8. Jones 1964 (1): 432; see also King 1980: 148; Delmaire 1989: 351–54; see also Delmaire 1989: 409–15 and King 1980: 148–50 for other taxes, such as state land revenues, fines, customs dues, and a tax on recovered hoards!
9. Jones 1964 (1): 435; Delmaire 1989: 547–48 suggests other occasions for the distribution of a donative would be the beginning of the new year, the accession of new consuls, royal marriages and births, before or after a battle – but not necessarily in coin. Other goods distributed would be textiles, gold jewelry, or armor. See also Whittaker 1980: 8 and note 47: "*donatives* were often paid in gold or silver," but "there is no evidence that the accession and quinqennial donations of all Augusti and Caesares were paid in all parts of the empire."
10. Delmaire 1989: 563–84; possibly some coins were distributed in an *adventus* (or entrance to the city) of an emperor, or at the games put on by the new consuls; these might primarily profit inhabitants of Rome

and Constantinople. More widespread might be the custom of distributing coins on accessions and the anniversaries of the emperor's reign; bronze coins marked VOT MVLT seem to testify to this practice.

11. Harl 1996: 217; see also Jones 1964 (1): 462. Harl argues that most salaries were not paid in gold coin, but in *billon* or bronze fractions, since gold was used by the government to pay off the barbarian federates. Harl also points out that we do not know the retirement pay of a legionary; nor do we know the pay of a civil servant in the fourth century.

12. *POxy* 3307, cited by Bowman 1980: 33. He left eight gold coins and one hundred ninety-nine half-talents of bronze; the will was made in the 320s.

13. Burnett 1987a: 120.

14. Yerushalmi Bava Mezia AK 5.6 and Yerushalmi Bava Mezia AL 4.1; see Sperber 1974: 149–51.

15. See Bagnall 1985: 49 ("there was not much gold or silver in the hands of most individuals at any one time") and 51 ("...Egypt's people had little gold or silver. The relatively few references to *solidi* before mid-century confirm this impression").

16. Arce 1987; see also the Chatby Hoard from Alexandria, which only has a few coins dating prior to 375. The bulk of the coins date from the reign of Justin I to Phocas; see Kent 1994 (*RIC* 10): lxxxix for a list. See also the small hoard from Tod (Egypt), published in Schwartz 1952: 96–98 and listed in *RIC* 10: cxiii: four coins of Valentinian I and nine of Valens, with one of Justinian. No mints were recorded.

17. *CH* VII no.330.

18. *CH* VII no.337; details are said to be on file at the British Museum; note that Kent, in *RIC* 10: c, calls this "a very unsatisfactory group." See also the "very unsatisfactory" group from Khirbet Deir Dassawi (Gaza Strip), consisting of three coins of Constans or Constantius II (my sources differ), one of Jovian, and one of Justinian (*RIC* 10: ci), originally published by Rahmani 1964: 19–23.

19. Munro-Hay 1989: 83–100; see also the listing in *RIC* 10: lxxxix.

20. *CH* II no.308.

21. *CH* III no. 224; *RIC* 10: lxxxviii; see also the hoard from Tell Nimrin, Jordan, published by Metcalf and Fulco 1995/96: 145–54. The hoard consists of thirty-four *solidi*, but is divided into two groups: Valens–Valentinian I, all from Antioch, and Leo I–Anastasius. Metcalf considers, but rejects, the proposition that these are two hoards. The Valens–Valentinian reverses are all RESTITVTOR REIPVBLICAE, and the coins come from six different *officinae*.

22. Casey 1974: 80–81, now superseded by Dürr and Bastien, 1984: 205–40; see also the note on a *solidi* hoard from Chemtou, Tunisia, consisting of 1646 *solidi* dating from the reigns of Valentinian I to Honorius. No other information is available; see *RIC* 10: xciv.

23. Personal communication, O. Storvick, draft of the JECM Preliminary Report of the Thirteenth and Fourteenth Seasons (1992, 1993).

24. Robertson 1986: 249.

Key to Comparison Sites

Totals do not include synagogue deposits or hoards, as these tend to be skewed to the higher denominations.

Samaria

Beth Shean: a "large number" of coins were found in the early twentieth-century excavations, most of bronze and badly corroded, most non-recognizable and not listed. Berman 1995; Peleg 1994; Berman 1992; Janai 1989/90; Fitzgerald 1958.

Caesarea: see additional reports Hohlfelder 1994; Hohlfelder 1992; Lampinen 1992; Levine and Netzer 1986; Hohlfelder 1985; Hohlfelder 1984; Hohlfelder 1981, Hohlfelder 1980; Frova 1966. Note the re-publication of statistics in Hohlfelder 1984 and Lampinen 1992.

Samaria (Neapolis): the earliest excavations report "large numbers" of third- and fourth-century C.E. bronzes, which were not published; Fulco and Zayadine 1981; Crowfoot *et al.* 1957; Reisner *et al.* 1924.

Coastal Sites

Dora: Stern 1930.

Jalame: Weinberg 1988.

Galilee/Decapolis

Capernaum: Tzaferis 1989; Spijkerman 1975; see Raynor and Meshorer 1988; Barag 1982/83.

Gamala: Syon 1992/93.

Gush Halav: Meyers, Meyers and Strange 1990; Meyers, Strange, Meyers and Hanson 1979.

Iotapata (Yodefat): Adan-Bayewitz and Aviam 1997.

Khirbet Shema: Meyers, Meyers and Strange 1990; Raynor and Meshorer 1988; E. Meyers *et al.* 1979. Totals are only of the coins found in the excavations outside of the synagogue.

Meiron: Raynor and Meshorer 1988. The coins were found in the area around, but not in, the synagogue.

Nabratein: C. Meyers *et al.* 1990; Meyers, Strange and Meyers 1981.

Sepphoris: Hendin 1986; Waterman 1960; see Raynor and Meshorer 1988 and Barag 1982/83.

Tel Anafa: Herbert 1994.

Judaea

Beer Sheba: Aharoni 1973.

Bethsaida: Arav and Freund 1995.

Herodium: Netzer 1981; Spijkerman 1972.

Jerusalem: Ariel 1982; Tushingham 1985; Wightman 1989; Ariel 1990; summarized, with new results added, in Gitler 1996.

Mambre: Mader 1957/58.

Eastern Cities

Antioch: Waage 1952.

Hama: Papanicolaou Christensen 1995

Gerasa: Bellinger 1938.

Pella: Sheedy, Carson and Walmsley 2001.

Pergamon: Voegtle 1993.

Sardis: Buttrey, Johnson, MacKenzie and Bates 1981.

Bibliography

Adan-Bayewitz, D., and Aviam, M.

1997 Iotapata, Josephus, and the Siege of 67: Preliminary Report on the 1992–94 seasons. *JRA* 10: 130–65.

Adelson, H., and Kustas, G.

1962 *A Bronze Hoard of the Period of Zeno I.* ANS Numismatic Notes and Monographs 148. New York: American Numismatic Society.

Aharoni, Y., ed.

1973 *Beer-Sheba I: Excavations at Tel Beer-Sheba 1969–1971 Seasons.* Tel Aviv: Institute of Archaeology.

Alföldi, A.

1938 Die römische Münzprägung und die historischen Ereignisse im Osten zwischen 260 und 270 n. Chr. *Berytus* 5: 47–92.

Alon, G.

1989 *The Jews and their Land in the Talmudic Age (70–640 C.E.).* Ed. and trans. G. Levi, from Hebrew. Cambridge, MA: Harvard University.

Appelbaum, S.

1976 The Organization of the Jewish Communities in the Diaspora. Pp.464–503 in *The Jewish People in the First Century,* 2 vols, eds. S. Safrai and M. Stern. Philadelphia, PA: Fortress.

Arav, R.

1989 *Hellenistic Palestine: Settlement Patterns and City Planning 337–31 B.C.E.* British Archaeological Reports International Series 485. Oxford: British Archaeological Reports.

Arav, R., and Freund, R., eds.

1995 *Bethsaida I.* Kirksville, MO: Thomas Jefferson University.

Arce, J.

1987 A Solidus Hoard from the Vicinity of Karanis. *SNR* 66: 181–87.

Ariel, D.

1982 A Survey of Coin Finds in Jerusalem [until the end of the Byzantine Period]. *LA* 32: 10–326.

1986 The Coins. Pp. 137–48 in *Excavations at Caesarea Maritima 1975, 1976, 1979: Final Report,* eds. L. Levine and E. Netzer, *Qedem* 21. Jerusalem: Institute of Archaeology, Hebrew University.

1990 *Excavations at the City of David 1978–1985 Directed by Yigal Shiloh, Vol. II: Imported Stamped Amphora Handles, Coins, Worked Bone and Ivory, and Glass*. Qedem 30. Jerusalem: Institute of Archaeology, Hebrew University.

Asolati, M.

1994/5 L'emissione Vandala con il palmizio: prototipi punici e l'evidenza dei ripostigli. *RIN* 96: 187–202.

Avi-Yonah, M.

1958 The Economics of Byzantine Palestine. *IEJ* 8: 39–51.

1975 *The World History of the Jewish People: the Herodian Period*. Series 1, v. 7. New Brunswick, NJ: Rutgers University.

1976 *The Jews of Palestine: A Political History from the Bar Kokhba War to the Arab Conquest*. Oxford: Blackwell.

1984 *The Jews under Roman and Byzantine Rule*. Jerusalem: Magnes.

Awad, H.

1972 Seventh Century Arab Imitations of Alexandrian Dodecanummia. *ANSMN* 18: 113–17.

Bagnall, R.

1985 *Currency and Inflation in Fourth Century Egypt*. Bulletin of the American Society of Papyrologists Supplement 5. Atlanta, GA: Scholars.

Bar, D.

2002 Was There a 3rd-c. Economic Crisis in Palestine? Pp. 43–54 in *The Roman and Byzantine Near East, vol.3*, ed. J. Humphrey. Journal of Roman Archaeology Supplement 49. Ann Arbor, MI: Journal of Roman Archaeology.

Barag, D.

1967 The Countermarks of the Legio Decima Fretensis. Pp. 117–35 in *International Numismatic Convention, Jerusalem 1963*, ed. A. Kindler. Tel Aviv: Schocken.

1969 A Note on the Geographical Distribution of Bar Kokhba Coins. *INJ* 4: 30–33.

1978 The Palestinian 'Judaea Capta' Coins of Vespasian and Titus and the Era on the Coins of Agrippa II minted under the Flavians. *NC* 128: 14–23.

1982/3 Tyrian Currency in Galilee. *INJ* 6/7: 7–13.

1992/3 New Evidence on the Foreign Policy of John Hyrcanus I. *INJ* 12: 1–12.

Barag, D., and Qedan, S.

1980 The Beginning of Hasmonean Coinage. *INJ* 4: 8–21.

Baramki, D.

1974 *The Coin Collection of the American University of Beirut Museum: Palestine and Phoenicia*. Beirut: American University of Beirut.

Bastien, P.

1985 *Le monnayage de l'atelier de Lyon: De la mort de Constantin à la mort de Julien (337–363)*. Numismatique Romaine 15. Wetteren: Edition Numismatique Romaine.

Bates, M.

1976 The "Arab-Byzantine" Bronze Coinage of Syria: An Innovation by 'Abd al-Malik. Pp. 16–27 in *A Colloquium in Memory of George Carpenter Miles*. New York: American Numismatic Society.

Bellinger, A. R.

1938 *Coins from Jerash, 1928–1934*. ANS Numismatic Notes and Monographs 81. New York: American Numismatic Society.

1966 *Catalogue of the Byzantine Coins in the Dumbarton Oaks Collection and the Whittemore Collection, Vol. 1: Anastasius I to Maurice, 491–602 A.D.* Washington, DC: Dumbarton Oaks Center for Byzantine Studies.

Bendall, S.

1976 An 'Eagle' Countermark on Sixth-Century Byzantine Coins. *NC* 136: 230.

Berman, A.

1992 The Numismatic Material from the 1991 Season [at Beth Shean]. *ESI* 11: 52.

1995 Beth Shean, the Citadel. *Hadashot Archaeologioth* 103: 31–36 (in Hebrew).

Biran, A., and Aviram, J., eds.

1993 *Biblical Archaeology Today, 1990. Proceedings of the 2nd International Congress of Biblical Archaeology.* Jerusalem: Israel Exploration Society.

Birley, A.

1981 The Economic Effects of Roman Frontier Policy. Pp. 39–53 in *The Roman West in the Third Century,* eds. A. King and M. Henig. British Archaeological Reports 109. Oxford: British Archaeological Reports.

Blakely, J.

1987 *Caesarea Maritima: the Pottery and Dating of Vault 1.* Lewistown, NY: Joint Expedition to Caesarea Maritima.

1988 Ceramics and Commerce: Amphorae from Caesarea Maritima. *BASOR* 271: 31–50.

Bland, R., and Abdy, R.

2002 Hoards of the Severan Period from Britain. Pp. 19–30 in *Coin Hoards of Roman Britain XI,* eds. R. Abdy, I. Leins, and J. Williams. Special Publication 36. London: Royal Numismatic Society.

Bowman, A.

1980 The Economy of Egypt in the Earlier Fourth Century. Pp. 23–40 in *Imperial Revenue, Expenditure, and Monetary Policy in the Fourth Century A.D.* Fifth Oxford Symposium on Coinage and Monetary History, ed. C. King. British Archaeological Reports International Series 76. Oxford: British Archaeological Reports.

Broshi, M.

1985 Fundamentals of the Economy of Israel during the Reign of Herod. Pp. 27–33 in *Jews in Economic Life: Collected Essays in Memory of A. Kahan,* ed. N. Gross. Jerusalem: Zalman Shazar Center for the Furtherance of the Study of Jewish History (in Hebrew).

Bruun, P.

1966 *The Roman Imperial Coinage. Vol. 7: Constantine and Licinius.* London: Spink.

Bull, R.

1973 Caesarea. *IEJ* 23: 260–62.
1974 Caesarea. *IEJ* 24: 280–82.
1975 Césarée Maritime. *Revue Biblique* 82: 278–80.
1982 Caesarea Maritima: The Search for Herod's City. *BA* 8: 24–40.

Bull, R.; Krentz, E.; and Storvick, O.

1986 The Joint Expedition to Caesarea Maritima: Ninth Season, 1980. Pp. 31–55 in *Preliminary Reports of ASOR-Sponsored Excavations,* ed. W. Rast. BASOR Supplement 24. Baltimore, MD: Johns Hopkins University/American Schools of Oriental Research.

Bull, R.; Krentz, E.; Storvick, O.; and Spiro, M.

1990 The Joint Expedition to Caesarea Maritima: Tenth Season, 1982. Pp. 69–94 in *Preliminary Reports of ASOR-Sponsored Excavations.,* ed. W. Rast. BASOR Supplement 27. Baltimore, MD: Johns Hopkins University/American Schools of Oriental Research.
1994 The Joint Expedition to Caesarea Maritima, Eleventh Season, 1984. Pp. 63–86 in *Preliminary Excavation Reports,* ed. W. Dever. AASOR 51. Boston, MA: American Schools of Oriental Research.

Bull, R.; and Toombs, L.

1972 Caesarea. *IEJ* 22: 178–80.
1973 Césarée Maritime. *Revue Biblique* 80: 582–85.

Burnett, A.

1987a *Coinage in the Roman World.* London: Seaby.
1987b Coinage of King Agrippa I of Judaea. Pp. 25–38 in *Mélanges de numismatique offerts à Pierre Bastien,* eds. H. Huvelin, M. Christol, and G. Gautier. Wetteren: Editions NR.

Burnett, A.; Amandry, M.; and Carradice, I.

1999 *Roman Provincial Coinage, Vol. 2: From Vespasian to Domitian (A.D. 69–96).* London: British Museum/ Paris: Bibliothèque Nationale.

Burnett, A.; Amandry M.; and Ripollès, P.

1992 *Roman Provincial Coinage, Vol. 1: From the Death of Caesar to the Death of Vitellius (44 B.C.–A.D. 69).* London: British Museum/Paris: Bibliothèque Nationale.

Bury, J.

1958 *History of the Late Roman Empire,* 2 vols. London: St. Martin's.

Butcher, K.

2000 Review of *Roman Provincial Coinage. Supplement I* and *Volume II* by A. Burnett, M. Amandry, and P. Ripollès and A. Burnett, M. Amandry, and I. Carradice. *SNR* 70: 199–204.

Buttrey, T.

1976 The Coins. Pp. 157–97 in *Excavations at Carthage 1975 Conducted by the University of Michigan,* Vol. 1, ed. J. Humphrey. Tunis: Ceres Productions.

1993 Calculating Ancient Coin Production: Facts and Fantasies (Presidential Address). *NC* 153: 335–51.

Buttrey, T.; Johnston, A.; MacKenzie, K.; and Bates, M.

1981 *Greek, Roman, and Islamic Coins from Sardis.* Archaeological Exploration of Sardis, Monograph 7. Cambridge, MA: Harvard University.

Buttrey, T. and Hitchner, R.

1978 The Coins—1976. Pp. 99–156 in *The Excavations at Carthage conducted by the University of Michigan,* Vol. 3, ed. J. Humphrey. Tunis: Ceres Productions.

Carradice, I.

1982/3 Coinage in Judaea in the Flavian Period, A.D. 70–96. *INJ* 6/7: 14–20.

Carson, R.

1967 The Inflation of the Third Century and its Monetary Influence in the Near East. Pp. 231–50 in *Proceedings of the International Numismatic Convention in Jerusalem 1963,* ed. A. Kindler. Jerusalem: Schocken.

Carson, R.; Hill, P.; and Kent, J.

1965 *Late Roman Bronze Coinage.* London: Spink (reprinted with corrections from the 1960 ed.).

Casey, P.

1974 The Interpretation of Romano-British Site Finds. Pp. 37–51 in *Coins and the Archaeologist,* eds. J. Casey and R. Reece. British Archaeological Reports 4. Oxford: British Archaeological Reports.

1986 *Understanding Ancient Coins.* Norman, OK: University of Oklahoma.

Cavada, E.

1994 *Archeologia a Mezzocorona: Documenti per la storia popolamento rustico di età romana nell'area atesina.* Trento: Servizio Beni Culturali della Provincia Autonoma.

Clarke, H., and Schia, E., eds.

1989 *Coins and Archaeology: Proceedings of the First Meeting of the Medieval Archaeology Research Group.* British Archaeological Reports International Series 556. Oxford: British Archaeological Reports.

Crowfoot, J.; Crowfoot, G; and Kenyon, K.

1957 *Samaria-Sebaste: Reports of the Work of the Joint Expedition in 1931–33 and the British Expedition of 1935: The Objects.* London: Palestine Exploration Fund.

Delmaire, R.

1989 *Largesses sacrées et "res privata:" l'ærarium impérial et son administration du IVe au VIe siècle. Collection de l'Ecole Française de Rome* 121: 509–17.

Di Segni, L.

1995 The Involvement of Local Municipal and Provincial Authorities in Urban Building in Late Antique Palestine and Arabia. Pp. 312–32 in *The Roman and Byzantine Near East: Some Recent Archaeological Research,* ed. J. Humphrey. Journal of Roman Archaeology Supplementary Series 14. Ann Arbor, MI: Journal of Roman Archaeology.

Duncan-Jones, R.

1990 *Structure and Scale in the Roman Economy*. Cambridge: Cambridge University.

1994 *Money and Government in the Roman Empire.* Cambridge: Cambridge University.

1999 The Monetization of the Roman Empire: Regional Variations in the Supply of Coin Types. Pp. 61–82 in *Roman Coins and Public Life under the Empire: the E. Togo Salmon Papers II,* eds. G. Paul and M. Ierardi. Ann Arbor, MI: University of Michigan.

Dürr, N., and Bastien, P.

1984 Trésor de solidi. *SNR* 63: 205–40.

Edbury, P., and Metcalf, D., eds.

1980 *Coinage in the Latin East*. British Archaeological Reports International Series 77. Oxford: British Archaeological Reports.

Evans, J. D.

1995 Ancient Coins from the Drew Institute of Archaeological Research Excavations of Caesarea Maritima, 1971–1984. *BA* 58: 156–66.

1993/4 Heraclian Countermarks on Coins found at Caesarea. *AJN* 5/6: 97–104.

Fitzgerald, G.

1931 *Beth Shan Excavations, 1921–23,* Vol. 3. Philadelphia, PA: University Press for the University of Pennsylvania Museum.

Foerster, G.

1975 The Early History of Caesarea. Pp. 9–22 in *The Joint Expedition to Caesarea Maritima, Vol. 1: Studies in the History of Caesarea Maritima,* ed. D. Freedman. Missoula, MT: *BASOR* Research Supplement 19.

Freeman-Grenville, G.

1992/3 Jerusalem, Aksum, and Aachen. *INJ* 12: 80–86.

Frova, A., ed.

1966 *Scavi di Caesarea Maritima*. Rome: "L'Erma" di Bretschneider.

Fulco, W., and Zayadine, F.

1981 Coins from Samaria-Sebaste. *ADAJ* 25: 197–225.

Fulford, M.

1984 The Long-Distance Trade and Communications of Carthage, c. A.D. 400 to c. A.D. 650. Pp. 255–62 in *Excavations at Carthage: The British Mission Vol. I, 2,* eds. M. Fulford and D. Peacock. Sheffield: British Academy.

Gitler, H.

1990/1 Numismatic Evidence on the Visit of Marcus Aurelius to the East. *INJ* 11: 36–51.

1996 A Comparative Study of Numismatic Evidence from Excavations in Jerusalem. *LA* 46: 317–62.

Goehring, J.

1983 Two New Examples of the Byzantine 'Eagle' Countermark. *NC* 143: 218–20.

Greene, K.

1986 *The Archaeology of the Roman Economy*. Berkeley, CA: University of California.

Grierson, P.

1967a *Catalogue of the Byzantine Coins in the Dumbarton Oaks Collection and the Whittemore Collection,* eds. A. R. Bellinger and P. Grierson, Vol. 2, Parts 1–2, *Phocas to Theodosius III, 602–717* AD. Washington, DC: Dumbarton Oaks Center for Byzantine Studies.

1967b The Monetary Reforms of Anastasius and their Economic Consequences. Pp. 283–301 in *International Numismatic Convention, Jerusalem 1963*, ed. A. Kindler. Tel Aviv: Schocken.

1982 *Byzantine Coins.* London: Methuen.

Hahn, W.

1973–81 *Moneta Imperii Byzantini,* 3 vols. Vienna: Österreichische Akademie der Wissenschaften.

1978 Alexandrian 3-nummi and 1-nummus Types under Heraclius. *NC* 138: 181–83.

1980 A Sixth-Century Hoard of Byzantine Small Change from Egypt and its Contribution to the Classification of African Minimi. *NC* 140: 64–70.

1983 Die Münzprägung des axumitischen Reiches. *Litterae Numismaticae Vindobonenses* 2: 113–80.

Hamburger, H.

1956 Minute Coins from Caesarea. *'Atiqot* 1: 115–38.

1970 The Coin Issues of the Roman Administration from the Mint of Caesarea Maritima. *IEJ* 20: 81–91.

Harl, K.

1996 *Coinage in the Roman Economy, 300* B.C. *to* A.D. *700*. Baltimore, MD: Johns Hopkins University.

Hayes, J.

1972 *Late Roman Pottery*. London: British School at Rome.

Hendin, D.

1986 Preliminary Report: Coins found at Sepphoris. *BA* 49: 8–9.

1990/91 A New Discovery on a Coin of Herod I. *INJ* 11: 32.

Hendy, M.

1985 *Studies in the Byzantine Monetary Economy c.300—1450.* Cambridge: Cambridge University.

Hengel, M.

1974 *Judaism and Hellenism,* 2 vols., trans. J. Bowden, from German. London: SCM.

Herbert, S.

1993 The Graeco-Phoenician Settlement at Tel Anafa: a Case Study in the Limits of Hellenization. Pp. 118–25 in *Biblical Archaeology Today: Proceedings of the Second International Congress on Biblical Archaeology, Jerusalem, 1990*, eds. A. Biran and J. Aviram. Jerusalem: Israel Exploration Society.

1994 *Tel Anafa I: Final Report.* Journal of Roman Archaeology Supplementary Series 10. Ann Arbor, MI: Kelsey Museum.

Hirschfeld, Y.

1997 *The Roman Baths of Hammat Gader: Final Report.* Jerusalem: Israel Exploration Society.

Hohlfelder, R.

1980 Crusader Coins and Finds of Caesarea Maritima, Israel: the Joint Expedition's Excavations, 1971–1979. Pp. 127–31 in *Coinage in the Latin East. Fourth Oxford Symposium on Coinage and Monetary History*, eds. P. Edbury and D. Metcalf. British Archaeological Reports International Series 77. Oxford: British Archaeological Reports.

1981 Appendix B: the Coin Finds. *BASOR* 244: 46–52.

1984 Caesarea Maritima in Late Antiquity. Pp. 261–85 in *Ancient Coins of the Graeco-Roman World, the Nickle Numismatic Papers*, eds. W. Heckel and R. Sullivan. Ontario: Wilfred Laurier University.

1985 Byzantine Coin Finds from the Sea: A Glimpse of Caesarea Maritima's Late History. Pp. 179–84 in *Harbour Archaeology: Proceedings of the First International Workshop on Ancient Mediterranean Harbours*, ed. A. Raban. British Archaeological Reports International Series 257. Oxford: British Archaeological Reports.

1992 The First Three Decades of Marine Explorations. Pp. 219–94 in *Caesarea Papers: Straton's Tower, Herod's Harbour, and Roman and Byzantine Caesarea*, ed. R. Vann. Journal of Roman Archaeology Supplementary Series 5. Ann Arbor, MI: Journal of Roman Archaeology.

1993 Anastasius I and the Restoration of Caesarea Maritima's Harbor: the Numismatic Evidence. Pp. 687–96 in *Biblical Archaeology Today, 1990. Proceedings of the 2nd International Congress of Biblical Archaeology*, eds. A. Biran and J. Aviram. Jerusalem: Israel Exploration Society.

1994 Coins. Pp. 77–82 in *The Harbours of Caesarea Maritima: Results of the Caesarea Ancient Harbour Excavation Project, 1980-1985, Vol. 2: the Finds and the Ship.* ed. J. Oleson. British Archaeological Reports International Series 594. Oxford: Tempus Reparatum.

2000 Anastasius I, Mud, and Foraminifera: Conflicting Views of Caesarea Maritima's Harbor in Late Antiquity. *BASOR* 317: 41–62.

Holum, K.

1989 The End of Classical Urbanism at Caesarea Maritima, Israel. Pp. 87–102 in *Studia Pompeiana and Classica in Honor of W. Jashemski*, vol.2, ed. R. Curtis. New Rochelle, NY: Caratzas.

1993 Caesarea in the Byzantine Period: Continuity and Change. Pp. 697–702 in *Biblical Archaeology Today, 1990. Proceedings of the Second International Congress of Biblical Archaeology*, eds. A. Biran and J. Aviram. Jerusalem: Israel Exploration Society.

1995 Inscriptions from the Imperial Revenue Office of Byzantine Caesarea Palaestinae. Pp. 333–45 in *The Roman and Byzantine Near East: Some Recent Archaeological Research*, ed. J. Humphrey. Journal of Roman Archaeology Supplementary Series 14. Ann Arbor, MI: Journal of Roman Archaeology.

Holum, K., and Raban, A.

1996 Introduction: Caesarea and Recent Scholarship. Pp. xxvii–xliv in *Caesarea Maritima: A Retrospective after two Millennia,* eds. A. Raban and K. Holum. Leiden: Brill.

Holum, K.; Hohlfelder, R.; Bull, R.; and Raban, A.

1988 *King Herod's Dream: Caesarea on the Sea.* New York: W.W. Norton.

Holum, K.; Raban, A.; and Patrich J., eds.

1999 *Caesarea Papers II.* Journal of Roman Archaeology Supplementary Series 35. Portsmouth, RI: Journal of Roman Archaeology.

Hopkins, K.

1980 Taxes and Trade in the Roman Empire, 200 B.C.–A.D. 400. *JRS* 70: 101–25.

Houghtalin, L.

1985 Roman Coins from the River Liri. *NC* 145: 67–81.

Howgego, C.

1985 *Greek Imperial Countermarks.* Special Publication 17. London: Royal Numismatic Society.

Humphrey, J.

1975 A Summary of the 1974 Excavations in the Caesarea Hippodrome. *BASOR* 218: 1–24.

1986 *Roman Circuses.* Berkeley, CA: University of California.

Humphrey, J., ed.

1995 *The Roman and Byzantine Near East: Some Recent Archaeological Research.* Journal of Roman Archaeology Supplementary Series 14. Ann Arbor, MI: Journal of Roman Archaeology.

Izmirlier, A.

1969 Some Unpublished Byzantine Copper Coins. *NumCirc* 12: 318–22.

Janai, J.

1989/90 Numismatic Material from the 1988/9 Season [of Beth Shean]. *ESI* 9: 128.

Jones, A. H. M.

1964 *The Later Roman Empire, 284—602: A Social, Economic, and Administrative Survey,* 2 vols. Oxford: Blackwell.

Kadman, L.

1957ff. *Corpus Nummorum Palaestinensium,* 4 vols. Tel Aviv: Schocken.

Kent, J.

1956 Gold Coinage in the Late Roman Empire. Pp. 190–204 in *Roman Coinage: Essays Presented to H. Mattingly,* eds. R. Carson and C. Sutherland. Oxford: Oxford University.

1981 *The Roman Imperial Coinage, Vol. 8. The Family of Constantine I: A.D. 337–364.* London: Spink.

1994 *The Roman Imperial Coinage, Vol. 10. The Divided Empire and the Fall of the Western Parts, A.D. 395–491.* London: Spink.

Kindler, A.

1980 *The Coinage of Bostra*. Warminster: Aris and Phillips.

King, C.

1980 The *Sacra Largitiones,* Revenues, Expenditure and the Production of Coin. Pp. 141–73 in *Imperial Revenue, Expenditure, and Monetary Policy in the Fourth Century A.D.* Fifth Oxford Symposium on Coinage and Monetary History, ed. C. King. British Archaeological Reports International Series 76. Oxford: British Archaeological Reports.

King, C., ed.

1980 *Imperial Revenue, Expenditure, and Monetary Policy in the Fourth Century A.D.* Fifth Oxford Symposium on Coinage and Monetary History. British Archaeological Reports International Series 76. Oxford: British Archaeological Reports.

King, C., and Wigg, D., eds.

1996 *Coin Finds and Coin Use in the Roman World.* Thirteenth Oxford Symposium on Coinage and Monetary History. Berlin: Gebr. Mann.

Klimosky, E.

1974 *On Ancient Palestinian and Other Coins: Their Symbolism and Metrology.* Tel Aviv: Israel Numismatic Society.

Kraeling, C., ed.

1938 *Gerasa: City of the Decapolis*. New Haven, CT: American Schools of Oriental Research.

Lampinen, P.

1992 The Coins, Preliminary Report, 1990. Pp. 169–72 in *Caesarea Papers: Straton's Tower, Herod's Harbour, and Roman and Byzantine Caesarea,* ed. R. Vann. Journal of Roman Archaeology Supplementary Series 5. Ann Arbor, MI: Journal of Roman Archaeology.

1999a The Gold Hoard of 4th-c. *Solidi* Found in 1993. Pp. 369–87 in *Caesarea Papers II,* eds. K Holum, A. Raban, and J. Patrich. Journal of Roman Archaeology Supplementary Series 35. Portmouth, RI: Journal of Roman Archaeology.

1999b Countermarked Byzantine *Folles* and the Identification of a New Imperial Family Member. Pp. 399–404 in *Caesarea Papers II,* eds. K. Holum, A. Raban, and J. Patrich. Journal of Roman Archaeology Supplementary Series 35. Portsmouth, RI: Journal of Roman Archaeology.

Lohmann, C., and Holum, K.

2000 *The Greek and Latin Inscriptions of Caesarea Maritima.* The Joint Expedition to Caesarea Maritima, Excavation Reports, vol. 5. Boston, MA: American Schools of Oriental Research.

Levine, L.

1972 Some Observations on the Coins of Caesarea Maritima. *IEJ* 22: 131–40.

1975a *Roman Caesarea. Qedem* 2. Jerusalem: Institute of Archaeology, Hebrew University.

1975b *Caesarea under Roman Rule*. Leiden: Brill.

Levine, L., ed.

1981 *The Jerusalem Cathedra: Studies in the History, Archeology, Geography, and Ethnography of the Land of Israel,* vol.1. Jerusalem: Izhak Ben Zvi Institute.

Levine, L., and Netzer, E.

1986 *Excavations at Caesarea Maritima 1975, 1976, 1979: Final Report. Qedem* 21. Jerusalem: Institute of Archaeology, Hebrew University.

Lindgren, H., and Kovacs, F.

1985 *Ancient Bronze Coins of Asia Minor and the Levant from the Lundgren Collection*. San Francisco, CA: Chrysopylon.

Mader, E.

1957–58 *Mambre: die Ergebnisse der Ausgrabungen in heiligen Râmet el-Halîl in Südpalästina, 1926–1928,* 2 vols. Freiburg: Wewel.

Magness, J.

1992 Late Roman and Byzantine Pottery: Preliminary Report, 1990. Pp. 129–53 in *Caesarea Papers: Straton's Tower, Herod's Harbour, and Roman and Byzantine Caesarea,* ed. R. Vann. Journal of Roman Archaeology Supplementary Series 5. Ann Arbor, MI: Journal of Roman Archaeology.

1995 The Pottery from Area V/4 at Caesarea. Pp. 133–37 in *Preliminary Excavation Reports,* ed. W. Dever. AASOR 52. Boston, MA: American Schools of Oriental Research.

Mattingly, H., and Sydenham, E.

1926 *Roman Imperial Coinage, Vol. 2. Vespasian to Hadrian.* London: Spink.

1930 *Roman Imperial Coinage, Vol. 3. Antoninus Pius to Commodus.* London: Spink.

Mattingly, H.; Sydenham, E.; and Sutherland, C.

1936 *The Roman Imperial Coinage, Vol. 4, Pt. 2. Macrinus to Pupienus.* London: Spink.

1949 *The Roman Imperial Coinage, Vol. 4, Pt. 3. Gordion III to Uranius Antoninus.* London: Spink.

McLean, M.

1981 The Initial Coinage of Alexander Jannaeus. *ANSMN* 26: 153–62.

Meshorer, Y.

1967 *Jewish Coins of the Second Temple Period,* trans. I. Levine, from Hebrew. Tel Aviv: Am Hassefer.

1981 Again on the Beginning of the Hasmonean Coinage. *INJ* 5: 11–16.

1982 *Ancient Jewish Coinage.* Dix Hills, NY: Amphora Books.

1986/87 The Coins of Dora. *INJ* 9: 59–72.

1990/91 *Ancient Jewish Coinage:* Addendum I. *INJ* 11: 104–32.

1998 *Ancient Means of Exchange: Weights and Coins, the Ruben and Edith Hecht Museum Collection*. Haifa: University of Haifa.

2001 *A Treasury of Jewish Coins from the Persian Period to Bar Kokhba,* trans. R. Amolis, from Hebrew. New York, NY: Amphora Books.

Metcalf, D. M.

1960 The Metrology of Justinian's Follis. *NC* 20: 209–19.

1961 The Organization of the Constantinian Mint for the Folles of the Anastasian Reforms. *NC* 1: 131–43.
1964 Some Byzantine and Arab-Byzantine Coins from Palaestina Prima. *INJ* 2: 32–46.
1969 *The Origins of the Anastasian Currency Reform.* Amsterdam: Hakkert.

Metcalf, W.

1974 Roman Coins from the River Liri II. *NC* 134: 42–52.
1975 A Heraclian Hoard from Syria. *ANSMN* 20: 109–37.
1982 The Coins – 1978. Pp. 63–168 in *Excavations at Carthage conducted by the University of Michigan,* vol.7, ed. J. Humphrey. Ann Arbor, MI: University of Michigan.
1987 The Michigan Finds at Carthage, 1975–79, an Analysis. *ANSMN* 32: 61–84.

Metcalf, W., and Fulco, W.

1995/96 Coins from the Excavations at Tell Nimrin. *AJN* 7/8: 145–54.

Metcalf, W., and Hitchner, R.

1980 The Coins – 1977. Pp. 185–270 in *Excavations at Carthage conducted by the University of Michigan,* vol.5, ed. J. Humphrey. Ann Arbor, MI: University of Michigan.

Meyers, C.; Meyers, E.; and Strange, J.

1990 *Excavations at the Ancient Synagogue of Gush Halav.* Meiron Excavations Project Vol. 5. Winona Lake, IN: American Schools of Oriental Research.

Meyers, E.

1983 Stratigraphic and Ceramic Observations from the Medieval Strata of Khirbet Shema, Israel: Assessment of the Value of Scientific Analysis. *BASOR* 260: 61–69.

Meyers, E., ed.

1997 *Oxford Encyclopedia of Archaeology in the Near East.* 4 vols. Oxford: Oxford University.

Meyers, E.; Kraabel, A.; and Strange, J.

1973 *Ancient Synagogue Excavations at Khirbet Shema, Upper Galilee, Israel, 1970—1972.* AASOR 42. Durham, NC: American Schools of Oriental Research.

Meyers, E.; Strange, J.; and Meyers, C.

1981 Preliminary Report on the 1980 Excavations at en-Nabratein, Israel. *BASOR* 244: 1–25.

Meyers, E.; Strange, J.; Meyers, C.; and Hanson, R.

1979 Preliminary Report on the 1977 and 1978 Seasons at Gush Halav (el-Jish). *BASOR* 233: 33–58.

Millar, F.

1993 *The Roman Near East.* Cambridge, MA: Harvard University.

Milne, J.

1993 *Oxford University, Ashmolean Museum Collection: Catalogue of the Alexandrian Coins.* Oxford: Oxford University.

Mørkholm, O.

1991 *Early Hellenistic Coinage, from the Accession of Alexander to the Peace of Apamea (336–188* B.C.*)*. Cambridge: Cambridge University.

Morrisson, C.

1970 *Catalogue des Monnaies Byzantines de la Bibliothèque Nationale,* vol.1. Paris: Bibliothèque Nationale.

Munro-Hay, S.

1989 The al-Madhariba Hoard of Gold Aksumite and Late Roman Coins. *NC* 149: 83–100.

Munro-Hay, S., and Juel-Jensen, B.

1995 *Aksumite Coinage.* London: Spink.

Negev, A.

1964 The High Level Aqueduct at Caesarea. *IEJ* 14: 237–49.

Netzer, E.

1981 *Greater Herodium*. Qedem 13. Jerusalem: Institute of Archaeology, Hebrew University.

Noeske, H.-C.

1998 Bemerkungen zur Problematik der Siedlungsfunde. Pp. 157–65 in *Studien zu Fundmünzen der Antike,* Bd.13, ed. D. Backendorf. Berlin: Gebr. Mann.

Olami, Y., and Peleg, Y.

1977 The Water Supply System of Caesarea Maritima. *IEJ* 27: 127–37.

Oleson, J.

1996 Artifactual Evidence for the History of the Harbors of Caesarea. Pp. 359–77 in *Caesarea Maritima: A Retrospective after two Millennia,* eds. A. Raban and K. Holum. Leiden: Brill.

Oleson, J., ed.

1994 *The Harbours of Caesarea Maritima: Results of the Caesarea Ancient Harbour Excavation Project, 1980–1985, Vol. 2: the Finds and the Ship*. British Archaeological Reports International Series 594. Oxford: Tempus Reparatum.

Papanicolaou Christensen, A.

1995 *Hama: Fouilles et Recherches, 1931–1938, Vol. 3 Part 3: The Graeco-Roman Objects of Clay, the Coins, and the Necropolis*. Copenhagen: Nationalmuseet.

Pastor, J.

1996 *Land and Economy in Ancient Palestine*. New York, NY: Routledge.

Patrich, J.

1999 The Warehouse Complex and Governor's Palace (Areas KK, CC, and NN, May 1993–December 1995). Pp. 70–107 in *Caesarea Papers II,* eds. K. Holum, A. Raban, and J. Patrich. Journal of Roman Archaeology Supplementary Series 35. Portsmouth, RI: Journal of Roman Archaeology.

Pearce, J.

1933 *The Roman Imperial Coinage, Vol. 9. Valentinian I to Theodosius I.* London: Spink.

Peleg, M.

1994 Bet Shean: A Paved Street and Adjacent Remains. *'Atiqot* 25: 139–55.

Phillips, J.

1962 The Byzantine Bronze Coins of Alexandria in the Seventh Century. *NC* 122: 225–41.

Phillips, M., and Goodwin, T.

1997 A Seventh-Century Hoard of Byzantine and Imitative Copper Coins. *NC* 157: 61–87.

Porath, Y.

1995 Herod's Amphitheatre at Caesarea: a Multi-purpose Entertainment Building. Pp. 15–27 in *The Roman and Byzantine Near East,* ed. J. Humphrey. Journal of Roman Archaeology Supplementary Series 14. Ann Arbor, MI: Journal of Roman Archaeology.

Qedar, S.

1988/89 Copper Coinage of Syria in the Seventh and Eighth Centuries A.D. *INJ* 10: 27–39.

Raban, A.

1992 Καισάρeia ἡ πρὸς Σebaστω Λιμένi: Two Harbours for Two Entities? Pp. 68–74 in *Caesarea Papers: Straton's Tower, Herod's Harbour, and Roman and Byzantine Caesarea,* ed. R. Vann. Journal of Roman Archaeology Supplementary Series 5. Ann Arbor, MI: Journal of Roman Archaeology.

1996 The Inner Harbor Basin of Caesarea: Archaeological Evidence for its Gradual Demise. Pp. 628–66 in *Caesarea Maritima: A Retrospective after two Millennia,* eds. A. Raban and K. Holum. Leiden: Brill.

1999 The Lead Ingots from the Wreck Site (Area K8). Pp. 179–88 in *Caesarea Papers II,* eds. K. Holum, A. Raban, and J. Patrich. Journal of Roman Archaeology Supplementary Series 35. Portsmouth, RI: Journal of Roman Archaeology.

Raban, A., ed.

1985 *Harbour Archaeology: Proceedings of the First International Workshop on Ancient Mediterranean Harbours.* British Archaeological Reports International Series 257. Oxford: British Archaeological Reports.

Raban, A.; Holum, K.; and Blakely, J.

1993 *The Combined Caesarea Expeditions: Field Report of the 1992 Season,* 2 vols. Haifa: University of Haifa.

Raban, A., and Holum, K., eds.

1996 *Caesarea Maritima: A Retrospective after two Millennia.* Leiden: Brill.

Rahmani, L.

1964 A 14th-Century Hoard from Tiberias. *INJ* 2: 19–23.

Rathbone, D.

1996 Monetisation, not Price-Inflation, in Third-Century A.D. Egypt? Pp. 321–39 in *Coin Finds and Coin Use in the Roman World,* Thirteenth Oxford Symposium on Coinage and Monetary History, eds. C. King and D. Wigg. Berlin: Gebr. Mann.

Raynor, J., and Meshorer, Y.

1988 *The Coins of Ancient Meiron.* Meiron Excavation Project Series, vol. 4. Winona Lake, IN: American Schools of Oriental Research.

Reece, R.

1982 Roman Coinage in the Western Mediterranean: A Quantitative Approach. *Opus* (Rome) 1: 341–50.

1996 The Interpretation of Site Finds: A Review. Pp. 341–55 in *Coin Finds and Coin Use in the Roman World.* Thirteenth Oxford Symposium on Coinage and Monetary History, eds. C. King and D. Wigg. Berlin: Gebr. Mann.

1998 Zur Auswertung und Interpretation römischer Fundmünzen aus Siedlungen. Pp. 175–95 in *Studien zu Fundmünzen der Antike,* Bd. 13, ed. D. Backendorf. Berlin: Gebr. Mann.

Reinhardt, E., and Patterson, R.

1999 Foraminiferal Analysis of Three Stratigraphic Sections from the Inner Harbour, Area I14. Pp. 346–49 in *Caesarea Papers II,* eds. K. Holum, A. Raban, and J. Patrich. Journal of Roman Archaeology Supplementary Series 35. Portsmouth, RI: Journal of Roman Archaeology.

Reisner, G.; Fisher, C.; and Lyon, D.

1924 *Harvard Excavations at Samaria, 1908–1910,* Vol. 1. Cambridge, MA: Harvard University.

Robertson, A.

1986 The Accidents of Survival. Pp. 245–52 in *Proceedings of the Tenth International Congress of Numismatics, London, 1986,* ed. I. Carradice. London: International Association of Professional Numismatists.

Roller, D.

1992 Straton's Tower: Some Additional Thoughts. Pp. 23–25 in *Caesarea Papers: Straton's Tower, Herod's Harbour, and Roman and Byzantine Caesarea,* ed. R. Vann. Journal of Roman Archaeology Supplementary Series 5. Ann Arbor, MI: Journal of Roman Archaeology.

Rosenberger, M.

1972–77 *City-Coins of Palestine: The Rosenberger Israel Collection,* 3 vols. Jerusalem: M. Rosenberger.

Rouvier, J.

1900 Numismatique des villes de la Phénicie. *Journal International d'Archéologie Numismatique* 3: 125–68.

Royal Numismatic Society

1976 *Coin Hoards II.* London: Royal Numismatic Society.

1977 *Coin Hoards III.* London: Royal Numismatic Society.

1985 *Coin Hoards VII.* London: Royal Numismatic Society.

Russell, J.

1983 A Coin Hoard of Maurice Tiberius from Anemurium, Isauria. *ANSMN* 28: 119–31.

Safrai, Z.

1994 *The Economy of Roman Palestine.* London: Routledge.

Schalit, A.

1972 *The World History of the Jewish People, vol. 6. The Hellenistic Age.* New Brunswick, NJ: Rutgers.

Schmitt-Korte, K.

1990 Nabataean Coinage – pt. II. New Coin Types and Variants. *NC* 150: 105–33.

Schubert, H.

1986 Beobachtungen zum frührömischen Münzumlauf am obergermanisch-rätischen Limes. Pp. 253–61 in *Proceedings of the Tenth International Congress of Numismatics, London, 1986,* ed. I. Carradice. London: International Association of Professional Numismatists.

Schulzki, H.-J.

1989 *Die Fundmünzen der römischen Strassenstation Flerzheim.* Beihefte der Bonner Jahrbücher, Band 48. Cologne: Rheinland.

Schwartz, J.

1952 Trésor de Monnaies de Tod. *Bulletin de l'Institut Français d'Archéologie Orientale* 51: 96–98.

Sheedy, K.; Carson, R.; and Walmsley, A.

2001 *Pella in Jordan 1979–1990: the Coins.* Sydney: Adapa.

Smallwood, E.

1976 *The Jews Under Roman Rule: from Pompey to Diocletian.* Leiden: Brill.

Sperber, D.

1974 *Roman Palestine, 200–400: Money and Prices,* second ed. Ramat-Gan: Bar-Ilan University.

1998 *The City in Roman Palestine.* Oxford: Oxford University.

Spijkerman, A.

1972 *Herodion III: Catalogo delle monete.* Jerusalem: Franciscan Printing.

1975 *Cafarnao III: Catalogo delle monete della città.* Jerusalem: Franciscan Printing.

1978 *The Coins of the Decapolis and Provincia Arabia.* Jerusalem: Franciscan Printing.

Stern, E.

1930 *Excavations at Dor, Final Report. Vol 1B: Areas A and C: The Finds. Qedem* Reports 2. Jerusalem: Institute of Archaeology, Hebrew University.

Stern, E., ed.

1993 *The New Encyclopedia of Archaeological Excavations in the Holy Land,* 4 vols. New York, NY: Simon and Schuster.

Stieglitz, R.

1993 Straton's Tower: the Name, the History, and the Archaeological Data. Pp. 646–51 in *Biblical Archaeology Today, 1990. Proceedings of the Second International Congress of Biblical Archaeology,* eds. A. Biran and J. Aviram. Jerusalem: Israel Exploration Society.

1996 Stratonos Pyrgos—Migdal Śar—Sebastos: History and Archaeology. Pp. 593–608 in *Caesarea Maritima: A Retrospective after two Millennia,* eds. A. Raban and K. Holum. Leiden: Brill.

1999 Straton's Tower and Demetrias Again: One Town or Two? Pp. 359–60 in *Caesarea Papers II*, eds. K. Holum, A. Raban, and J. Patrich. Journal of Roman Archaeology Supplementary Series 35. Portsmouth, RI: Journal of Roman Archaeology.

Sussman, V.

1996 Caesarea Illuminated by its Lamps. Pp. 346–58 in *Caesarea Maritima: A Retrospective after two Millennia*, eds. A. Raban and K. Holum. Leiden: Brill.

Sutherland, C.

1967 The Patterns of Monetary Development in Phoenicia and Palestine in Antiquity. Pp. 88–105 in *Proceedings of the International Numismatic Convention in Jerusalem, 1963*, ed. A. Kindler. Tel Aviv: Schocken.

1973 *The Roman Imperial Coinage, Vol. 6. Diocletian to Maximinus.* London: Spink.

1984 *The Roman Imperial Coinage, Vol. 1, revised. 31 B.C.–A.D. 69.* London: Spink.

Syon, D.

1992/93 The Coins from Gamala: Interim Report. *INJ* 12: 34–55.

Toombs, L.

1978 The Stratigraphy of Caesarea Maritima. Pp. 223–32 in *Archaeology in the Levant: Essays for Kathleen Kenyon*, eds. R. Moorey and P. Parr. Warminster: Aris and Phillips.

Tsafrir, Y.

1995 The Synagogues of Capernaum and Meroth and the Dating of the Galilean Synagogue. Pp. 151–61 in *The Roman and Byzantine Near East: Some Recent Archaeological Research*, ed. J. Humphrey. Journal of Roman Archaeology Supplementary Series 14. Ann Arbor, MI: Journal of Roman Archaeology.

Tushingham, A.

1985 *Excavations in Jerusalem, 1961–1967, Vol. 1.* Toronto: Royal Ontario Museum.

Tzaferis, V.

1989 *Excavations at Capernaum, Vol. 1.* Winona Lake, IN: American Schools of Oriental Research.

Vann, R., ed.

1992 *Caesarea Papers: Straton's Tower, Herod's Harbour, and Roman and Byzantine Caesarea.* Journal of Roman Archaeology Supplementary Series 5. Ann Arbor, MI: Journal of Roman Archaeology.

Voegtle, H.

1993 *Die Fundmünzen aus der Stadtgrabung von Pergamon.* Berlin: de Gruyter.

Waage, D.

1952 *Antioch-on-the-Orontes IV pt. 2: Greek, Roman, Byzantine and Crusader Coins.* Princeton, NJ: Princeton University.

Walmsley, A.

1996 Byzantine Palestine and Arabia: Urban Prosperity in Late Antiquity. Pp. 126–58 in *Towns in Transition: Urban Evolution in Late Antiquity and the Early Middle Ages*, eds. N. Christie and S. T. Loseby. Aldershot: Scolar.

Waterman, L.

1960 *Preliminary Report of the University of Michigan Excavations at Sepporis in Palestine*. Ann Arbor, MI: University of Michigan.

Webb, P.

1927 *Roman Imperial Coinage, Vol. 5, Pt. 1. Valerian to Florian.* London: Spink.

1933 *Roman Imperial Coinage, Vol. 5., Pt. 2. Probus to Amandus.* London: Spink.

Weinberg, G., ed.

1988 *Excavations at Jalame: Site of a Glass Factory in Late Roman Palestine*. Columbia, MO: University of Missouri.

Weiss, Z., and Netzer, E.

1995 New Evidence for Late-Roman and Byzantine Sepphoris. Pp. 167–76 in *The Roman and Byzantine Near East: Some Recent Archaeological Research,* ed. J. Humphrey. Journal of Roman Archaeology Supplementary Series 14. Ann Arbor, MI: Journal of Roman Archaeology.

Whittaker, C.

1980 Inflation and the Economy in the Fourth Century A.D. Pp. 1–22 in *Imperial Revenue, Expenditure, and Monetary Policy in the Fourth Century A.D.,* Fifth Oxford Symposium on Coinage and Monetary History, ed. C. King. British Archaeological Reports International Series 76. Oxford: British Archaeological Reports.

1993 *Land, City and Trade in the Roman Empire.* Brookfield, VT: Variorum.

Wiemken, R., and Holum, K.

1981 The Joint Expedition to Caesarea Maritima: Eighth Season, 1979. *BASOR* 244: 53–72.

Wightman, G.

1989 *The Damascus Gate, Jerusalem: Excavations by C.-M. Bennett and J. B. Hennessy at the Damascus Gate, Jerusalem, 1964–66.* British Archaeological Reports International Series 519. Oxford: British Archaeological Reports.

Yule, B., and Barham, A.

1999 Caesarea's Inner Harbour: the Potential of the Harbour Sediments. Pp. 262–84 in *Caesarea Papers II,* eds. K. Holum, A. Raban, and J. Patrich. Journal of Roman Archaeology Supplementary Series 35. Portsmouth, RI: Journal of Roman Archaeology.

Catalogue of Coins from the JECM Excavations 1971–1987

The second line of the catalogue entry reads: metal, denomination (if known), weight in grams, diameter in mm, inventory number, locus (beginning with the letter L). An asterisk after the weight means that the coin was fragmentary, halved or pierced (asterisks are also used in the description to denote stars in the types). The inventory number shows the Year. Field. Area. Bucket. Field number. Unknown field is marked 'X'; unknown area or bucket is marked '0.' The full locus should be obtained by ascertaining the Field and Area number (e.g., the locus for coin one is G.18 000); '000' means that the coin was either from the surface or baulk cleaning, or that the locus is lost or unknown. Coins that are missing or otherwise unavailable are marked "inventory only."

Greek, including Roman Provincial, Judaic, Nabatean, Arabian, and Axumite

Aeolis

Cyme

350–320 B.C.E.

Eagle standing r. | KY; One-handled vase | *BMC Troas* p. 106: 16–20

1. AE 0.87 9 84.G.18.192.88 L 000

Pamphylia

Side

300–200 B.C.E.

Athena head r. | Pomegranate | *BMC Lycia* p. 150: 59–61

2. AE 3.00 13 72.A.1.291.3 L 143 Plate 1

Syria

Gaba

161–168 B.C.E. Lucius Verus

Verus head r.; AVPOYHPOC KAICAP | Faustina minor bust r.; ...EINA CEB ΓAB | *BMC Galatia* p. 300: 2

3. AE 8.10 24 79.L.1.67.79 L 021 Plate 1

COMMAGENE?

19–20 C.E. TIBERIUS

Obverse	Reverse	Reference
Tiberius bust r. laur.; TI CAESAR DIVI AVGVSTI F AVGVSTVS	Double cornucopiae, caduceus; PONT MAXIM COS III IMP VII TR POT XXI	*RPC 1*: 3868, *RIC 1*: 89

No.	Metal	Denom.	Weight	mm	Reg. no.	Locus	Remarks	Plate
4.	AE	Dup.	16.01	30	74.H.3.121.11	L 306	cm on obv: male head r., 10 × 7 mm	Plate 1

Obverse	Reverse	Reference
Tiberius bust r. laur.; TI CAESAR DIVI AVGVSTI F AVGVSTVS	Double cornucopiae, caduceus; PONT MAXIM COS III IMP VII TR POT XXI or XXII	*RPC 1*: 3868–69, *RIC 1*: 89–90

No.	Metal	Denom.	Weight	mm	Reg. no.	Locus
5.	AE	Dup.	14.04	25	80.G.9.317.164	L005
6.			10.47	28	72.C.2.104.2	L 274

DAMASCUS?

114–95 B.C.E.? ANTIOCHUS IX (?)

Obverse	Reverse	Reference
Antiochus IX(?) head r.	Cornucopiae; ΒΑΣΙΛΕΩΣ ΑΝΤΙΟΧΟΥ ΦΙΛΟΠΑΤΟΡΟΣ	*ACNAC* 4: 884?

No.	Metal	Denom.	Weight	mm	Reg. no.	Locus
7.	AE	Hemidr.	2.46	16	78.G.7.56.8	L 029

COELE SYRIA

ANTIOCH AD ORONTES

268–261 B.C.E.? ANTIOCHUS I?

Obverse	Reverse	Reference
Antiochus I? head r.	Apollo seated on omphalos; ΒΑΣΙ ΑΝΤΙ	*ACNAC* 4: 31?

No.	Metal	Weight	mm	Reg. no.	Locus
8.	AE	0.65	8	80.G.7.177.25	L 106

222–187 B.C.E. ANTIOCHUS III

Obverse	Reverse	Reference
Apollo head r.	Apollo standing holding bow; ΒΑΣΙΛΕΩΣ ΑΝΤΙΟΧΟΥ	*ACNAC* 4: 70–71

No.	Metal	Weight	mm	Reg. no.	Locus
9.	AE	1.57	9	80.C.25.137.11	L 075
10.		1.31	11	80.G.12.5.2	L 004
11.		1.13	10	87.G.22.15.2	L 001
12.		1.11	9	80.G.7.178.26	L 106

280–187 B.C.E ANTIOCHUS I OR III

Obverse	Reverse	Reference
Head r.	Apollo seated on omphalos	*ACNAC* 4: 31–33, 66–67

No.	Metal	Weight	mm	Reg. no.	Locus
13.	AE	1.24	12	80.G.8.491.24	L 121

175–164 B.C.E. ANTIOCHUS IV

Obverse	Reverse	Reference
Apollo head r., monogram	Apollo seated holding bow, aphlaston to l.; ΒΑΣΙΛΕΩΣ ΑΝΤΙΟΧΟΥ, serrate	*ACNAC* 4: 115–16

No.	Metal	Weight	mm	Reg. no.	Locus	Plate
14.	AE	2.38	12	78.G.6.142.28	L 080	Plate 1
15.		1.96	14	80.G.8.488.21	L 119	
16.		1.93	14	78.G.6.63.14	L 045	

Antiochus IV head r. | Zeus standing holding wreath; ANTIOXEΩN TΩN ΠΡΟΣ ΔΑΦΝΗΙ [sic obv. description] | *ACNAC* 4: 129–33

17. AE 4.46 17 78.G.6.7.39.7 L 016

150–145 B.C.E. *ALEXANDER I BALAS*

Dionysos head r. | Tyche standing with cornucopiae and rudder; ΒΑΣΙΛΕΩΣ ΑΛΕΞΑΝΔΡΟΥ | *ACNAC* 4: 199

18. AE 5.27 18 78.G.6.148.30 L 083

128–122 B.C.E. *ALEXANDER II ZABINAS*

Eros bust r. | Inverted anchor; ΒΑΣΙΛΕΩΣ ΑΓΕΞΑΝΔΡΟΥ | *ACNAC* 4: 300

19. AE 3.11 16 80.G.8.488.20 L 119

125–121 B.C.E. *ANTIOCHUS VIII*

Antiochus VIII head r. | Owl on amphora | *ACNAC* 4: 317–18

20. AE 4.60 19 80.G.7.0.33 L 069

1–100 C.E.

Head r. | SC in wreath

21. AE 14.62 29 80.C.27.80.8 L 031

22. AE 6.54 25 72.A.2.30.6 L 107

81–83 C.E. *DOMITIAN*

Domitian head r. laur. | SC in wreath; IMP DOMITIANVS CAES AVG | *RPC* 2: 2021–23

23. AE 1.04 9 72.A.1.248.3 L 143

97 C.E. *NERVA*

Nerva head r. laur.; IMP CAESAR NERV AVG III COS | SC in wreath; I | *BMC Galatia* p. 182: 264

24. AE 3.80 29 72.A.1.285.5 L 042 Plate 1

KANATA

93/4 C.E. *DOMITIAN*

Domitian head l. laur. | Tyche head l.; KANATA ZNP DOMITI KAICAP | *RPC* 2: 2092

25. AE 2.33 14 72.A.1.295.23 L 143

Phoenicia

Berytus

30 B.C.E.–14 C.E.

Eagle on fulmen — Lituus; AVG — *RPC* I: 4538

26. AE 2.41 15 72.A.1.298.5 L 143

218–222 C.E. Elagabalus

Elagabalus head r. laur.; IMP CAES M AVR ANTONINVS — Arched gateway supporting figure on panther: Silenus statue in arch; COL IVL AVG FEL BER — *BMC Phoenicia* pp. 81: 192–83: 206

27. AE 13.02 30 79.L.1.13.6 L 004

Elagabalus head r.?; IMP CAES M AVR ANTONINVS AVG — Astarte in galley; COL IVL FEL BER — Rouvier 1900: 587

28. AE 7.87 20 72.A.1.298.6 L 143

Ake-Ptolemais

175–164 B.C.E. Antiochus IV

Antiochus IV head r.; ΒΑΣΙΛΕΩΣ ΑΝΤΙΟΧΟΥ — Artemis standing holding torch, bow — *ACNAC* 4: 788–89

29. AE dilepton 1.42 13 82.G.13.319.17 L 079 inventory only

Antiochus IV head r. — Veiled female standing holding scepter — *ACNAC* 4: 791–93

30. AE dilepton serrate 2.46 13 80.G.8.500.30 L 123

31. 2.37 13 80.G.8.490.22 L 119

32. 2.31 13 87.G.22.7.1 L 000 inventory only

33. 1.91 14 80.G.8.492.25 L 121 Plate 1 (rev.)

34. 1.60 13 80.G.8.497.28 L 119

35. 1.33 13 80.G.8.502.29 L 000

Similar? — Similar?

36. 1.72 14 71.X.0.0.18 L 000

66–67 C.E. Nero

Nero head r. laur.; IMP NER CLA CAES AVG GERM PM TR POT — Man ploughing, 4 vexilla; DIVOS CLAVD STAB GER FELIX P COL CLA III VI X XI — *RPC* 1: 4750

37. AE 7.87 20 72.A.1.296.6 L 143

211–215 C.E. Caracalla

Caracalla head r.; M…ANTONI — Caduceus with club and harpa; COL PTOLO — *CNP* 4: 134

38. AE 1.92 13 74.H.5.23.1 L 007

Sidon

10–9 B.C.E.

Zeus head r. laur.; ΣΙΔΩΝΟΣ ΘΕΑΣ					Nike on prow; L BP		*RPC* 1: 4600
39.	AE		3.79	18	72.A.1.46.27 L 090		

Tyre

222–187 B.C.E. Antiochus III

Antiochus III head r.					Palm tree; ΒΑΣΙΛΕΩΣ ΑΝΤΙΟΧΟΥ		*ACNAC* 4: 729
40.	AE		1.75	15	80.G.8.490.23 L 119		
41.	AE		1.53	13	72.A.2.157.4 L 068		
Antiochus III head r.					Club; ΒΑΣΙΛΕΩΣ ΑΝΤΙΟΧΟΥ		*ACNAC* 4: 730
42.	AE		1.33	13	80.G.9.319.166 L 057		

204–198 B.C.E. Ptolemy V

Zeus Ammon head r.					Eagle l. on fulmen, cornucopiae, club, monogram; ΠΤΟΛΕΜΑΙΟΥ ΒΑΙΣΛΕΩΣ		*BMC Ptolemaic* p. 73: 56–58
43.	AE		6.27	18	78.G.7.19.3 L 008	inventory only	

175–164 B.C.E. Antiochus IV

Antiochus IV head r.					Palm tree; ΒΑΣΙΛΕΩΣ ΑΝΤΙΟΧΟΥ		*ACNAC* 4: 735
44.	AE		1.69	15	80.G.8.472.14 L 118		

222–164 B.C.E. Antiochus III or IV

Head r.					Palm tree; ΒΑΣΙΛΕΩΣ ΑΝΤΙΟΧΟΥ		*ACNAC* 4: 729 or 735
45.	AE		2.28	15	72.A.1.196.8 L 135		
46.			1.53	13	87.G.19.232.9 L 076		
47.			1.45	15	84.G.12.68.5 L 010	inventory only	
48.			1.23	19	80.G.8.488.18 L 119		
49.			1.17	14	80.G.8.492.26 L 121		

138–129 B.C.E. Antiochus VII

Antiochus VII head r.					Eagle on galley prow, palm branch		
50.	AR	tetradrachm	13.8	26	76.G.3.256.1 L 145	inventory only	

64/5–119 C.E. Autonomous City

Tyche head r.					Palm tree, monogram of Tyre; ΙΕΡ ΑΣ		*RPC* 2: 2077–80
51.	AE		0.57*	13	71.A.1.102.88 L 049	date uncertain	

93/4 C.E.

Tyche bust r					Palm tree, monogram of Tyre; ΙΕΡ ΑΣ ΘΙΣ		*RPC* 2: 2083
52.	AE		1.37	13	76.H.6.1.1 L 001	inventory only	

98/9 C.E.

Tyche head r. | Astarte standing on galley, monogram of Tyre; ΔKE | *BMC Phoenicia* p. 26: 1303–4

53. AE 1.52 12 72.A.1.291.4 L 143

104–109 C.E.

Tyche head r. | Palm tree, monogram of Tyre; ΜΗΤΡΟΠΟΛΕωΣ ΙΕΡΑΣ ΛΕ | *BMC Phoenicia* p. 265: 338

54. AE 0.71 14 72.A.1.60.5 L 101 inventory only

108/9 C.E.

Tyche head r. | Palm tree, monogram of Tyre; ΜΗΤRΟΠΟΛΕωΣ ΙΕΡΑΣ ΔΛΕ | *BMC Phoenicia* p. 265: 340–42

55. AE 3.36 18 74.C.12.39.1 L 042

56. AE 2.64 15 72.A.1.57.10 L 102

114/5 C.E.

Tyche head r. | Astarte standing on galley, monogram of city; MC | *BMC Phoenicia* p. 262: 309

57. AE 1.07 13 76.G.3.57.1 L 036 inventory only

115–119 C.E.

Tyche bust r. | Palm tree, monogram of city; ΜΗΤΡΟΠΛΕωΣ ΙΕΡΑΣ ?ΜΣ | *BMC Phoenicia* p. 266: 343–45

58. AE 2.87 15 72.A.1.295.17 L 143

218–222 C.E. *ELAGABALUS*

Elagabalus bust r. laur.; IMP CAES M AV ANTONINVS AVG TVPIORUM | Astarte with trophy, Nike, palm tree | *BMC Phoenicia* p. 275: 401

59. AE 16.99 29 71.A.2.178.410 L 042

60. 12.34 27 71.A.1.21.10 L 011

251–252 C.E. *TREBONIUS GALLUS*

Trebonius bust r. laur.?; IMP C G VIBIVS TREBO GALLVS AVG | Bull r., legionary standard, murex; LEG III GAL COL TV ROME TRO | *BMC Phoenicia* p. 285: 443

61. AE 8.26 27 82.G.14.30.5 L 009 inventory only

253–268 C.E. *SALONINA*

Salonina bust r. *BMC Phoenicia* p. 295: 494 | Astarte crowned by Nike in temple *BMC Phoenicia* p. 291: 475 (Gallienus) | Lindgren and Kovacs no. 2400

62. AE 15.24 29 74.C.10.216.6 L 109 Plate 1

200–300 C.E.

Tyche bust r. | Palm tree | Hamburger 1956: 21

63. AE 0.66 12 72.A.1.64.9 L 101

Tyche bust r. | Palm tree, inscr. obscure | *BMC Phoenicia* p. 253: 246–47

64. AE 0.71 12 72.A.1.117.4 L 103

1–300 C.E. Autonomous City

Tyche bust r. | Palm tree | Hamburger 1956: 1–13

65. AE 0.42 11 72.A.1.150.3 L 130

Tyche bust r. | Palm tree | Hamburger 1956: 23

66. AE 0.35 11 80.G.8.378.2 L 088

Uncertain | Palm tree

67. AE 0.88 12 72.A.1.229.24 L 135

Dora

64–63 B.C.E. Autonomous City

Tyche bust r., veiled, turreted | Ear of barley; LA ΔΩ | *BMC Phoenicia* p. 113: 2

68. AE 3.35 16 72.A.1.261.3 L 135

111–112 C.E. Trajan

Trajan head r. laur.; AVTOK KAIC NEP TRAIANOC CEB ΓΕΡΜΑΝ | Tyche bust, veiled, turreted; ΔωΡΙ(?) ΡΟΕ | *BMC Phoenicia* p. 117: 33

69. AE 10.64 25 72.A.1.10.8 L 079 inventory only

Trajan head r. laur.; AVTOKP KAIC NEP TRAIANC CEB ΓΕΡΜ ΔΑΚ | Tyche standing on galley, holding standard and cornucopiae; ΔΑΦΝΑ..C.NL, ΔΟΡ? | *BMC Phoenicia* p. 117: 34ff var

70. AE 8.55 23 72.A.1.229.16 L 135 Plate 1

144/5 C.E. Antoninus Pius

Pius bust r. laur.; AVT KAI ANTωNEINOC CEBEY | Tyche head r. laur., aphlaston; ΔωΡ ΙΕΡΑC ΑΥΤΝΑΥ ΑΡΧΙC LCZ | *BMC Phoenicia* p. 118: 40

71. AE 8.63 25 72.A.1.193.16 L 105 inventory only

Paneas

4 B.C.E.–34 C.E. Herod Philip II

Augustus bust r. laur.; KAICAP CEBACT(Ω) | Tetrastyle temple?; ΦΙΛΙΠΠΟΥ ΤΕΤΡΑΡΧΟΥ | *RPC* 1: 4940–42; *TJC* p. 228: 97–99

72. AE 6.79 21 78. C.23.181.15 L 066

74/5 C.E. Domitian

Domitian head r. laur.; ΔΟ…KAICAP | Nike standing writing on shield; ΕΤΟΥ ΙΕ ΒΑCΙ ΑΓΡΙΠΠΑ | *RPC* 1: 2253; *TJC* p. 235: 141 (dated 75/6)

73. AE 4.81 21 72.A.1.298.2 L 143

70–75 C.E.

Domitian head r. laur. | Nike writing on shield | *RPC* 2: 2250–51, 2253, 2256, 2259, 2264; *TJC* pp. 234: 139; 235: 141, 144, 147; 236: 152

74. AE 6.45 19 72.A.1.238.28 L 114 date uncertain

75. 5.63* 23 72.A.2.1.1 L 090

76. 5.03 19 72.A.1.260.9 L 132

77. 4.81 20 72.A.1.296.2 L 143

83/4 C.E.

Domitian head r. laur.; ΔΟΜΕΤ ΚΑΙϹ ΓΕRΜΑΝ | Nike writing on shield; ΕΤΟ ΚΔ ΒΑ ΑΓΡΙΠΠ | *RPC* 1: 2264; *TJC* p. 236: 151 (dated 84/5)

78. AE 4.31 17 72.A.1.295.12 L 143

PALESTINE

GALILEE

SEPPHORIS

98–119 C.E. TRAJAN

Trajan bust r. laur.; ΤΡΑΙΑΝΟΣ ΑVΤΟ ΚΕ ΔΩΚΕΝ | Ears of barley; ΣΕΠΦΩ ΡΗΝΩΝ | *BMC Palestine* p. 3: 17–20

79. AE 2.27 16 72.A.1.298.3 L 143

Trajan bust r. laur.; ΤΡΑΙΑΝΟΣ ΑVΤΟΚΡΑΤΩΡ ΕΔΩΚΕΝ | Palm tree; ΣΕΠΦΩΡΗΝΩΝ | *BMC Palestine* p. 1–2: 5–11

80. AE 3.34 20 71.B.2.0.892 L 000 inventory only

Trajan bust r. laur.; TRAIANOΣ ΑVΤΟΚΡΑΤΩΡ ΕΔΩΚΕΝ | Caduceus; ΣΕΠΦΩΡΗΝΩΝ | *BMC Palestine* p. 2: 12–6

81. AE 4.53 20 76.C.5.95.2 L 111 inventory only

GADARA

214–215 C.E. CARACALLA

Caracalla bust r.; ΑVΤΚΑΙ ΑΝΤΟΝΕΙΝΟϹ | Tetrastyle temple, within Zeus enthroned; ΠΟΜ ΚϹVΤΑ ΓΑΔΑΡΕ ΗΟϹ | Spjikerman 1978: 146 no. 73

82. AE 11.44 26 76.A.5.272.5 L 037 inventory only

SAMARIA

CAESAREA MARITIMA

68 C.E. NERO

Nero bust r. laur.; ΝΕΡΩΝ ΚΑΙϹΑΡ ΣΕΒΑΣΤΟΣ | Standing Tyche holding bust and standard; ΚΑΙϹΑΡΙΑ Η ΠΡΟΣ ΣΕΒΑΣΤΣ ΩΙΜΕΝΙ ΛΙΔ | *RPC* 1: 4862

83. AE 10.72 23 79.L.1.149.128 L 050

84. 8.90 22 73.C.8.71.2 L 040 inventory only

85. 5.84 23 87.G.20.327.31 L 012 3 cm on rev: ΚΑΙ (7 × 6); male head r. (3 × 5); *GIC* 115

86. 7.29 19 72.A.4.35.1 L 017 diameter probable

87. 6.03* 23 72.A.1.7.11 L 078 cm on obv: Athena? in circular punch; diameter probable

71 C.E. *TITUS*

Titus head r. laur.; ΑΥΤΟΚΡ ΤΙΤΟΣ ΚΑΙΣΑΡ — Nike, foot on helmet, writing on shield set on palm tree; ΙΟΥΔΑΙΑΣ ΕΑΛΩΚΥΙΑΣ — *RPC* 2: 2311; *TJC* p. 265: 381–85

88. AE 8.05 21 71.A.2.201.458 L 074

72 C.E.

Titus head r. laur.; ΑΥΤΟΚΡ ΤΙΤΟΣ ΚΑΙCΑΡ — Captive bound beneath trophy; ΙΟΥΔΑΙΑΣ ΕΑΛΩΚΥΙΑΣ — *RPC* 2: 2313; *TJC* p. 265: 384–85

89. AE 11.07 24 72.A.1.229.15 L 135 inventory only

90. 72.A.1.229.17 L 135 inventory only

83–93 C.E. *DOMITIAN*

Domitian head r. laur.; IMP CAES DOMIT AVG GERM PM TRP XII — Nike advancing l. with wreath, trophy; IMP XXIII COS XVI CENS PPR — *RPC* 2: 2308; *TJC* p. 267: 395a (dated 93)

91. AE 9.46 25 72.A.1.296.1 L 143 cm on obv.: *GIC* 133 or 160; Plate 1

92. 7.65 25 72.A.1.229.1 L 135 cm on obv.: male head r., rectangular punch 6×4

Domitian head r. laur.; IMP… — Female advancing l. with wreath, trophy — *RPC* 2: 2306 or 2308; *TJC* p. 267: 393 or 395

93. AE 3.64 22 71.A.2.217.511 L 087 2 cms on obv.: *GIC* 135, 281; Plate 1 (obv.)

Domitian head r. — Uncertain

94. AE 8.74 23 87.G.23.16.2 L 008 cm on obv.: *GIC* 133; Plate 1 (obv.)

79–96 C.E. *UNCERTAIN FLAVIAN*

Bust r. — Tyche standing

95. AE 3.92 19 87.G.19.237.10 L 078

114–117 C.E. *TRAJAN*

Trajan bust r. laur.; IMP CAES NER TRAIANO OP AVG GER DAC COS VI PP — Trajan pouring libation over altar; COL PRI FL AVG CAESARENSIS — *BMC Palestine* p. 17–18: 42–48

96. AE 9.03 21 72.A.1.291.7 L 049 Plate 1 (rev.)

117–138 C.E. *HADRIAN*

Hadrian bust r. laur.; IMP TRA HADRIANO CAES AVG — Serapis bust r.; COLI FL AVG CAESARENS — *BMC Palestine* p. 19–20: 58–63

97. AE 11.69 22 72.A.1.291.1 L 143

Hadrian bust r. laur.; IMP TRA HADRIANOC AA — Apollo standing before altar and serpent; C I F AVG CAESAR — *BMC Palestine* p. 21: 69–75

98. AE 6.04 19 80.G.9.37.40 L 004

99. 4.03 19 79.K.1.78.54 L 013 Plate 1

98–138 C.E. TRAJAN OR HADRIAN

Hadrian bust r. laur.; ?IM TRA HADRIANOC AA — Lion walking r.?; C I F A C — *BMC Palestine* p. 21: 76–77

100. AE 2.25 11 72.A.1.152.2 L 104

Head r. — Animal r. — Hamburger 1956: 36–58

101. AE 1.43 11 72.A.1.261.4 L 135

Head r. — Boar r. — Hamburger 1956: 38, 40, 44–46

102. AE 0.77 9 72.A.1.233.13 L 142

103. AE 0.56 10 72.A.1.32.26 L 089

104. AE 0.52 8 72.A.1.238.27 L 114

Hercules head r. — Boar; SC — Hamburger 1956: 40

105. AE 0.77 9 72.A.3.166.57 L 058

Head r. — Goat? — Hamburger 1956: 41?

106. AE 1.50 15 72.A.1.1.3 L 034 inventory only

Head of Hercules? — Animal r. — Mint not certain

107. AE 0.82 8 79.L.1.14.11 L 004

Bust r. — Animal? — Mint not certain

108. AE 1.19 11 82.N.1.80.16 L 033 inventory only

109. 0.89 12 72.A.1.46.45 L 090

Uncertain — Animal? — Mint not certain

110. AE 0.52 12 72.A.1.74.8 L 109

161–189 C.E. AURELIUS

Aurelius head r.; AVRELIO ANTON AVG PF — Serapis head r.; COL PRIM FL AVG CAESAREA — *BMC Palestine* p. 22–23: 79–91

111. AE 12.11 24 72.A.2.282.1 L 208

161–189 C.E. AURELIUS OR VERUS

Head r. — Serapis head r.

112. AE 14.06 24 79.K.2.202.39 L 097

217–218 C.E. DIADUMENIANUS

Diadumenian head r. laur.; MOP DIADVMENIA CAE — Serapis head r.; COLI F AV F C CAESAR — *BMC Palestine* p. 26: 110–15

113. AE 7.17 20 74.C.16.92.62 L 045

114. 6.86 19 79.L.1.10.5 L 004 cm on rev.: standing female l.? in circular punch

115. 6.15 21 74.C.16.92.60 L 045

116. 5.32 20 74.C.16.100.1 L 048

117. 4.87 20 72.A.1.50.7 L 097

218–222 c.e. *Elagabalus*

Obverse	Reverse	Reference
Elagabalus head r. laur.; IMP CA.. V ANTON	Serapis head r.; COLI FLA..C CAES	*BMC Palestine* p. 27: 116–17

No.	Metal	Weight	Diam.	Registration	Locus	Notes
118.	AE	5.01	17	72.A.1.263.2	L 142	

117–222 c.e. *Uncertain Emperor*

Obverse	Reverse	Reference
Head r.	Serapis head r.	

No.	Metal	Weight	Diam.	Registration	Locus	Notes
119.	AE	9.82	23	74.C.16.92.54	L 045	
120.		7.13	21	74.C.16.92.57	L 045	
121.		6.60	18	80.C.27.20.3	L 005	
122.		6.48	19	72.A.2.109.9	L 129	
123.		6.10	18	73.C.8.92.2	L 046	
124.		4.37	23	74.C.16.92.63	L 045	
125.		4.10	16	72.A.2.79.11	L 097	

222–235 c.e. *Severus Alexander*

Obverse	Reverse	Reference
Severus Alexander head r. laur.	Eagle, SPQR in wreath	*BMC Palestine* p. 27–29: 118–37

No.	Metal	Weight	Diam.	Registration	Locus	Notes
126.	AE	14.82	31	80.C.30.36.74	L 026	
127.		12.52	24	78.G.8.97.13	L 010	
128.		10.37	20	76.H.7.52.1	L 022	inventory only
129.		9.39	20	72.A.1.285.6	L 042	
130.		9.31	22	72.B.2.128.1	L 096	
131.		7.67	23	78.C.23.181.17	L 066	
132.		7.07	20	80.E.42.80.1	L 000	Plate 1
133.		5.19	23	72.A.3.131.2	L 042	
134.		5.03	17	78.B.8.44.2	L 006	
135.		5.03*	17	74.H.1.65.1	L 024	
136.		4.90	20	80.G.9.0.148	L 000	
137.		4.14	19	72.B.2.14.4	L 060	
138.		3.57	17	87.C.42.104.80	L 000	
139.		3.31	17	79.K.2.106.6	L 012	

Obverse	Reverse	Reference
Severus Alexander head r.?	Uncertain	Mint not certain

No.	Metal	Weight	Diam.	Registration	Locus	Notes
140.	AE	10.23	24	79.L.1.61.74	L 021	

244/5 c.e. *Otacilia*

Obverse	Reverse	Reference
Otacilia head r.; OTAC SEVERA AVG	Eagle supporting wreath enclosing Tyche bust; SC	Combination not recorded

No.	Metal	Weight	Diam.	Registration	Locus	Notes
141.	AE	23.10	29	74.C.16.100.3	L 031	Plate 1

247–249 c.e. *Philip II*

Obverse	Reverse	Reference
Philip II head r. laur.; ..PHILIPVS PF AVG	Dionysos riding a panther; COL PRI… AVF C CAES..	*BMC Palestine* p. 29: 138–39 var

No.	Metal	Weight	Diam.	Registration	Locus	Notes
142.	AE	14.25	30	80.G.9.40.34	L 012	rev. not previously paired with obv.

Obverse				Reverse		Reference
Philip II head r. rad.; ....NECNIVSPHILIP..				Seated Minerva hands victoriola to Philip; ...LAVG MET		Rosenberger 1972–77: III no. 108
143. AE	24.71	28		74.C.12.54.1 L 021	Plate 1	

249–250 C.E. *DECIUS*

Obverse				Reverse		Reference
Decius head r. rad.; IMP C G MES Q T R A DEC				Tyche standing foot on prow, with bust, spear; river god beneath; COL PR FL AVG CAES METROP		*BMC Palestine* p. 32: 150–51
144. AE	6.28	20		74.H.4.89.6 L 054		
145.	5.55	20		72.A.1.61.8 L 101		
Decius head r.; IMP C G MES Q T R				Tyche head r.; COL P F AVF C CAES METRP		*BMC Palestine* p. 34: 166
146. AE	5.83	18		71.X.0.0.7 L 000		
Decius head r. rad.; ...TRAIANVS DECIUS AVG				Tyche head r.; uncertain inscription		*BMC Palestine* p. 34: 167
147. AE	3.63*	19		72.A.1.219.2 L 142		
Decius head r.? (or Herrenius Etruscus?)				Roma? seated holding Nike		Rosenberger 1972–77: II pp. 19–25, nos. 122, 145
148. AE	16.74	27		80.C.25.146.25 L 072		
149.	8.41*	26		79.L.1.24.20 L 010		

249–250 C.E. *HOSTILIAN*

Obverse				Reverse		Reference
Hostilian head r. rad.; HOSTILIANVS QVINTOC				Serapis standing r.; COL PF AVG...TRP		*BMC Palestine* p. 37: 189–90
150. AE	8.30	20		72.A.1.85.54 L 095		

250–251 C.E. *HERENNIUS ETRUSCUS*

Obverse				Reverse		Reference
Herennius head r. rad.; MES Q EREN ETRVSCO DECIO CAES				Tyche head r.; ...COL F AV F C CAES METRP		*BMC Palestine* p. 36–37: 183–88
151. AE	6.79	20		72.C.3.46.1 L 019		
152.	6.31	20		72.A.1.244.31 L 115	(types not certain)	
153.	5.19	20		76.H.7.14.1 L 003	inventory only	
154.	4.46	18		74.C.16.92.56 L 045		

66–256 C.E. *MINT NOT CERTAIN*

Obverse				Reverse		Reference
Head r.				Uncertain		
155. AE	12.20	25		72.A.4.24.4 L 010	cm on obv.: *GIC* 133 (first century?)	
156.	12.20	24		75.PA.4.1.1 L 002	inventory only; Domitian? head r.; cm obv.: prob. *GIC* 133	
157.	10.97	21		73.C.8.71.1 L 040	cm on obv.: prob. *GIC* 133 (first century?) Plate 1 (obv.)	
158.	10.00	22		72.A.1.233.6 L 142	cm on obv.: *GIC* 133 (first century?)	
159.	8.71	24		72.A.1.265.6 L 042	cm on obv.: *GIC* 133 (first century?)	

160. 8.48 23 71.X.0.0.1 L 000 cm on obv.: *GIC* 133 (first century?)
161. 8.37 24 72.A.1.0.6 L 104 cm on obv.: *GIC* 133 (first century?); Plate 1 (obv.)
162. 7.95 24 72.A.1.285.7 L 042 cm on obv.: *GIC* 133 (first century?); Plate 1 (obv.)
163. 5.82 20 72.A.1.60.2 L 101 two cms on obv.: *GIC* 135, 409? (first century?)
164. 10.70 24 72.A.2.292.5 L 148
165. 6.25 18 72.A.1.219.3 L 142
166. 2.48* 18 80.C.25.147.38 L 075

Uncertain — Tyche standing on prow?
167. AE 3.34* 21 72.A.1.295.26 L 143

Head r. — Figure at altar
168. AE 2.85 17 79.L.1.106.107 L 021

Uncertain — Uncertain
169. AE 3.46 19 72.A.1.296.9 L 143

200–256 C.E. *Mint not certain*

Head r. — Tyche bust r.
170. AE 3.94 19 75.PS.6.6.3 L 007 inventory only

Head r. — Serapis head r.?
171. AE 6.07 19 71.X.0.0.3 L 000
172. 4.19 17 71.A.1.225.15 L 000 inventory only

Head r. — Uncertain
173. AE 11.55 26 72.B.3.48.3 L 017
174. 10.64 24 80.G.8.468.12 L 100

Tyche head r. — Galley — Hamburger 1956: 59ff
175. AE 1.00 11 72.A.1.233.21 L 142
176. 0.45 10 75.PA.2.21 L 003 inventory only
177. 0.36 10 74.B.3.36.1 L 212

222–256 C.E.

Head r. — Eagle in wreath
178. AE 6.43 23 72.A.1.74.6 L 109

Head r. — Eagle, SPQR
179. AE 4.53 22 72.A.1.50.9 L 097
180. 4.28 21 71.A.2.174.406 L 084

Head r. — Tyche head r.
181. AE 3.63 19 72.A.1.219.2 L 142

Head r. — Two eagles, addorced
182. AE 3.75 19 72.A.2.267.1 L 121

183.			3.45	20	78.C.23.183.19	L 066
184.			2.25	15	78.C.21.228.28	L 055

Radiate head r. — Serapis bust r.? — Mint not certain

185.	AE		5.17	18	71.B.2.114.800	L 066

Neapolis

238–240 C.E. *Philip I*

Philip I head r. rad.; IMP C MI IVL PHILIPPO PF AVG — Mt. Gerazim supported by eagle; COL IVL NEAPOL — *BMC Palestine* p. 63: 117

186.	AE		11.85	27	79.K.1.157.147	L 055

Judaea

Jerusalem

103–76 B.C.E. *Alexander Jannaeus*

Anchor; ΑΛΕΧΑΝΔΡΟΥ ΒΑΣΙΛΕΩΣ — Wheel, diadem or star; הדבתן המלך' — *TJC* p. 209: K

187.	AE	prutah	1.15	14	72.A.1.117.5	L 103
188.			0.58	13	74.C.16.73.2	L 099
189.			0.56	12	72.A.4.39.2	L 013

103–58 B.C.E. *Hasmonean*

Uncertain — Uncertain

190.	AE	prutah	2.22	17	84.G.18.237.169	L 046
191.			2.08	15	80.G.9.78.46	L 020
192.			0.77	15	84.G.18.264.187	L 060

40–4 B.C.E. *Herod the Great*

Double cornucopiae and caduceus — Anchor; ΒΑCΙΛΕ ΗΡωΔΟΥ — *RPC* 1: 4910; *TJC* p. 222: 59

193.	AE	prutah	1.92	16	80.G.7.220.38	L 126
194.			1.67	17	78.G.6.14.3	L 010
195.			1.51	16	72.A.1.321.6	L 143
196.			1.45	14	78.G.6.14.1	L 010
197.			1.41	17	80.C.28.92.12	L 016
198.			1.37	16	80.G.7.177.24	L 106
199.			1.36	15	80.G.9.279.118	L 057
200.			1.29	16	78.G.6.141.29	L 078
201.			1.23	15	80.G.7.198.32	L 116
202.			1.17	15	79.L.1.156.130	L 055
203.			1.11	14	84.G.18.311.287	L 073
204.			1.08	14	72.A.1.90.6	L 115
205.			1.04	15	80.G.7.139.19	L 082
206.			1.04	14	80.G.7.218.37	L 122
207.			0.93	13	78.G.5.214.17	L 047

208. 0.47 11 80.G.8.436.6 L 041

4 B.C.E.–6 C.E. *Herod Archelaus*

Double cornucopiae, caduceus; ΕΘΝΑΡΧ Anchor; ΗΡωΔΟΥ *RPC* 1: 4912; *TJC* p. 224: 67

209. AE prutah 1.12 15 84.G.18.186.62 L 046

Anchor in wreath; ΗΡωΔΟΥ ΕΘΝΑΡΧΟΥ in wreath *RPC* 1: 4913; *TJC* p. 224: 69

210. AE prutah 1.27 15 74.H.4.3.2 L 002
211. 1.19 14 80.G.9.371.183 L 084
212. 1.01 14 80.G.9.336.173 L 005
213. 0.48 12 72.C.2.156.3 L 318
214. 0.38 11 78.G.6.56.13 L 038

Double cornucopiae; ΗΡωΔΗϹ Galley; ΕΘΝΑΡΧΗ(.) *RPC* 1: 4914–15; *TJC* p. 224: 70

215. AE prutah 1.66 15 72.A.1.321.9 L 143
216. 1.45 14 74.B.6.81.1 L 033
217. 0.99 14 78.G.7.91.10 L 051
218. 0.80 15 80.G.9.320.165 L 005

Prow l.; ΗΡω ΕΘΝ in wreath *RPC* 1: 4916; *TJC* p. 225: 72

219. AE prutah 1.43 15 82.G.9.457.3 L 112 inventory only
220. 1.38 15 78.G.6.73.19 L 052
221. 1.33 15 78.G.5.110.4 L 042
222. 1.25 15 78.G.6.115.26 L 070
223. 1.23 14 76.A.6.84.1 L 026 inventory only
224. 1.06 14 80.C.26.309.31 L 094
225. 1.04 13 72.A.1.57.9 L 052
226. 0.85 14 80.G.9.371.182 retrograde letters L 084
227. 0.83 14 80.G.14.321.242 L 122
228. 0.78 13 80.C.26.219.19 retrograde letters L 094

Bunch of grapes; ΗΡωΔΟΥ Helmet; ΕΘΝΑΡΧΟΥ *RPC* 1: 4917; *TJC* p. 226: 73

229. AE prutah 2.36 17 80.C.26.309.30 L 094 inventory only
230. 2.23 17 78.G.6.81.21 L 000
231. 2.04 16 82.G.9.427.1 L 101 inventory only
232. 1.99 17 78.G.6.73.18 L 052 inventory only
233. 1.90 17 78.G.6.44.9 L 028
234. 1.79 17 72.C.2.152.2 L 314
235. 1.64 16 80.G.9.296.137 L 067
236. 1.49 16 78.B.8.48.3 L 000
237. 1.32 16 78.G.6.63.15 L 045
238. 1.30 18 78.G.6.63.16 L 045
239. 0.82 13 82.C.31.3.1 L 001 inventory only

6 C.E. AUGUSTUS (COPONIUS)

Ear of barley; KAICAPOC			Palm tree; LΛς		*RPC* 1: 4954; *TJC* p. 256: 311
240. AE prutah	2.21	17	82.G.14.220.84 L 091	inventory only	
241.	0.65*	17	71.X.0.0.2 L 000		

9 C.E. (AMBIBULUS)

Ear of barley; KAICAPOC			Palm tree; LΛΘ		*RPC* 1: 4955; *TJC* p. 256: 313
242. AE prutah	1.63	17	78.G.6.104.25 L 062		
243.	1.46	16	78.G.7.88.9 L 051		
244.	1.40	17	80.G.9.371.179 L 084		

10 C.E.

Ear of barley; KAICAPOC			Palm tree; LM(.)		*RPC* 1: 4956–57 *TJC* p. 256: 313–15
245. AE prutah	0.83*	13	80.G.9.339.175 L 005		

11 C.E.

Ear of barley; KAICAPOC			Palm tree; LMA		*RPC* 1: 4957; *TJC* p. 256: 315
246. AE prutah	1.68	16	72.A.1.271.3 L 148		

6–9 C.E. (COPONIUS OR AMBIBULUS)

Ear of barley; KAICAPOC			Palm tree; LΛ.		*RPC* 1: 4954–55 *TJC* p. 256: 311–15a
247. AE prutah	1.94	17	80.G.9.279.127 L 057		
248.	1.13	15	82.G.14.198.82 L 085	inventory only	

6–12 C.E. (COPONIUS OR AMBIBULUS)

Ear of barley; KAICAPOC			Palm tree; L..		*RPC* 1: 4954–57 *TJC* p. 256: 311–15a
249. AE prutah	2.81	18	72.A.1.322.3 L 143		
250.	2.15	17	76.C.19.112.3 L 078	inventory only	
251.	1.79	18	82.G.14.323.245 L 123	inventory only	
252.	1.43	17	71.A.2.194.450 L 068		
253.	1.35	16	72.A.2.166.13 L 160		

15 C.E. TIBERIUS (GRATUS)

IOYΛIA in wreath			Laurel branch; LB		*RPC* 1: 4959; *TJC* p. 256: 316
254. AE prutah	1.40*	18	80.G.9.336.172 L 005		

16. C.E.

KAICAP in wreath			Double cornucopiae, caduceus; TIBEPIOY LΓ		*RPC* 1: 4960; *TJC* p. 257: 320
255. AE prutah	1.84	15	76.A.6.297.2 L 115	inventory only	
256.	1.44	16	80.G.9.336.171 L 005		

16 C.E.

Obverse				Reverse		Reference
ΙΟΥΛΙΑ in wreath				Three lilies; LΓ		*RPC* 1: 4961; *TJC* p. 257: 321
257.	AE prutah	1.58	17	80.G.9.368.178 L 081		
258.		1.54	17	74.C.17.45.2 L 035		

17 C.E.

Obverse				Reverse		Reference
Vine branch with grapes; TIBEPIOY				Amphora; LΔ		*RPC* 1: 4962; *TJC* p. 257: 326
259.	AE prutah	1.89	16	82.G.14.61.38 L 030	inventory only	

17–24 C.E.

Obverse				Reverse		Reference
TIB KAICAP in wreath				Palm branch; ΙΟΥΛΙΑ L.		*RPC* 1: 4964–66 *TJC* pp. 257: 327–258: 329c
260.	AE prutah	2.61	17	80.G.9.347.176 L 005		
261.		2.11	16	73.C.9.0.4 L 045		
262.		1.62	16	74.B.3.4.25 L 201		
263.		1.43	15	72.C.2.74.1 L 256		

18 C.E.

Obverse				Reverse		Reference
TIB KAICAP in wreath				Palm branch; ΙΟΥΛΙΑ LE		*RPC* 1: 4965; *TJC* p. 257: 328
264.	AE prutah	2.25	15	72.A.1.261.5 L 135		
265.		1.87	16	72.A.2.233.2 L 167		
266.		1.53	15	80.G.7.172.23 L 103		
267.		1.53	15	72.A.1.7.5 L 078		

24 C.E.

Obverse				Reverse		Reference
TIB KAICAP in wreath				Palm branch; ΙΟΥΛΙΑ LIA		*RPC* 1: 4966; *TJC* p. 258: 329
268.	AE prutah	2.06	16	78.C.22.209.20 L 159		

29 C.E. *(Pilate)*

Obverse				Reverse		Reference
Simpulum; TIBEPOY KAICAPOC LIϛ				Three ears of barley; ΙΟΥΛΙΑ KAICAPOC		*RPC* 1: 4967; *TJC* p. 258: 331
269.	AE prutah	2.00	15	76.A.5.55.2 L 020		
270.		1.74	20	80.C.26.39.3 L 001		
271.		1.54	16	87.G.24.26.4 L 015		

30 C.E.

Obverse				Reverse		Reference
Lituus; TIBEPIOY KAICAPOC				LIZ in wreath		*RPC* 1: 4968; *TJC* p. 258: 333
272.	AE prutah	2.12	15	76.C.20.3.1 L 003	inventory only	
273.		1.65	15	72.C.2.172.1 L 336		
274.		1.45	21	84.C.20.140.20 L 000		
275.		1.37	17	74.H.4.80.2 L 050		
276.		1.36	14	78.G.99.0.2 L 000		

31 C.E.

Lituus; ΤΙΒΕΡΙΟΥ ΚΑΙCΑΡΟC					LIH in wreath			*RPC* 1: 4969; *TJC* p. 258: 334
277.	AE	prutah	2.11	15	76.C.5.87.1	L 102	inventory only	

30–31 C.E.

Lituus; ΤΙΒΕΡΙΟΥ ΚΑΙCΑΡΟC					LI. in wreath			*RPC* 1: 4968-69 *TJC* p. 258: 333–35d
278.	AE	prutah	2.47*	17	80.G.9.297.141	L 068		
279.			2.42	17	74.H.4.65.16	L 045		
280.			2.14*	17	84.C.20.130.18	L 045		
281.			2.13	17	80.C.27.31.4	L 014		
282.			2.08	18	78.G.5.186.11	L 054		
283.			2.01	15	80.C.29.21.2	L 006		
284.			1.54*	15	80.C.21.1216.10	L 137		
285.			1.46	15	72.A.2.165.12	L 158		
286.			0.99*	15	80.G.8.438.7	L 109		

41–42 C.E. *AGRIPPA I*

Canopy; ΒΑCΙΛΕωS ΑΓΡΙΠΠΑ					Three ears of barley; Lς			*RPC* 1: 4981; *TJC* p. 231: 120
287.	AE	prutah	3.30	19	80.G.8.462.9	L 111		
288.			2.61	18	84.G.18.146.51	L 037		
289.			2.51	17	74.H.4.97.10	L 060		
290.			2.44	17	74.H.5.17.1	L 007		
291.			2.14	17	71.A.1.109.162	L 025		
292.			2.07	16	74.H.4.48.37	L 031		
293.			2.00	16	72.A.2.178.2	L 073		
294.			1.98	17	72.A.2.178.1	L 073		
295.			1.95	16	74.H.5.26.1	L 007		
296.			1.90	20	80.C.26.308.29	L 094		
297.			1.91	16	73.C.7.18.1	L 013		
298.			1.84	16	82.G.14.83.47	L 004	inventory only	
299.			1.77	17	74.C.8.0.1	L 081		
300.			1.74	17	76.H.7.36.1	L 015	inventory only	
301.			1.72	14	72.A.2.264.3	L 039		
302.			1.72	18	76.C.19.115.4	L 080	inventory only	
303.			1.71	17	74.H.4.76.4	L 041	Plate 1	
304.			1.68	15	71.A.1.0.240	L 000		
305.			1.67	16	76.H.6.17.5	L 012		
306.			1.63	16	82.G.14.330.246	L 087	inventory only	
307.			1.53	14	72.A.3.186.2	L 062		
308.			1.52	17	78.G.8.200.18	L 040	inventory only	
309.			1.49	18	74.H.4.75.5	L 041		
310.			0.71	12	72.A.2.161.11	L 146		

54 c.e. *Claudius (Antonius Felix)*

ΙΟΥΛΙΑ ΑΓΡΙΠΠΙΝΑ in wreath					Two palm branches, crossed; LIΔ TI ΚΛΑVΔΙΟϹ ΚΑΙϹΑΡ ΓΕRΜ		*RPC* 1: 4970 *TJC* p. 259: 342
311.	AE	prutah	2.37	17	76.E.3.56.2 L 054	inventory only	
312.			2.04	16	80.G.8.466.11 L 100		
313.			1.34	17	72.A.1.268.14 L 143		
314.			1.25	17	71.A.2.198.453 L 072		

59 c.e. *Nero (Festus)*

ΝΕΡωΝΟϹ in wreath					Palm branch; ΚΑΙϹΑΡΟϹ LE		*RPC* 1: 4972, *TJC* p. 260: 345
315.	AE	prutah	2.89	15	72.A.1.273.4 L 149		
316.			2.47	18	72.A.1.7.18 L 078		
317.			2.18	16	71.A.2.202.465 L 074		
318.			2.04	17	71.A.1.27.14 L 013	Plate 1	
319.			2.04	17	71.A.1.224.14 L 013	inventory only	
320.			2.04	17	71.A.2.175.396 L 058		
321.			1.94	15	72.A.1.268.15 L 143		
322.			1.94	15	72.A.1.322.1 L 143		
323.			1.72	17	74.H.4.75.4 L 041		
324.			1.64	15	72.A.1.273.2 L 149		
325.			1.61	16	72.A.1.296.11 L 143		
326.			1.60	15	72.A.1.300.11 L 143		
327.			1.59	15	2.A.1.296.13 L 143		
328.			1.57	15	72.A.1.301.13 L 143		
329.			1.50*	16	72.A.1.295.22 L 143		
330.			1.45	15	72.A.1.296.12 L 143		
331.			1.43	15	72.A.1.301.12 L 143		
332.			1.38	15	72.A.1.272.8 L 135		
333.			1.36	17	72.A.1.295.16 L 143		
334.			1.28	16	71.A.2.201.459 L 074		
335.			1.27	15	72.A.1.272.9 L 135		
336.			1.09	15	72.SP.2.1.4 L 003		
337.			1.01	16	72.A.1.273.3 L 149		
338.			0.94*	15	72.A.1.248.6 L 143		
339.			0.65*	15	72.A.1.322.2 L 143		
340.			0.52*	12	80.C.28.53.5 L 030		
341.			0.37*	13	72.A.1.270.5 L 149		

5–58 c.e. *Uncertain Procurator*

342.	AE	prutah	2.08	15	72.C.4.21.1 L 018	
343.			1.61	16	82.G.14.173.58 L 009	inventory only
344.			1.56	17	74.C.12.94.2 L 097	
345.			1.11	15	80.C.29.56.4 L 023	

346. 0.76* 15 78.G.6.57.31 L 041

67 C.E. *JEWISH WAR*

Amphora; שנת שת'ם — Vine leaf; חדות ע'ון — *TJC* pp. 241: 196–247: 199

347. AE 3.06 18 75.PA.2.2.2 L 003 inventory only

69 C.E.

Chalice; לגאלת צ'ון — Lulav, 2 ethrogs; שנתאדכע — *TJC* p. 243: 214

348. AE 3.92 20 80.G.8.479.17 L 100 inventory only

249–250 C.E. *DECIUS*

Decius head r. rad.; ...DECIVS AVG — COL AEL KAP COMM P F in wreath — *BMC Palestine* p. 100: 102

349. AE 12.04 27 84.G.18.43.4 L 001

249–250 C.E. *HOSTILIAN*

Hostilian bust r. rad.; G VALOST MES QVINTVS — She-wolf and suckling twins, legionary eagle; COLA EL...PF — *BMC Palestine* p. 102: 111

350. AE 12.61 26 72.A.1.74.1 L 109

351. 8.39 25 72.A.2.226.1 L 177

ASCALON

72/3 C.E.

Tyche bust r. — Galley; AC, date: ϛoP — *BMC Palestine* p. 112: 46

352. AE 3.46 15 72.A.1.277.1 L 149

150/1–218/9 C.E.

Head r. — Temple with four doorways — *BMC Palestine* p. 129: 191

353. AE 11.97 27 80.G.10.169.20 L 056

GAZA

132–133 C.E. *HADRIAN*

Hadrian head laur. r.; A KATP AΔPIANCE — Herakles standing facing; ΓA A ΔEΠ II•• — *BMC Palestine* p. 151: 49

354. AE 4.15 12 72.A.1.57.12 L 102

NABATAEA

16 C.E.? *ARETAS IV*

Jugate busts of Aretas and Shaquilat — Cornucopiae crossed, wreath; — Schmitt-Korte 1990: 122, no. 77

355. AE 2.71 17 72.A.1.261.2 L 135

Arabia

Bostra

222–235 C.E. Severus Alexander

Obverse	Reverse	Reference
Bust of Severus Alexander r. laur.; IMP CAES M AVR SEVE ALEXANDER PF AVG	Bust of Tyche l.; COLONIA BOSTRA	Kindler 1983: 118, no. 36

No.	Metal	Weight	Diam.	Reg. no.	Locus	Note
356.	AE as	5.33	21	84.G.18.140.46	L 032	

Egypt

Alexandria

113/4 C.E. Trajan

Obverse	Reverse	Reference
Trajan head r. laur.	Hemhem crown; LIZ	*BMC Alexandria* p. 68: 561

No.	Metal	Weight	Diam.	Reg. no.	Locus	Note
357.	AE	1.46	14	72.A.1.265.11	L 042	
358.		1.11	12	72.A.1.296.4	L 143	Plate 2
359.		0.86	11	72.A.1.221.4	L 143	inventory only
360.		0.45	10	71.A.2.151.550	L 031	
361.		0.36	9	72.A.1.271.4	L 148	
362.		0.15*	8	71.A.2.160.563	L 054	

117–135 C.E. Hadrian

Obverse	Reverse	Reference
Hadrian head r. laur.	Cornucopiae; L..	*BMC Alexandria* p. 104: 895–97

No.	Metal	Weight	Diam.	Reg. no.	Locus	Note
363.	AE	4.60	9	72.A.1.74.3	L 109	

Obverse	Reverse	Reference
Hadrian head r. laur.	Hemhem crown; I LI	*BMC Alexandria* p. 105: 902

No.	Metal	Weight	Diam.	Reg. no.	Locus	Note
364.	AE	1.46	14	71.B.2.123.896	L 070	

Obverse	Reverse	Reference
Hadrian head r. laur.	Oenochoe; LΔE	*BMC Alexandria* p. 105: 913

No.	Metal	Weight	Diam.	Reg. no.	Locus	Note
365.	AE	2.08	13	72.A.1.285.9	L 402	

Obverse	Reverse	Reference
Hadrian head r. laur.	Ibis r.	Hamburger 1956: 82–84

No.	Metal	Weight	Diam.	Reg. no.	Locus	Note
366.	AE	0.54	13	72.A.1.229.3	L 135	

Obverse	Reverse	Reference
Hadrian head r. laur.	Three ears of wheat	Hamburger 1956: 89–90

No.	Metal	Weight	Diam.	Reg. no.	Locus	Note
367.	AE	0.41	10	80.G.8.442.8	L 112	

Obverse	Reverse	Reference
Hadrian head r.; AVT KAIC TRAIAN AΔPIANOC CEB	Ptah standing facing; LΔωΔE KATOV	*BMC Alexandria* p. 76: 637

No.	Metal	Weight	Diam.	Reg. no.	Locus	Note
368.	AE	0.97	10	72.B.3.32.1	L 007	inventory only

150–200 C.E.

Obverse	Reverse	Reference
Bust of Herakles?	Wolf?	Hamburger 1956: 55–58

No.	Metal	Weight	Diam.	Reg. no.	Locus	Note
369.	AE	0.54	7	72.A.2.103.8	L 134	

1–300 C.E.

Obverse	Reverse	Reference
Ibis	Crocodile l.	Milne 1933: 5254–55

No.	Metal	Weight	Diam.	Reg. no.	Locus	Note
370.	AE	0.52	10	72.A.1.46.65	L 090	

Bust r.?				Three ears of wheat		Milne 1933: 5265–66
371.	AE	1.12	12	72.A.1.233.10 L 142		
Uncertain				Uncertain		
372.	AE	0.82	10	72.A.1.269.1 L 042		

200–300 C.E.

Head r.?				Hemhem crown		Hamburger 1956: 103
373.	AE	0.67	10	72.A.1.74.4 L 109		

AXUMITE KINGS

330–358 C.E.

Bust r.; BACIΛEUC				Cross; TOYTO APECH TH XωPA		Munro-Hay 1995: 141 no. 51–52
374.	AE	0.31	9	72.A.1.46.25 L 090	Plate 2	

400–450 C.E.

Bust r.; BASI ΛEVS				Cross in circle; TOYTΩ APECH TH XωPA		Hahn 1983: 166 no. 33
375.	AE	0.43	11	78.C.21.595.97 L 078		
376.		0.42	11	80.G.9.27.28 L 005		
377.		0.28	10	78.C.21.416.66 L 078		
378.		0.21	11	74.C.13.128.1 L 116		
379.		0.21	9	72.B.1.119.14 L 096		
380.		0.12	9	80.C.21.1449.93 L 159		
381.		0.09	9	80.C.21.1449.53 L 159		
Uncertain				Cross		Hahn 1983: 166 no. 33, 167 no. 36, 172 no. 43, 174 no. 47, 175 no. 53, 177 nos. 59, 61
382.	AE	0.35	10	84.G.18.202.98 L 051		

UNCERTAIN MINT

300–200 B.C.E. *PTOLEMAIC*

Zeus head r.				Eagle standing on thunderbolt		
383.	AE	6.36	19	72.C.2.131.2 L 297		
Zeus(?) head r.				Uncertain		
384.	AE	6.64	18	80.G.8.471.13 L 118		

300–100 B.C.E. *AUTONOMOUS CITY*

Zeus(?) head r.				Standing figure		
385.	AE	4.32	17	72.A.1.265.10 L 042		
Zeus(?) head r.				Uncertain		
386.	AE	3.12	16	72.A.1.261.1 L 135		

280–40 B.C.E. *Uncertain Seleucid*

Obverse				Reverse	
Uncertain				Uncertain	
387.	AE	2.40	10	72.A.1.203.1 L 087	
388.		2.32	13	78.G.6.75.17 L 050	
389.		2.23	13	72.A.1.299.10 L 143	
390.		2.11	16	82.G.13.316.16 L 079	inventory only
391.		2.05	13	72.A.1.298.7 L 143	
392.		1.88	11	72.A.2.287.2 L 223	
393.		1.57	15	80.G.8.488.19 L 119	
394.		1.34	10	72.A.2.117.10 L 141	
395.		1.18	10	87.G.20.359.35 L 039	
396.		0.93	10	78.G.6.119.27 L 070	
397.		0.56	13	78.G.8.108.15 L 011	

81–96 C.E. *Uncertain Domitianic*

Obverse				Reverse	
Domitian bust r.				Uncertain	
398.	AE	14.16	28	78.C.24.22.8 L 007	cm over face of emperor, type obscure (4×3) Plate 2 (obv.)
399.		4.11	18	71.A.2.178.409 L 092	cm on obv.: *GIC* 135; Plate 2 (obv.)

100 B.C.E.–256 C.E. *Autonomous City*

Obverse				Reverse	
Uncertain				Tyche bust r.	
400.	AE	0.76	11	72.A.1.201.10 L 135	
Tyche? bust				Standing figure? (mint in Phoenicia?)	
401.	AE	4.25	19	72.A.1.0.1bis L 142	
Bust r.				Standing figure?	
402.	AE	0.81*	9	72.A.1.240.26 L 135	
Animal?				...NωN?	
403.	AE	0.94	15	72.A.1.0.1 L 142	
Trajan? bust r.				Uncertain	
404.	AE	3.28	20	71.B.2.23.33 L 013	
Trajan? bust r.				Standing figure?	
405.	AE	6.28	29	71.A.1.132.206 L 060	
Bust r.				Standing figure	
406.	AE	5.16	28	72.A.2.197.2 L 114	
Bust r.				Tetrastyle temple	
407.	AE	20.03	35	72.A.4.90.3 L 044	
408.		3.95	20	76.A.6.292.2 L 127	inventory only

Bust r.				Uncertain	
409. AE	12.98	28	80.G.9.32.32	L 005	
410.	9.59	20	80.C.21.1186.9	L 141	
411.	7.86*	25	76.C.19.29.1	L 024	
412.	7.45	18	76.H.7.3.3	L 002	inventory only
413.	7.24	20	74.B.5.224.1	L 166	
414.	6.84	18	82.G.13.180.13	L 003	inventory only
415.	4.73	20	79.L.1.70.86	L 021	
416.	4.37*	23	74.C.16.92.55	L 045	
417.	4.33	17	76.H.7.5.5	L 003	inventory only
418.	4.30	15	76.A.5.117.1	L 023	inventory only
419.	4.15	18	72.A.1.0.9	L 142	
420.	4.13	17	76.H.7.2.2	L 001	inventory only
421.	1.78	14	72.A.3.174.186	L 058	
422.	0.70	8	72.A.3.174.278	L 058	
Radiate bust r.				Uncertain (third century C.E.)	
423. AE	16.63	28	72.A.1.74.2	L 109	
424.	2.15	23	72.A.1.51.1	L 085	
Bust r.				Uncertain (third century C.E.)	
425. AE	4.27	18	72.B.2.31.1	L 060	
426.	3.38	21	84.G.18.196.85	L 046	*antoninianus*?
427.	0.64*	15	79.L.1.56.61	L 022	
Gallienus bust r.?				Standing figure (253–256 C.E.?)	
428. AE	2.74	19	72.A.2.77.3	L 121	
Uncertain				Uncertain	
429. AE	4.75	23	73.C.8.23.1	L 016	
430.	4.54	22	80.G.8.466.10	L 100	
431.	2.98	18	80.G.7.164.20	L 090	
432.	1.60*	20	71.B.2.67.216	L 034	
433.	0.34	10	72.A.1.1.37	L 034	

Roman Imperial Coinage

Hadrian

121–122 C.E.

Rome

Hadrian head l. laur.; IMP CAESAR TRAIANVS HADRIANVS AVG | Minerva dropping incense on burner; PM TRP COS III SC | *RIC* 2 p. 42: 61, 1a

434. AE Sest 19.01 22 87.G.20.36.5 L 006

134–135 C.E.

Hadrian head r. laur.; HADRIANVS AVG COS III PP | Aegyptos reclining; AEGYPTOS SC | *RIC* 2 p. 446: 839

435. AE Aes/Dup 8.60 25 74.C.8.244.3 L 181

Sabina

117–135 C.E.

Rome

Sabina head r. diad.; SABINA AVGVSTA HADRIANI AVG PP | Venus standing; VENERI GENETRICI SC | *RIC* 2 p. 477: 1035

436. AE Sest 21.45 29 76.H.7.14.2 L 012 inventory only

Diva Faustina

141 C.E.

Rome

Faustina head r. | Concordia; DIV FAVSTINA | *RIC* 3 p. 72: 381–82?

437. AE Dup 8.42 24 78.G.99.0.9 L 000 Mint uncertain

Divus Aurelius (Commodus)

181 C.E.?

Rome

Aurelius head r.; DIVVS M ANTONINVS PIVS | Eagle standing by altar; CONSECRATIO SC | *RIC* 3 p. 441: 657

438. AE Sest 15.94 30 74.C.16.73.8 L 037

Maximinus I

235–238 C.E.

Rome

Maximinus head r. laur.; IMP MAXIMINVS PIVS AVG | Salus seated feeding serpent; SALVS AVGVSTI SC | *RIC* 4.2 p. 145: 64

439. AE Sest 18.13 29 84.G.18.235.168 L 046

MAXIMUS

236–238 C.E.

ROME

Maximus head r.; MAXIMVS CAES GERM | Maximus standing l.; PRINCIPI IVVENTVTIS SC | *RIC* 4.2 p. 156: 13

440. AE Sest 18.93 30 80.G.9.90.51 L 018

GORDIAN III

240 C.E.

ROME

Gordian III head r. laur.; IMP GORDIANVS PIVS FEL AVG | Sol standing; AETERNITATI AVG SC | *RIC* 4.3 p. 48: 297b

441. AE Aes 8.95 23 78.G.99.0.3 L 000

PHILIP I

244–246 C.E.

ROME

Philip I head r. laur.; IMP M IVL PHILIPPVS AVG | Annona standing l.; ANNONA AVGG SC | *RIC* 4.3 p. 90: 168a

442. AE Sest 16.68 27 74.C.11.16.1 L 016 inventory only

as above; IMP PHILIPPVS AVG | *RIC* 4.3 p. 90: 168d

443. AE Sest 17.98 29 84.G.18.196.83 L 046 Plate 2

GALLIENUS JOINT REIGN

254–255 C.E.

UNCERTAIN WESTERN MINT

Gallienus head r. laur.? | Soldier standing l. with shield, spear; VIRTVS AVGG

444. AE Sest 12.20* 33 84.G.18.126.28 L 032 Rome or Mediolanum

255–259 C.E.

"ASIA"

Gallienus head r. rad. cuir.; IMP CP LIC GALLIENVS PF AVG | 2 emperors standing, *, wreath; VIRTVS AVGG | *RIC* 5.1 p. 104: 456

445. Bi Ant 3.73 20 72.A.1.120.7 L 107

Gallienus head r. rad.; IMP CP LIC GALLIENVS PF AVG | Roma seated, emperor standing *, wreath; ROMAE AETERNAE | *RIC* 5.1 p. 103: 449

446. Bi Ant 3.40 21 76.H.7.1.2 L 001 inventory only

Gallienus sole reign

257–267 c.e.

"Asia"

Obverse	Reverse	Reference
Gallienus head r. rad.; GALLIENVS AVG	Soldier standing with shield, spear; VIRTVS AVG	*RIC* 5.1 p. 189: 668

447. Bi Ant 2.88 21 76.H.7.10.5 L 004 inventory only

266/7 c.e.

Obverse	Reverse	Reference
Gallienus head r. rad.; GALLIENVS AVG	Emperor sacrificing at tripod; PIETAS AVG VIIC	*RIC* 5.1 p. 186: 618

448. Bi Ant 5.28 28 72.B.2.61.8 L 074

Obverse	Reverse	Reference
Gallienus head r. rad.; GALLIENVS AVG	Fortuna standing l.; FORTVNA REDUX VIIC	*RIC* 5.1 p. 185: 613

449. Bi Ant 3.35 21 72.A.1.46.39 L 090 Plate 2

267–268 c.e.

Obverse	Reverse	Reference
Gallienus head r. rad.; GALLIENVS AVG	Sol standing l.; SOLI INVICTO	*RIC* 5.1 p. 185: 611 or 189: 658

450. Bi Ant 2.82 22 72.A.1.120.8 L 107

Salonius as Caesar

256 c.e.

Antioch

Obverse	Reverse	Reference
Saloninus head r. rad.; SALON VALERIANVS NOB CAES	Spes, emperor standing; SPES PVBLICA	*RIC* 5.1 p. 127: 36

451. Bi Ant 2.94 21 74.H.4.255.3 L 151 Plate 2

Salonina

255–258 c.e.

"Asia"

Obverse	Reverse	Reference
Salonina head r. diademed, on crescent; CORN SALONINA AVG	Emperor and empress, standing; CONCORDIA AVGG	*RIC* 5.1 p. 114: 63

452. Bi Ant 2.76 20 75.PW.1.0.4 L 009 inventory only

Claudius Gothicus

268–270 c.e.

Antioch

Obverse	Reverse	Reference
Claudius head r. rad.; IMP C CLAVDIVS AVG	Aequitas standing; AEQVITAS AVG	*RIC* 5.1 p. 228: 197

453. Bi Ant 2.88 21 84.G.18.4.1 L 001

Obverse	Reverse	Reference
Claudius head r. rad.; IMP C CLAVDIVS AVG	Sol standing l.; SOL AVG, no dot in exergue	*RIC* 5.1 p. 230: 221

454. Bi Ant 3.39 21 74.H.4.4.5 L 003

			dot in exergue		
455. Bi Ant	3.57	21	71.A.1.142.217 L 063		

Obverse			Reverse		Reference
Claudius head l. rad.; IMP C CLAVDIVS AVG			Jupiter, Juno standing; CONSER AVG, no mintmark		Alföldi 1938: 58 no. 5
456. Bi Ant	3.27	21	84.G.18.204.102 L 051	Plate 2	

Aurelian

270–275 C.E.

Antioch

Obverse			Reverse		Reference
Aurelian head r. rad.; IMP C AVRELIANVS AVG			Vabalathus bust r. laur.; VABALATHVS VCRIMDR, unc. officina		*RIC* 5.1 p. 308: 381
457. Bi Ant	3.50*	21	74.C.10.230.1 L 136	(pierced)	
458.	3.09	21	80.C.25.153.30 L 087	off.: Γ	
459.	2.60	20	76.H.7.5.7 L 003	inventory only; unc. off.	

Obverse			Reverse		Reference
Aurelian head r. rad.; IMP C AVRELIANVS AVG			Emperor, woman presenting wreath; RESTITVT ORBIS		*RIC* 5.1 p. 308: 386
460. Bi Ant	2.47	23	79.K.1.79.49 L 023		

Tripolis

Obverse			Reverse		Reference
Aurelian head l. rad.; IMP C AVRELIANVS AVG			Sol and captive; SOLI INVICTO, * in field only		*RIC* 5.1 p. 309: 390
461. Bi Ant	3.10	21	84.G.18.215.113 L 054		

Uncertain mint

Obverse			Reverse		Reference
Aurelian head r. rad.			Emperor, woman presenting wreath; RESTITVT ORBIS		
462. Bi Ant	2.65*	23	72.A.1.50.6 L 097		

Probus

276–280 C.E.

Antioch

Obverse			Reverse		Reference
Probus head r. rad.; IMP C M AVR PROBVS PF AVG			Jupiter and emperor standing; CLEMENTIA TEMP		*RIC* 5.2 p. 120: 922
463. Bi Ant	3.84	22	79.L.1.41.47 L 004	B/XXI	
464.	3.43	23	80.C.29.112.13 L 064	Δ•/XXI	

281–282 C.E.

Siscia?

Obverse			Reverse		Reference
Aurelian head r. rad.; IMP C PROBVS PF AVG			Emperor, woman presenting wreath; RESTITVT ORBIS		*RIC* 5.2 p. 96: 733
465. Bi Ant	3.10	21	72.A.1.106.5 L 097	A?/XXI	

Carinus

282–283 C.E.

Antioch

Obverse	Reverse	Reference
Carinus head r. rad.; IMP CM AVR CARINVS PF AVG	Jupiter and emperor standing; VIRTVS AVGG	*RIC* 5.2 p. 179: 325

No.	Metal	Denom.	Wt.	Diam.	Inv.	Locus	Notes
466.	Bi	Ant	3.42	21	84.G.18.187.69	L 048	E?/XXI

Diocletian

284 C.E.

Antioch

Obverse	Reverse	Reference
Diocletian head r. rad.; IMP CC VAL DIOCLETIANVS PF AVG	Jupiter and emperor standing; IOVI CONSERVATORI AVG	*RIC* 5.2 p. 256: 324

No.	Metal	Denom.	Wt.	Diam.	Inv.	Locus	Notes
467.	Bi	Ant	3.53	21	84.G.18.187.71	L 048	unc. mintmark

285 C.E.

Obverse	Reverse	Reference
Diocletian head r. rad.; IMP CC VAL DIOCLETIANVS PF AVG	Jupiter and Hercules standing; IOV ET HERCV CONSER AVGG	*RIC* 5.2 p. 256: 323

No.	Metal	Denom.	Wt.	Diam.	Inv.	Locus	Notes
468.	Bi	Ant	3.14	23	76.H.6.36.1	L 027	Γ/XXI; inventory only

284 C.E.

Tripolis

Obverse	Reverse	Reference
Diocletian head r. rad.; IMP CC VAL DIOCLETIANVS PF AVG	Jupiter and Hercules standing; IOVI CONSERVATORI AVG	*RIC* 5.2 p. 257: 328

No.	Metal	Denom.	Wt.	Diam.	Inv.	Locus	Notes
469.	Bi	Ant	3.90	22	84.G.18.187.68	L 048	TR/XXI

295–296 C.E.

Cyzicus

Obverse	Reverse	Reference
Diocletian head r. rad.; IMP CC VAL DIOCLETIANVS PF AVG	Jupiter and emperor standing; CONCORDIA MILITVM	*RIC* 6 p. 531–32: 13 or 21

No.	Metal	Denom.	Wt.	Diam.	Inv.	Locus	Notes
470.	AE	Rad Frac	2.27	22	84.G.18.207.107	L 051	KΔ; inventory only
471.			1.76	22	72.A.1.38.50	L 085	KΓ; *RIC* 6 p. 581: 15a

300 C.E.

Alexandria

Obverse	Reverse	Reference
Diocletian head r. rad.; IMP CC VAL DIOCLETIANVS PF AVG	Genius standing holding patera; GENIO POPVLI ROMANI XXI	*RIC* 6 p. 665: 30a

No.	Metal	Denom.	Wt.	Diam.	Inv.	Locus	Notes
472.	AE	Fol	8.40	26	76.H.6.10.1	L 008	Δ/ALE; inventory only

Maximianus as Caesar

285–286 C.E.

Uncertain mint

Obverse	Reverse	Reference
Maximian head r. rad.; GAL VAL MAXIMIANVS NOB CAES	Jupiter and emperor standing; CONCORDIA MILITVM	

No.	Metal	Denom.	Wt.	Diam.	Inv.	Locus	Notes
473.	Bi	Ant	2.14	22	72.B.3.141.2	L 020	

MAXIMIANUS AS AUGUSTUS

292–295 C.E.

HERACLEIA

Maximianus head r. rad.; IMP CMA MAXIMIANVS PF AVG | Jupiter and emperor standing; CONCORDIA MILITVM | *RIC* 5.2 p. 289: 595

474. Bi Ant 4.21 22 84.G.18.187.70 L 048 ΗΓ•XXI•

295–296 C.E.

Maximianus head r. rad.; IMP CMA MAXIMIANVS PF AVG | Jupiter and emperor standing; CONCORDIA MILITVM | *RIC* 6 p. 581: 15b

475. AE Rad Frac 1.12* 19 74.H.4.249.1 L 109 ΚΔ

293 C.E.

CYZICUS

Maximianus head r. rad.; IMP CMAV MAXIMIANVS PF AVG | Jupiter and emperor standing; CONCORDIA MIILITVM | *RIC* 5.2 p. 291: 607 var

476. Bi Ant 3.60 21 84.G.18.197.86 L 046 Є/XXI•

300–301 C.E.

ANTIOCH

Maximianus head r. laur.; IMP CMA MAXIMIANVS PF AVG | Genius standing holding patera; GENIO POPVLI ROMANI | *RIC* 6 p. 620: 54b

477. AE Fol 11.11 28 72.A.4.0.8 L 002 ΚΓ V/ANT

296–297 C.E.

ALEXANDRIA

Maximianus head r. rad.; IMP CMA MAXIMIANVS PF AVG | Jupiter and emperor standing; CONCORDIA MILITVM | *RIC* 6 p. 667: 46b

478. AE Frac 2.02 20 72.A.1.46.7 L 090 B/ALE; Plate 2

308 C.E.

Maximianus head r. laur., hand raised; DN MAXIMIANO BAEATISSIM | Providentia and Quies standing; PROVIDENTIA DEORVM | *RIC* 6 p. 676: 86

479. AE Frac 2.54 21 74.B.5.6.1 L 031 Γ/ALE

286–311 C.E.

UNCERTAIN MINT

Maximianus head r. rad. | Uncertain

480. AE Rad Frac 2.17* 24 74.C.17.0.1 L 000

Carausius

287–290 C.E.

Britain

Carausius head r. rad.; IMP CARAVSIVS PF AVG | Sol standing l., captive to l.; ORIENS AVG | *RIC* 5.2 p. 534: 869

481. Bi Ant 4.24 23 87.G.19.205.8 L 060

Maxentius

307 C.E.

Aquileia

Maxentius head r. rad.; IMP C MAXENTIVS PF INV AVG | Roma and emperor in tetrastyle temple; CONSER VRB SVAE | *RIC* 6 p. 325: 113

482. AE Rad Fol 5.50 25 74.C.8.249.5 L 086 /AQΓ

Maximinus as Caesar

308–310 C.E.

Thessalonica

Maximinus head r. laur.; MAXIMINVS FIL AVGG | Genius standing; GENIO CAESARIS | *RIC* 6 p. 514: 32a

483. AE Fol 5.17 25 72.A.3.194.1 L 064 Δ/SMTS

Maximinus as Augustus

310–313 C.E.

Siscia

Maximinus head r. laur.; IMP MAXIMINVS PF AVG | Genius standing holding patera; GENIO AVGVSTI | *RIC* 6 p. 480: 207c

484. AE Fol 4.07 25 72.A.1.112.10 L 097 Є/SIS

Heracleia

Maximinus head r. laur.; IMP C GAL VAL MAXIMINO PF INV AVG | Genius standing holding patera; GENIO IMPERATORIS | *RIC* 6 p. 537: 49a

485. AE Fol 4.50 25 72.A.1.106.6 L 097 HTΔ

310 C.E.

Uncertain mint

Maximinus head r. laur. | Genius standing holding patera; GENIO AVGVSTI

486. AE Fol 1.10* 19 72.A.1.102.22 L 097

Constantine I as Augustus

312–313 C.E. ruling with Licinius

Rome

Constantine head r. laur.; IMP CONSTANTINVS PF AVG — Sol standing; SOLI INVICTO COMITI — *RIC* 6 p. 388: 323a

487. AE Fol 2.46 21 80.G.9.52.41 L 004 /RP

Uncertain mint

Constantine head r. laur. — Sol standing; SOLI INVICTO COMITI

488. AE Fol 2.48 19 82.G.14.184.75 mintmark unclear; inventory only

313 C.E. as sole ruler

Rome

Constantine head r. laur.; IMP CONSTANTINVS PF AVG — Sol standing; SOLI INVICTO COMITI — *RIC* 7 p. 296: 2

489. AE Fol 2.72* 21 80.C.26.218.20 L 093 R|F/RS

490. 2.17* 20 84.G.18.268.222 L 061 R|F/RQ; *RIC* 7 p. 296: 2–4

Ticinum

Constantine head r. laur.; CONSTANTINVS PF AVG — Sol standing; SOLI INVICTO COMITI — *RIC* 7 p. 360: 3

491. AE Fol 2.46 22 72.A.1.50.8 L 097 /PT

313–314 C.E.

Uncertain mint

Constantine head r. laur. — Sol standing; SOL INVICTO COMITI

492. AE Fol 1.25* 20 72.A.1.106.3 L 097 mintmark unclear

314 C.E.

Rome

Constantine head r. laur.; IMP CONSTANTINVS PF AVG — Sol standing; SOL INVICTO COMITI — *RIC* 7 p. 298: 19

493. AE Fol 2.11 20 74.C.17.58.4 L 049 R|F/R*T

314–315 C.E.

Rome

Constantine head r. laur.; IMP CONSTANTINVS PF AVG — Sol standing; SOLI INVICTO COMITI — *RIC* 7 p. 299: 27

494. AE Fol 2.28 21 80.G.9.38.36 L 005 RX|F/RS

316 C.E.

Arles

Constantine head r. laur.; IMP CONSTANTINVS PF AVG | Sol standing; SOLI INVICTO COMITI | *RIC* 7 p. 243: 102

495. AE Fol 1.98* 20 74.C.8.130.1 L 081 unc off.

317 C.E.

Rome

Constantine head r. laur.; IMP CONSTANTINVS PF AVG | Sol standing; SOL INVICTO COMITI | *RIC* 7 p. 306: 78

496. AE Fol 1.96 29 82.G.14.44.29 L 030 A/RP; inventory only

Aquileia

Constantine head r. laur.; IMP CONSTANTINVS PF AVG | Sol standing; SOL INVICTO COMITI | *RIC* 7 p. 392–93: 3–5

497. AE Fol 1.50 17 79.L.1.46.51 L 004 /AQP

322–323 C.E.

Arles

Constantine head r. laur.; CONSTANTINVS AVG | VOT XX in wreath; DN CONSTANTINI MAX AVG | *RIC* 7 p. 261: 252

498. AE Fol 2.96 20 84.G.18.216.117 L 054 /P*AR; inventory only

499. 2.68 19 72.A.3.168.308 L 063

Licinius

314 C.E.

Rome

Licinius head r. laur.; IMP LICINIVS PF AVG | Sol standing; SOLI INVICTO COMITI | *RIC* 7 p. 298: 22

500. AE Fol 2.83 20 72.A.1.103.20 L 122 R|F/R*T

314–315 C.E.

Licinius head r. laur.; IMP LICINIVS PF AVG | Sol standing; SOLI INVICTO COMITI | *RIC* 7 p. 299: 29, 31

501. AE Fol 2.27 21 80.G.9.25.15 L 001 RX|F/F/RT

320 C.E.

Thessalonica

Licinius head r. laur.; IMP LICINIVS AVG | VOT XX in wreath; DN LIC LICINI AVGVSTI | *RIC* 7 p. 510: 102

502. AE Fol 3.00 19 76.C.18.137.1 L 151 /TSAVI; inventory only

321–324 C.E.

NICOMEDIA

Licinius head r. rad.; IMP C VAL LINCIN LICINIVS PF AVG | Jupiter and captive; IOVI CONSERVATORI | *RIC* 7 p. 607: 44

503. AE Fol 3.31 20 84.G.18.216.120 L 054 X II /SMNA

504. 2.95 19 78.G.5.64.1 L 027

CRISPUS CAESAR

317–322 C.E.

LYON

Crispus head l. laur.; DN CRISPO NOB CAES | VOT X in wreath; CAESARVM NOSTRORVM | *RIC* 7 p. 136: 223

505. AE Fol 2.35 18 74.C.10.126.1 L 036 •I•/•PLGC•

321 C.E.

ROME

Crispus head r. laur.; CRISPVS NOB CAES | VOT X in wreath; CAESARVM NOSTRORVM | *RIC* 7 p. 321: 239

506. AE Fol 2.13 18 87.G.20.174.15 L 031 /RT; inventory only

320 C.E.

AQUILEIA

Crispus bust r., shield, cuir.; CRISPVS NOB CAES | Captive and standard; VIRTVS EXERCIT | *RIC* 7 53: 63 var

507. AE Fol 2.31 18 82.G.13.135.8 L 001 /AQT; inventory only

321–322 C.E.

ALEXANDRIA

Crispus head r. laur.; DN FL IVL CRISPVS NOB CAES | Jupiter and Nike; IOVI CONSERVATORI | *RIC* 7 p. 708: 29

508. AE Fol 2.71 20 72.A.1.85.50 L 095 I XII N /SMAL.

UNCERTAIN EMPEROR, UNCERTAIN MINT

294–305 C.E.

Laureate bust r. | Uncertain

509. AE Fol 4.01 24 74.B.7.9.4 L 009

250–300 C.E.

UNCERTAIN WESTERN MINT

Radiate bust r. | Fides standing, 2 standards; .....AVG

510. AE Barb Rad 1.45* 14 80.G.9.114.55 L 005

Uncertain Emperor, western mint

257–300 C.E.

Radiate bust r. — Woman presenting wreath to emperor; RESTITVTOR ORBIS

511. Bi Ant (broken) 78.E.5.137.89 L 116

Late Roman Coins (all bronzes, except no. 899)

Constantine I ruling alone, 324–337 C.E.

Thessalonica — VOT XX in wreath; DN CONSTANTINI MAX AVG — *RIC* 7 p. 513: 123

512. AE Fol 324 3.17 20 72.A.1.285.1 L 042; Plate 2 — Off: TSAVI

Heracleia — GLORIA EXERCITVS; two soldiers, two standards — *RIC* 7 p. 557: 111

513. AE Fol 330–335 2.05 19 72.A.1.265.9 L 042

Constantinople — GLORIA EXERCITVS • two soldiers, one standard — *RIC* 7 p. 590: 149

514. AE Fol 336–337 0.48* 14 72.C.2.165.1 L 329 — Off: Δ

Nicomedia — PROVIDENTIAE AVGG; Camp gate — *RIC* 7 p. 615: 90

515. AE Fol 324–325 2.20 18 82.G.14.41.9 L 026; inventory only — Off: A

Antioch — GLORIA EXERCITVS; two soldiers, two standards — *RIC* 7 p. 693: 86

516. AE Fol 330–335 2.29 16 71.A.1.114.183 L 050 — Off: B (1), unc. (1)

517. 1.95 18 80.G.9.28.18 L 001

GLORIA EXERCITVS; two soldiers, one standard — *RIC* 7 p. 697: 108

518. AE Fol 335–337 1.50 15 79.K.2.165.28 L 074 — Off: A (1), H (1), unc. (2)

519. 1.42 16 74.B.3.3.2 L 201

520. 1.36 16 74.B.6.104.1 L 052

521. 0.86 14 72.A.1.265.12 L 042

Uncertain mint — GLORIA EXERTICVS; two soldiers, two standards

522. AE Fol 330–335 1.53 17 74.B.5.0.3 L 098

523. frag. 15 72.A.1.46.61 L 090

Constantine I posthumous

Lyon? — AETERNA PIETAS; emperor holding spear, globe — *RIC* 8 p. 178: 10–12?

524. AE Fol 337–341 1.41 14 84.G.18.268.230 L 061; inventory only

CONSTANTINOPLE				Quadriga r.			*RIC* 8 p. 450: 39
525.	AE	Fol	337–341	1.70	17	74.H.3.106.8 L 033	
				VN MR; emperor standing, veiled			*RIC* 8 p. 453: 68
526.	AE	Fol	347–348	frag.	17	72.C.4.114.1 L 114	
NICOMEDIA				GLORIA EXERCITVS; two soldiers, one standard			*RIC* 8 p. 471: 9
527.	AE	Fol	337–340	1.27	18	87.G.20.170.12 L 030	
ANTIOCH				Quadriga r.			*RIC* 8 p. 515: 39
528.	AE	Fol	337–340	1.23	14	82. G.14.42.10 L 027; inventory only	Off: A, Θ
529.				1.08	15	72.A.1.37.22 L 085a	
				VN MR; emperor standing, veiled			*RIC* 8 p. 521: 112
530.	AE	Fol	347–348	1.04	15	72.A.3.174.246 L 058	Off: A
				VN MR; emperor standing, veiled			*RIC* 8 p. 521: 117
531.	AE	Fol	347–348	1.51	14	80.G.9.27.20 L 005	Off: A
				VOT XX MVLT XXX in wreath			*RIC* 8 p. 521: 118
532.	AE	Fol	347–348	1.29	15	84.G.18.268.242 L 061	Off: ΔI
533.				1.00	16	84.G.18.267.212 L 061	
534.				frag.	14	72.B.1.8.6 L 080	
ALEXANDRIA				Quadriga r.			*RIC* 8 p. 539: 12
535.	AE	Fol	337–340	1.64	15	74.H.3.170.4 L 334; Plate 2	Off: Γ
				VN MR; emperor standing, veiled			*RIC* 8 p. 541: 32
536.	AE	Fol	347–348	1.61	16	74.C.14.68.4 L 062	Off: A
				VN MR; emperor standing, veiled			*RIC* 8 p. 541: 35
537.	AE	Fol	347–348	1.11	15	80.G.10.165.21 L 055	Off: A•
UNCERTAIN MINT				AETERNA PIETAS; emperor holding spear, globe			
538.	AE	Fol	337–341	2.01	15	72.A.3.168.254 L 063; inventory only	
539.				1.47	14	72.A.1.285.14 L 042	
				VOTA XX MVLT XXX in wreath			
540.	AE	Fol	341–346	frag.	13	87.G.20.311.29 L 012	
				Quadriga r.			
541.	AE	Fol	337–347	1.24	16	72.A.1.238.9 L 114	
542.				0.88	14	72.A.1.238.23 L 114	
543.				0.86*	16	78.C.22.149.9 L 133	
544.				0.69*	19	74.H.3.106.10 L 033	
545.				0.25*	11	78.C.21.652.224 L 097	
546.				frag.	14	87.G.22.61.3 L 053	

VICTORIAE DD AVGGQ NN; two victories

547. AE Fol 347–348 1.70 14 72.A.3.175.284 L 063

548. 1.55 13 72.A.3.162.104 L 060

549. 1.52 14 79.L.1.23.17 L 004

550. 1.33 14 72.A.3.161.55 L 059

VN MR; standing emperor, veiled

551. AE Fol 347–348 1.36 15 84.G.18.305.283 L 066

552. 1.22 15 72.A.2.103.2 L 134

553. 1.13 15 74.H.3.123.15 (poss.) L 307

VOT XX MVLT XXX in wreath

554. AE Fol 347–348 1.76 17 82.G.14.75.41 L 009; inventory only

555. 1.54 13 72.A.3.176.358 L 063

556. 1.17 15 72.A.1.85.14 L 095

557. 1.09 14 72.A.1.238.8 L 114

558. 0.56 15 78.C.22.224.21 L 164

559. frag.* 17 72.A.1.46.15 L 090

560. frag. 13 78.C.21.416.61 L 078

Urbs Roma

Constantinople — Wolf and twins — *RIC* 7 p. 579: 62

561. AE Fol 330–333 2.40 15 80.G.9.273.104 L 056 — Off: IA, E

562. 2.11 18 80.G.9.270.103 L 001

563. frag. 18 71.B.1.94.3 L 022

Cyzicus — GLORIA EXERCITVS; two soldiers, one standard — *LRBC* I: 1271

564. AE Fol 336–337 1.13 19 80.G.9.27.19 L 005 — Off: A

Antioch — Wolf and twins — *RIC* 7 p. 693: 91

565. AE Fol 330–337 0.85 14 76.H.6.27.4 L 018; inventory only — Off: Θ

Constantinopolis

Cyzicus — Victory on prow l. — *RIC* 7 p. 657: 108

566. AE Fol 332–335 1.71 14 84.G.17.55.14 L 003 — Off: B?

Uncertain mint — Victory on prow

567. AE Fol 330–335 2.14 16 72.A.3.176.357 L 063

568. 1.00 13 72.A.3.156.5 L 051

GLORIA EXERCITVS; two soldiers, one standard

569. AE Fol 335–341 1.57 15 78.G.99.0.4 L 000

Constantine II as Caesar

Cyzicus				GLORIA EXERCITVS; two soldiers, two standards	*RIC* 7 p. 655: 80–83
570.	AE	Fol	331–334	2.39 19 74.C.14.68.3 L 062	Off: Δ

Constantius II as Caesar

Heracleia				GLORIA EXERCITVS; two soldiers, two standards	*RIC* 7 p. 558: 117
571.	AE	Fol	330–333	2.03 18 71.B.1.128.20 L 016	Off: Δ
572.				1.77 18 76.H.6.26.2 L 015; inventory only	
Constantinople				GLORIA EXERCITVS; two soldiers, one standard	*RIC* 8 p. 449: 28
573.	AE	Fol	330	frag. 16 72.A.1.285.3 L 042	
				GLORIA EXERCITVS; two soldiers, two standards	*RIC* 7 p. 579: 61
574.	AE	Fol	330–335	2.27 16 80.C.26.196.18 L 059	Off: A
				GLORIA EXERCITVS • two soldiers, one standard	*RIC* 7 p. 590: 151
575.	AE	Fol	336–337	1.67 16 72.A.1.85.32 L 095	Off: B, Δ
576.				1.67 14 72.C.4.114.3 L 114	
Cyzicus				GLORIA EXERCITVS; two soldiers, one standard	*RIC* 7 p. 659: 139–41
577.	AE	Fol	336–337	1.37 15 76.H.6.5.2 L 005; inventory only	Off: Γ
Antioch				GLORIA EXERCITVS; two soldiers, two standards	*RIC* 7 p. 693: 88
578.	AE	Fol	330–335	1.84 20 72.A.1.85.49 L 095	Off: E, Z
579.				2.29 17 71.A.1.114.183 L 050; Plate 2	
				VOT XX MVLT XXX in wreath	*RIC* 8 p. 521: 113
580.	AE	Fol	341–346	1.83 15 80.G.10.68.3 L 010	Off: AI
Alexandria				GLORIA EXERCITVS; two soldiers, two standards	*RIC* 7 p. 633: 188
581.	AE	Fol	333–335	2.62 16 84.G.17.86.27 L 033	Off: B
582.				2.02 15 72.A.4.66.2 L 012	

Constantius II as Augustus

Arles				FEL TEMP REPARATIO; Virtus spearing horseman FH3 (raising arms)	*RIC* 8 p. 219: 215
583.	AE	AE3	353–355	1.52 18 80.G.9.317.162 L 005	Off: Γ
Rome				SECVRITAS REIPVB; victory left	*RIC* 8 p. 249: 6–7
584.	AE	AE3	337–340	1.07 16 72.A.3.174.168 L 058	

				VICTORIAE DD AVGGQ NN; two victories	*RIC* 8 p. 253: 79
585.	AE	Fol	347–348	1.26 15 71.A.1.103.107 L 023	Off: R? T
586.				1.19 16 80.G.9.90.50 L 018	
				FEL TEMP REPARATIO; Virtus spearing horseman FH3 (raising arms)	*RIC* 8 p. 274: 272
587.	AE	AE3	352–355	2.24 18 79.K.1.45.34 L 002; obv. reads PF AVG DN CONSTANTIVS	Off: Q
AQUILEIA				VICTORIAE DD AVGGQ NN; two victories	*RIC* 8 p. 322: 76, 78, 80, 82, 84, 86, 88, 90;
588.	AE	Fol	347–348	0.59 13 72.A.1.285.2 L 042	Off: P
				FEL TEMP REPARATIO; Virtus spearing horseman FH3 (raising arms)	*RIC* 8 p. 334: 199
589.	AE	AE3	352–355	2.32 17 72.A.1.85.20 L 095	Off: P (2)
590.				1.54* 17 84.C.20.82.8 L 059	
THESSALONICA				FEL TEMP REPARATIO; Virtus spearing horseman FH4 (clutching neck)	*RIC* 8 p. 421: 211
591.	AE	AE3	355–361	2.44 15 72.A.1.85.27 L 095	Off: A
				SPES REIPVBLICE; Virtus holding globe and spear	*RIC* 8 p. 422: 213
592.	AE	AE4	355–361	2.23 13 87.G.21.110.5 L 041; Plate 2	Off: A, B
593.				1.66 16 75.PS.6.0.2 L 000; inventory only	
594.				1.21 16 79.K.1.45.29 L 002	
HERCLEIA				GLORIA EXERCITVS; two soldiers, one standard	*RIC* 8 p. 431: 22
595.	AE	Fol	337–340	1.64 16 72.A.1.0.78 L 096	Off: A
				FEL TEMP REPARATIO; Virtus spearing horseman FH3 (raising arms)	*RIC* 8 p. 436: 82
596.	AE	AE3	351–355	1.74 18 72.A.1.46.71 L 090	Off: E
				FEL TEMP REPARATIO; Virtus spearing horseman FH3 (raising arms)	*RIC* 8 p. 436: 86
597.	AE	AE2	351–355	3.65 19 80.G.9.28.17 L 001	Off: B
				FEL TEMP REPARATIO; Virtus spearing horseman FH3 (raising arms)	*RIC* 8 p. 436: 90
598.	AE	AE3	351–355	3.20 18 72.A.3.157.2 L 010	Off: B
				FEL TEMP REPARATIO; Virtus spearing horseman FH3 (raising arms)	
599.	AE	AE3	351–361	4.56 19 87.G.20.56.8 L 006	
CONSTANTINOPLE				FEL TEMP REPARATIO; Virtus spearing horseman FH4 (clutching neck)	*RIC* 8 p. 456: 106
600.	AE	AE2	351–355	4.91 23 79.K.1.150.102 L 052	

				FEL TEMP REPARATIO; Virtus spearing horseman FH4 (clutching neck)	*RIC* 8 p. 457: 116
601.	AE	AE2	351–355	2.65 19 79.K.1.150.91 L 052	Off: A
				FEL TEMP REPARATIO; Virtus spearing horseman FH3 (raising arms)	*RIC* 8 p. 458: 1185 Off: A, E,Θ
602.	AE	AE3	351–355	3.32 17 79.L.1.67.81 L 021	
603.				2.32 17 84.G.12.142.13 L 011	
604.				2.03 13 84.G.18.271.255 L 061	
605.				1.39 15 72.A.3.176.361 L 063	
				FEL TEMP REPARATIO; Virtus spearing horseman FH3 (raising arms)	*RIC* 8 p. 458: 121 Off: Z
606.	AE	AE3	351–355	1.74 17 79.K.1.110.61 L 032	
NICOMEDIA				VOT XX MVLT XXX in wreath	*RIC* 8 p. 474: 49
607.	AE	Fol	347–348	frag. 15 72.A.1.209.4 L 142	
				FEL TEMP REPARATIO; Emperor, 2 captives	*RIC* 8 p. 476: 71
608.	AE	AE2	347–348	– – 82.G.14.164.53 L 009; inventory only	Off: E
				FEL TEMP REPARATIO; Virtus spearing horseman FH3 (raising arms)	*RIC* 8 p. 479: 96
609.	AE	AE3	351–355	2.09 15 72.A.1.85.53 L 095; inventory only	
				FEL TEMP REPARATIO; Virtus spearing horseman FH3 (raising arms)	
610.	AE	AE3	351–361	1.69* 16 84.G.18.271.256 L 061	Off: A
				SPES REIPVBLICE; Virtus holding globe and spear	*RIC* 8 p. 482: 112
611.	AE	AE4	355–361	1.71 15 79.K.1.78.52 L 013	Off: A
CYZICUS				GLORIA EXERCITVS; two soldiers, one standard	*RIC* 8 p. 490: 16
612.	AE	Fol	337–340	1.24 11 74.B.1.112.1 L 571	Off: Δ
				GLORIA EXERCITVS; two soldiers, one standard	*RIC* 8 p. 491: 21
613.	AE	Fol	337–340	0.96 14 76.H.6.21.3 L 012; inventory only	Off: E•
				VOT XX MVLT XXX in wreath	*RIC* 8 pp. 493: 47–49, 494: 55–56, 58, 60, 63;
614.	AE	Fol	347–348	frag, 18 72.A.1.85.48 L 095	Off: Γ
				VOT XX MVLT XXX in wreath	*RIC* 8 p. 493: 48
615.	AE	Fol	347–348	1.43 17 74.C.14.27.3 L 000	Off: A
				FEL TEMP REPARATIO; Virtus spearing horseman FH3 (raising arms)	*RIC* 8 p. 496: 89
616.	AE	AE2	347–348	5.82 21 72.A.1.263.1 L 142	

No.	Metal	Denom.	Date	Description / Data	Reference
				FEL TEMP REPARATIO; Virtus spearing horseman FH3 (raising arms)	*RIC* 8 p. 497: 92
617.	AE	AE2	351–354	5.46 20 72.A.4.54.1 L 033	Off: A
				FEL TEMP REPARATIO; Virtus spearing horseman FH3 (raising arms)	*RIC* 8 p. 498: 104
618.	AE	AE3	351–361	2.10 18 79.K.1.0.149 L 016	Off: A
				FEL TEMP REPARATIO; Virtus spearing horseman FH3 (raising arms)	*RIC* 8 p. 499: 115
619.	AE	AE3	351–354	2.02 17 74.C.10.154.1 L 053	Off: B
				SPES REIPVBLICE; Virtus holding globe and spear	*RIC* 8 p. 499: 119
620.	AE	AE4	355–361	1.68 17 72.A.1.85.4 L 095	Off: Δ
Antioch				GLORIA EXERCITVS; two soldiers, one standard	*RIC* 8 p. 515: 40
621.	AE	Fol	337–340	1.15 16 80.G.9.23.13 L 003	Off: E
				GLORA EXERCITVS; two soldiers, one standard	*RIC* 8 p. 515: 44–46, 49, 52, 54;
622.	AE	Fol	337–341	1.39 15 82.G.14.173.60 L 009; inventory only	Off: AI
				GLORIA EXERCITVS; two soldiers, one standard	*RIC* 8 p. 515: 49
623.	AE	Fol	337–340	1.03* 16 78.G.5.115.3 L 025	Off: A
				GLORIA EXERCITVS; two soldiers, one standard	*RIC* 8 p. 515: 54
624.	AE	Fol	337–340	0.88 11 78.C.23.170.13 L 060	Off: EI
				VOT XX MVLT XXX in wreath	*RIC* 8 p. 521: 113
625.	AE	Fol	350–355	1.71 16 72.A.1.269.2 L 042	Off: A, E
626.				1.70 14 74.C.10.69.23 L 021	
627.				1.00* 16 74.C.10.218.7 L 125	
628.				0.81* 15 84.G.18.219.138 L 054	
				FEL TEMP REPARATIO; Virtus spearing horseman FH4 (clutching neck)	*RIC* 8 p. 522: 123 Off: Z
629.	AE	AE3	348–350	5.30 25 72.A.2.9.2 L 098	
				FEL TEMP REPARATIO; Virtus spearing horseman FH4 (clutching neck)	*RIC* 8 p. 524: 155 Off: Γ
630.	AE	AE3	347–348	2.00 17 72.B.3.247.3 L 085	
				FEL TEMP REPARATIO; Virtus spearing horseman	*RIC* 8 p. 524: 155 or p. 528: 188
631.	AE	AE3	347–361	2.19 16 79.L.1.39.45 L 004	Off: A (2)
632.				1.91 15 87.G.20.164.11 L 030	
633.				1.75 15 74.C.10.204.1 L 115	
				FEL TEMP REPARATIO; Virtus spearing horseman FH4 (clutching neck)	*RIC* 8 p. 523: 135 Off: B
634.	AE	AE3	350–355	4.64 22 78.C.24.28.11 L 008; inventory only	

No.					
635.				2.51 16 79.K.2.0.30 L 071	
636.				1.51 17 72.A.1.39.7 L 085b	
				FEL TEMP REPARATIO; Virtus spearing horseman FH3 (raising arms)	*RIC* 8 p. 524: 148 Off: A
637.	AE	AE2	350–355	4.72 19 72.A.3.176.356 L 063	
638.				1.80* 17 78.E.4.74.104 L 071	
				FEL TEMP REPARATIO; Virtus spearing horseman FH3 (raising arms)	*RIC* 8 p. 524: 153 Off: Γ, Δ
639.	AE	AE3	350–355	1.64 15 74.C.14.63.5 L 032	
640.				1.26 17 74.C.14.51.15 L 032	
				FEL TEMP REPARATIO; Virtus spearing horseman FH4 (clutching neck)	*RIC* 8 p. 528: 191 Off: A, B
641.	AE	AE3	355–361	2.34 16 72.A.1.85.52 L 095	
642.				frag. 15 72.A.1.85.6 L 095	
				SPES REIPVBLICE; Virtus holding globe and spear	*RIC* 8 p. 528: 193
643.	AE	AE4	355–361	1.36 14 80.G.7.119.14 L 075	Off: A (2)
644.				1.09 14 74.C.14.39.13 L 014	
Alexandria				GLORIA EXERCITVS; two soldiers, one standard	*RIC* 8 p. 539: 14
645.	AE	Fol	337–340	1.65 16 72.A.1.238.2 L 114	
				GLORIA EXERCITVS; two soldiers, one standard	*RIC* 8 p. 539: 19
646.	AE	Fol	340–341	1.40 15 82.C.31.147.6 L 070; inventory only	Off: Δ
				FEL TEMP REPARATIO; Emperor, 2 captives	*RIC* 8 p. 542: 54
647.	AE	AE2	348–350	– – 84.C.36.0.5 L 000; inventory only	Off: Γ
				FEL TEMP REPARATIO; Virtus spearing horseman FH3 (raising arms)	*RIC* 8 pp. 544: 80–545: 82; Off: B
648.	AE	AE3	351–361	0.80* 16 78.C.21.842.158 L 086	
				FEL TEMP REPARATIO; Virtus spearing horseman FH3 (raising arms)	*RIC* 8 p. 543: 72f–73
649.	AE	AE3	351–361	3.05 16 72.A.1.265.1 L 042	
				FEL TEMP REPARATIO; Virtus spearing horseman FH3 (raising arms)	*RIC* 8 p. 545: 84 Off: Γ
650.	AE	AE3	355–361	1.43 16 71.X.0.0.4 L 000	
651.				1.42* 13 84.C.20.82.7 L 059; inventory only	
				SPES REIPVBLICE; Virtus holding globe and spear	*RIC* 8 p. 545: 87
652.	AE	AE4	355–361	1.53 12 84.C.0.0.1 L 000; inventory only	Off: A
Uncertain mint				GLORIA EXERCITVS; two soldiers, one standard	
653.	AE	Fol	337–341	1.58 15 79.L.1.60.72 L 024	

654. 1.37 13 72.A.3.168.319 L 063

FEL TEMP REPARATIO; Virtus spearing horseman
FH 3 (raising arms)

655. AE AE3 347–361 3.30 16 79.K.1.43.28 L 002
656. 2.47 17 72.A.1.85.11 L 095
657. 1.83 15 80.G.7.0.11 L 060
658. 1.80 18 4.C.27.147.1 L 075; inventory only
659. 1.77 17 74.C.14.62.2 L 034
660. 1.70 18 72.A.1.244.32 L 115
661. 1.66 16 79.K.1.158.133 L 055
662. 1.63 16 74.H.3.128.3 L 312
663. 1.55 16 79.K.1.65.40 L 018

FEL TEMP REPARATIO; Virtus spearing horseman

664. AE AE3 346–361 2.34 16 82.G.14.184.77 L 009; inventory only
665. 1.57 17 72.A.2.64.237 L 097
666. 1.40* 12 74.C.14.51.10 L 032
667. 1.20 15 74.C.14.62.1 L 028
668. 1.14 17 80.G.9.314.158 L 057
669. 0.98* 16 80.C.5.404.4 L 404
670. 0.81 17 79.L.1.92.93 L 024
671. 0.79* 13 79.L.1.51.71 L 019

VOT XX MVLT XXX in wreath

672. AE Fol 347–348 0.61 16 71.A.2.10.5 L 001

FEL TEMP REPARATIO; Emperor, 2 captives

673. AE AE2 348–351 6.43 23 72.A.1.74.5 L 109; (unc. emp.)

FEL TEMP REPARATIO; Virtus spearing horseman
FH4 (clutching neck)

674. AE AE3 351–361 1.46 16 72.A.1.196.2 L 135

SPES REIPVBLICE; Virtus holding globe and spear (emp. unc.)

675. AE AE4 355–363 2.00 17 76.H.7.5.4 L 003; inventory only
676. 1.36 11 80.C.27.82.10 L 037
677. 1.29 14 74.B.4.39.2 L 324
678. 1.17 13 78.C.21.844.159 L 086

Constans

Rome GLORIA EXERCITVS; two soldiers, one standard — *RIC* 8 p. 249: 8

679. AE Fol 337–340 0.95 13 72.A.1.85.34 L 095 — (mint unc.)

VICTORIAE DD AVGGQ NN; two victories — *RIC* 8 p. 253: 77, 79

680. AE Fol 347–348 1.50 11 80.G.9.0.61 L 000 — Off: Γ

VICTORIAE DD AVGGQ NN; two victories — *RIC* 8 p. 254: 88

681. AE Fol 347–348 1.12 17 74.C.16.95.44 L 998 — Off: Γ

Aquileia GLORIA EXERCITVS; two soldiers, one standard — *RIC* 8 p. 317: 34

682. AE Fol 340 1.00 16 72.C.3.144.1 L 077 — Off: P

Siscia GLORIA EXERCITVS; two soldiers, one standard *RIC* 7 p. 460: 264–65

683. AE Fol 337 2.07 18 82.G.13.216.14 L 058; inventory only Off: H

Thessalonica VICTORIAE DD AVGGQ; NN two victories *RIC* 8 p. 411: 100

684. AE Fol 347–348 1.73 16 74.C.10.69.20 L 021 Off: A

Heracleia FEL TEMP REPARATIO; Emperor on galley *RIC* 8 p. 434: 66

685. AE AE2 348–351 4.14 25 72.A.1.134.13 L 002

Constantinople GLORIA EXERCITVS; two soldiers, one standard *RIC* 8 p. 449: 29

686. AE Fol 330 1.77 15 84.G.18.137.47 L 012 Off: Γ

GLORIA EXERCITVS; two soldiers, one standard *RIC* 8 p. 450: 45

687. AE Fol 330 1.39 14 76.H.6.25.1 L 017; inventory only

Cyzicus GLORIA EXERCITVS; two soldiers, one standard *RIC* 8 p. 490: 18

688. AE Fol 337–340 1.68 17 74.C.14.35.7 L 010 Off: Δ

VOT XX MVLT XXX in wreath *RIC* 8 p. 494: 51

689. AE Fol 347–348 1.64 16 80.G.7.190.30 L 110 Off: E

VOT XX MVLT XXX in wreath *RIC* 8 p. 494: 58

690. AE Fol 347–348 1.29 15 76.C.19.149.3 L 090; inventory only Off: Θ

FEL TEMP REPARATIO; Virtus leading barbarian from hut *RIC* 8 p. 495: 72

691. AE AE2 348–350 3.70 22 71.A.1.100.86 L 030 Off: Δ

Antioch GLORIA EXERCITVS; two soldiers, one standard *RIC* 8 p. 515: 47

692. AE Fol 337–347 1.49 15 76.H.6.5.3 L 005; inventory only Off: Θ

GLORIA EXERCITVS; two soldiers, one standard *RIC* 8 p. 515: 53

693. AE Fol 337–340 1.43 15 84.G.18.218.133 L 054; (emp. unc.) Off: I

VOT XV MVLT XXX in wreath *RIC* 8 p. 521: 116

694. AE Fol 347–348 0.78 14 72.A.2.122.2 L 143 Off: Γ, E

695. 1.35 14 72.X.0.0.1 L 000

Alexandria GLORIA EXERCITVS; two soldiers, one standard *RIC* 8 p. 539: 7

696. AE Fol 337–341 1.41 16 84.C.5.232.3 L 178; inventory only Off: B

GLORIA EXERCITVS; two soldiers, one standard *RIC* 8 p. 539: 21

697. AE Fol 340 1.57 17 74.C.10.69.10 L 021 Off: A

VOT XX MVLT XXX in wreath *RIC* 8 p. 541: 34

698. AE Fol 347–348 2.08 15 74.C.10.214.5 L 123 Off: B

				FEL TEMP REPARATIO; Emperor, 2 captives				*RIC* 8 p. 542: 64
699.	AE	AE2	348–350	4.36	21	79.K.1.24.2	L 006	Off: A
UNCERTAIN MINT				VICTORIAE DD AVGGQ NN; two victories				
700.	AE	Fol	347–348	0.98	15	80.G.9.296.138	L 067	
701.				frag	13	71.A.2.151.144	L 031	
				VOT XX MVLT XXX in wreath				
702.	AE	Fol	347–348	1.13	14	76.H.6.15.2	L 010; inventory only	

DELMATIUS?

UNCERTAIN MINT				GLORIA EXERCITVS; two soldiers, one standard				
703.	AE	Fol	335–337	0.69*	15	71.A.1.97.75	L 043	

CONSTANTIUS GALLUS

CONSTANTINOPLE				FEL TEMP REPARATIO; Virtus spearing horseman FH4 (clutching neck)				*RIC* 8 p. 456: 107
704.	AE	AE2	351–355	5.13	23	87.G.20.12.3	L 001; Plate 2	Off: B
				FEL TEMP REPARATIO; Virtus spearing horseman FH3 (raising arms)				*RIC* 8 p. 457: 110 or 113
705.	AE	AE2	351–355	2.79	20	72.A.1.97.7	L 076	
				FEL TEMP REPARATIO; Virtus spearing horseman FH3 (raising arms)				*RIC* 8 p. 458: 121–24
706.	AE	AE3	351–355	1.76	18	80.G.10.1.1	L 001	
				FEL TEMP REPARATIO; Virtus spearing horseman FH3 (raising arms)				*RIC* 8 p. 458: 124
707.	AE	AE3	351–355	1.53	18	79.K.1.150.90	L 052	Off: Δ
NICOMEDIA				FEL TEMP REPARATIO; Virtus spearing horseman FH3 (raising arms)				*RIC* 8 p. 479: 97
708.	AE	AE3	351–355	2.24	17	72.A.1.0.11	L 095	
CYZICUS				FEL TEMP REPARATIO; Virtus spearing horseman FH3 (raising arms)				*RIC* 8 p. 498: 103
709.	AE	AE2	351–355	4.44	21	84.G.17.3.1	L 001	Off: Δ
ALEXANDRIA				FEL TEMP REPARATIO; Virtus spearing horseman FH3 (raising arms)				*RIC* 8 p. 544: 79
710.	AE	AE2	351–355	4.35	23	79.K.1.23.3	L 002; Plate 2	Off: A

Uncertain mint FEL TEMP REPARATIO; Virtus spearing horseman FH3 (raising arms)

711.	AE	AE3	351–361	1.78 17 84.G.17.45.12 L 013	
712.				1.46 18 72.A.1.46.72 L 090	

FEL TEMP REPARATIO; Virtus spearing horseman

713.	AE	AE3	351–361	4.27 19 76.A.5.119.3 L 045; inventory only	

Julian as Caesar

Arles SECVRITAS REIPVB; bull and eagle — *RIC* 8 p. 229: 318–23

714.	AE	AE1	360–363	6.49 25 80.C.27.70.6 L 024	

Sirmium FEL TEMP REPARATIO; Virtus spearing horseman FH3 (raising arms) — *RIC* 8 p. 390: 74

715.	AE	AE3	355–361	1.06* 15 72.A.3.169.176 L 062	

Constantinople SPES REIPVBLICE; Virtus holding globe and spear — *RIC* 8 p. 461: 151–53

716.	AE	AE4	355–361	1.07 14 74.C.10.0.4 L 103	

Cyzicus SPES REIPVBLICE; Virtus holding globe and spear — *RIC* 8 p. 499: 118

717.	AE	AE4	355–361	1.46* 15 74.C.14.51.8 L 032	Off: A

Antioch FEL TEMP REPARATIO; Virtus spearing horseman FH4 (clutching neck) — *RIC* 8 p. 528: 189 Off: Γ , I

718.	AE	AE3	355–361	2.02 16 80.C.27.82.9 L 037	
719.				1.71 17 74.C.10.205.3 L 116	

Alexandria SPES REIPVBLICE; Virtus holding globe and spear — *RIC* 8 p. 545: 89

720.	AE	AE4	361–363	2.07 14 72.A.1.88.4 L 114; inventory only	Off: A (2)
721.				1.25* 16 84.C.1.103.3 L 103; inventory only; (mint unc.)	

Uncertain mint FEL TEMP REPARATIO; Virtus spearing horseman FH3 (raising arms)

722.	AE	AE3	351–361	1.86 17 78.C.21.416.51 L 078	

FEL TEMP REPARATIO; Virtus spearing horseman

723.	AE	AE3	355–361	2.69 15 78.C.21.442.81 L 080	
724.				1.86 13 74.H.3.112.4 L 038	
725.				0.68 14 74.C.14.11.5 L 002	(emp. unc.)
726.				1.65 16 72.X.0.0.6 (poss.) L 000	

SPES REIPVBLICE; Virtus holding globe and spear

727.	AE	AE4	355–363	1.37 16 72.A.3.174.175 L 058	
728.				1.13 15 74.C.10.69.19 L 021	

No.	Metal	Denom.	Date	Weight	Axis	Inventory	Locus	Reference
729.				0.92*	16	72.B.4.26.1	L 015	
730.				1.48	14	79.L.1.52.55	L 014	(emp. unc.)
731.				1.41	11	74.C.10.121.3	L 036	(emp. unc.)
732.				1.00	15	74.H.3.117.3	L 041	(emp. unc.)
				VOT XX MVLT XXX in wreath				
733.	AE	AE3	360–363	1.12*	16	72.A.3.169.177	L 062	

JULIAN AS AUGUSTUS

No.	Metal	Denom.	Date	Weight	Axis	Inventory	Locus	Reference
ROME				VIRT EXERC ROMANOR; Virtus with captive and trophy				*RIC* 8 p. 280: 327
734.	AE	AE4	361–363	1.43	14	80.G.9.261.92	L 057; inventory only	
735.				1.57*	12	74.H.4.49.41	L 028	(rev. unc.)
ANTIOCH				SECVRITAS REIPVB; bull, 2 stars				*RIC* 8 p. 532: 216 or 217
736.	AE	AE1	361–363	8.52	29	72.A.1.19.12	L 084; inventory only	Off: A (2)
737.				6.77	25	72.B.1.119.13	L 096	
UNCERTAIN MINT				VOT XX MVLT XXX				
738.	AE	AE3	361–363	2.84	16	72.A.3.176.353	L 063	

HOUSE OF CONSTANTINE

No.	Metal	Denom.	Date	Weight	Axis	Inventory	Locus	Reference
CONSTANTINOPLE				FEL TEMP REPARATIO; Virtus spearing horseman				
739.	AE	AE3	346–361	0.52*	13	80.C.25.142.19	L 080	
				GLORIA EXERCITVS; two soldiers, one standard				*RIC* 7 pp. 589: 137–44, 590: 149–55
740.	AE	Fol	336–337	1.78	15	74.C.14.68.1	L 062	
NICOMEDIA				PROVIDENTIA AVGG; camp gate				
741.	AE	Fol	324–330	0.69	13	71.A.2.160.301	L 054	Off: A
				GLORIA EXERCITVS; two soldiers, one standard				*RIC* 7 p. 635: 199–206
742.	AE	Fol	336–337	0.23*	14	71.X.0.0.24	L 000	Off: A
				FEL TEMP REPARATIO; Virtus spearing horseman FH3 (raising arms)				
743.	AE	AE3	351–361	1.62	15	72.A.1.88.2	L 114	
CYZICUS				VOT XX MVLT XXX in wreath				*RIC* 8 p. 493: 48 or 51
744.	AE	Fol	347–348	1.32	16	79.K.1.158.137	L 055	Off: A
ANTIOCH				GLORIA EXERCITVS; two soldiers, one standard				*RIC* 8 p. 515: 51–52
745.	AE	Fol	337–347	1.28	14	72.A.1.244.30	L 115	

FEL TEMP REPARATIO; Virtus spearing horseman FH4 (clutching neck). — *RIC* 8 p. 521: 123 Off: Γ

746. AE AE2 348–350 3.44 21 79.L.1.23.19 L 004
747. 1.57 19 74.C.10.69.22 L 021

FEL TEMP REPARATIO; Virtus spearing horseman FH3 (raising arms) — *RIC* 8 p. 523: 132

748. AE AE3 350–355 1.48 15 75.PC.4.21.1 L 020; inventory only

VOT XX MVLT XXX in wreath — mint not certain

749. AE Fol 347–348 0.46* 15 72.A.3.174.176 L 058 — Off: B

ALEXANDRIA

SPES REIPVBLICE; Virtus holding globe and spear — *RIC* 8 p. 545: 87–89

750. AE AE4 351–363 1.53 13 74.C.10.69.24 L 021 — Off: A (2), B
751. 1.49 15 74.C.10.131.3 L 036
752. 1.35 17 74.C.14.51.23 L 032

UNCERTAIN MINT

FEL TEMP REPARATIO; Virtus leading barbarian from under tree

753. AE AE2 346–361 1.75 19 72.A.1.85.5 L 095

FEL TEMP REPARATIO; Virtus spearing horseman

754. AE AE2 346–361 3.33 21 79.K.1.150.101 L 052
755. 2.00* 20 84.G.18.206.104 L 051

FEL TEMP REPARATIO; Virtus spearing horseman; FH3 (raising arms)

756. AE AE3 346–361 2.92 14 84.G.18.99.13 L 018
757. 2.78 17 72.A.1.85.10 L 095
758. 2.10 15 80.G.9.314.159 L 057
759. 1.95 16 72.A.1.85.35 L 095
760. 1.94 15 75.PC.6.3.4 L 008; inventory only
761. 1.78 16 84.G.18.218.136 L 054
762. 1.78 17 74.C.14.62.3 L 034
763. 1.58 17 84.G.18.187.74 L 048
764. 1.30 14 78.G.99.0.5 L 000
765. 0.88 15 79.K.1.158.139 L 055
766. 0.63* 14 78.E.4.74.138 L 071
767. 0.61* 13 84.G.18.218.135 L 054
768. frag. 17 84.G.17.162.33 L 007
769. frag. 15 80.G.9.279.121 L 057

FEL TEMP REPARATIO; Virtus spearing horseman; FH2 (sitting on ground)

770. AE AE3 351–361 1.05 12 78.B.8.75.6 L 013

FEL TEMP REPARATIO; Virtus spearing horseman; FH4 (clutching neck)

771. AE AE3 351–361 4.14 12 72.B.2.72.3 L 080
772. 2.03 17 84.G.18.281.273 L 056
773. 1.53 16 1.53 80.G.7.116.12 L 075
774. 1.36 13 84.C.36.1.1 L 000
775. 1.35 14 78.C.21.416.67 L 078
776. 1.19 14 84.G.18.125.29 L 012
777. 0.77 14 78.C.21.416.45 L 078

FEL TEMP REPARATIO; Virtus spearing horseman

778. AE AE3 346–361 2.36 17 80.G.10.205.44 L 065
779. 2.17 17 72.A.3.174.255 L 058
780. 2.17 14 79.K.3.0.58 L 009
781. 2.14 14 84.G.18.112.18 L 019
782. 2.13 15 72.A.1.46.59 L 090

783. 1.95 16 76.A.5.227.1 L 104
784. 1.94 14 72.A.4.61.7 L 037
785. 1.93 17 72.A.1.102.19 L 097
786. 1.87* 14 84.G.18.270.220 L 062
787. 1.84 15 74.C.8.146.2 L 095
788. 1.81* 16 75.PS.6.0.3 L 000; inventory only
789. 1.78* 17 72.A.3.168.255 L 063
790. 1.74 17 72.A.1.46.14 L 090
791. 1.72 16 72.A.1.85.15 L 095
792. 1.70 15 74.C.10.131.2 L 036
793. 1.67 13 80.G.9.294.131 L 066
794. 1.61 17 84.G.18.268.249 L 061
795. 1.61* 18 74.C.14.51.9 L 032
796. 1.56 15 84.G.18.137.35 L 012
797. 1.54 13 79.K.1.158.128 L 055
798. 1.48 15 72.A.1.49.14 L 085
799. 1.35 14 79.K.2.169.27 L 077
800. 1.32 15 72.A.3.174.258 L 058
801. 1.32 13 72.A.3.161.98 L 059
802. 1.32 13 72.A.2.64.230 L 097
803. 1.27 16 82.G.14.46.35 L 030; inventory only
804. 1.27 15 72.A.1.0.10 L 095
805. 1.17 15 74.C.10.200.7 L 113
806. 1.17* 13 79.L.1.107.109 L 021
807. 1.13 16 80.G.9.297.143 L 068
808. 1.08 14 78.C.21.605.163 L 078
809. 1.07 15 71.X.0.0.23 L 000
810. 1.07 15 72.A.3.174.172 L 058
811. 1.07* 16 74.C.10.190.3 L 093
812. 1.04 13 76.A.5.64.3 L 005; inventory only
813. 1.02* 15 74.C.10.69.11 L 021
814. 0.89* 17 80.G.9.302.150 L 057
815. 0.81 13 72.A.1.250.5 L 117
816. 0.78* 15 80.G.10.206.50 L 065
817. 0.76 14 80.G.10.187.28 L 056
818. 0.74 13 74.C.16.0.5 L 000
819. 0.67 12 82.G.14.82.44 L 044; inventory only
820. 0.65* 16 72.A.3.174.193 L 058
821. 0.55 15 72.A.3.174.190 L 058
822. 0.51 13 82.G.14.323.243 L 123; inv. only
823. 0.50* 15 72.A.3.169.178 L 062
824. 0.47 12 80.G.9.5.2 L 001
825. frag. 13 82.G.14.232.210 L 095
826. – 16 78.G.8.30.9 L 000; inventory only

GLORIA EXERCITVS; two soldiers, one standard

827. AE Fol 335–341 1.24 14 72.A.3.168.256 L 063
828. 1.23 14 74.H.3.169.1 L 333
829. 0.67 17 72.A.1.85.33 L 095
830. 0.60 13 76.C.19.174.2 L 108; inventory only

GLORIA EXERCITVS; two soldiers, one or two standards

831. AE Fol 330–341 0.67* 13 72.B.1.58.1 L 087

VICTORIAE DD AVGGQ NN; two victories

832. AE Fol 347–348 1.57 13 72.A.1.85.37 L 095
833. 1.44 14 72. A.1.238.10 L 114; inventory only
834. 0.93 12 74.H.3.92.1 L 027
835. 0.90* 14 72.A.1.0.12 L 095
836. 0.62* 13 72.B.2.61.5 L 074

VOT XX MVLT XXX in wreath

837. AE Fol 347–348 1.73 13 72.A.1.85.51 L 095
838. 1.34 14 72.A.1.46.31 L 090
839. 1.33 13 72.A.1.88.3 L 114
840. 1.31 14 78.C.21.605.167 L 078
841. 1.22 15 74.H.3.123.16 L 307
842. 1.20 15 72.A.3.174.171 L 058
843. 1.17 14 74.C.10.131.4 L 036
844. 1.02 15 72.A.1.238.19 L 114
845. 0.79 13 78.E.4.78.149 L 071
846. 0.78 18 72.A.1.37.18 L 085a
847. 0.70 15 80.G.10.309.68 L 078
848. 0.68 9 71.A.2.151.150 L 031
849. 0.65 13 71.A.2.160.296 L 054

850. 0.31* 12 72.A.3.175.295 L 063; inventory only

Victory advancing left

851. AE Fol 330–346 1.63 15 84.G.18.57.6 L 000

SPES REIPVBLICE; Virtus holding globe and spear

852. AE AE4 355–363 1.98 15 74.C.14.35.4 L 010

853. 1.73 13 72.A.2.103.3 L 134

854. 1.70 11 78.C.21.605.173 L 078

855. 1.65 14 74.C.14.35.14 L 010

856. 1.61 12 74.C.10.121.2 L 036

857. 1.59 16 72.A.1.238.20 L 114

858. 1.55 13 74.C.14.24.6 L 004

859. 1.54 12 74.C.14.51.4 L 032

860. 1.51 11 80.C.21.1091.6 L 137

861. 1.48 13 79.K.2.169.31 L 077

862. 1.42 12 80.C.21.1097.7 L 137

863. 1.41 14 72.A.1.49.3 L 085

864. 1.24 13 74.C.14.35.3 L 010

865. 1.24 14 74.C.14.39.10 L 014

866. 1.22 12 74.C.10.69.17 L 021

867. 1.13 15 78.C.21.624.109 L 086

868. 1.12 11 84.G.17.33.8 L 003

869. 1.07 13 82.G.14.17.3 L 009; inv. only

870. 1.05 13 74.C.14.35.15 L 010

871. 1.00* 16 80.C.21.1449.86 L 159

872. 0.98 13 80.G.8.476.15 L 023

873. 0.94 13 74.H.3.120.2 L 042

874. 0.94 13 74.C.10.193.10 L 104

875. 0.91 11 74.C.14.51.18 L 032

876. 0.91* 15 72.A.3.167.97 L 062

877. 0.87 13 80.G.9.275.107 L 057

878. 0.82 12 84.C.27.168.3 L 085

879. 0.81 11 84.G.18.180.57 L 046

880. 0.81* 14 84.C.20.54.2 L 038

881. 0.76* 15 80.C.5.404.5 L 404

882. 0.73 12 74.C.10.69.18 L 021

883. 0.69* 12 78.C.21.416.48 L 078

884. 0.63 11 79.K.1.45.30 L 002

885. 0.53 12 78.C.21.605.176 L 078

886. 0.44 11 79.K.1.158.125 L 055

887. 1.16 12 72.A.3.174.268 (poss.) L 058

888. frag. 13 72.A.1.88.5 (poss.) L 114

JOVIAN

ANTIOCH VOT V MVLT X in wreath *RIC* 8 p. 534: 232–33

889. AE AE3 363–364 1.58 17 72.A.2.64.244 L 097; inventory only

UNCERTAIN MINT VOT V MVLT X in wreath

890. AE AE3 363–364 2.65 15 79.K.1.150.84 L 052

891. 1.77 16 74.C.14.63.7 L 032

VALENS

ARLES SECVRITAS REPVBLICAE; victory left *RIC* 9 p. 64: 9b (ii a)

892. AE AE3 364–367 1.86 13 80.G.8.240.1 L 046; Plate 2 Off: OF II

ROME? SECVRITAS REIPVBLICAE; victory left *RIC* 9 p. 121: 24b or 28a

893. AE AE3 367–378 2.24 20 72.B.1.88.2 L 089

THESSALONICA SECVRITAS REIPVBLICAE; victory left *RIC* 9 p. 178: 27b

894. AE AE3 367–375 2.03 17 76.H.7.7.4 L 003; inventory only

CONSTANTINOPLE GLORIA ROMANORVM; emperor dragging captive *RIC* 9 p. 214: 16b–c

895. AE AE3 364–375 1.55 18 74.H.3.106.9 L 033 Off: Δ

SECVRITAS REIPVBLICAE; victory left *RIC* 9 p. 221: 42

896. AE AE3 367–375 1.88 17 82.G.14.47.33 L 028; inventory only Off: A

NICOMEDIA GLORIA ROMANORVM; emperor dragging captive *RIC* 9 p. 252: 9b–c

897. AE AE3 364–367 1.98 16 84.G.17.14.3 L 001

CYZICUS RESTITVTOR REIP; emperor holding standard *RIC* 9 p. 241: 10b

898. AE AE3 364–367 1.27 17 79.L.1.21.13 L 004 Off: A

ANTIOCH RESTITVTOR REIPVBLICAE; emperor standing *RIC* 9 p. 272: Zc

899. AV solidus 364–367 3.59 20 74.C.16.90.1 L 044; inventory only Off: Θ

GLORIA ROMANORVM; emperor dragging captive *RIC* 9 p. 281: 35

900. AE AE3 364–367 2.36 17 72.A.3.178.1 L 068; (emp. unc.)

GLORIA ROMANORVM; emperor dragging captive *RIC* 9 p. 274: 10b–c or 35b

901. AE AE3 364–375 2.16 15 72.A.2.64.241 L 097; (emp. unc.)

ALEXANDRIA SECVRITAS REIPVBLICAE; victory left *RIC* 9 p. 298: 3b

902. AE AE3 364–375 2.51 15 87.G.20.303.27 L 029; inventory only Off: A (2)

903. 1.55 14 72.A.1.285.4 L 042

UNCERTAIN MINT SECVRITAS REIPVBLICAE; victory left

904. AE AE3 364–378 1.83 12 72.A.1.46.35 L 090

905. 1.71 14 87.G.20.249.20 L 031; inventory only

906. 1.67 15 74.H.3.123.14 L 307

907. 1.55* 15 72.A.3.168.127 L 063

908. 1.47 17 72.X.0.0.5 L 000

909. 1.31 12 72.A.3.174.154 L 058

VALENTINIAN I

ARLES SECVRITAS REPVBLICAE; victory left *RIC* 9 p. 64: 9a

910. AE AE3 364–367 1.93 16 72.X.0.0.3 L 000

ROME SECVRITAS REIPVBLICAE; victory left *RIC* 9 p. 120: 17a (v)

911. AE AE3 364–367 1.80 13 72.C.3.126.1 L 063 Off: P

Aquileia GLORIA ROMANORVM; emperor dragging captive *RIC* 9 p. 96: 11a (xvii a)
912. AE AE3 367–375 1.41 18 72.A.3.161.69 L 059 Off: P

Siscia GLORIA ROMANORVM; emperor dragging captive *RIC* 9 p. 146: 5a (iii)
913. AE AE3 364–367 2.23 18 72.A.3.174.245 L 058 Off: C

SECVRITAS REIPVBLICAE; victory left *RIC* 9 p. 146: 7 (x a)
914. AE AE3 364–367 1.46 17 72.A.3.174.153 L 058 Off: • A

Constantinople SECVRITAS REIPVBLICAE; victory left *RIC* 9 p. 215: 21a
915. AE AE3 364–367 1.82 19 72.A.2.64.243 L 097 Off: PA

Alexandria SECVRITAS REIPVBLICAE; victory left *RIC* 9 p. 298: 3a or 5a
916. AE AE3 364–375 1.45 14 74.C.14.39.12 L 014 Off: A, Γ
917. 1.63 15 74.C.14.37.8 L 008

Uncertain mint GLORIA ROMANORVM; emperor dragging captive
918. AE AE3 364–367 1.63 18 72.A.3.169.175 L 062
919. 1.63* 18 72.B.4.32.9 L 016
920. 0.73 20 82.G.9.460.5 L 109; inventory only

SECVRITAS REIPVBLICAE; victory left
921. AE AE3 364–378 2.45 16 74.H.2.15.1 L 002
922. 1.78 16 74.H.3.121.12 L 306
923. 1.10 15 72.A.2.103.4 L 134

uncertain reverse
924. AE AE3 364–392 1.64* 15 72.B.2.59.3 L 083

Gratian

Constantinople REPARATIO REIPVB; emperor raising fallen woman *RIC* 9 p. 226: 54a
925. AE AE2 378–383 4.38 22 74.C.16.105.1 L 031; Plate 2 Off: Γ

Nicomedia VOT XX MVLT XXX in wreath *RIC* 9 p. 259: 39a
926. AE AE4 378–383 0.74 13 80.C.21.1004.3 L 128

Antioch SECVRITAS REIPVBLICAE; victory left *RIC* 9 p. 281: 36c
927. AE AE3 364–367 2.67 14 74.C.17.59.6 L 050; (emp. unc.)

VOT V MVLT X in wreath *RIC* 9 p. 288: 52
928. AE AE4 378–383 1.00 14 76.A.6.96.2 L 041; inventory only Off: Θ

Valens, Valentinian I or Gratian

No.	Metal	Denom.	Date	Wt.	Diam.	Inv.	Notes	Reference
Siscia				GLORIA ROMANORVM; emperor dragging captive				*RIC* 9 pp. 147: 14, 149: 21, 154: 38; Off: C
929.	AE	AE3	364–375	1.38	15	72.A.3.175.293	L 063; inventory only	
				SECVRITAS REIPVBLICAE; victory left				*RIC* 9 p. 147: 15a (xxxff)
930.	AE	AE3	364–375	2.46	15	87.G.20.269.24	L 022; inventory only + in field r.	
Thessalonica				SECVRITAS REIPVBLICAE; victory left				*RIC* 9 pp. 178: 27, 179: 32; Off: A
931.	AE	AE3	364–374	1.61	14	72.C.2.24.4	L 214	
Constantinople				SECVRITAS REIPVBLICAE; victory left				*RIC* 9 p. 215: 21 or 42
932.	AE	AE3	364–375	0.91	16	72.A.2.110.1	L 127	
933.				0.86	12	79.K.1.109.59	L 032	
Antioch				GLORIA ROMANORVM; emperor dragging captive				*RIC* 9 p. 274: 10 or 35 Off. A
934.	AE	AE3	364–375	1.40*	13	74.C.14.39.11	L 014	
				SECVRITAS REIPVBLICAE; victory left				*RIC* 9 p. 275: 12 or 36
935.	AE	AE3	364–375	1.08	14	84.G.12.19.1	L 011	
936.				2.05	15	87.G.20.14.4	L 001; inventory only	
Alexandria				SECVRITAS REIPVBLICAE; victory left				*RIC* 9 p. 298: 3a or 5a Off: Γ
937.	AE	AE3	364–375	1.72	16	84.G.18.305.284	L 066	
Uncertain mint				GLORIA ROMANORVM; emperor dragging captive				
938.	AE	AE3	364–375	2.70	18	79.K.1.150.82	L 052	
939.				2.54	16	78.C.23.183.18	L 066	
940.				2.23	13	74.C.14.29.1	L 004	
941.				2.13	14	82.G.14.323.244	L 123; inv. only	
942.				2.13	16	80.G.9.315.160	L 005	
943.				2.05	15	72.A.3.174.179	L 058	
944.				1.99	13	72.A.2.64.227	L 097	
945.				1.98	16	72.A.3.174.167	L 058	
946.				1.94	16	74.C.10.82.2	L 016	
947.				1.87*	18	72.A.3.168.321	L 063	
948.				1.78	13	74.C.14.51.16	L 032	
949.				1.72	13	74.C.17.8.2	L 001	
950.				1.63	14	72.A.3.174.274	L 058	
951.				1.43	16	80.G.9.245.86	L 005	
952.				1.42	13	72.C.4.114.2	L 114	
953.				1.40	14	74.C.11.38.1	L 046	
954.				1.38	15	72.A.3.174.272	L 058; inv. only	
955.				1.37	13	84.C.1.0.4	L 000	
956.				1.32	13	84.G.18.260.183	L 052	
957.				1.29	16	72.A.3.176.368	L 063	
958.				1.22*	15	72.A.1.0.2	L 000	
959.				1.16	13	80.G.9.312.155	L 037	
960.				1.13	14	72.B.3.187.3	L 059	
961.				1.12*	14	74.C.14.63.6	L 032	
962.				1.04*	12	79.K.1.87.55	L 025	
963.				1.00	14	72.A.3.174.280	L 058	
964.				0.97*	15	74.C.10.69.21	L 021	
965.				0.96*	15	84.G.18.216.119	L 054	
966.				0.95	13	78.C.21.605.177	L 078	
967.				0.84*	14	80.G.9.174.59	L 034	
968.				frag.	12	84.G.18.189.67	L 046	
969.				1.74	20	73.C.9.0.3	L 000; (unc rev.)	
970.				1.40	15	72.A.1.141.2	L 104; (unc rev)	

971. 0.81 13 72.A.3.174.201 L 058; (unc rev)

972. 0.66 12 74.H.4.94.6 L 057; (unc rev)

SECVRITAS REIPVBLICAE; victory left

973. AE AE3 364–378 2.04 14 82.G.14.179.72 L 080; inventory only

974. 2.02 12 74.C.14.51.5 L 032

975. 2.00 13 74.C.14.24.5 L 004

976. 1.92 14 78.G.6.14.2 L 010

977. 1.81 13 74.C.10.68.9 L 020

978. 1.80 17 82.G.14.178.69 L 080; inv. only

979. 1.78 12 72.A.3.176.355 L 063

980. 1.68 14 72.B.2.65.1 L 080

981. 1.65 14 72.A.1.39.8 L 085b

982. 1.63 15 87.G.20.253.22 L 041; inv. only

983. 1.60 16 74.C.14.51.12 L 032

984. 1.60 15 84.G.17.86.26 L 031

985. 1.55 17 79.K.1.150.104 L 052

986. 1.55 13 74.C.10.69.15 L 021

987. 1.54 13 74.C.14.51.13 L 032

988. 1.53 18 72.X.0.0.2 L 000

989. 1.53 13 74.C.14.51.17 L 032

990. 1.50 14 79.K.1.150.92 L 052

991. 1.50* 15 80.C.26.286.25 L 101

992. 1.46 17 71.X.0.0.9 L 000; inventory only

993. 1.46 11 74.H.3.51.1 L 010

994. 1.43* 13 76.A.5.82.13 L 037

995. 1.41 13 72.A.3.176.359 L 063

996. 1.34 15 74.H.4.89.1 L 054

997. 1.32 14 78.C.21.605.182 L 078

998. 1.32 16 80.G.7.187.29 L 110

999. 1.28 15 72.A.3.176.354 L 063

1000. 1.28 13 72.A.1.40.91 L 090

1001. 1.28 15 78.C.21.605.162 L 078

1002. 1.27 13 74.C.10.199.5 L 112

1003. 1.24 14 74.H.3.121.3 L 306

1004. 1.24 16 72.A.1.37.7 L 085a

1005. 1.24 13 80.G.11.98.2 L 010

1006. 1.24 12 80.C.25.136.13 L 073

1007. 1.24* 16 72.A.3.161.97 L 059

1008. 1.17 14 80.G.9.296.140 L 067

1009. 0.93 14 80.G.9.190.63 L 045

1010. 0.93 13 79.L.1.96.98 L 024

1011. 0.80* 14 80.C.21.1356.176 L 157

1012. 0.76 14 74.C.14.63.11 L 032

1013. 0.75 13 78.B.8.209.42 L 053

1014. 0.74* 14 72.A.1.27.24 L 045

1015. 0.74* 12 79.K.1.78.48 L 013

1016. 0.73* 13 76.C.19.144.1 L 048

1017. 0.71 14 79.K.1.110.60 L 032

1018. 0.62 13 74.C.10.68.8 L 020

1019. 0.58* 14 72.A.3.174.189 L 058

1020. 1.86 13 72.A.2.64.240 L 097; (unc rev)

1021. 1.79 15 72.A.1.49.5 L 085; (unc rev)

1022. 1.53 15 72.A.1.50.13 L 097; (unc rev)

1023. 0.78 12 72.A.1.40.59 L 090; (unc rev)

VALENTINIAN II

AQUILEIA — CONCORDIA AVGGG; Roma seated facing — *RIC* 9 p. 101: 32c

1024. AE AE3 378–383 1.97 18 72.A.3.166.34 L 058 — Off. S

SALVS REIPVBLICAE; victory dragging captive; Chi-rho in field — *RIC* 9 p. 106: 58a

1025. AE AE4 388–398 1.05 13 84.G.18.264.190 L 060 — Off: S

CONSTANTINOPLE — VOT X MVLT XX in wreath — *RIC* 9 p. 229: 63a

1026. AE AE4 378–388 0.73 14 74.H.4.9.3 L 008 — Off: Δ

SALVS REIPVBLICAE; victory dragging captive; Chi-rho in field — *RIC* 9 p. 234: 86 or 90, Off: B, Γ (2)

1027. AE AE4 388–392 1.12 14 74.H.3.112.3 L 038

No.	Metal	Denom.	Date	Description	Reference
1028.				1.39 14 72.A.1.37.8 L 085a	(*RIC* 86a)
1029.				1.20 12 72.A.1.132.3 L 126	(*RIC* 86a)
Nicomedia				SALVS REIPVBLICAE; victory dragging captive	*RIC* 9 p. 262: 45a2
1030.	AE	AE4	388–392	0.93 12 78.B.2.168.1 L 304	Off: B′
Cyzicus				VOT XX MVLT XXX in wreath	*RIC* 9 p. 244: 22b
1031.	AE	AE4	378–383	0.92 13 72.A.2.64.242 L 097	Off: Δ
				SALVS REIPVBLICAE; victory dragging captive; Chi-rho in field	*RIC* 9 p. 246: 26a
1032.	AE	AE4	388–392	1.28 13 72.A.3.166.54 L 050; inventory only	Off: B
Antioch				VOT X MVLT XX in wreath	*RIC* 9 p. 289: 56b
1033.	AE	AE4	378–383	1.30 13 72.A.3.174.164 L 058	Off: A (2)
1034.				1.15 12 72.A.3.175.289 L 063; inventory only	
				VOT X MVLT XX in wreath	*RIC* 9 p. 292: 65a
1035.	AE	AE4	383–388	1.40 16 72.A.2.55.69 L 097	Off: A (2)
1036.				1.36 12 72.C.2.199.1 L 357	
1037.				1.33 13 72.A.3.168.317 L 063	
1038.				1.31 13 84.C.10.205.1 L 202	
1039.				0.68 14 74.H.3.101.1 L 031	
				SALVS REIPVBLICAE; victory dragging captive; unc. symbol in r. field	*RIC* 9 p. 292: 67a Off: A (2), Γ
1040.	AE	AE4	383–388	1.21 12 72.A.3.174.158 L 058	
1041.				1.13 11 82.G.9.454.4 L 109; inventory only	
1042.				1.22 13 72.A.3.174.163 L 058	+ in r. field (*RIC* 67a3)
Alexandria				SALVS REIPVBLICAE; victory dragging captive	*RIC* 9 p. 303: 20a
1043.	AE	AE4	383–392	1.06 13 72.A.3.169.275 L 062	Off: A
1044.				0.93 14 71.B.2.32.893 L 014	
1045.				1.43 12 87.G.20.327.32 L 001; inventory only	(*RIC* 9 20a5)
				Uncertain reverse	
1046.	AE	AE4	378–392	0.88 12 72.A.1.46.4 L 090; inventory only	Off: Γ
Uncertain mint				VOT X MVLT XX	
1047.	AE	AE4	378–392	1.17 13 84.G.18.210.111 L 051	
1048.				1.12 13 72.A.2.64.235 L 097	
1049.				0.61 12 74.C.13.127.12 L 116	
				SALVS REIPVBLICAE; victory dragging captive	
1050.	AE	AE4	383–392	1.75 12 80.G.10.188.31 L 048	
1051.				1.30 11 82.G.9.454.2 L 109; inventory only	

No.			Date	Wt.	Axis	Reg. no.	Locus / remarks	Reference
1052.				1.12	11	82.G.14.184.73	L 009; inventory only	
1053.				1.04	14	72.A.3.162.121	L 060	
1054.				0.96	12	80.C.25.142.22	L 080	
1055.				0.73	14	72.A.1.89.1	L 116	
1056.				0.54	14	72.A.1.46.62	L 090	
1057.				0.53	14	72.A.1.40.54	L 090	
				SALVS REIPVBLICAE; victory dragging captive; chi-rho in field				
1058.	AE	AE4	383–392	1.65	13	72.B.2.7.1	L 060	
1059.				0.90	12	80.G.9.61.44	L 005	

Theodosius I

No.			Date	Wt.	Axis	Reg. no.	Locus / remarks	Reference
Thessalonica				VICTORIA AVG; two victories facing each other				*RIC* 9 p. 187: 63b
1060.	AE	AE4	383–388	1.37	11	72.A.3.162.103	L 060	Off: B (in r. field)
				SALVS REIPVBLICAE; victory dragging captive				*RIC* 9 p. 188: 65b
1061.	AE	AE4	383–388	0.92	14	74.H.3.112.2	L 038	Off: Δ
Heracleia				VOT X MVLT ++				*RIC* 9 p. 196: 19c note
1062.	AE	AE4	378–383	0.41	9	74.H.4.19.2	L 014	Off: A
Constantinople				SALVS REIPVBLICAE; victory dragging captive; Chi-rho in field				*RIC* 9 p. 234: 86b or 90b
1063.	AE	AE4	388–392	1.17	12	76.C.19.174.1	L 108; inventory only	Off: A
1064.				0.93	13	74.H.3.123.13	L 307	
				GLORIA ROMANORVM; emperor on horseback				*RIC* 9 p. 236: 89
1065.	AE	AE4	392–395	1.24	14	72.A.3.174.160	L 058	
Nicomedia				VOT XX MVLT XXX in wreath				*RIC* 9 p. 259: 39c
1066.	AE	AE4	378–383	1.14	13	84.G.18.218.126	L 054	
				SALVS REIPVBLICAE; victory dragging captive				*RIC* 9 p. 262: 45b
1067.	AE	AE4	388–392	1.19	14	82.G.14.190.79	L 080; inventory only, pellet on rev.	Off: A (3)
1068.				1.02	13	72.A.3.174.159	L 058	(*RIC* 45b1)
1069.				1.09	12	72.A.3.162.143	L 060	(*RIC* 45b2)
Cyzicus				VOT V in wreath				*RIC* 9 p. 244: 20c
1070.	AE	AE4	378–383	0.93	13	72.A.3.169.274	L 062	Off: A
1071.				0.89	14	72.C.2.3.1	L 201	
				SALVS REIPVBLICAE; victory dragging captive; chi-rho in field				*RIC* 9 p. 246: 26b or 30b
1072.	AE	AE4	388–392	1.21	13	84.G.18.131.33	L 011; Plate 2	Off: B (2)

1073.				0.99	13	72.A.3.174.156 L 058	(poss *RIC* 26c or 30c)
ANTIOCH				VOT X MVLT XX in wreath			*RIC* 9 p. 289: 56c
1074.	AE	AE4	378–383	1.27	12	72.A.1.39.3 L 085b	Off: A
1075.				1.27	13	72.A.1.49.13 L 085	
1076.				0.97	11	84.G.18.168.53 L 046	
1077.				0.95	12	74.C.14.35.5 L 010	
1078.				0.93	14	72.A.1.1.4 L 034	
				VOT X MVLT XX in wreath			*RIC* 9 p. 292: 65b
1079.	AE	AE4	383–388	1.47	13	80.G.9.29.22 L 005	Off: Γ
				SALVS REIPVBLICAE; victory dragging captive			*RIC* 9 p. 292: 67a
1080.	AE	AE4	383–388	1.25	11	76.G.4.63.4 L 004; inventory only	Off: A (7), B (3)
1081.				1.11	11	72.A.3.174.260 L 058	
1082.				1.06	12	72.A.3.163.140 L 061	(*RIC* 67b)
1083.				0.78*	13	84.G.18.265.193 L 060	(*RIC* 67b)
1084.				0.62	13	74.H.4.36.1 L 028	(*RIC* 67b)
1085.				1.49	12	84.G.18.268.227 L 061	(*RIC* 67b–c)
1086.				1.12	13	72.A.3.176.366 L 063	(*RIC* 67b–c)
1087.				1.00	13	72.A.3.174.161 L 058	(*RIC* 67b–c)
1088.				0.87	12	71.A.1.103.110 L 023	(*RIC* 67b–c)
1089.				0.77	12	74.H.3.121.1 L 306	(*RIC* 67b–c)
1090.				0.93	11	76.G.4.81.1 L 004; inventory only	(or *RIC* 70)
1091.				0.88	13	84.G.18.241.173 L 046	(or *RIC* 70)
ALEXANDRIA				VOT X MVLT XX in wreath			*RIC* 9 p. 302: 19b
1092.	AE	AE4	383–388	0.73	12	72.A.3.161.73 L 059	Off: A
				SALVS REIPVBLICAE; victory dragging captive			*RIC* 9 p. 303: 20
1093.	AE	AE4	388–392	1.27	11	79.L.1.75.88 L 021; pellet beneath	Off: P
UNCERTAIN MINT				VOT X MVLT XX in wreath			
1094.	AE	AE4	378–392	1.15	13	74.H.3.106. 11 L 033	
1095.				1.37	12	72.A.3.175.288 L 063; inventory only	
1096.				1.04	12	72.A.3.174.252 L 058	
1097.				0.96	13	78.C.21.416.69 L 078	
1098.				0.83	10	72.A.2.116.4 L 140	
				SALVS REIPVBLICAE; victory dragging captive			
1099.	AE	AE4	383–392	1.68	13	76.A.5.109.3 L 023; inventory only	
1100.				1.25	13	72.A.3.174.250 L 058	
1101.				1.22	11	74.C.15.33.4 L 015	
1102.				1.15	12	84.G.18.220.148 L 054	
1103.				1.14	12	72.A.1.1.15 L 034	
1104.				1.13	11	84.G.18.218.125 L 054	
1105.				1.06	12	78.C.21.611.105 L 085	
1106.				1.04	14	82.G.14.47.34 L 028; inv. only	
1107.				1.00	14	79.K.2.79.3 L 030	

1108. 0.95 12 74.H.3.106.12 L 033
1109. 0.86 12 72.A.1.27.17 L 045
1110. 0.84 14 79.K.2.166.29 L 075
1111. 0.77 10 72.A.3.166.60 L 058
1112. 0.60 13 78.C.21.605.187 L 078
1113. 0.54 13 72. A.1.40.84 L 090; inv. only
1114. 0.47 13 72.A.1.40.83 L 090

SALVS REIPVBLICAE; victory dragging captive; chi-rho in field
1115. AE AE4 383–392 1.34 14 74.C.14.32.6 L 006
1116. 1.25 13 72.B.3.183.1 L 056
1117. 1.05 11 72.A.3.162.130 L 060
1118. 1.02 12 72.B.3.0.1 L 000
1119. 0.94* 12 84.G.18.270.219 L 062
1120. 0.88 12 78.C.21.605.169 L 078
1121. 0.74* 12 72.A.1.40.90 L 090

GLORIA ROMANORVM; emperor on horseback
1122. AE AE4 392–395 1.09 15 72.A.3.161.87 L 059

uncertain reverse
1123. AE AE4 378–395 0.90 11 72.A.1.1.9 L 034
1124. 0.84 11 79.K.3.0.89 L 029
1125. 0.67 13 71.X.0.0.19 L 000
1126. 0.45 12 72.A.1.40.81 L 090

FLACILLA

CONSTANTINOPLE SALVS REIPVBLICAE; seated victory writing *RIC* 9 p. 233: 81
1127. AE AE2 388–392 0.65 13 82.G.13.144.9 L 038; inventory only Off: E

NICOMEDIA SALVS REIPVBLICAE; seated victory writing *RIC* 9 p. 259: 36
1128. AE AE4 378–383 1.46 12 72.A.1.49.6 L 085; inventory only Off: E

MAGNUS MAXIMUS

ROME SPES ROMANORVM; camp gate, star above *RIC* 9 p. 131: 59
1129. AE AE4 387–388 1.01 14 79.L.1.156.131 L 055; Plate 2 Off: P (2)
1130. 0.81 13 72.B.1.88.4 L 089
1131. 0.40* 11 72.C.2.43.1 L 238

ARCADIUS

HERACLEIA VOTA V in wreath *RIC* 9 p. 196: 18b4
1132. AE AE4 378–383 1.36 13 74.C.14.27.5 L 006 Off: •B

CONSTANTINOPLE SALVS REIPVBLICAE; victory dragging captive; Chi-rho in field *RIC* 9 p. 234: 86c
1133. AE AE4 388–392 0.72 13 78.C.21.828.156 L 086 Off: A
1134. 1.00 12 76.G.4.63.3 L 004; inventory only (*RIC* 90c)

No.	Metal	Denom.	Date	Description / Weight, Size, Inventory, Locus	Reference
				VIRTVS EXERCITI; victory crowning emperor	*RIC* 10 p. 246: 60
1135.	AE	AE3	395–401	2.21 17 72.A.1.19.19 L 084	
				CONCORDIA AVG; cross	*RIC* 10 p. 249: 108
1136.	AE	AE4	404–406	0.92 13 74.H.3.121.10 L 306	Off. A
Nicomedia				VOT V in wreath	*RIC* 9 p. 259: 37c
1137.	AE	AE4	378–383	1.15 15 72.A.3.175.285 L 063	Off: A (2)
1138.				1.05 13 72.A.3.174.247 L 058	
Cyzicus				VOT V in wreath	*RIC* 9 p. 244: 20d
1139.	AE	AE4	378–383	1.11 13 72.A.3.174.157 L 058	Off: B, Δ
1140.				0.94 13 78.C.21.605.185 L 078	
				SALVS REIPVBLICAE; victory dragging captive; Chi-rho in field	*RIC* 9 p. 24:6 26b or 30b
1141.	AE	AE4	388–392	1.01 12 84.G.18.233.165 L 046	Off: A (2)
1142.				1.11 12 84.G.18.122.21 L 032	(*RIC* 26c or 30c)
				GLORIA ROMANORVM; 3 emperors facing	*RIC* 10 p. 251: 148
1143.	AE	AE3	406–408	frag. 16 71.B.1.136.32 L 053	Off: B
Antioch				VOT X MVLT XX in wreath	*RIC* 9 p. 292: 65c
1144.	AE	AE4	383–388	1.75 12 72.A.3.174.249 L 058	Off: A, Γ, S
1145.				0.85 12 74.H.3.106.13 L 033	
1146.				0.73 12 72.A.4.89.1 L 031	
				SALVS REIPVBLICAE; victory dragging captive	*RIC* 9 p. 293: 67d
1147.	AE	AE4	383–392	0.92 13 72.A.3.168.318 L 063	Off: chi-rho in field
1148.				1.33 11 74.H.3.120.1 L 042	l. and A + in field l. and A (3)
1149.				1.30 11 74.H.3.51.2 L 010	
1150.				0.87 13 79.L.1.101.104 L 021	
1151.				1.07 12 72.A.3.174.251 L 058	chi-rho in field l.
1152.				1.03 12 76.G.4.128.1 L 004; inventory only	and Γ (3)
1153.				0.77 21 76.G.4.137.1 L 004; inventory only	
				CONCORDIA AVGGG; cross	*RIC* 10 p. 251: 136–38
1154.	AE	AE4	404–406	0.90 11 78.C.22.149.8 L 133	Off: Γ
1155.				0.48 10 72.B.3.187.2 L 059	
Alexandria				VOT X MVLT XX in wreath	*RIC* 9 p. 302: 19d
1156.	AE	AE4	383–388	1.22 12 84.G.18.219.161 L 054	Off: Δ
1157.				1.14 13 72.A.3.174.165 L 058	

SALVS REIPVBLICAE; victory dragging captive — *RIC* 9 p. 303: 20c1

1158. AE AE4 388–392 1.14 17 74.C.14.51.7 L 032 — Off: chi-rho in field l. Γ

1159. 0.96 13 74.H.3.132.1 L 316 — (*RIC* 9 20c2) + in field l. Γ

GLORIA ROMANORVM; emperor holding standard — *RIC* 9 p. 304: 21

1160. AE AE2 392–395 3.94 21 74.C.10.67.13 L 020 — Off: A

CONCORDIA AVGGG; cross — *RIC* 10 p. 251: 139

1161. AE AE4 404–406 0.66 10 72.A.3.161.32 L 059 — Off: A (2)

1162. 0.61 12 72.C.2.31.4 L 226

UNCERTAIN MINT

VOT X MVLT XX in wreath

1163. AE AE4 378–392 1.01 12 72.A.1.40.88 L 090

1164. 0.93 12 78.G.5.66.2 L 029

1165. 0.92 12 74.C.17.55.4 L 049

SALVS REIPVBLICAE; victory dragging captive

1166. AE AE4 383–395 0.51* 15 72.A.3.169.174 L 062

1167. 0.80 14 87.G.24.16.2 L 008; inventory only

SALVS REIPVBLICAE; victory dragging captive; Chi-rho in field

1168. AE AE4 383–392 1.07 13 78.B.8.191.35 L 045

1169. 0.97 14 82.G.14.166.54 L 009; inv. only

1170. 0.82 12 84.G.18.216.123 L 054

1171. 0.77 12 72.A.3.174.256 L 058

1172. 0.64 15 84.G.18.141.48 L 011

VIRTVS EXERCITI; victory crowning emperor

1173. AE AE3 395–401 2.01 16 80.G.10.314.77 L 078

1174. 1.85 13 84.G.18.133.34 L 035

1175. 1.16 12 74.C.14.33.2 L 010

1176. 1.16 12 74.B.3.6.14 L 201

1177. 0.74* 14 80.C.25.135.6 L 073

CONCORDIA AVG; cross

1178. AE AE4 404–406 0.60 13 71.A.2.158.270 L 050

1179. 0.92 11 76.C.5.93.1 L 108; inventory only

CONCORDIA AVGGG; cross

1180. AE AE4 404–406 0.90 14 72.A.3.171.13 L 056

Uncertain reverse

1181. AE AE4 375–435 1.13 11 72.A.3.161.71 L 059

1182. 0.92* 13 71.X.0.0.8 L 000

1183. 0.90 12 72.B.1.133.26 L 101

HONORIUS

ROME

VICTORIA AVGG; victory left, wreath and palm — *RIC* 10 p. 338: 1357

1184. AE AE3 408–423 0.97 10 84.G.18.308.286 L 066 — Off: S

Constantinople				GLORIA ROMANORVM; 2 emperors with globe				*RIC* 10 p. 272: 409
1185.	AE	AE3	408–423	1.67	13	72.C.5.56.3	L 045	Off: A
Cyzicus				SALVS REIPVBLICAE; victory dragging captive				*RIC* 9 p. 247: 30c
1186.	AE	AE4	388–392	1.38	13	72.A.3.161.70	L 059	Chi-rho in field l.
Antioch				CONCORDIA AVGGG; cross				*RIC* 10 p. 251: 137
1187.	AE	AE4	404–406	0.86	11	78.C.23.174.14	L 045; Plate 2	Off: Γ
				GLORIA ROMANORVM; 3 emperors facing				*RIC* 10 p. 252: 153–54
1188.	AE	AE3	406–408	1.36	14	80.G.9.27.25	L 005	Off: B
Uncertain mint				SALVS REIPVBLICAE; victory dragging captive				
1189.	AE	AE4	383–392	1.29	15	72.A.1.39.17	L 085b	
1190.				0.75	13	72.A.1.190.10 (prob.)	L 095	
				GLORIA ROMANORVM; Emperor, 2 captives				
1191.	AE	AE3	408–423	1.68	16	72.A.2.64.233	L 097	
1192.				0.41*	9	74.H.4.53.2 (poss.)	L 035	
				VIRTVS EXERCITI; victory crowning emperor				
1193.	AE	AE3	395–401	1.34	17	72.A.2.103.1	L 134	
				GLORIA ROMANORVM; 3 emperors standing				
1194.	AE	AE3	406–408	1.03	14	72.A.3.174.262	L 058	
				GLORIA ROMANORVM; 2 emperors with shields				
1195.	AE	AE3	408–423	1.70	15	71.B.2.32.134	L 014	
				Uncertain reverse				
1196.	AE	AE3	392–423	1.56	10	72.A.3.161.88	L 059	
1197.				1.06	12	78.B.8.191.30	L 045	
1198.				0.54	15	79.L.1.23.15	L 004	

Honorius, Arcadius, Theodosius I or Valentinian II

Rome				CONCORDIA AVGGG; cross				
1199.	AE	AE4	378–383	1.53	13	74.C.10.65.1	L 015	
				VICTORIA AVGGG; two victories facing				*RIC* 9 p. 130: 57
1200.	AE	AE4	383–388	1.07	12	72.A.3.174.155	L 058	Off: B
				SPES REPVBLICAE; Virtus standing with captive				*RIC* 9 p. 133: 63
1201.	AE	AE4	388–394	1.05*	13	72.B.4.121.3	L 077	
				SALVS REIPVBLICAE; victory dragging captive; Chi-rho in field				*RIC* 9 p. 136: 69
1202.	AE	AE4	394–395	0.88	12	76.G.4.63.5	L 004; inventory only	Off: P

No.	Metal	Denom.	Date	Weight	Axis	Reg. no.	Locus	Reference
Thessalonica				VICTORIA AVG; two victories facing				*RIC* 9 p. 187: 63
1203.	AE	AE4	383–388	1.08	12	78.C.21.605.174	L 078	Off: A
Constantinople				SALVS REIPVBLICAE; victory dragging captive; Chi-rho in field				
1204.	AE	AE4	388–392	0.90	14	80.G.9.38.37	L 005	Off: A
1205.				0.53*	13	72.A.3.161.56	L 059	
1206.				0.42	13	71.A.1.103.103	L 023	
Nicomedia				SALVS REIPVBLICAE; victory dragging captive				*RIC* 9 pp. 265: 45, 266: 48
1207.	AE	AE4	388–392	1.35	10	72.A.3.174.257	L 058	
Cyzicus				VOT V in wreath				*RIC* 9 p. 244: 20
1208.	AE	AE4	378–383	1.53	12	74.H.3.121.2	L 306	Off: A
1209.				0.60*	12	84.G.18.281.271	L 056	
Antioch				VOT X MVLT XX in wreath				*RIC* 9 p. 289: 56, 65
1210.	AE	AE4	378–388	1.05	13	72.A.3.174.261	L 058	Off: A (3), Γ, Δ
1211.				1.00	14	80.G.10.0.41	L 064	
1212.				0.98	12	72.A.3.166.55	L 058	
1213.				0.96	13	84.G.17.20.7	L 003	
1214.				0.96	13	79.K.2.102.5	L 036	
1215.				0.78	14	72.A.3.174.162	L 058	
				SALVS REIPVBLICAE; victory dragging captive				
1216.	AE	AE4	383–392	1.43	12	72.A.3.174.248	L 058	Off: Γ (2)
1217.				1.26	13	72.A.3.166.5	L 058	
1218.				0.69	11	84.G.18.126.30	L 032	
Alexandria				VOT X MVLT XX in wreath				*RIC* 9 p. 301: 13
1219.	AE	AE4	378–383	1.43	11	72.A.3.162.132	L 060	
				VOT XX MVLT XXX in wreath				*RIC* 9 p. 301: 14
1220.	AE	AE4	378–383	0.97	12	72.B.1.2.3	L 016	Off: A
1221.				0.63	11	72.A.3.168.322	L 060	
				SALVS REIPVBLICAE; victory dragging captive				*RIC* 9 p. 303: 20
1222.	AE	AE4	388–392	1.18	12	79.L.1.34.37	L 004	Off: A (1), • in field l., A (2)
1223.				1.06	12	72.A.1.46.50	L 090	
1224.				0.97	12	82.G.14.0.248	L 125; inventory only	
Uncertain western mint				VICTORIA AVGGG; two victories facing each other				
1225.	AE	AE4	375–465	1.99	13	72.A.3.114.10	L 020	
1226.				1.62	13	80.G.9.302.149	L 057	
1227.				0.82	13	80.G.9.80.47	L 018	
1228.				0.50	10	72.A.3.174.266	L 058	

Uncertain mint victory left

1229. AE AE4 375–465 1.60 11 87.C.42.91.74 L 037; inventory only

1230. 1.58 13 72.A.3.175.286 L 063

1231. 1.56 12 76.C.19.173.2 L 107

1232. 1.52 13 74.C.14.51.11 L 032

1233. 1.35 12 72.A.3.174.279 L 058

1234. 1.27 10 87.C.42.25.14 L 032; inv. only

1235. 1.25 14 74.H.3.101.2 L 031

1236. 1.25 12 74.C.14.51.22 L 032

1237. 1.20 10 72.A.3.161.72 L 059

1238. 1.13 12 84.G.18.68.7 L 017

1239. 1.12 10 72.A.1.40.60 L 090

1240. 1.07 11 78.C.21.416.44 L 078

1241. 1.07 10 79.K.3.0.40 L 005

1242. 1.07 10 72.B.1.120.7 L 094

1243. 1.06 10 71.A.2.160.298 L 054

1244. 0.96 12 74.C.14.51.3 L 032

1245. 0.96 12 74.C.10.82.1 L 016

1246. 0.91 11 74.C.14.51.14 L 010

1247. 0.89 10 72.A.2.124.3 L 129

1248. 0.83 10 74.C.14.62.4 L 032

1249. 0.82 12 76.G.3.24.1 L 004

1250. 0.82 11 78.E.5.125.94 L 109; inv. only

1251. 0.82 10 78.C.21.605.190 L 078

1252. 0.80 12 74.B.3.77.1 L 218

1253. 0.77 11 79.K.3.0.39 L 005

1254. 0.76 10 78.E.6.24.120 L 001

1255. 0.76* 12 74.B.4.70.1 L 337

1256. 0.74 12 80.C.28.0.7 L 041; inventory only

1257. 0.74 9 80.C.21.1447.112 L 157

1258. 0.73 10 78.C.21.605.215 L 078

1259. 0.73 9 72.A.2.14.2 L 097

1260. 0.71 10 78.B.8.190.26 L 044

1261. 0.70 9 84.G.18.194.81 L 046

1262. 0.67 10 72.A.3.171.15 L 056

1263. 0.66 9 72.B.3.201.3 L 065

1264. 0.66 11 80.C.26.277.24 L 099

1265. 0.64 9 78.E.6.54.201 L 034

1266. 0.63 11 84.G.18.220.145 L 054

1267. 0.63 11 74.B.5.193.1 L 118

1268. 0.62 9 78.E.4.84.150 L 000

1269. 0.61 9 72.A.3.174.173 L 058

1270. 0.60 11 78.C.21.605.213 L 078

1271. 0.57 12 80.C.21.1449.96 L 159

1272. 0.55 8 79.K.3.17.29 L 011

1273. 0.47* 9 80.G.9.262.94 L 057

1274. 0.45 11 79.K.1.154.111 L 055

1275. 0.45 11 87.G.19.167.5 L 054; inv. only

1276. 0.45 12 72.A.1.40.68 L 090; inventory only

1277. 0.34 8 72.B.1.133.25 L 101

1278. 0.33 10 74.H.4.4.6 L 003

1279. 0.31 10 75.PW.1.20.1 L 045

1280. 0.31 9 78.E.5.137.92 L 116

1281. frag. 11 78.C.21.605.197 L 078

CONCORDIA AVGGG; Roma seated facing

1282. AE AE3 378–406 1.73 14 80.C.21.1449.82 L 159

VRBS ROMA; Roma seated holding victoriola and spear

1283. AE AE4 378–484 0.61* 13 80.G.11.106.6 L 016 (unc. rev.)

VOT XX MVLT XXX in wreath

1284. AE AE4 378–392 1.41 13 72.A.3.161.96 L 059

1285. 1.07 13 82.G.14.180.70 L 009; inv. only

1286. 1.03 12 72.A.1.49.16 L 085

1287. 1.01 13 80.G.9.27.26 L 005

1288. 0.95 12 72.B.1.133.22 L 101

1289. 0.90 11 72.A.2.95.2 L 127

1290. 0.87 12 72.A.1.40.74 L 090

1291. 0.85 11 78.C.21.605.99 L 078

1292. 0.84 14 79.K.1.154.109 L 055

1293. 0.84 15 78.G.6.92.23 L 057

1294. 0.84 12 80.C.21.1447.138 L 157

1295. 0.81 11 78.G.5. 111.5 L 044

1296. 0.81 10 80.C.21.1449.60 L 159

1297. 0.76 11 78.C.24.24.10 L 008

1298. 0.75 13 72.A.3.174.253 L 058

1299. 0.75 9 78.E.5.74.38 L 063

1300. 0.74 13 71.B.2.12.7 L 005

1301. 0.74 13 74.H.3.1221.4 L 306

1302. 0.66 14 72.A.1.95.15 L 085

1303. 0.52 9 71.A.2.160.304 L 054

1304. 0.51* 12 72.B.1.135.1 L 101

1305. 0.47 10 84.C.20.65.4 L 025; inventory only

1306. 0.45 9 72.B.1.129.19 L 094

1307. 0.44* 11 78.E.4.84.151 L 000

1308. 0.43* 10 71.X.0.0.15 L 000

1309. 0.41* 13 80.C.21.1447.137 L 157

1310. 0.27 8 78.C.21.444.82 L 081

SALVS REIPVBLICAE; victory dragging captive

1311. AE AE4 383–395 1.83 12 79.K.3.0.49 L 005

1312. 1.54 13 84.G.18.271.260 L 061

1313. 1.46 13 80.C.26.33.2 L 001

1314. 1.39 11 82.G.14.168.56 L 009; inv. only

1315. 1.34 12 84. G.18.122.24 L 032

1316. 1.33 13 80.G.11.98.4 L 010

1317. 1.31 11 72.A.3.174.170 L 058

1318. 1.30 13 79.K.3.30.64 L 005

1319. 1.28 11 72.A.3.175.294 L 063; inv. only

1320. 1.23 12 84.G.18.216.124 L 054

1321. 1.20 13 84.C.20.82.9 L 064; inventory only

1322. 1.20 12 72.A.1.74.7 L 109

1323. 1.18 15 73.C.9.7.52 L 000

1324. 1.17 12 74.H.3.115.1 L 033

1325. 1.16 14 84.G.18.122.25 L 032

1326. 1.15 13 72.A.3.174.275 L 058

1327. 1.15 15 80.G.7.223.39 L 128

1328. 1.14 15 78.C.21.851.160 L 110

1329. 1.13 12 74.C.14.63.9 L 032

1330. 1.10 11 84.G.18.122.22 L 032

1331. 1.10 14 72.A.1.39.10 L 085b

1332. 1.08 13 84.G.18.270.218 L 062

1333. 1.08 12 72.A.3.175.287 L 063; inv. only

1334. 1.08 11 80.G.10.307.65 L 079

1335. 1.07 10 78.C.21.416.65 L 078

1336. 1.05 16 79.K.1.158.132 L 055

1337. 1.03 12 74.B.5.63.1 L 049

1338. 1.03 11 72.A.3.169.234 L 062

1339. 1.03 13 76.E.3.0.1 L 000

1340. 1.02 14 72.A.3.174.265 L 058

1341. 1.01 12 72.B.1.143.2 L 109

1342. 0.96 10 79.K.2.204.38 L 098

1343. 0.95 13 72.A.1.46.51 L 090

1344. 0.95 12 76.A.5.121.9 L 036

1345. 0.94 13 72.A.3.174.263 L 058

1346. 0.94 10 72.A.1.46.26 L 090

1347. 0.92 14 80.G.10.200.35 L 063

1348. 0.92 13 72.A.1.37.13 L 085a

1349. 0.92 12 72.A.4.61.1 L 037

1350. 0.91 11 72.A.1.223.5 L 090

1351. 0.91 11 79.K.1.74.43 L 023

1352. 0.90 12 84.G.18.271.261 L 061

1353. 0.90 10 72.A.3.166.56 L 058

1354. 0.86 15 76.E.1.30.1 L 026; inventory only

1355. 0.86 11 72.A.3.166.6 L 058

1356. 0.85 13 79.L.1.46.50 L 004

1357. 0.84 12 82.G.14.84.46 L 009; inv. only

1358. 0.84 11 72.A.1.40.92 L 090

1359. 0.84 13 72.A.1.46.57 L 090

1360. 0.82* 12 72.A.3.162.134 L 060

1361. 0.78 13 78.C.21.798.149 L 078

1362. 0.78 12 79.K.3.0.92 L 033

1363. 0.78 13 80.C.30.30.35 L 022

1364. 0.78 13 75.PS.6.1.1 L 001; inventory only

1365. 0.77 11 76.H.6.5.1 L 005; inventory only

1366. 0.76 12 74.H.4.85.1 L 054

1367. 0.73* 12 80.C.29.98.11 L 046

1368. 0.72 12 72.A.3.161.75 L 059

1369. 0.70 13 79.L.1.14.10 L 000

1370. 0.70 12 82.G.14.1.1 L 001; inventory only

1371. 0.65 9 73.C.9.35.2 L 055

1372. 0.62 11 72.A.3.174.264 L 058

1373. 0.58 12 72.A.3.60.3 L 009

1374. 0.54 12 72.A.1.1.17 L 034

1375. 0.52 11 72.A.3.166.58 L 058

1376. 0.51* 12 72.A.3.174.194 L 058

1377. 0.51 10 79.L.1.28.31 L 004

1378. 0.48 12 74.H.5.23.2 L 007

1379. 0.47 12 72.A.3.174.181 L 058

1380. 0.45 12 72.A.1.46.68 L 090
1381. 0.43 11 2.A.1.46.11 L 090
1382. 0.42 12 82.G.9.460.6 L 109; inv. only
1383. 0.42 10 78.C.21.579.96 L 078
1384. 0.40 10 72.A.1.49.17 L 085
1385. 0.37 11 84.G.18.268.244 L 061; inv. only
1386. 0.33 9 76.C.19.149.4 L 090
1387. 0.32 12 72.A.1.1.18 L 034
1388. 0.30* 10 80.C.28.87.9 L 049

SALVS REIPVBLICAE; victory dragging captive; Chi-rho in field

1389. AE AE4 383–395 1.64 13 84.G.18.194.82 L 046
1390. 1.48 13 84.G.18.267.204 L 061
1391. 1.45 12 72.A.1.1.21 L 034
1392. 1.27 11 80.G.9.22.10 L 004
1393. 1.24 12 72.A.3.174.254 L 058
1394. 1.14 11 74.H.3.123.17 L 307
1395. 1.07 11 78.E.5.98.44 L 068
1396. 1.01* 12 74.H.3.92.2 L 027
1397. 0.93 11 84.G.18.204.100 L 051
1398. 0.92 11 72.A.3.175.292 L 063; inv. only
1399. 0.84 12 78.C.21.621.107 L 079
1400. 0.79 13 80.C.25.137.15 L 075
1401. 0.75 11 84.G.18.219.139 L 054
1402. 0.74 13 71.A.2.151.154 L 031
1403. 0.65 11 72.A.3.174.169 L 058
1404. 0.55 11 72.A.1.40.71 L 090
1405. 0.23 9 78.C.22.149.13 L 133

GLORIA ROMANORVM; emperor on galley

1406. AE AE2 383–392 1.28 21 73.C.9.5.20 L 019

GLORIA ROMANORVM; emperor on horseback

1407. AE AE4 392–395 0.65 12 71.X.0.0.17 L 000

VIRTVS EXERCITI; victory crowning emperor

1408. AE AE3 395–402 2.55 19 84.C.20.96.15 L 000; inventory only
1409. 1.90 14 78.C.22.149.11 L 133
1410. 1.87 12 79.L.1.125.119 L 022
1411. 1.84 15 84.G.18.219.141 L 054
1412. 1.47 11 79.K.1.79.47 L 023
1413. 1.19 13 82.N.1.85.23 L 033; inv. only
1414. 0.97 13 72.A.1.132.5 L 126
1415. 0.94 14 76.C.19.148.2 L 094; inv. only
1416. frag. 15 71.A.2.93.102 L 032

Cross

1417. AE AE4 395–450 0.65 9 73.C.10.0.1 L 000

GLORIA ROMANORVM; 3 emperors standing

1418. AE AE3 400, 402 frag. 13 73.C.9.60.27 L 044

THEODOSIUS II

CONSTANTINOPLE VOT X MVLT XX in wreath *RIC* 9 p. 229: 63b

1419. AE AE4 378–383 0.56 12 71.A.2.134.129 L 001

Cross in wreath *RIC* 10 p. 275: 443–45

1420. AE AE3/4 425–435 0.91 12 71.B.2.99.352 L 052
1421. 0.65 10 79.K.3.9.6 L 005
1422. 0.48 12 72.A.1.22.15 L 076

Cyzicus Cross in wreath *RIC* 10 p. 275: 449 or 451

1423. AE AE3/4 425–435 1.15 11 80.C.25.136.10 L 073 Off: A

Antioch GLORIA ROMANORVM; 3 emperors standing *RIC* 10 p. 252: 155

1424. AE AE3 406–408 1.51 14 72.A.1.46.23 L 090 Off: A

Cross in wreath *RIC* 10 p. 275: 453-54

1425. AE AE3/4 425–435 0.61 11 72.A.3.174.267 L 058

Alexandria CONCORDIA AVG; cross *RIC* 10 p. 250: 122

1426. AE AE4 404–406 0.68 11 72.A.3.169.233 L 062

Uncertain mint CONCORDIA AVGGG; cross

1427. AE AE4 402–408 0.50 11 87.C.42.44.42 L 010; inventory only

1428. 0.65 10 84.G.18.219.143 L 054

CONCORDIA AVG; victory facing, 2 wreaths

1429. AE AE4 425–435 1.39 12 72.A.1.39.99 L 085b

1430. 0.88 11 72.A.3.175.296 L 063; inventory only

1431. 0.53 10 72.A.3.166.36 L 058

Cross in wreath

1432. AE AE4 425–435 0.94 12 74.C.10.65.4 L 015

1433. 0.85 10 80.G.9.5.6 L 001

1434. 0.82 12 80.K.4.2.1 L 003

1435. 0.70 10 74.H.4.94.1 L 057

1436. 0.53 10 80.C.21.1449.62 L 159

1437. 0.48 10 79.K.1.78.45 L 013

1438. 0.33 10 72.A.1.1.34 L 034

1439. 0.29* 10 74.B.3.6.6 L 201

Eudoxia

Alexandria SALVS REIPVBLICE; victory left with wreath, palm *LRBC* II: 2919

1440. AE AE4 401–403 0.96 13 79.L.1.101.101 L 021 Off: A

Valentinian III

Rome SALVS REIPVBLICE; victory left with wreath, palm *RIC* 10 p. 376: 2107–8

1441. AE AE4 425–435 0.94 10 78.B.8.96.14 L 016 Off: P

VICTORIA AVGG; two victories holding a wreath *RIC* 10 p. 378: 2131

1442. AE AE4 425–435 0.94 13 72.A.3.161.46 L 059 Off: P

1443. 0.86 12 72.A.2.301.2 L 148

Victory left

1444. AE AE4 425–450 0.89 17 80.G.9.317.163 L 005

No.	Metal	Denom.	Date	Type / Weight, Die axis, Inventory, Locus	Reference
				Cross in wreath	
1445.	AE	AE4	425–455	0.72 12 78.C.21.605.166 L 078	
Uncertain mint				Victory left	
1446.	AE	AE4	425–455	0.50 9 78.E.5.0.62 L 109	

Honorius, Theodosius II or Valentinian III

No.	Metal	Denom.	Date	Type / Weight, Die axis, Inventory, Locus	Reference
Rome				VRBS ROMA FELIX; Roma standing holding trophy	*RIC* 10 p.327: 1271–83
1447.	AE	AE3	404–408	1.52 13 72.A.1.40.35 L 090; inventory only	Off: Q (2)
1448.				1.03 13 72.A.3.174.182 L 058	
				VICTORIA AVGG; victory left	
1449.	AE	AE4	410–455	0.74 10 84.G.17.15.5 L 001	
				CASTRA; camp gate	*RIC* 10 p. 380: 2160–61
1450.	AE	AE3/4	425–435	1.50 14 80.C.21.1447.123 L 159	
1451.				0.67 11 78.C.21.814.150 L 078	
Nicomedia				GLORIA ROMANORVM; 2 emperors with globe	*RIC* 10 p. 272: 412–13 var.
1452.	AE	AE3	408–423	1.29 15 78.C.21.855.161 L 112	MM: SNMA
Cyzicus				Cross in wreath	*RIC* 10 p. 275: 449ff
1453.	AE	AE3/4	425–435	0.66 10 84.G.18.252.181 L 046	Off: A
Antioch				CONCORDIA AVGGG; cross	*RIC* 10 p. 251: 136–38
1454.	AE	AE4	404–406	0.48 11 84.G.18.218.131 L 054	Off: A
1455.				0.48 10 76.E.1.57.6 L 049; inventory only	
				GLORIA ROMANORVM; 3 emperors facing	*RIC* 10 p. 252: 151–55
1456.	AE	AE3	406–408	1.35 13 72.A.3.174.177 L 058	Off: A
1457.				0.83 14 72.C.2.129.1 L 295	
Alexandria				CONCORDIA AVG; cross	*RIC* 10 p. 250: 120ff
1458.	AE	AE4	404–406	0.34 10 74.C.17.23.1 L 020	Off: Λ
Uncertain western mint				VICTORIA AVGG; victory left	
1459.	AE	AE4	410–455	1.18 10 84.G.18.137.42 L 012	
1460.				0.45 9 80.G.9.203.64 L 005	
				VICTORIA AVGGG; two victories, each with wreath	
1461.	AE	AE4	428–455	0.48 11 84.G.18.197.87 L 046	
1462.				1.00 12 78.C.21.444.83 L 081	

UNCERTAIN MINT

CONCORDIA AVG; cross

1463.	AE	AE4	404–406	0.50	9	75.PW.1.0.1 L 000; inventory only
1464.				0.62	10	82.G.14.167.55 L 009; inventory only

CONCORDIA AVGGG; cross

1465.	AE	AE4	404–406	1.81	10	72.A.2.77.13 L 121
1466.				1.59	12	78.C.21.605.102 L 078
1467.				1.75	14	72.A.1.1.12 L 034
1468.				1.15	10	78.C.21.416.72 L 078
1469.				1.08	12	80.C.26.307.28 L 096
1470.				0.88	11	79.K.1.43.27 L 002
1471.				0.81	12	72.A.3.174.271 L 058
1472.				0.75	10	79.K.1.132.64 L 045
1473.				0.74	14	78.C.21.798.129 L 078
1474.				0.70	10	79.L.1.46.52 L 004
1475.				0.59	10	78.C.23.189.21 L 071
1476.				0.52	9	79.L.1.19.12 L 004
1477.				0.48	8	76.E.1.31.2 L 027; inventory only
1478.				0.45	11	72.B.2.61.7 L 074
1479.				0.43*	11	80.C.25.135.3 L 075
1480.				0.38	10	79.K.3.17.16 L 011
1481.				0.36*	10	84.G.18.219.142 L 054
1482.				0.22	8	72. A.2.77.12 L 121; inventory only
1483.				0.33	9	72.A.1.3.1 L 071

Cross

1484.	AE	AE4	404–454	1.10	12	78.C.21.595.98 L 078
1485.				0.77	8	79.L.1.67.82 L 021
1486.				0.72	8	74.B.4.88.1 L 501
1487.				0.40	9	71.A.2.151.149 L 031
1488.				0.23	9	74.B.7.9.3 L 009
1489.				0.18*	9	71.A.2.151.152 L 031

SPES REPVBLICE; Virtus holding globe and spear

1490.	AE	AE3	404–408	2.36	20	82.G.14.81.45 L 009; inventory only

GLORIA ROMANORVM; 3 emperors facing

1491.	AE	AE3	406–408	2.00	15	80.C.25.137.14 L 075
1492.				1.87	13	80.G.9.312.154 L 037
1493.				1.84	14	84.G.18.218.129 L 054
1494.				1.71	15	76.G.4.184.1 L 002; inv. only
1495.				1.59	10	84.G.18.218.127 L 054
1496.				1.48	16	80.C.26.275.21 L 093
1497.				1.44	13	84.G.18.267.211 L 061
1498.				1.37	14	78.B.8.189.25 L 043
1499.				1.20	15	80.G.9.235.77 L 005
1500.				1.20	14	72.A.3.169.155 L 062
1501.				1.14	13	76.C.19.86.2 L 066; inventory only
1502.				1.09	13	74.H.4.47.24 L 028
1503.				1.05	14	78.C.21.605.192 L 078
1504.				0.92*	13	72.A.3.168.128 L 063
1505.				0.76	12	78.C.21.605.103 L 078
1506.				0.73	13	80.G.9.27.21 L 005
1507.				0.28*	13	74.H.3.49.2 L 010

GLORIA ROMANORVM; 2 emperors holding globe

1508.	AE	AE3	408–423	1.59	13	74.H.4.9.4 L 008
1509.				1.36	12	71.X.0.0.21 L 000
1510.				0.97	14	71.X.0.0.14 L 000; inventory only

GLORIA ROMANORVM; 2 or 3 emperors

1511.	AE	AE3	408–423	0.70	14	78.B.8.224.50 L 067

CONCORDIA AVG; victory facing, 2 wreaths

1512.	AE	AE4	425–435	1.64	12	72.A.3.161.74 L 059

1513. 1.06 10 72.A.2.168.1 L 146

1514. 0.94 11 80.C.21.1449.90 L 159

1515. 0.51 10 84.G.18.265.195 L 060

1516. 0.34* 11 84.G.18.268.231 L 061

Cross in wreath

1517. AE AE4 425–455 1.01 10 78.C.22.152.14 L 134

1518. 0.82 11 71.A.2.160.299 L 054

1519. 0.78 12 79.L.1.56.63 L 022

1520. 0.76 10 72.A.3.174.259 L 058

1521. 0.75 10 78.C.21.416.75 L 078

1522. 0.71 10 74.H.4.48.38 L 031

1523. 0.70 8 79.L.1.27.26 L 004

1524. 0.68 9 72.B.1.111.11 L 084

1525. 0.63 10 71.X.0.0.29 L 000

1526. 0.60 11 72.B.1.145.3 L 098

1527. 0.54 10 78.C.22.149.5 L 133

1528. 0.53 11 78.C.21.605.196 L 078

1529. 0.46 10 80.G.12.102.12 L 000

1530. 0.43 8 72.A.3.166.59 L 058

1531. 0.40 9 74.C.16.24.2 L 013

1532. 0.39* 9 80.C.25.142.18 L080

1533. 0.39 9 71.A.2.160.295 L 054

1534. 0.29 9 71.A.2.160.302 L 054

1535. 0.22 11 71.B.2.118.801 L 069

Marcian

Thessalonica — Monogram type 1, CHES — *RIC* 10 p. 282: 535

1536. AE AE4 450–457 1.37 10 72.A.3.160.22 L 058

Heracleia — Monogram type 1, SMHA — *RIC* 10 p. 282: 537

1537. AE AE4 450–457 0.85 10 78.C.21.605.207 L 078

Monogram type 1 var, with star and cross

1538. 0.83 10 72.A.3.171.14 L 056; inventory only

Constantinople — Monogram type 2, CON — *RIC* 10 p. 282: 543

1539. AE AE4 450–457 0.91 11 78.C.21.605.168 L 078

1540. 0.77 10 78.E.6.24.125 L 001

1541. 0.48 10 74.C.14.29.7 L004

Monogram type 2, + above, CON — *RIC* 10 p. 282: 545

1542. AE AE4 450–457 1.42 11 78.E.6.24.121 L 001

1543. 0.39 10 80.C.21.1389.24 L 144

Monogram type 2 or 5, CON

1544. AE AE4 450–457 0.65 10 76.C.19.174.4 L 108; inventory only

Nicomedia — Monogram type 5, NIC(A) — *RIC* 10 p. 282: 547–48

1545. AE AE4 450–457 0.85 9 72.A.1.1.25 L 034

Monogram type 2, above +, NIC — *RIC* 10 p. 282: 551

1546. 1.17 10 84.G.12.141.14 L 011

Monogram type 4, NIC — *RIC* 10 p. 282: 553

1547. 1.26 11 78.C.21.416.49 L 078

Monogram type 1 — Adelson and Kustas 1962

1548. 0.63 0 71.A.1.0.226 L 000; inventory only

CYZICUS

Monogram, uncertain type — *RIC* 10 p. 283: 561–65

1549. AE AE4 450–457 1.47 12 80.C.25.155.34 L 062

Monogram type 2, CVZ — *RIC* 10 p. 283: 563

1550. 0.27 9 72.A.3.171.17 L 056

ANTIOCH

Monogram type 2, ANTA, uncertain mark — *RIC* 10 p. 283: 567–68

1551. AE AE4 450–457 0.77 10 79.L.1.13.8 L 004

1552. 0.42 9 72.B.2.58.2 L 084

UNCERTAIN EASTERN MINT

Monogram in wreath, *RIC* 10 type 1, cross above

1553. AE AE4 450–457 0.36 11 78.C.21.605.186 L 078

Monogram *RIC* 10 type 1

1554. 1.55 10 78.C.21.605.191 L 078

Monogram *RIC* 10 type 2

1555. 0.61 10 71.A.1.30.17 L 014

Monogram *RIC* 10 type 5

1556. 0.63 9 74.H.4.48.39 L 031

1557. 0.25* 10 78.C.21.416.73 L 078; (Variant)

Monogram, uncertain type

1558. AE AE4 450–457 1.02 11 84.G.18.107.16 L 019*

1559. 0.99 10 76.H.7.7.3 L 003; inventory only

1560. 0.77 11 78.C.21.792.121 L 078

1561. 0.72 10 84.G.18.220.147 L 054

1562. 0.71 10 76.C.19.90.1 L 066; inventory only

1563. 0.71 10 76.G.5.2.1 L 001; inventory only

1564. 0.67 9 80.C.25.145.24 L 072

1565. 0.65 9 80.G.10.185.23 L 048

1566. 0.63 10 76.C.19.174.3 L 108; inv. only

1567. 0.63 10 72.A.3.174.209 L 058

1568. 0.57 11 78.C.21.605.165 L 078

1569. 0.51 8 84.G.18.218.137 L 054

1570. 0.47 8 78.E.6.23.113 L 001

1571. 0.41 9 72.A.3.60.8 L 009

1572. 0.40 8 78.E.4.74.130 L 071

1573. 0.36 8 76.E.1.57.5 L 049; inventory only

1574. 0.31 9 76.C.19.146.3 L 094; inv. only

MAJORIAN?

ROME OR RAVENNA

VICTORIA AVGGG; victory holding wreath and palm — *RIC* 10 p. 401: 2515–18

1575. AE AE3/4 457–461 1.20 12 72.A.3.161.26 L 059

Leo I

Rome?				VICTORIA AVGG; victory left, with wreath and palm				*RIC* 10 p. 396: 2528?
1576.	AE	AE4	465–467	0.63	11	78.C.21.605.188	L 078	
Thessalonica?				Empress b/E				*RIC* 10 p. 295: 713
1577.	AE	AE4	457–474	0.59	11	73.C.9.53.5	L 044	
Constantinople				Monogram, *RIC* 10 type 1 or 2, CON				*RIC* 10 p. 293: 683–88
1578.	AE	AE4	457–474	1.44	10	80.G.10.122.7	L 034	
1579.				0.68	10	80.C.21.1449.72	L 159	
				Monogram, *RIC* 10 type 6 in wreath, KOC				*RIC* 10 p. 296: 720
1580.				0.64	11	78.C.21.605.201	L 078	
1581.				0.47	9	78.C.21.605.211	L 078	
				Emperor and captive, CN				*RIC* 10 p. 294: 703
1582.	AE	AE4	457–474	0.86	10	72.B.1.129.18	L 094; inventory only	
1583.				0.67	10	74.H.3.41.1	L 007	(*RIC* 10 p. 294: 703–4)
				With cross in l., CN				
1584.				0.78	10	84.G.18.220.154	L 054	(*RIC* 10 p. 294: 704)
				Lion in wreath, CON				*RIC* 10 p. 293: 673ff
1585.	AE	AE4	457–474	0.81	10	74.H.4.40.54	L 030	
1586.				0.33	9	76.C.19.146.4	L 094; inventory only	
				Two emperors enthroned, KOC				*RIC* 10 p. 296: 724
1587.	AE	AE4	473–474	0.45	11	80.C.21.1449.77	L 159	
Nicomedia				Emperor and captive, NIC				*RIC* 10 p. 295: 705–10
1588.	AE	AE4	457–474	0.67	11	80.C.21.1449.92	L 159	
1589.				0.50	9	80.G.10.198.33	L 063; obv: DN LEOS PF AVG	(*RIC* 10 p. 295: 710)
Uncertain eastern mint				Monogram, *RIC* 10 type 1				
1590.	AE	AE4	457–474	0.58	9	71.X.0.0.27	L 000	
1591.				0.52	10	72.A.2.251.2	L 071	
1592.				0.32	8	78.B.8.151.19	L 028	
				Monogram *RIC* 10 type 1 or 3				
1593.				0.83	10	78.E.6.25.134	L 001	
				Monogram *RIC* 10 type 5				
1594.				0.62	11	78.C.21.605.209	L 078	
1595.				0.36*	9	72.A.1.27.10	L 04	

Monogram, *RIC* 10 type 1or 2

1596. 1.01 10 79.K.1.158.115 L 055

Monogram, uncertain type

1597. 0.48* 8 80.C.21.1447.140 L 157

Emperor and captive

1598. AE AE4 457–474 frag. 14 71.A.2.178.404 L 092

Lion in wreath

1599. AE AE4 457–474 0.93 10 74.C.13.115.3 L 103

Empress b/E

1600. AE AE4 457–474 1.59 9 78.C.21.416.63 L 078
1601. 1.24 11 80.C.21.1449.67 L 159
1602. 1.09 11 78.C.21.605.202 L 078
1603. 1.02 9 72.A.1.51.2 L 085
1604. 0.95* 11 78.C.21.416.54 L 078
1605. 0.91 11 84.G.18.267.206 L 061
1606. 0.86 12 78.C.21.416.59 L 078
1607. 0.82 11 84.C.20.88.10 L 025; inv. only
1608. 0.77 9 78.C.21.605.210 L 078
1609. 0.77 9 80.C.21.1449.81 L 159; Plate 2
1610. 0.73 9 74.H.4.40.52 L 030
1611. 0.73 10 80.C.21.1449.59 L 159
1612. 0.70 9 72.B.1.118.3 L 023
1613. 0.70 10 71.X.0.0.28 L 000
1614. 0.59 9 72.A.3.169.156 L 062
1615. 0.58 15 78.C.21.416.62 L 078
1616. 0.52 8 74.H.4.65.21 L 045
1617. 0.52 8 78.E.6.7.3 L 001
1618. 0.38* 7 76.G.4.185.3 L 004
1619. 0.36 9 74.H.3.101.3 L 031
1620. 0.35 8 78.G.7.27.4 L 013
1621. 0.14* 9 78.B.9.33.3 L 019

Lion

1622. AE AE4 457–474 1.23 11 78.E.5.134.77 L 116
1623. 0.74 8 79.L.1.27.30 L 004
1624. 0.84 9 71.X.0.0.5 L 000
1625. 0.82 10 80.G.9.54.42 L 013
1626. 0.54 10 80.C.21.1449.76 L 159
1627. 0.44 8 74.H.4.50.84 L 033
1628. 0.43 9 80.G.9.5.5 L 001
1629. 0.41 9 78.E.6.51.176 L 030
1630. 0.36 9 78.E.6.15.28 L 001
1631. 0.31 8 74.H.4.67.3 L 020
1632. 0.30 10 72.A.3.161.76 L 059; inv. only

Uncertain reverse

1633. AE AE4 457–474 0.98 10 72.A.1.27.7 L 045
1634. 0.94 8 72.A.1.37.24 L 085a, inventory only
1635. 0.54 11 84.G.18.192.89 L 000
1636. 0.52 11 72.A.1.18.18 L 071
1637. 0.27 8 84.C.20.122.19 L 024; inventory only

LIBIUS SEVERUS

ROME Monogram (no wreath) *RIC* 10 p. 408: 2715–17

1638. AE AE4 461–465 0.55 8 79.K.1.132.69 L 045

Anthemius

Rome				Monogram in wreath, type 3, RM			*RIC* 10 p. 415: 2859
1639.	AE	AE4	467–472	1.08	11	78.C.21.416.52 L 078	

Zeno

Constantinople				Monogram in wreath, type 5, KOC			*RIC* 10 p. 314: 962
1640.	AE	AE4	476–491	0.91	8	74.H.4.49.44 L 028	
1641.				0.71	9	80.C.21.1449.69 L 159	
1642.				0.68	8	72.X.0.0.7 L 000	
1643.				0.66	8	74.C.14.13.6 L 003	
1644.				0.57	9	79.K.2.108.7 L 050	
1645.				0.57	9	84.G.12.71.6 L 011	

Cyzicus				Monogram in wreath, type 14, CVZ			*RIC* 10 p. 314: 967
1646.	AE	AE4	476–491	1.07	9	72.A.3.159.2 L 057	
1647.				0.98	9	74.B.3.6.15 L 201	
1648.				0.76	10	74.H.4.67.10 L 020	

Uncertain eastern mint				Monogram in wreath, *RIC* 10 type 1		
1649.	AE	AE4	476–491	1.02	9	84.G.18.224.160 L 055
1650.				0.96	8	71.X.0.0.13 L 000
1651.				0.84	8	79.K.2.165.20 L 074
1652.				0.68	9	72.A.3.178.2 L 068
1653.				0.52	8	80.C.21.1459.44 L 159
				Monogram in wreath, *RIC* 10 type 1 or 14		
1654.				0.82	7	78.E.6.67.231 L 039
				Uncertain reverse		
1655.	AE	AE4	476–491	0.38	11	84.G.17.59.16 L 018

Uncertain Monogram

Constantinople						
1656.	AE	AE4	445–518	0.58	8	72.A.1.46.37 L 090

Uncertain eastern mint				Monogram		
1657.	AE	AE4	445–518	1.07	11	72.A.3.159.1 L 057

1658.	1.06	10	78.B.8.224.51 L 067	**1661.**	0.97	8	72.A.3.171.16 L 056
1659.	1.03	12	74.C.14.56.1 L 038	**1662.**	0.96	9	72.C.4.59.4 L 054
1660.	1.01	9	80.G.10.200.34 L 101	**1663.**	0.95	9	84.G.18.216.122 L 054

1664.	0.92	9	72.A.1.18.17 L 071
1665.	0.92	10	78.E.6.56.198 L 035
1666.	0.91	9	78.E.6.13.26 L 011
1667.	0.91	10	84.C.36.0.4 L 000; inventory only
1668.	0.90	10	72.A.1.37.10 L 085a
1669.	0.86	9	79.L.1.13.9 L 004
1670.	0.83	8	74.H.4.9.7 L 008
1671.	0.82*	10	76.C.19.86.4 L 066
1672.	0.81	10	84.G.18.292.281 L 068
1673.	0.81	8	82.G.14.42.16 L 027; inv. only
1674.	0.78	9	72.A.1.40.29 L 090
1675.	0.78	9	79.K.3.0.38 L 000
1676.	0.78	9	84.G.18.184.60 L 046
1677.	0.78	9	74.H.4.40.96 L 030
1678.	0.76	9	78.C.21.90.16 L 036
1679.	0.75	10	78.B.2.270.4 L 217
1680.	0.74	9	72.A.3.155.1 L 049
1681.	0.74	10	80.C.21.1449.70 L 159
1682.	0.74	9	82.G.14.275.220 L 100; inv. only
1683.	0.74	8	79.K.2.132.8 L 074
1684.	0.73	7	78.E.6.20.63 L001
1685.	0.72	10	78.G.6.28.6 L 004
1686.	0.72	8	74.C.14.14.7 L 003
1687.	0.72	8	72.C.2.119.1 L 283
1688.	0.71	8	76.C.19.146.6 L 094
1689.	0.70	8	79.L.1.28.33 L 004
1690.	0.70	8	79.K.3.34.76 L 026
1691.	0.68	8	78.E.5.137.85 L 116
1692.	0.67	8	72.A.1.21.8 L 083
1693.	0.64	9	78.E.6.21.103 L 001
1694.	0.64	8	78.E.6.67.223 L 039
1695.	0.64	8	76.G.4.190.3 L 004
1696.	0.63	8	72.A.3.166.38 L 058
1697.	0.63	8	79.L.1.25.25 L 004
1698.	0.62	8	78.E.6.36.150 L 018
1699.	0.62	9	78.C.21.798.147 L 078
1700.	0.61	7	72.B.1.60.6 L 087
1701.	0.61	10	84.G.18.264.191 L 060
1702.	0.61	8	78.E.4.74.120 L 071
1703.	0.61	8	72.A.3.167.68 L 062; inv. only
1704.	0.61	9	78.E.5.131.70 L 113
1705.	0.60	8	84.G.18.266.201 L 078
1706.	0.57	10	76.C.19.146.5 L 094
1707.	0.56	7	84.G.18.305.285 L 066
1708.	0.54*	7	72.A.3.167.98 L 062
1709.	0.54	7	78.E.6.15.49 L 001
1710.	0.54	7	84.G.18.221.159 L 055; inv. only
1711.	0.54	11	73.C.9.7.45 L 000
1712.	0.53	7	82.G.13.16.2 L 006; inventory only
1713.	0.53	9	80.C.21.1356.177 L 157
1714.	0.53	8	84.G.18.268.232 L 061
1715.	0.51	9	78.E.6.23.117 L 001
1716.	0.50	7	78.E.6.21.98 L 001
1717.	0.50	7	78.C.21. 794.122 L 078
1718.	0.50	9	78.E.5.131.68 L 113
1719.	0.49	10	80.C.21.1449.56 L 159
1720.	0.49	10	84.G.18.247.177 L 046
1721.	0.49	9	78.C.22.0.18 L 154
1722.	0.48*	7	78.E.4.74.114 L 071
1723.	0.48	10	72.A.3.174.198 L 058
1724.	0.48	10	74.C.15.7.3 L 001
1725.	0.48	9	71.X.0.0.22 L 000
1726.	0.47	8	78.B.8.147.17 L 025
1727.	0.47	12	82.G.13.22.3 L 006; inventory only
1728.	0.47	8	79.K.3.0.108 L 009
1729.	0.46*	9	79.K.3.0.62 L009
1730.	0.46	10	79.K.1.33.11 L 008
1731.	0.45	11	78.C.21.605.189 L 078
1732.	0.45	8	74.H.3.106.15 L 033
1733.	0.45	7	79.K.3.9.7 L 005
1734.	0.45	10	74.H.4.41.6 L 028
1735.	0.44	9	72.B.2.33.7 L 003
1736.	0.44	10	78.C.21.817.153 L 078
1737.	0.42	10	78.C.21.605.179 L 078
1738.	0.42	7	72.B.2.33.8 L 003
1739.	0.41	9	74.H.4.19.3 L 014; inventory only
1740.	0.41	9	74.C.13.128.2 L 116
1741.	0.40	7	79.K.3.17.28 L 011
1742.	0.40	9	72.A.3.174.205 L 058
1743.	0.39*	8	76.G.4.64.6 L 006
1744.	0.38	9	76.E.3.73.2 L 074
1745.	0.38	9	84.C.20.153.21 L 064; inv. only
1746.	0.37	8	84.G.18.220.155 L 054
1747.	0.36*	8	74.B.4.61.4 L 337

1748.	0.36	10	78.E.5.137.93 L 116
1749.	0.36	8	78.E.6.23.107 L 001
1750.	0.36	10	71.B.2.101.471 L 055
1751.	0.35*	7	74.C.15.59.3 L 036
1752.	0.35	8	79.K.3.0.51 L 005
1753.	0.33	8	78.E.6.54.204 L 034
1754.	0.33	9	74.H.4.45.46 L 032
1755.	0.32	9	79.K.3.0.44 L 005
1756.	0.31	8	78.E.6.59.214 L 034
1757.	0.29	9	84.G.18.268.234 L 061
1758.	0.28*	8	78.E.6.68.217 L 037
1759.	0.28	7	72.A.3.174.204 L 058
1760.	0.27	10	80.G.9.23.11 L 003
1761.	0.27	10	78.C.21.416.74 L 078
1762.	0.25	9	80.G.10.320.82 L 079
1763.	0.25	9	78.C.21.605.220 L 078
1764.	0.25	8	74.B.4.61.3 L 337
1765.	0.24	7	87.C.42.44.47 L 010; inv. only
1766.	0.24	10	78.E.5.137.80 L 116
1767.	0.22	10	78.C.21.798.130 L 078
1768.	0.21	9	72.B.1.88.3 L 089
1769.	0.17	8	74.H.4.46.36 L 031
1770.	0.16	11	74.C.14.14.8 L 003
1771.	0.15	8	72.B.1.132.4 L 094
1772.	0.13	7	79.K.2.204.37 L 098
1773.	0.09*	8	80.C.21.1449.61 L 159
1774.	frag.	8	71.B.2.101.472 L 055
1775.			82.G.13.140.12 L 005; inv. only
1776.			80.G.10.206.56 L 065 inv. only

Vandalic

Carthage			Victory left				*BMC Vandal* p. 22: 44–48?
1777.	AE	425–455	1.07	10	79.K.2.0.10 L 012		
			Bust r./Pax standing				*BMC Vandals* p. 23: 51
1778.	AE	423–451	0.95	11	74.H.4.50.83 L 033		
			Bust r./Victory left				*RIC* 10 p. 468: 3805
1779.	AE	423–451	0.92	12	74.C.14.63.8 L 032		
1780.			0.35	9	76.H.7.6.1 L 002; inventory only		
			DOMINO NOSTRO bust r./ emperor standing VICTORI…				*BMC Vandal* p. 24: 54
1781.	AE	423–533	0.52	10	76.E.3.44.4 L 047; inventory only		
1782.			0.27	8	76.E.1.28.2 L 023; inventory only		
			Bust r./Emperor standing, arms outstretched				*BMC Vandal* p. 25: 57–60
1783.	AE	423–533	0.24	8	72.A.1.39.18 L 085b		
			Male standing/Horsehead l. (Gaiseric)				*BMC Vandal* p. 4: 14–16
1784.	AE	439–477	0.32	10	80.C.21.1352.14 L 138		
1785.			0.13*	9	74.H.4.36.3 L 028		
			Bust r./D in wreath				*BMC Vandal* p. 35: 150–51
1786.	AE	428–533	0.47	10	74.B.7.9.2 L 009		
1787.			0.47	9	80.C.21.1449.91 L 159		
			Bust r. /Chi-rho				*BMC Vandal* p. 37: 159–60
1788.	AE	428–533	0.73	8	72.A.3.60.5 L 009		
1789.			0.57	10	72.B.4.28.3 L 016		

No.	Metal	Date	Weight	Axis	Reg. no. / Locus	Reference
1790.			0.56	9	80.G.10.172.22 L 058; inventory only	
1791.			0.56	9	72.A.3.166.37 L 058	
1792.			0.51	8	79.K.3.0.60 L 009	
1793.			0.21*	8	78.E.6.20.75 L 001	
			Facing bust/Star in wreath			*BMC Vandal* p. 38: 165
1794.	AE	428–533	0.39	8	78.E.4.74.137 L 071	
1795.			0.34	9	78.G.5.181.13 L 031	
1796.			0.23	8	72.A.1.18.15 L 071	
			Bust r./Cross potent in wreath			*BMC Vandal* p. 40: 182–85
1797.	AE	428–533	0.46	9	82.G.14.241.128 L 047; inventory only	
1798.			0.31	8	80.C.21.1461.50 L 161	
1799.			0.12	8	82.G.14.61.39 L 030; inventory only	
1800.			frag.	12	79.L.1.56.58 L 022	
			Bust r. DN/Victory left			*BMC Vandal* p. 21: 32–36
1801.	AE	428–533	0.82	10	74.H.4.67.2 L 020	
1802.			0.50	9	80.G.9.82.48 L 018	
1803.			0.49	9	76.E.1.57.7 L 049; inventory only	
1804.			0.48	9	80.C.2.151.28 L 081	
1805.			0.43*	10	78.E.6.44.171 L 018	
1806.			0.42	7	74.H.4.0.1 L 001	
1807.			0.34	8	72.A.3.174.207 L 058	
1808.			0.34	9	72.B.1.129.16 L 094	
1809.			0.31	7	74.C.14.18.2 L 003	
1810.			0.31	8	74.H.4.40.78 L 030	
1811.			0.30	9	74.H.5.4.2 L 002	
1812.			0.30	9	78.E.6.67.227 L 039	
1813.			0.29	9	78.E.6.54.202 L 034	
1814.			0.28	8	80.C.21.1447.153 L 157	
1815.			0.24	10	78.E.6.15.36 L 001	
1816.			0.23	6	72.B.1.119.19 L 096	
1817.			0.22	7	80.K.4.7.3 L 005	
1818.			0.15	9	71.X.0.0.16 L 000	
1819.			0.15	6	71.B.2.99.345 L 052	
			Bust r./palm tree			*BMC Vandal* p. 26: 68
1820.	AE	428–533	0.72	8	76.E.1.42.2 L 035; inventory only	
1821.			0.67	8	80.G.10.185.25 L 048	
1822.			0.66	7	79.L.1.56.59 L 022	
1823.			0.65	9	78.E.6.20.74 L 001	
1824.			0.65	8	87.C.42.23.4 L 003; inventory only	
1825.			0.62	7	74.H.4.49.43 L 028	
1826.			0.60	10	80.G.9.245.83 L 005	
1827.			0.58	9	71.X.0.0.26 L 000	
1828.			0.54*	9	74.H.4.41.99 L 028	
1829.			0.49	7	78.E.6.67.219 L 039	
1830.			0.46	7	76.E.1.28.1 L 023; inventory only	
1831.			0.46	8	72.A.2.122.5 L 143; inv. only	
1832.			0.46	9	87.C.42.19.3 L 006; inventory only	
1833.			0.45	7	78.E.5.137.81 L 116; inv. only	
1834.			0.44	8	78.E.4.74.135 L 071	
1835.			0.43*	7	72.B.2.134.1 L 060	
1836.			0.43	7	72.X.0.0.4 L 000	
1837.			0.43	9	79.L.1.56.66 L 022	
1838.			0.43	8	74.H.4.67.6 L 020	
1839.			0.43	7	78.E.6.36.146 L 018	
1840.			0.42	8	78.E.5.82.37 L 064	
1841.			0.41	7	78.E.4.74.101 L 071	
1842.			0.40	7	71.A.2.151.148 L 031	
1843.			0.39	8	72.C.3.43.2 L 015	
1844.			0.39	7	73.C.9.42.4 L 044	
1845.			0.38	7	72.B.1.111.5 L 084	
1846.			0.38	7	74.H.4.24.2 L 018	
1847.			0.37	7	74.H.4.73.9 L 045	
1848.			0.37	9	76.H.7.7.2 L 003; inventory only	

1849. 0.35 9 78.E.5.99.49 L 073
1850. 0.35 9 78.E.4.74.129 L 071
1851. 0.33 8 78.E.6.21.91 L 001
1852. 0.33 7 78.E.6.21.101 L 001
1853. 0.32 8 74.H.4.45.50 L 032
1854. 0.32 7 78.E.6.54.186 L 034
1855. 0.32 9 78.E.4.74.107 L 071; Plate 2 (rev.)
1856. 0.32 7 78.E.6.20.72 L 001
1857. 0.32 7 80.G.10.185.26 L 048
1858. 0.31 7 74.B.5.141.2 L 118
1859. 0.31 7 78.E.6.15.46 L 001
1860. 0.31 7 78.E.5.66.20 L 037
1861. 0.30 7 78.E.6.67.230 L 039
1862. 0.29 7 78.E.6.20.69 L 001
1863. 0.27* 10 71.B.2.99.346 L 052
1864. 0.27 8 72.B.1.119.27 L 096
1865. 0.27* 7 72.A.1.17.7 L 072; inventory only
1866. 0.23 8 79.L.1.56.64 L 022
1867. 0.22 7 76.A.5.81.12 L 036; inv. only
1868. 0.22 8 78.E.6.67.221 L 039
1869. 0.22 8 74.B.3.145.12 L 201
1870. 0.22* 8 72.B.1.132.5 L 094
1871. 0.22 7 78.E.6.54.207 L 034
1872. 0.11 7 74.H.4.40.53 L 030
1873. frag. 11 71.A.1.103.232 L 023

uncertain/exploding star — Hahn 1980: 250

1874. AE 428–533 0.47 8 78.E.4.75.145 L 071; Plate 2 (rev.)
1875. 0.37 9 80.C.21.1449.52 L 159

uncertain/lion, pillar? — *BMC Vandal* p. 26: 67?

1876. AE 428–533 0.50 9 78.E.5.78.31 L 052

Huneric bust r./N/IIII palm branch — *BMC Vandal* p. 14: 12–14

1877. AE 477–484 0.88 10 79.L.1.73.84 L 005; Plate 2
1878. tetranummium 0.60 9 72.SP.7.19.5 L 003

bust of Hilderic?/ Cross potent — *BMC Vandal* p. 14: 9–10?

1879. AE nummus 523–530 0.81 9 71.X.0.0.31 L 000

bust of Gelimir?/monogram? — *BMC Vandal* p. 16: 4–6

1880. AE 530–533 0.70 10 74.H.4.47.25 L 028
1881. nummus 0.42 9 79.K.1.104.58 L 032

Ticinum

type C (Baduila); bust r./DN REX B — *BMC Vandal* p. 90: 28–36

1882. AE 541–549 0.59 9 72.B.4.128.3 L 080
1883. nummus 0.56 9 78.E.4.74.116 L 071
1884. 0.48 8 78.E.6.21.104 L 001

Uncertain western mint

Athlaric bust r./monogram — Hahn *MIB* 80

1885. AE nummus 526–535 0.62 11 78.C.21.605.200 L 078

Unidentifiable

1886–1911. 4th century (26)
1912–2151. 5th–early 6th century (240)

BYZANTINE COINS (ALL BRONZES, EXCEPT NO. 2215)

ANASTASIUS I (11 APRIL 491 – 1 JULY 518)

CONSTANTINOPLE

Nummus 491–498 diademed bust r. monogram DOC 1 p. 11: 15

No.		Wt.	Diam.	Reg. no.	Locus
2152.	AE	1.53	10	80.G.9.122.56	L 005
2153.		0.92	11	80.C.21.1449.79	L 159
2154.		0.84	9	78.E.5.111.55	L 105
2155.		0.81	9	72.X.0.0.12	L 000; inv. only
2156.		0.81	8	72.B.1.135.3	L 101
2157.		0.74	8	72.B.2.33.4	L 003
2158.		0.72	8	72.A.3.168.126	L 063
2159.		0.71	8	72.A.4.27.1	L 010
2160.		0.70	10	71.A.2.151.145	L 031
2161.		0.68	10	72.K.1.55.36	L 004
2162.		0.67	8	79.L.1.117.114	L 021
2163.		0.66	9	78.E.6.43.162	L 021
2164.		0.66	8	78.E.5.120.58	L 109
2165.		0.65	9	78.C.21.798.131	L 078
2166.		0.63	10	80.C.21.1459.48	L 159
2167.		0.62	8	78.E.5.137.84	L 116
2168.		0.62	9	72.A.3.162.131	L 060
2169.		0.62	8	80.C.26.61.6	L 024
2170.		0.61	10	84.G.18.265.192	L 060; inv. only
2171.		0.61	8	74.H.4.41.10	L 028
2172.		0.58	10	72.X.0.0.8	L 000
2173.		0.56	8	74.H.4.40.75	L 030
2174.		0.56	8	78.C.21.798.142	L 078
2175.		0.54*	9	79.K.2.165.17	L 074
2176.		0.52	9	72.A.3.159.17	L 057
2177.		0.52	8	74.B.3.6.2	L 201
2178.		0.51	9	74.H.4.66.18	L 044
2179.		0.50	8	74.H.4.40.74	L 030
2180.		0.49	8	72.A.3.168.125	L 063
2181.		0.47	8	79.L.1.10.4	L 004
2182.		0.47	8	74.H.4.50.82	L 033
2183.		0.47	7	74.H.4.40.76	L 030
2184.		0.46	8	72.A.3.185.1	L 064
2185.		0.46	9	74.B.6.0.1	L 000
2186.		0.46	6	78.E.5.83.39	L 052
2187.		0.44	9	78.E.5.137.82	L 116
2188.		0.43	7	78.G.5.151.7	L 043
2189.		0.35	8	76.A.5.100.3	L 048; inv. only
2190.		0.33	8	72.B.1.101.5	L 048
2191.		0.32	9	78.E.6.18.53	L 001
2192.		0.32	8	78.E.5.134.76	L 116
2193.		0.31*	7	74.H.4.65.20	L 045
2194.		0.30	9	82.G.14.42.22	L 027; inv. only
2195.		0.27	9	74.H.4.42.35	L 012
2196.		0.27	8	78.E.6.15.50	L 001
2197.		0.21	8	78.E.5.125.59	L 109

Reformed follis first period 498–518 bust r., M *DOC* 1 p. 12: 16

No.		Wt.	Diam.	Reg. no.	Locus
2198.	AE	5.89	24	74.B.1.0.1	L 529

Reformed half-follis first period 498–518 bust r., K *DOC* 1 p. 13: 18

No.		Wt.	Diam.	Reg. no.	Locus
2199.	AE	5.76	21	79.K.1.46.33	L 004
2200.		5.50	21	79.L.1.87.92	L 015
2201.		3.18	21	78.B.8.161.20	L 022

Reformed follis second period 498–518 bust r., M *DOC* 1 p. 16; 20e

No.		Wt.	Diam.	Reg. no.	Locus
2202.	AE	7.87	21	87.C.42.23.5	L 003

Half-follis; second period			498–518	bust r., K ANNO garbled on rev.	*DOC* 1 p. 17: 21b, yet no inscrip. on obv.
2203.	AE	2.60	19	80.C.21.987.2 L 127	
Large follis third period			498–518	bust r., M	*DOC* 1 p. 18: 23a
2204.	AE	16.00	32	76.E.99.0.1 L 000; inventory only	
Large follis third period			498–518	bust r., M	Off. Γ
2205.	AE	15.72	34	73.C.9.0.1 L 000	*DOC* 1 p. 19: 23d
2206.		14.11	35	72.B.1.111.14 L 084	
2207.		9.39	37	75.PC.3.0.1 L 001; overstruck?; c/m twice on rev. Hahn *MIB* 1a and 1b (634, Evans 1993/4)	
Large follis third period			498–518	bust r., M	Off. Δ
2208.	AE	11.83	33	71.A.2.171.321 L 058	*DOC* 1 p. 21: 23g
2209.		frag.	35	73.H.1.25.1 L 015	*DOC* 1 p. 20: 23f–g
Large follis third period			498–518	bust r., M	Off. E
2210.	AE	17.92	40	79.K.2.81.2 L 034	*DOC* 1 p. 22: 23j1
2211.		14.11	32	72.A.2.40.12 L 099	*DOC* 1 p. 22: 23k
2212.		16.73	33	74.C.14.8.3 L 002	*DOC* 1 p. 22: 23k1

Nicomedia

Small half-follis			498–518	bust r., K	*DOC* 1 p. 28: 31
2213.	AE	3.58	19	74.H.3.0.1 L 003	

Justin I (10 July 518 – 1 August 527)

Thessalonica

Trinummium			518–527	bust r., Γ	*DOC* 1 p. 47: 26
2214.	AE	1.01	14	71.A.2.134.130 L 001	

Constantinople

Tremissis			518–527	bust r., VICTORIA AVGVSTORVM; victory walking r. with wreath and globus cruciger	*DOC* 1 p. 37: 4
2215.	AV			80.G.9.158.185 L 036; inventory only	
Follis			518–527	bust r., M	
2216.	AE	13.43	31	82.G.14.173.59 L 009; inventory only	*DOC* 1 p. 39: 8
2217.		10.43	29	72.C.2.99.1 L 267	*DOC* 1 p. 39: 8a
2218.		11.04	29	80.C.26.136.16 L 037; c/m on rev., eagle (613–17, Evans 1993/4); Plate 2	*DOC* 1 p. 39: 8a or d
2219.		15.02	30	76.A.5.45.1 L 021; inventory only	*DOC* 1 p. 39: 8c
2220.		14.86	30	84.G.18.178.56 L 046; c/m on rev., Hahn *MIB* 1a (630, Evans 1993/4); Plate 3	*DOC* 1 p. 40: 8d

2221.		14.44	30	84.G.17.49.13 L 012; inventory only; c/m on obv., Arabic	*DOC* 1 p. 40: 8e
2222.		15.92	31	74.H.4.249.2 L 109	*DOC* 1 p. 40: 9a2
2223.		14.85	33	80.C.30.30.5 L 022	*DOC* 1 p. 40: 9b
2224.		16.42	34	78.C.21.350.34 L 074; Off. Γ	*DOC* 1 p. 41: 10

Pentanummium 518–527 bust r., Chi-rho

2225.	AE	1.42	12	72.B.2.159.1 L 078	*DOC* 1 p. 45: 21
2226.		2.29	14	72.B.1.0.11 L 084	*DOC* 1 p. 45: 21b
2227.		2.29	14	72.B.1.133.11 L 101	
2228.		1.99	13	79.L.1.32.40 L 004	
2229.		0.79	11	78.E.5.75.27 L 064	
2230.		1.34	12	79.K.3.38.79 L 001	*DOC* 1 p. 45: 21d

Pentanummium 518–527 Bust r., Chi-rho, pellets

2231.	AE	1.12	10	79.L.1.11.3 L 006	*DOC* 1 p. 46: 22

NICOMEDIA

Follis 518–527 Bust r., M

2232.	AE	15.83	31	74.B.1.109.1 L 571	*DOC* 1 p. 48: 28b
2233.		9.53	32	74.B.3.3.1 L 201	*DOC* 1 p. 48: 29a
2234.		16.46	30	84.G.17.49.15 L 012; Off. A	*DOC* 1 p. 49: 32
2235.		16.80	32	72.A.2.186.11 L 039	*DOC* 1 p. 49: 33b1

Pentanummium 518–527 Bust r., Chi-rho

2236.	AE	1.35	12	79.L.1.49.54 L 014	*DOC* 1 p. 50: 36
2237.		frag.	10	71.A.2.151.147 L 031	

ANTIOCH

Follis 518–527 Bust r., M (MM reads ANTIX)

2238.	AE	15.40	36	74.C.15.10.7 L 005	*DOC* 1 p. 53: 47 note

ALEXANDRIA

Dodecanummium 518–527 Bust r., I + B

2239.	AE	3.04	15	72.A.2.95.1 L 127	*DOC* 1 p. 56: 58

UNCERTAIN MINT

Nummus 518–527 Bust r., monogram — Hahn *MIB* 34

2240.	AE	0.24	8	78.E.6.34.142 L 001	
2241.		0.35	8	78.E.6.21.88 (variant) L 001	

Anastasius through Justin I (418–527)

Constantinople

Follis 498–527 Bust r., M

2242.	AE	9.60	31	74.B.3.6.1 L 201	**2244.**		5.88	30	79.K.99.0.3 L 000
2243.		7.54	29	74.C.14.1.2 L 000	**2245.**		frag.	31	73.C.9.2.6 L 000

Antioch

Follis 498–527 Bust r., M

2246. AE 8.25 31 74.B.3.4.24 L 201

Uncertain mint

Follis 498–527 Bust r., M

2247. AE frag. 35 73.C.9.1.2 L 000

Justin I and Justinian I (4 April 527 – 1 August 527)

Constantinople

Follis Bust of Justin r., M *DOC* 1 p. 60: 11

2248. AE 14.81 30 71.A.2.158.268 L 050 Off. Δ

Nicomedia

Follis Bust of Justin r., M *DOC* 1 p. 60: 12

2249. AE 15.27 30 79.K.1.99.57 L 032

Justinian I (1 August 527 – 14 November 565)

Carthage?

Nummus 534–565 Facing bust, helmeted, cross suspending A, ω, in wreath *DOC* 1 p. 193: 373

2250. AE 0.71 8 72.A.2.64.236 L 0097

2251. 0.55 11 74.H.4.42.2 L 012

2252. 0.40 8 78.E.6.43.170 L 021; inventory only

Nummus 534–565 Facing bust, helmeted, P as cross suspending A, ω, in wreath *DOC* 1 p. 193: 374

2253. 1.85 11 71.A.1.109.160 L 025

2254.	0.60	10	78.E.6.38.144 L 001	**2263.**	0.36	8	79.K.3.0.117 L 005
2255.	0.55	9	71.B.2.99.349 L 052	**2264.**	0.36	9	74.B.1.94.1 L 570
2256.	0.49	7	72.B.1.111.6 L 084	**2265.**	0.33	7	78.E.6.21.102 L 001
2257.	0.48	9	71.B.2.99.347 L 052	**2266.**	0.31	8	74.C.13.124.7 L 110
2258.	0.48	9	76.A.5.86.1 L 034; inv. only	**2267.**	0.29	8	78.E.6.24.136 L 001
2259.	0.46	8	78.E.6.15.27 L 001	**2268.**	0.25	7	74.B.7.4.1 L 002
2260.	0.45	7	78.E.6.15.45 L 001	**2269.**	frag.	9	78.E.4.74.108 L 071
2261.	0.42	8	78.E.6.18.55 L 001	**2270.**	frag.	8	72.B.1.130.9 L 098
2262.	0.37	8	78.E.6.54.184 L 034	**2271.**	frag.	7	72.B.2.6.5 L 003

Nummus 534–539 Bust r., A, beneath C *DOC* 1 p. 170: 308

2272. AE 0.52 9 71.B.2.99.348 L 052
2273. 0.49 8 72.A.3.158.16 L 054
2274. 0.46 8 74.C.14.14.15 L 003
2275. 0.28 8 78.E.4.75.141 L 071
2276. frag. 8 72.A.2.121.1 L 129
2277. 0.40 9 72.B.3.166.3 (prob) L 002

Nummus 534–539 Bust r., A *DOC* 1 p. 170: 309

2278. AE 0.53 9 78.E.5.103.54 L 066
2279. 0.49 8 78.E.6.20.64 L 001
2280. 0.36 9 78.E.5.111.56 L 105; Plate 3
2281. 0.33 8 78.E.5.49.16 L 043
2282. 0.31 8 78.E.6.20.65 L 001
2283. 0.26 7 79.L.1.39.44 L 004
2284. 0.26 8 80.C.25.32.35 L 004
2285. 0.18 7 78.E.6.7.20 L 001
2286. frag. 9 78.E.6.51.178 L 030
2287. frag. 9 76.G.3.74.5 L 036

Nummus 534–539 Facing bust, A *DOC* 1 p. 170: 309 var

2288. AE 0.64 9 74.H.4.41.7 L 028

Nummus 534–539 Bust r., A *DOC* 1 p. 170: 308 or 309

2289. AE 0.49 8 74.B.1.87.1 L 568

Nummus 534–565 Bust r. NO, cross with four pellets *Carthage* 1975: 218

2290. AE 0.39 9 78.E.6.15.33 L 001
2291. 0.38 8 78.E.6.47.173 L 029
2292. 0.36 9 80.G.9.212.70 L 005
2293. frag. 9 78.C.21.605.203 L 078
2294. frag. 8 78.E.6.72.234 L 039

Nummus 534–565 Bust r., cross with two pellets *Carthage* 1978: 1012

2295. AE 0.41 10 80.C.21.1449.84 L 159

Nummus 534–565 Bust r., cross potent *Carthage* 1978: 1014

2296. AE 1.11 11 78.E.5.134.73 L 116
2297. 0.69 9 80.C.25.42.36 L 002
2298. 0.48 9 78.E.4.74.112 L 071
2299. 0.45 9 79.K.1.144.76 L 052
2300. 0.26 8 79.K.3.17.30 L 011
2301. frag. 9 78.C.21.90.25 L 036

Nummus 534–565 Bust r., CN Hahn *MIB* 212

2302. AE 0.36 9 71.A.2.151.146 L 031 (mint uncertain)

Nummus 534–565 Bust r., CN (N retrograde) Hahn *MIB* 212 var

2303. AE 0.40 8 72.B.1.120.26 L 094 (mint uncertain)

Half-follis 539/40 Bust facing, K *DOC* 1 p. 165: 294

2304. AE 10.39 29 80.G.9.222.74 L 005

Nummus 539/40 Bust r., VOT XIII *DOC* 1 p. 167: 302

2305. AE 0.75 9 78.E.6.20.78 L 001
2306. 0.67 9 73.C.9.48.8 L 044
2307. 0.48 9 80.G.10.308.73 L 079

Nummus			539–541	Bust r, VOT XIII[I]	*DOC* 1 p. 167–68: 302–3
2308. AE	0.72	9	71.A.2.151.151 L 031		
2309.	0.62	8	79.K.2.165.22 L 074		
Half-follis			542/3	Bust facing, K	*DOC* 1 p. 165: 295
2310. AE	13.57	33	84.G.18.49.5 L 003		
Nummus			548–565	Facing bust, A	
2311. AE	0.61	8	78.E.6.23.106 L 001		*DOC* 1 p. 170: 310
2312.	0.46	8	73.C.9.60.26 L 044		
2313.	0.43	8	78.E.6.54.196 L 034		
2314.	0.41	9	74.H.4.40.51 L 030		
2315.	0.34	10	78.E.6.54.203 L 034		
2316.	0.34	8	78.E.6.67.220 L 039		
2317.	0.32	7	74.B.3.6.3 L 201		
2318.	frag.	8	78.E.6.21.84 L 001		
2319.	0.37	9	84.C.20.89.12 L 064		*DOC* 1 p. 170: 310.1
2320.	0.58	8	82.G.14.31.8 L 009; inventory only		*DOC* 1 p. 170: 310.2
2321.	0.51	8	72.B.1.118.1 L 023		
2322.	0.37	7	76.E.4.40.2 L 043; inventory only		
Nummus			548–565	bust r., Chi-rho	*DOC* 1 p. 170: 311
2323. AE	1.00	11	78.G.99.0.10 L 000		

2324.	0.81	10	78.E.5.93.41 L 070	**2330.**	0.41	8	78.E.5.131.69 L 113
2325.	0.74	10	74.C.14.5.1 L 002	**2331.**	0.39	9	72.X.0.0.9 L 000
2326.	0.73	8	71.B.2.99.344 L 052; Plate 3	**2332.**	0.34	8	78.E.6.54.195 L 034
2327.	0.68	8	79.K.3.0.41 L 005	**2333.**	0.33	9	78.C.21.90.18 L 036
2328.	0.56	9	74.H.4.63.3 L 044	**2334.**	frag.	8	71.B.2.99.351 L 052
2329.	0.46	7	79.L.1.56.68 L 022				

Nummus			552–557	Facing bust, * in wreath	Hahn *MIB* 211
2335. AE	0.41	8	74.C.17.51.1 L 048		

Thessalonica

Duanummum			527–562	Bust r., B	*DOC* 1 p. 108: 102
2336. AE	0.72	11	78.E.6.34.140 L 000		

Constantinople

Follis			527–538	Blank, M	*DOC* 1 p. 78: 28a
2337. AE	9.13	27	72.A.1.27.8 L 045		
Follis			527–538	Bust r., M	
2338. AE	16.23	30	80.C.26.123.11 L 017		*DOC* 1 p. 79: 28c
2339.	12.86	31	71.A.1.20.7 L 010		*DOC* 1 p. 79: 28c4
2340.	15.16	30	72.A.4.30.7 L 014		*DOC* 1 p. 79: 28d1–3

2341.		15.62	31	72.A.2.76.2 L 024	*DOC* 1 p. 79: 28d4
2342.		16.26	30	72.A.3.143.1 L 050; Off. E	*DOC* 1 p. 79: 29b1
Follis			527–538	Bust r., + M *	
2343.	AE	17.18	29	80.G.10.24.2 L 003; Off. E	*DOC* 1 p. 80: 30h var
Follis			527–538	Bust r., M	
2344.	AE	13.62	31	72.C.2.87.1 L 230; Off. h	*DOC* 1 p. 80: 31b2
Follis			527–565	Bust r., M* L+ Mintmark CON (off. E); barbarous style	
2345.	AE	8.31	28	72.A.4.10.1 L 002	
Half-follis			527–538	Bust r., K, to r., B	
2346.	AE	7.02	24	79.K.2.0.12 L 022	*DOC* 1 p. 81: 33 var
Pentanummium			527–538	Bust r., Chi-rho	*DOC* 1 p. 82: 35
2347.	AE	1.14	13	72.C.3.24.2 L 008	
2348.		frag.	12	71.A.1.20.8 L 010	
Small pentanummium			534–565	Bust r., E	
2349.	AE	1.15	9	79.L.1.41.49 L 004	*DOC* 1 p. 103: 97
2350.		1.87	12	78.C.21.90.21 L 036	*DOC* 1 p. 103: 97e
Decanummium			547/8	Bust r., I	
2351.	AE	1.81	14	78.E.6.28.127 L 015	*DOC* 1 p. 99: 82

NICOMEDIA

Pentanummium			527–538	Bust r., Chi-rho	*DOC* 1 p. 111: 114
2352.	AE	1.73	12	72.A.2.103.5 L 134	
Decanummium			556/7	Bust r., I	*DOC* 1 p. 122: 156
2353.	AE	2.50	19	71.A.2.158.271 L 050	
Half-follis			558/9	Bust facing, K	*DOC* 1 p. 122: 154
2354.	AE	6.61	20	80.G.10.135.13 L 043	

CYZICUS

Half-follis			545/6	Facing bust, K XYMI/I	Izmirlier 1969: 318, 8
2355.	AE	7.93	27	74.B.1.95.3 L 571	
Decanummium			563/4	Bust r., I	*DOC* 1 p. 132: 197
2356.	AE	4.31	15	78.E.6.7.4 L 001	

ANTIOCH

Follis, class 1			527/8	Bust r., M	*DOC* 1 p. 134: 202a2
2357.	AE	8.85	30	76.A.5.122.7 L 045	

Follis, class 2			529–533	Bust r., M	*DOC* 1 p. 136: 206b
2358. AE	16.58	32		74.H.4.49.79 L 028	
Follis, class 3			533–537	Bust r., M	*DOC* 1 p. 138: 210a
2359. AE	15.34	33		74.C.15.0.2 L 000; inventory only	
2360.	14.46	33		84.C.5.152.1 L 143; c/m on rev.: eagle (613–17, Evans 1993/4)	
2361.	13.37	33		87.C.42.6.2 L 003	
2362.	8.57	30		78.E.5.50.18 L 043	
2363.	14.33	26		80.G.10.153.16 L 050; c/m on rev.: eagle (613–17, Evans 1993/4) Plate 3	*DOC* 1 p. 138: 210b
Half-follis, class 3			533–537	Bust r., K	*DOC* 1 p. 139: 211c1
2364. AE	8.99	28		72.A.4.12.2 L 002	
Follis, class 4			537–539	Bust r., M	
2365. AE	11.18	29		76.A.6.299.1 L 128; inventory only	*DOC* 1 p. 140: 212c
2366.	9.07	30		78.B.8.96.12 L 016	*DOC* 1 p. 139: 212–13
Decanummium class D			551/2	Bust r., I	
2367. AE	3.47	21		71.A.2.136.131 L 001	*DOC* 1 p. 152: 256

Alexandria

Dodecanummium			527–565	Bust r., I + B	*DOC* 1 p. 157: 274
2368. AE	3.17	16		72.A.2.141.9 L 146	

2369.	3.30	16	74.H.4.62.2 L 044	**2373.**	0.95	13	74.H.4.41.4 L 028
2370.	2.24	15	74.B.5.21.1 L 042	**2374.**	0.52	11	76.A.5.100.2 L 048
2371.	2.19	18	71.A.2.11.6 L 001	**2375.**	0.71	14	72.C.3.96.1 L 028 (prob.)
2372.	1.87	15	76.E.1.96.1 L 076; inv. only	**2376.**	frag.	17	74.C.16.28.2 L 020 (prob.)

Dodecanummium			527–565	Bust r.?, I + B, pellets over +
2377. AE	2.62	15		75.PW.1.0.2 L 001; inventory only

Uncertain mint

Follis			527–538	Bust facing, M
2378. AE	12.88	30		72.B.1.35.10 L 085
Decanummium			538–565	Bust r., I
2379. AE	2.27	13		76.E.4.0.1 L 000; inventory only
2380.	1.73	14		74.H.4.36.2 L 028
Nummus			538–565	Bust r., monogram (Constantinople?)
2381. AE	0.80	10		72.A.1.7.9 L 078;
2382.	0.73	9		79.L.1.28.34 L 004
Decanummium			556/7	Bust r., I, year 30
2383. AE	4.04	17		79.K.1.60.38 L 013

ANASTASIUS THROUGH THE UNREFORMED COINAGE OF JUSTINIAN (418–538)

CONSTANTINOPLE

Follis 498–538 Bust r., M

2384. AE 15.32 33 72.A.2.141.8 L 146; Off. E

2385. 11.88 31 74.H.4.65.15 L 045; Off. Δ

2386. 9.47 29 71.A.2.158.269 L 050; Off. B

2387. 7.20 30 74.C.16.86.1 L 040

UNCERTAIN MINT

Follis 498–538 Bust r., M

2388. AE 12.60 31 72.C.3.6.1 L 002

2389. 10.55 28 71.A.2.176.391 L 059

2390. 7.15 30 74.C.16.8.1 L 013

2391. 6.22* 30 71.B.2.123.849 L 070

2392. frag. 30 79.K.0.0.3 L 000; inv. only

JUSTIN I THROUGH JUSTINIAN I (527–565)

CONSTANTINOPLE

Follis 518–538 Bust r., M

2393. AE 12.89 30 78.C.24.30.13 L 008; Off. B

2394. 12.53 31 71.B.1.130.23 L 048; Off. B; c/m on rev.: eagle (613–17, Evans 1993/4), Plate 3

2395. 10.18 29 71.A.2.73.21 L020; Off. Δ; inventory only; c/m on obv., Arabic

Pentanummium 518–538 Bust r., Chi-rho

2396. AE 1.35 14 76.A.5.116.1 L 052; inventory only

2397. 1.09 12 72.C.4.32.2 L 028

2398. 1.05 12 84.G.18.174.55 L 046

UNCERTAIN MINT

Pentanummium Bust r., Chi-rho

2399. AE 1.91 14 80.G.9.208.66 L 005

2400. 1.36 12 84.C.20.122.17 L 024

JUSTIN II (15 NOVEMBER 565 – 5 OCTOBER 578)

CARTHAGE

Half-follis 572/3 Justin and Sophia, K — *DOC* 1 p. 255: 199

2401. AE 10.37 23 72.B.1.49.2 L 087

THESSALONICA

Half-follis 566/7 Facing bust, K — *DOC* 1 p. 220: 62

2402. AE 4.48 23 74.C.17.0.1 L 000

Half-follis 576/7 Justin and Sophia, K

2403. AE 4.68 22 78.G.99.0.1 L 000 — *DOC* 1 p. 225: 84

Half-follis 568/9 Justin and Sophia, K

2404. AE 5.78 22 74.H.4.0.2 L 006 — *DOC* 1 p. 221: 65

2405. 5.94 22 79.K.1.0.145 L 000 — *DOC* 1 p. 221: 65.2

Half-follis 574/5 Justin and Sophia, K

2406. AE 4.37 20 76.A.5.52.5 L 019; inventory only *DOC* 1 p. 223: 78

Constantinople

Follis 566/7 Justin and Sophia, M

2407. AE 13.40 24 78.B.2.268.3 L 217 *DOC* 1 p. 205: 23a

Follis 568/9 Justin and Sophia, M

2408. AE 12.88 29 72.B.4.32.7 L 016 *DOC* 1 p. 206: 25b

Follis 569/70 Justin and Sophia, M

2409. AE 11.98 31 76.E.3.52.1 L 055; inventory only; Off. A *DOC* 1 p. 206: 26c

Follis 570/1 Justin and Sophia, M

2410. AE 12.67 32 78.E.5.44.14 L 041; Off. Δ *DOC* 1 p. 207: 28c

2411. 13.07 31 74.B.5.6.2 L 031 *DOC* 1 p. 208: 29c

Half-follis 572/3 Justin and Sophia, K

2412. AE 5.83 23 84.C.20.88.11 L 025; inventory only; date reads IϚ/I *DOC* 1 p. 216: 52b var

Follis 573/4 Justin and Sophia, M *DOC* 1 p. 210: 36b1

2413. AE 11.16 30 74.B.1.54.1 L 545

2414. 9.19 29 74.B.3.4.26 L 201

Half-follis 574/5 Justin and Sophia, K

2415. AE 3.15 23 71.A.2.85.28 L 032 *DOC* 1 p. 217: 56

Follis 576/7 Justin and Sophia, M

2416. AE 10.06 29 87.G.21.103.4 L 040; inventory only *DOC* 1 p. 213: 42b

2417. 9.54 31 71.A.1.35.20 L 013 *DOC* 1 p. 213: 42e

Nicomedia

Follis 568/9 Justin and Sophia, M

2418. AE 11.37 29 72.B.4.121.4 L 077 *DOC* 1 p. 227: 94b

Follis 572/3 Justin and Sophia, M

2419. AE 9.13 28 78.C.24.18.5 L 003 *DOC* 1 p. 229: 98d

Half-follis 572–575 Justin and Sophia, K

2420. AE 6.39 22 76.A.5.57.4 L 020; inventory only *DOC* 1 p. 233: 110–12

Cyzicus

Follis 574/5 Justin and Sophia, M *DOC* 1 p. 236: 123a

2421. AE 12.08 30 76.A.5.119.5 L 045; inventory only

2422. 4.55 21 71.B.1.133.29 L 038

ANTIOCH

Nummus 565–578 Bust r, monogram

2423. AE 0.75 8 79.K.3.0.50 L 005 *DOC* 1 p. 242: 149

2424. 0.72 10 80.G.9.5.3 L 001 *DOC* 1 p. 242: 149 var

Follis 571/2 Justin and Sophia, M

2425. AE 7.13 31 78.C.24.18.4 L 003 *DOC* 1 p. 243: 152

Half-follis 571/2 Justin and Sophia, K

2426. AE 7.94 25 72.C.2.20.2 L 213; inventory only; date reads: *X *DOC* 1 p. 247: 170 var

Half-follis 575/6 Justin and Sophia, K

2427. AE 7.11 24 79.L.1.76.89 L 029 *DOC* 1 p. 247: 171

JUSTIN I THROUGH JUSTIN II (518–578)

ALEXANDRIA

Pentanummium 518–578 Bust r., I + B

2428. AE 2.85 15 80.G.9.63.45 L 005

2429. 2.74 13 74.B.5.0.4 L 098

2430. 1.74 15 79.K.1.37.25 L 004

TIBERIUS II (26 SEPTEMBER 578 – 14 AUGUST 582)

CONSTANTINOPLE

Half-follis 579–582 Bust r., XX

2431. AE 5.55 24 84.C.20.27.1 L 025; inventory only *DOC* 1 p. 274: 17d

Follis 580/1 Bust r., M

2432. AE 10.63 30 71.B.2.49.140 L 021; inventory only *DOC* 1 p. 271: 13d

Follis 581/2 Bust r., M; obv. inscrip. reads: CON STANT...

2433. AE 9.65 31 71.A.2.95.61 L 042 *DOC* 1 p. 272: 14d

NICOMEDIA

Follis 579/80 Bust r., M

2434. AE 14.46 34 76.E.3.58.1 L 061; inventory only *DOC* 1 p. 278: 29

Follis 581/2 Bust r., M

2435. AE 11.11 29 74.C.15.46.1 L 001 *DOC* 1 p. 279: 31b

Three-quarter follis 579–582 Bust r., XXX

2436. AE 6.77 31 74.C.10.117.1 L 005 *DOC* 1 p. 280: 32a

Half-follis 579–582 Bust r., K

2437. AE 5.15 19 72.B.1.129.28 L 094 *DOC* 1 p. 280: 33a

Antioch

Follis 581/2 Bust r., M *DOC* 1 p. 283: 44

2438. AE 10.78 29 76.A.5.51.2 L 019; inventory only

Alexandria

Duodecanummium 578–582 Bust r., I + B *DOC* 1 p. 286: 55

2439. AE 5.99 15 72.C.2.145.1 L 297

2440. 4.97 15 87.C.42.5.1 L 003; inv. only

2441. 3.83 15 87.G.20.351.34 L 031

2442. 2.05 15 72.C.2.25.5 L 214

Uncertain mint

Half-follis 578–582 Bust r., XX

2443. AE frag. 17 74.C.16.28.1 L 020

Maurice (13 august 582 – 25 november 602)

Thessalonica

Half-follis 582–585 Bust r., K

2444. AE 5.72 22 74.B.7.1.1 L 001

Half-follis 584/5 Bust r., K; obv.: emp. helmeted

2445. AE 4.35 21 72.B.1.2.2 L 016 *DOC* 1 p. 321: 74

Half-follis 586/7 Bust r., K

2446. AE 5.06 22 78.E.5.37.9 L 031 *DOC* 1 p. 321: 77

Half-follis 589/90 Bust r., K

2447. AE 5.02 19 74.B.5.119.1 L 110 *DOC* 1 p. 322: 80

Half-follis 601/2 Bust r., K; c/m rev.: Hahn *MIB* 1a (630, Evans 1993/4)

2448. AE 5.21 21 74.C.15.51.2 L 028 *DOC* 1 p. 323: 89

Constantinople

Follis 583/4 Bust r., M

2449. AE 9.19 30 71.A.2.93.533 L 032 *DOC* 1 p. 303: 22d

Follis 584/5 Bust r., M

2450. AE 10.87 32 71.B.2.69.219 L 035 *DOC* 1 p. 304: 26b1

Half-follis 584/5 Bust r., K; blundered inscrip. obv

2451. AE 5.87 22 78.E.5.74.26 L 063 *DOC* 1 p. 311: 48

Follis 585/6 Bust r., M; c/m rev.?: Hahn *MIB* 1a (630, Evans 1993/4)

2452. AE 11.58 31 74.C.99.0.1 L 000; inventory only *DOC* 1 p. 304: 27b

Follis 588/9 Bust r., M; obv. defaced with chisel cuts c/m rev.: Hahn *MIB* 1a (630, Evans 1993/4)

2453. AE 12.24 36 80.C.25.150.27 L 000; Plate 3 *DOC* 1 p. 306: 30d

Follis			590/1	Bust r., M		
2454.	AE	10.39	31	71.A.2.158.184 L 010; Off. Δ		*DOC* 1 p. 307: 32b
Follis			591/2	Bust r., M; c/m obv.: Hahn *MIB* 1a (630, Evans 1993/4)		
2455.	AE	12.16	29	84.G.17.20.6 L 003; Off. Γ; Plate 3		*DOC* 1 p. 307: 33b
2456.		10.46	33	71.A.2.34.15 L 013; Off. B; c/m on rev. Hahn *MIB* 1a (630, Evans 1993/4); Plate 3		Russell 1983: 10
Half-follis			594/5	Bust r., K		
2457.	AE	10.38	31	78.C.22.195.16 L 150		*DOC* 1 p. 308: 36
Half-follis			594/5	Bust r., K (date reads: IX); o/s on decanummium of Maurice, 582–602, Constantinople (*DOC* 1 p. 317: 66c)		
2458.	AE	4.07	22	73.C.9.65.2 L 055		*DOC* 1 p. 314: 57 var
Follis			596/7	Bust r., M		
2459.	AE	10.07	30	87.G.20.230.18 L 031; inventory only; Off. A		*DOC* 1 p. 308: 38 var
Follis			596/7	Bust r., M; c/m rev.: Hahn *MIB* 1a (630, Evans 1993/4)		
2460.	AE	8.80	30	74.B.6.273.1 L 116; Off. E		*DOC* 1 p. 308: 38c
Follis			599/600	Bust r., M; c/m rev.: Hahn *MIB* 1a (630, Evans 1993/4)		
2461.	AE	10.52	28	72.C.4.59.1 L 054; Plate 3		*DOC* 1 p. 309: 41
Follis			582–602	Bust r., M; blundered obv. inscrip.; c/m on rev., Hahn *MIB* 1a (630, Evans 1993/4)		
2462.	AE	9.93	30	71.A.2.21.8 L 001; Plate 3 (rev.)		
2463.		9.10	34	74.C.15.28.2 L 011; inventory only; c/m on obv., Hahn *MIB* 1a, over face (630, Evans 1993/4)		
2464.		11.05	32	78.E.6.85.241 L 049 (prob.)		
Nicomedia						
Follis			584/5	Bust r., M		
2465.	AE	11.45	28	76.A.6.236.1 L 102; inventory only		*DOC* 1 p. 324: 93?
Follis			587–595	Bust facing, M; obv.: *DOC* 1 p. 326: 102–3, rev.: *DOC* 1 p. 325: 96a		
2466.	AE	9.64	27	72.A.1.153.1 L 012		
Follis			589/90	Bust facing, M		
2467.	AE	11.18	32	80.G.9.266.101 L 059; c/m obv.: Hahn *MIB* 1a (630, Evans 1993/4) Plate 3		*DOC* 1 p. 325: 98a
2468.		9.46	30	76.A.5.57.7 L 020; inventory only		
Follis			587–591	Bust facing, M		
2469.	AE	4.89	29	76.A.5.80.18 L 034; inventory only		*DOC* 1 p. 325: 96a–99a
Cyzicus						
Follis			587/8	Bust r., M		
2470.	AE	11.29	28	76.H.6.14.4 L 011; inventory only		*DOC* 1 p. 331: 122a

Half-follis			588/9	Bust r., K	
2471. AE	5.32	23		72.C.3.110.3 L 015	*DOC* 1 p. 334: 139
2472.	6.70	24		84.G.17.90.30 L 001; o/s on Justinian I half-follis, 538–557, Constantinople (*DOC* 1 p. 130: 182–92)	*DOC* 1 p. 334: 139a
ANTIOCH					
Follis			582–584	Facing bust, m	
2473. AE	11.51	30		72.A.3.153.1 L 049	*DOC* 1 p. 338: 152–53
Follis			586/7	Facing bust, m; c/m rev.: Hahn *MIB* 1a (630, Evans 1993/4)	
2474. AE	10.58	31		72.B.4.28.2 L 016; Plate 3 (rev.)	*DOC* 1 p. 339: 156
Follis			588/9	Facing bust, m	
2475. AE	11.93	30		72.A.2.74.11 L 119	*DOC* 1 p. 339: 158b
Follis			589/90	Facing bust, m; (date reads: y/IH)	
2476. AE	10.35	29		72.A.2.20.2 L 097	*DOC* 1 p. 340: 159 var
Follis			591/2	Facing bust, M	
2477. AE	9.77	30		76.A.6.0.1 L 000; inventory only	*DOC* 1 p. 341: 162c
Follis			592/3	Facing bust, M	
2478. AE	11.37	28		80.G.9.132.57 L 005	*DOC* 1 p. 341: 163a
Follis			593/4	Facing bust, M	
2479. AE	10.58	29		84.G.18.4.2 L 001	*DOC* 1 p. 342: 164a
Follis			594/5	Facing bust, M	
2480. AE	10.30	28		76.A.5.131.1 L 045; inventory only	*DOC* 1 p. 343: 165b
Follis			594/5	Facing bust, M; year 13, Off. A	
2481. AE	25.29	35		74.H.4.80.1 L 050; inventory only; combination unpublished	
Follis			595/6	Facing bust, M	
2482. AE	10.80	28		76.A.6.227.1 L 096; inventory only	*DOC* 1 p. 343: 166c
Half-follis			595/6	Facing bust, K	
2483. AE	4.47	22		76.C.18.65.1 L 068; inventory only	*DOC* 1 p. 348: 189
Follis			596/7	Facing bust, M; Off. E	
2484. AE	8.61	27		72.C.3.115.2 L 048	*DOC* 1 p. 343: 167c
Half-follis			596/7	Facing bust, K	
2485. AE	5.50	20		74.C.15.34.3 L 016	*DOC* 1 p. 348: 190
Follis			599/600	Bust facing, M; Off. Γ	
2486. AE	7.18	27		76.A.5.105.1 L 045; inventory only	*DOC* 1 p. 344: 170b1
Half-follis				Bust facing, K X/ϛ, mintmark P (not R)	
2487. AE	4.06	25		74.B.5.127.2 L 120	*DOC* 1 p. 348: 190 var

Follis 601/2 Facing bust, m

2488. AE 9.25 25 71.A.1.62.58 L 030 — *DOC* 1 p. 345: 172; unc. off.

ALEXANDRIA

Dodecanummium 582–602 Bust r., I + B

2489. AE 1.45 14 79.K.3.0.67 L 001 — *DOC* 1 p. 352: 213.3

Dodecanummium 582–700 Bust r., I + B — Hahn *NC* 1980: 67 nos. 81–83

2490. AE 2.23 12 79.L.1.0.46 L 000

UNCERTAIN MINT

Follis 588/9 Facing bust, M

2491. AE 10.15 30 72.C.2.72.2 L 254

Follis 597/8? Facing bust, M

2492. AE 5.93 27 71.A.2.106.113 L 001

Half-follis 582–602 Facing bust, K

2493. AE 2.30 21 71.A.2.77.25 L 023

JUSTINIAN THROUGH MAURICE (527–602)

UNCERTAIN MINT

Half-follis 543–600 Facing bust, K; date: IX/IϚ; Off. Δ

2494. AE 4.65 22 78.E.5.39.11 L 031

PHOCAS (23 NOVEMBER 602 – 4 OCTOBER 610)

CONSTANTINOPLE

Follis, class 1 602/3 Phocas and Leontia, m — *DOC* 2.1 p. 163: 24c

2495. AE 7.97 32 71.A.1.76.62 L 035

NICOMEDIA

Half-follis, class 2 606/7 Bust r., XX — *DOC* 2.1 p. 180: 66b

2496. AE 4.49 23 72.B.1.74.1 L 047

CYZICUS

Half-follis, class 2 606?–610 Bust r., XX — *DOC* 2.1 p. 185: 81a1

2497. AE 5.12 22 72.C.2.176.1 L 340

Half-follis, class 2 606?–610 Bust facing (instead of r.), XX — *DOC* 2.1 p. 185: 81a var

2498. AE 5.44 21 74.H.4.249.4 L 109

ANTIOCH

Follis, class 1 602–608 Phocas and Leontia, m

2499. AE 10.92 29 76.A.5.52.4 L 019; inventory only — *DOC* 2.1 pp. 187: 83–188: 89

Follis, class 1 | 603/4 | Phocas and Leontia, m | *DOC* 2.1 p. 187: 84

No.	Metal	Wt.	Size	Details
2500.	AE	9.66	29	78.C.24.39.19 L 039
2501.		9.56	29	76.A.5.52.3 L 019; inventory only
2502.		8.68	25	76.E.4.24.1 L 033; inventory only

Half-follis, class 1 | 603/4 | Phocas and Leontia, XX | *DOC* 2.1 p. 189: 92.1

No.	Metal	Wt.	Size	Details
2503.	AE	4.23	22	78.C.21.121.26 L 049; Plate 3

Alexandria

Dodecanummium class 1 | 603? | Bust r. with beard, I + B | *DOC* 2.1 p. 192: 105 var

No.	Metal	Wt.	Size	Details
2504.	AE	2.40	14	78.E.5.50.17 L 043

Dodecanummium class 2 | 602–608 | Bust r., I + B | *DOC* 2.1 p. 192: 106

No.	Metal	Wt.	Size	Details
2505.	AE	3.78	13	74.C.17.2.1 L 002; Plate 3
2506.		3.37	14	76.A.5.100.4 L 048; inv. only
2507.		2.86	14	74.B.7.1.3 L 001
2508.		2.72	14	75.PC.6.0.1 L 000; inv. only
2509.		2.67	12	76.E.3.0.3 L 000; inventory only
2510.		2.57	14	72.B.1.114.24 L 084
2511.		2.55	14	71.A.1.112.167 L 055
2512.		2.43	12	80.G.9.203.65 L 005
2513.		2.36	13	74.C.15.33.1 L 015
2514.		2.32	10	74.C.16.59.4 L 000
2515.		2.22	12	73.C.9.38.2 L 044
2516.		2.17	13	72.L.1.107.110 L 021
2517.		2.15	14	84.G.17.15.4 L 001
2518.		2.15	12	72.C.3.27.4 L 008
2519.		2.12	13	79.L.1.51.70 L 019
2520.		2.11	14	74.B.4.48.1 L 331
2521.		2.10	14	72.C.3.113.1 L 047; ALEX reversed
2522.		2.06	13	74.C.13.122.4 L 110
2523.		2.05	13	74.B.5.164.3 L 135
2524.		1.98	15	76.A.5.100.5 L 048; inv. only
2525.		1.98	13	72.C.4.33.3 L 029
2526.		1.97	14	74.B.4.34.1 L 320
2527.		1.91	12	74.C.15.1.1 L 001
2528.		1.90	14	79.L.1.39.43 L 004
2529.		1.89	14	84.G.18.193.78 L 046
2530.		1.87	11	79.K.3.0.68 L 001
2531.		1.86	13	79.L.1.27.23 L 004
2532.		1.84	12	74.B.5.159.1 L 112
2533.		1.82	13	84.G.18.205.110 L 000
2534.		1.82	12	87.G.23.13.1 L 006
2535.		1.80	14	80.G.7.226.40 L 000
2536.		1.78	13	74.B.6.202.1 L 116
2537.		1.76	11	87.G.21.72.3 L 021
2538.		1.73	14	76.A.5.122.11 L 045; inv. only
2539.		1.73	11	79.L.1.27.29 L 004
2540.		1.68	12	78.B.99.0.5 L 000
2541.		1.68	10	79.L.1.10.1 L 004
2542.		1.67	13	74.B.5.103.1 L 094
2543.		1.66	12	80.G.10.188.29 L 048
2544.		1.62	13	79.K.3.0.122 L 000
2545.		1.60	9	78.E.6.7.7 L 001
2546.		1.55	13	80.G.10.158.17 L 050
2547.		1.55	12	72.C.2.63.1 L 248
2548.		1.52	12	80.C.28.47.3 L 009
2549.		1.51	12	74.H.4.21.1 L 016
2550.		1.50	11	73.L.1.21.16 L 004; inv. only
2551.		1.50	11	76.A.5.106.2 L 048e; inv. only
2552.		1.47	12	82.C.31.95.4 L 066; inv. only
2553.		1.46	13	71.X.0.0.10 L 000
2554.		1.46	13	79.K.1.0.150 L 030
2555.		1.44	13	71.A.1.22.13 L 011
2556.		1.44	12	80.G.9.91.52 L 005
2557.		1.42	15	80.C.26.125.12 L 020
2558.		1.41	12	79.L.1.27.21 L 004
2559.		1.37	13	72.A.1.7.14 L 078
2560.		1.37	12	74.H.4.3.3 L 002

2561.	1.36	12	74.C.15.42.2 L 001	**2576.**	0.99	13	72.A.3.168.124 L 063
2562.	1.35	13	78.C.24.20.7 L 003	**2577.**	0.98	15	76.E.1.27.1 L 023; inv. only
2563.	1.32	14	82.G.14.30.6 L 009; inv. only	**2578.**	0.98	13	82.G.14.267.219 L 100; inv. only
2564.	1.31	13	87.C.41.47.2 L 015	**2579.**	0.95	14	72.A.3.120.3 L 020
2565.	1.30	12	84.G.17.69.18 L 003	**2580.**	0.92	13	74.H.4.54.4 L 036
2566.	1.30	12	72.C.2.10.4 L 204	**2581.**	0.91	13	74.B.5.141.1 L 118
2567.	1.29	12	76.A.5.100.1 L 048; inv. only	**2582.**	0.88	14	84.C.36.0.3 L 000
2568.	1.24	12	72.B.4.128.5 L 080	**2583.**	0.73	14	78.E.6.25.133 L 001
2569.	1.19	15	78.E.5.137.83 L 116; inv. only	**2584.**	0.68	13	78.B.9.16.2 L 003
2570.	1.16	12	76.A.5.80.20 L 034; inv. only	**2585.**	0.56	13	72.B.3.106.2 L 001
2571.	1.15	12	79.L.1.67.76 L 021	**2586.**	0.46	11	72.B.1.129.25 L 094
2572.	1.14	12	72.SP.7.11.8 L 003	**2587.**	0.39	10	78.E.6.7.6 L 001
2573.	1.10	13	80.G.9.212.68 L 005	**2588.**	0.31	8	78.E.6.54.197 L 034
2574.	1.07	11	76.A.5.238.3 L 080	**2589.**	0.15	9	78.E.6.14.22 L 001
2575.	1.01	13	79.L.1.71.85 L 021	**2590.**	frag.	11	74.B.5.180.1 L 139

Justin I through Phocas (518–610)

Alexandria

Pentanummium Bust r., I + B

2591. AE	2.94	16	74.B.5.130.3 L 113	**2603.**	1.40	11	79.L.1.99.103 L 015
2592.	2.64	15	72.B.3.233.2 L 071	**2604.**	1.32	12	71.B.1.116.9 L 016
2593.	2.62	14	79.K.1.0.62 L 037	**2605.**	1.11	15	71.A.1.109.159 L 025
2594.	2.32	16	72.B.4.30.5 L 016	**2606.**	1.04	14	71.B.2.96.243 L 049
2595.	2.19	13	71.A.2.11.6 L 001	**2607.**	frag.	13	71.A.1.34.25 L 016
2596.	2.13	14	79.L.1.27.22 L 004	**2608.**	frag.	15	72.A.3.164.1 L 053
2597.	1.92	13	74.H.5.23.1 L 007	**2609.**	frag.	16	71.A.1.21.11 L 011
2598.	1.87	13	72.B.4.142.12 L 080	**2610.**	frag.	18	72.B.4.30.6 L 016
2599.	1.87	12	71.A.1.0.160 L 025	**2611.**	frag.	13	80.C.28.7.1 L 004
2600.	1.62	15	71.B.2.12.8 L 005	**2612.**	frag.	13	72.A.3.155.3 L 049
2601.	1.61	13	72.B.3.134.1 L 042	**2613.**	frag.	15	72.A.3.155.2 L 049
2602.	1.49	13	72.A.3.171.12 L 056	**2614.**	frag.	17	78.E.5.74.30 L 063

Justinian through Phocas (527–610)

Constantinople

Half-follis 538–610 Bust r., K

2615. AE 3.15 22 71.B.1.128s.21 L 016

Uncertain mint

Half-follis 538–610 Bust r., K

2616. AE 4.28 21 80.C.21.872.1 L 121

Decanummium 538–610 Bust r., I

2617. AE 2.30 15 79.L.1.124.116 L 022

Justin II through Phocas (565–610)

Constantinople

Follis 566–612 Uncertain obverse, M

2618. AE 8.06 30 87.C.24.0.1 L 000

Uncertain mint

Follis 565–614 Two figures, M; overstruck?

2619. AE 9.46 29 71.A.1.109s.161 L 025

Heraclius (5 October 610 – 11 February 641)

Thessalonica

Half-follis, class 2 619/20 2 standing figures, K *DOC* 2.1 p. 312: 145

2620. AE 5.23 27 72.C.3.70.1 L 020; c/m rev., 2 times: Hahn *MIB* 1a, 1b (634, Evans 1993/4) Plate 4

2621. 2.18 19 79.K.0.0.2 L 000

Constantinople

Follis, class 1 610–613 Bust facing, M

2622. AE 11.20 28 74.C.15.51.1 L 028; inventory only; c/m obv.: Hahn *MIB* 1a (630, Evans 1993/4)

Follis, class 1 611/12 Bust facing, M *DOC* 2.1 p. 275: 70a

2623. AE 12.94 32 74.C.15.28.1 L 011; inventory only; c/m rev.: Hahn *MIB* 1a (630, Evans 1993/4)

Follis, class 1 611–613 Bust r., M *DOC* 2.1 p. 275: 70 or 71d

2624. AE 9.50 30 71.A.1.70.228 L 028

Follis, class 1 613 Bust r., M

2625. AE 9.49 33 74.B.5.119.3 L 110; o/s on ? *DOC* 2.1 p. 276: 71

Half-follis 610–614 Bust facing, K

2626. AE 3.43 25 74.B.1.21.1 L 513 *DOC* 2.1 p. 277: 72–74

Follis, class 2 613–616 2 standing figures, M

2627. AE frag. 31 79.L.1.49.53 L 014; Plate 4 (rev.) *DOC* 2.1 p. 279: 76–82

Follis, class 2 614/5 2 standing figures, M *DOC* 2.1 p. 284: 80b

2628. AE 11.08 32 80.G.9.18.9 L 001; o/s on Heraclius class 1 follis, 610–613, Nicomedia (*DOC* 2.1 p. 315: 153–55); itself o/s on Phocas class 2 follis, 606/7, Nicomedia (*DOC* 2.1 p. 178: 58a)

Follis, class 2 614/5 2 standing figures, M *DOC* 2.1 p. 284: 80d

2629. AE 10.35 31 71.A.2.71.19 L 020; o/s on Maurice follis, 586/7, Constantinople (*DOC* 1 p. 304: 28); itself o/s on Justin II follis; c/m rev.: Hahn *MIB* 1a (630, Evans 1993/4) Plate 4 (rev.)

2630. 10.14 28 74.C.15.10.4 L 005; o/s on Phocas XXX, 607/8; itself o/s on Maurice? half-follis

Half-follis 615/6 2 standing figures, K *DOC* 2.1 p. 286: 84

2631. AE 4.81 29 72.C.4.28.1 L 025; o/s on Heraclius follis

2632. frag. 22 71.B.1.121s.14 L 016

2633. 2.22 22 80.C.27.46.5 L 001; no obv. inscrip. *DOC* 2.1 p. 286: 84 var

Follis, class 3			615/6	3 standing figures, M	
2634.	AE	6.48	31	84.C.20.121.16 L 024	*DOC* 2.1 p. 288: 89
Half-follis, unc. class			619/20?	Bust r., K	
2635.	AE	4.55	24	71.A.2.161.340 L 001	
Follis, class 4			624–629	3 standing figures, M	
2636.	AE	5.14	20	74.C.15.7.2 L 001; o/s?	
Follis, class 4			625/6	3 standing figures, M	*DOC* 2.1 p. 293: 100b?
2637.	AE	3.13	24	74.B.5.55.1 L 061; o/s on uncertain type	
Half-follis, class 4			625/6	3 standing figures, K	*DOC* 2.1 p. 294: 104 var
2638.	AE	2.01	18	87.G.19.73.1 L 017; inventory only; ANNO K X/ ςI, cross above, but nothing beneath	
Large follis, class 5			629/30	2 standing figures, M	
2639.	AE	7.15	28	72.C.2.19.1 L 208; o/s on Heraclius class 2 follis, Constantinople	*DOC* 2.1 p. 295: 105a
2640.		8.00	28	72.B.1.106.3 L 048	*DOC* 2.1 p. 296: 105c
2641.		7.32	23	71.A.2.91.32 L 035	
2642.		–	28	74.C.15.28.3 L 011; o/s on Heraclius class 1 follis, Constantinople, 611/2 (*DOC* 2.1 p. 275: 70b); c/m rev. twice: Hahn *MIB* 1b, (634 Evans 1993/4) inventory only	
2643.		9.15	32	72.C.2.34.5 L 228; o/s on Justin II? follis, Thessalonica?; c/m rev: Hahn *MIB* 1a (630, Evans 1993/4)	*DOC* 2.1 p. 296: 105d
2644.		10.75	40	75.PC.6.9.1 L 009; c/m rev, twice:  second indistinguishable; inventory only	*DOC* 2.1 p. 296: 105d2
Small follis, class 5			631/2	2 standing figures, M	*DOC* 2.1 p. 297: 107a
2645.	AE	5.92	26	72.A.1.31.3 L 071; o/s on Phocas follis, Antioch; c/m rev.: Hahn *MIB* 1a (630, Evans 1993/4) Plate 4 (rev.)	
Large follis, class 5			631–34	2 standing figures, M	*DOC* 2.1 p. 297: 107–11 1b
2646.	AE	5.07	21	76.A.5.64.1 L 005; inventory only; c/m rev. three times: Hahn *MIB* 1b (twice), 1a (once; 634, Evans 1993/4)	
Large follis, class 5			632/3	2 standing figures, M	*DOC* 2.1 p. 297: 108
2647.	AE	6.37	25	73.C.9.0.1 L 044; o/s on uncertain type; c/m rev.: Hahn *MIB* 1a (630, Evans 1993/4) Plate 4 (rev.)	
Large follis, class 5			629–641	2 standing figures, M	
2648.	AE	5.52	24	72.C.4.2.1 L 002; o/s?; inventory only	
2649.		4.63	26	72.B.1.0.1 L 048; o/s on follis, Constantinople	
2650.		4.96	22	73.C.9.52.1 L 044; o/s?	
Small follis, class 5			634–640	2 standing figures, M	
2651.	AE	5.37	27	72.C.2.102.3 L 273; o/s on uncertain type; c/m rev., twice: Hahn *MIB* 1a, 1b (634, Evans 1993/4) Plate 4	

Large three-quarter follis			629/30	2 standing figures, Λ	
2652.	AE	3.83	24	74.C.15.53.3 L 534; inventory only; c/m rev: Hahn *MIB* 1b (634, Evans 1993/4)	*DOC* 2.1 p. 301: 117a
2653.		4.94	26	74.C.15.33.2 L 515; o/s on half-follis?	*DOC* 2.1 p. 301: 117b
2654.		6.25	24	74.C.15.56.4 L 041; c/m rev.: Hahn *MIB* 1b, 634 (Evans 1993/4) Plate 4 (rev.)	*DOC* 2.1 p. 301: 117
Large half-follis class 5			629/30	2 standing figures, K	
2655.	AE	6.37	20	80.G.10.142.15 L 041; o/s on class 5 half- follis, 629–631	*DOC* 2.1 p. 302: 118b
2656.		4.06	23	72.C.4.59.3 L 059; o/s on uncertain type	*DOC* 2.1 p. 302: 118c
2657.		5.19	25	84.C.5.228.2 L 172; o/s on follis, Constantinople	*DOC* 2.1 p. 302: 118d
2658.		6.19	25	72.C.4.13.1 L 011; o/s on follis, Constantinople	
2659.		5.54	28	72.A.2.79.10 L 097; o/s on half-follis, mm CONOB	*DOC* 2.1 p. 302: 118
2660.		frag.	24	72.C.3.34.1 L 010	
Large half-follis class 5			630/1	2 standing figures, K	
2661.	AE	5.35	23	74.B.5.29.1 L 051	*DOC* 2.1 p. 303: 119a
2662.		6.21	24	72.C.4.29.1 L 025; o/s on Heraclius, follis, Cyzicus, 628/9 (*DOC* 2.1 p. 327: 178)	*DOC* 2.1 p. 303: 119c
Small half-follis class 5			631/2	2 standing figures, K	*DOC* 2.1 p. 304: 120b
2663.	AE	2.88	21	74.B.5.144.2 L 098	
Small half-follis class 5			639/40	2 standing figures, K (date ϛI)	*DOC* 2.1 p. 304: 122 var
2664.	AE	2.53	18	79.L.1.23.18 L 004	
Large half-follis class 5			629–631	2 standing figures, K	
2665.	AE	5.80	23	72.C.5.56.2 L 045; o/s on half-follis, class 5, 629–631; c/m rev.: Hahn *MIB* 1b (634, Evans 1993/4) Plate 4 (rev.)	
2666.		3.98	27	74.C.15.0.1 L 000; o/s on class 4 follis, 624–626; c/m rev.: Hahn *MIB* 1b (634, Evans 1993/4)	
Large follis, class 5			631–640	2 standing figures, M	
2667.	AE	11.20	31	82.C.32.194.2 L 120; o/s on unc. type; c/m rev., three times: Hahn *MIB* 1b (twice), third obscure (634, Evans 1993/4) inventory only	
Small follis, class 5			631–640	2 standing figures, M	
2668.	AE	6.15	27	78.C.24.35.18 L 037	
2669.		3.96	26	76.A.6.208.1 L 083w; o/s on unc. type; c/m rev.? "many times," Hahn *MIB* 1a (630, Evans 1993/4) inventory only	
Large half-follis class 5			631–640	2 standing figures, K	*DOC* 2.1 p. 303: 120–24
2670.	AE	2.60	14	76. A.5.80.21 L 034	

Small half-follis class 5 631–640 2 standing figures, K

2671. AE 4.98 20 73.C.9.65.3 L 051; o/s on uncertain type

Nicomedia

Follis, class 1 610/11 Bust facing, M *DOC* 2.1 p. 315: 153b

2672. AE 9.00 30 73.C.9.23.2 L 044; c/m obv: Hahn *MIB* 1a? (630, Evans 1993/4) Plate 4 (obv.)

Follis, class 2 612/3 2 standing figures, M

2673. AE 10.11 29 78.C.22.208.19 L 160; o/s on year 1 follis of uncertain ruler, Antioch *DOC* 2.1 p. 318: 158b2

Follis 612/3 mule?: obv. Maurice?, rev. M

2674. AE 12.26 28 72.A.4.12.1 L 002; o/s on Phocas follis, Constantinople; c/m rev.: Hahn *MIB* 1a (630 Evans 1993/4) Plate 4 *DOC* 2.1 p. 316: 154b (rev.)

Follis, class 1 610–613 Bust facing, M *DOC* 2.1 p. 315: 153–55

2675. AE 12.36 28 75.PW.1.6.3 L 005; inventory only

Cyzicus

Follis, class 1 612/3 Bust facing, M

2676. AE 10.44 30 84.C.5.251.4 L 192; inventory only; c/m rev.: Hahn *MIB* 1a (630, Evans 1993/4) *DOC* 2.1 p. 322: 169a9–b6

Follis, class 1 613/4 Bust r., M

2677. AE 9.35 32 74.C.11.0.1 L 001 *DOC* 2.1 p. 323: 170a

Alexandria

Dodecanummium class 1 613–618 2 busts facing, I + B *DOC* 2.1 p. 334: 189

2678. AE 6.12 16 79.L.1.71.87 L 021

2679. 6.04 16 80.G.9.215.72 L 005

2680. 3.66 16 72.A.3.60.7 L 009

Dodecanummium class 2 618–628 Facing bust (Chosroes II?), I + B *DOC* 2.1 p. 336: 191

2681. AE 4.11 19 76.A.5.119.4 L 045; inventory only

2682. 3.80 15 76.A.5.129.3 L 045; inventory only

Hexanummium class 1 613–618 Cross potent, S *DOC* 2.1 p. 340: 198

2683. AE 2.60 17 72.C.4.59.2 L 059; o/s on Phocas, dodecanummium, Alexandria, 602–608 (*DOC* 2.1 p. 192: 106)

2684. 2.30 15 80.G.9.0.76 L 000; o/s on Phocas, dodecanummium, Alexandria, 602–608 (*DOC* 2.1 p. 192: 106)

2685. 2.30 14 74.B.5.162.1 L 134

2686. 2.28 16 71.B.2.99.350 L 052

2687.		2.16	14	72.A.3.143.2 L 050	
2688.		2.10	15	72.B.4.121.1 L 077	
2689.		2.09	16	76.A.5.122.10 L 045; inventory only	
2690.		2.09	15	80.G.10.188.27 L 048; (obv. inscrip: domh er) o/s on Phocas, dodecanummium, Alexandria, 602–608 (*DOC* 2.1 p. 192: 106) inventory only	
2691.		2.06	11	74.B.6.0.3 L 122; o/s on Phocas, dodecanummium, Alexandria, 602–608 (*DOC* 2.1 p. 192: 106)	
2692.		2.04	15	79.L.1.28.35 L 004	
2693.		1.88	16	71.A.1.20.221 L 010; o/s on Heraclius class 1 dodecanummium, 613–618, Alexandria (*DOC* 2.1 p. 334: 189–90)	
2694.		1.87	13	84.G.2.0.89.14 L 064 (obv. inscrip: domh er)	
2695.		1.84	14	80.G.10.185.24 L 048	
2696.		1.82	11	84.G.18.268.225 L 061	
2697.		1.78	15	79.L.1.14.7 L 001; o/s on Phocas, dodecanummium, Alexandria, 602–608 (*DOC* 2.1 p. 192: 106)	
2698.		1.71	13	72.B.1.133.27 L 101; o/s on Phocas, dodecanummium, Alexandria, 602–608 (*DOC* 2.1 p. 192: 106)	
2699.		1.70	16	72.SP.1.3.9 L 005	
2700.		1.60	16	80.G.9.94.53 L 005	
2701.		1.40	16	71. A.1.20.114 L 010	
2702.		1.21	15	71.B.1.128s.19 L 016	
2703.		1.16	13	80.G.9.204.67 L 049	
2704.		0.94	15	71.A.1.109.157 L 028	
2705.		frag.	15	71.A.1.103.233 L 000	
2706.		frag.	11	84.G.18.185.61 L 046	
Hexanummium class 2		628/9?		2 standing figures, S	*DOC* 2.1 p. 342: 199
2707.	AE	1.88	14	74.B.6.0.2 L 000; o/s on Phocas, dodecanummium, Alexandria, 602–608 (*DOC* 2.1 p. 192: 106)	
2708.		3.09	19	87.G.21.159.8 L 059; with obv. inscription: …CLI	

Uncertain mint

Follis, class 2		613–616		2 standing figures, M	
2709.	AE	10.92	30	74.B.5.112.2 L 098; o/s on Maurice follis, Constantinople	
Half-follis, class 1		614–616		Bust facing, K	
2710.	AE	4.11	23	72.B.4.140.1 L 055	
Half-follis, class 1		625–640		Facing bust, K	
2711.	AE	3.44	24	78.E.6.88.242 L 051; o/s on Heraclius follis, 624/5, Constantinople (*DOC* 2.1 p. 292: 99)	
Follis, class 5		629–641		2 standing figures, M	
2712.	AE	frag.	21	72.B.1.16.1 L 048; o/s?	

Follis, class 5 630–641 2 standing figures, M

2713. AE 8.77 28 76.C.19.32.1 L 023; inventory only; o/s on Justinian class E half-follis, 556/7, Antioch (*DOC* 2.1 p. 150: 245); c/m obv. Hahn *MIB* 1a (630, Evans 1993/4)

UNCERTAIN RULER

CONSTANTINOPLE

Follis 518–640 Bust r., M

2714. AE 6.68 32 78.C.24.40.20 L 041

UNCERTAIN MINT

Follis 498–640 Bust r., M

2715. AE frag. 24 74.C.8.151.1 L 102

Follis 518–640 Bust r., M

2716. AE frag. 20 78.E.5.82.35 L 064

Half-follis 498–640 Bust r., K

2717. AE 4.20 18 71.A.1.27.15 L 013

2718. 3.21 23 71.A.1.129.214 L 061

2719. 1.78 21 71.X.0.0.20 L 000

2720. 1.36 18 71.X.0.0.6 L 000

Half-follis 518–640 Bust r., K

2721. AE 8.64 21 76.A.5.116.2 L 052

HERACLONAS (APRIL–OCTOBER? 641)

CONSTANTINOPLE

Follis 641 Bust facing, M *DOC* 2.2 p. 396: 5e

2722. AE 3.00 25 80.C.26.183.17 L 070; Plate 4 (obv.)

CONSTANS II (SEPTEMBER 641 – 15 JULY 668)

CONSTANTINOPLE

Follis 646/7 Standing figure, m; Off. B, date ϛ *DOC* 2.2 p. 447: 65 var

2723. AE 5.60 23 80.G.10.130.12 L 039

Follis, class 5 651/2? Standing figure, M, A beneath *DOC* 2.2 p. 450: 69

2724. AE 3.40 22 72.A.4.26.5 L 011; o/s on Heraclonas class 1 follis

Follis, class 6 655–657 Standing figure, M *DOC* 2.2 p. 452: 75–76

2725. AE frag. 20 72.B.1.75.2 L 089

Follis, class 11 666–668 Bust facing, M *DOC* 2.2 p. 459: 88–89

2726. AE frag. 17 71.X.0.0.2 L 000

UNCERTAIN MINT

Follis 651–658 Standing figure, M

2727. AE frag. 24 74.C.8.148.3 L 097; Plate 4

Constantine IV (13 April 654 – 10 July 685)

Carthage

Follis, class 2 674–681 Bust facing, M *DOC* 2.2 p. 549: 52

2728. AE 1.63 21 71.A.2.25.9 L 001

Fals, 7th century

Standing emperor, M Hahn *MIB:* pl.29 x23–33

2729. AE 0.95 22 82.G.14.258.218 L 073; inventory only

Three emperors standing, M

2730. AE 4.08 13 80.G.7.163.21 L 097

Facing bust, M

2731. AE 2.51 20 73.C.7.3.1 L 001

Standing figure, M

2732. AE 3.06 32 71.A.1.105.150 L 025

Uncertain, M, c/m rev., Arabic

2733. AE 2.70 23 71.A.2.192.418 L 065

Follis Uncertain date, mint, 5th–7th century

2734. AE frag. – 73.C.9.37.2 L 000

Index of Loci

The Locus Index is arranged by Fields, the positions of which are shown on the Map, Figure 1. Fields PA, PC, PS, PW and SP are probes within the lettered Fields, as explained in the Introduction. Within the field, the excavation was done in 10 × 10 meter squares, which are designated with numbers after the Field letter; these are called Areas. The Locus, or specific stratigraphic unit, is designated by the three-digit number after the Area number. Sealed loci are marked with an asterisk. All dates (in italics) are C.E., unless marked B.C.E. The numbers after the colon are the catalog numbers. In cases of vague definitions ("unidentified 5th–6th century"), or where the coin was not part of the catalog, the numbers in parentheses are the number of coins in this category at this locus. Note that countermarked coins are placed in the era when they last left the mint.

A.1

079 *Trajanic:* 69

083 *445–518:* 1692; *5th–early 6th century* (1)

084 *361–401:* 736, 1135

085 *200–300:* 424, 471; *300–361:* 798, 863; *361–400:* 1021, 1075, 1128, 1286, 1301, 1384; *457–474:* 1603; *5th–early 6th century* (2)

085a *300–361:* 529, 846; *361–400:* 1004, 1028, 1348; *450–518:* 1634, 1668

085b *350-355:* 636; *364–400:* 981, 1074, 1189, 1331; *425–450:* 1429; *423–533:* 1783

087 *280–40 B.C.E.:* 387

089 *98–138:* 103

090 *Augustan:* 39; *Trajan/Hadrian:* 109; *250–310:* 449, 478; *100–300:* 370; *300–361:* 374, 523, 559, 596, 712, 782, 790, 838; *361–404:* 904, 1000, 1023, 1046, 1056, 1057, 1113, 1114, 1121, 1126, 1163, 1223, 1290, 1343, 1346, 1350, 1358, 1359, 1380, 1381, 1404; *375–465:* 1239, 1276; *4th century* (1); *404–450:* 1424, 1447; *445–518:* 1656, 1674; *5th–early 6th century* (2); *7th–8th century* (1)

095 *249–250:* 150; *300–361:* 508, 556, 575, 578, 589, 591, 609, 614, 620, 641, 642, 656, 679, 708, 753, 757, 759, 791, 804, 829, 832, 835, 837; *383–392:* 1190

096 *337–340:* 595

097 *217–256:* 117, 179; *270–280:* 462, 465; *310–314:* 484, 485, 486, 491, 492; *346–378:* 785, 1022

101 *Trajan/Hadrian:* 54; *66–256:* 163; *200–300:* 63, 145

102 *Trajan/Hadrian:* 56, 354

103 *Hasmonaean:* 187; *200–300:* 64, *5th–early 6th century* (1)

104 *Trajan/Hadrian:* 100; *66–256:* 161; *364–375:* 970

105 *Pius:* 71

107 *255–268:* 445, 450

109 *Trajan/Hadrian:* 110, 363; *222–256:* 178, 350; *200–300:* 373, 423; *300–361:* 673; *361–400:* 1322

114 *Flavian:* 74; *Trajan/Hadrian:* 104; *300–361:* 541, 542, 557, 645, 743, 833, 839, 844, 857, 888; *361–375:* 720

115 *Augustan:* 204; *250–300:* 152; *300–361:* 660, 745

116 *383–392:* 1055

117 *346–361:* 815

122 *314:* 500

126 *388–401:* 1029, 1414

130 *100–300:* 65

132 *Flavian:* 76

135 *300–100 B.C.E.:* 386; *Seleucid:* 45; *Augustan:* 355; *Tiberian:* 264; *Neronian:* 68, 332, 335; *Flavian:* 89, 90, 92; *Trajan/Hadrian:* 101, 366; *100 B.C.E.–256 C.E.:* 400, 402; *100–200:* 70; *1–300:* 67; *350–375:* 674

142 *Trajan/Hadrian:* 102; *Severan:* 118; *100 B.C.E.–256 C.E.:* 147, 158, 165, 175, 181, 371, 401, 403, 419; *347–348:* 607, 616

143 *300–200 B.C.E.:* 2; *Seleucid:* 389, 391; *Augustan:* 26; *Herod:* 195; *Archelaus:* 215; *Procurators:* 249, 313, 321, 322, 325, 326, 327, 328, 329, 330, 331, 333, 338, 339; *Neronian:* 37; *Flavian:* 23, 25, 73, 77, 78, 91; *Trajan/Hadrian:* 53, 58, 79, 97, 358, 359, 389, 391; *Severan:* 28; *66–256:* 167, 169

148 *Augustan:* 246; *Trajan/Hadrian:* 361

149 *Neronian:* 315, 324, 337, 341

402 *Hadrian:* 365

A.2

001 *300–361:* 672; *361–400:* 1419; *518–565:* 2214, 2367, 2371; *597–620?:* 2462, 2492, 2595, 2635; *modern* (1)

010 *590/1:* 2454

013 *591/2:* 2456

020 *518–538:* 2395; *614/5:* 2629

023 *582–602:* 2493

024 *527–538:* 2341

031 *Trajan/Hadrian:* 360; *300–361:* 701, 848; *361–400:* 1402; *404–454:* 1487, 1489; *428–533:* 1842; *491–518:* 2160; *518–565:* 2237, 2302, 2308; *5th–6th century* (1)

032 *395–401:* 1416; *574–584:* 2415, 2449

A.3

060 *347–395:* 548, 1060, 1069, 1117, 1219, 1221, 1360; *491–498:* 2168; *5th–early 6th century* (1)

061 *383–388:* 1082

062 *Augustan:* 307; *300–361:* 715, 733, 823, 876; *361–404:* 918, 1043, 1070, 1166, 1338; *404–450:* 1426, 1500; *450–518:* 1614, 1703, 1708

063 *322–363:* 499, 538, 547, 555, 567, 605, 637, 654, 738, 789, 827, 850; *364–395:* 907, 929, 947, 957, 979, 995, 999, 1034, 1037, 1086, 1095, 1137, 1147, 1319, 1333, 1398; *4th century* (2); *375–465:* 1230, 1430, 1504; *491–498:* 2158, 2180; *5th–early 6th century* (2); *602–608:* 2576

064 *308–310:* 483; *491–498:* 2184

068 *364–367:* 900; *476–491:* 1652; *5th–early 6th century* (1)

A.4

002 *300–301:* 477; *527–613:* 2345, 2674

010 *66–256:* 155; *491–498:* 2159

011 *651/2?:* 2724

012 *333–335:* 582

013 *Hasmonaean:* 189

014 *527–538:* 2340

017 *Neronian:* 86

030 *7th–8th century* (1)

031 *383–388:* 1146

033 *351–354:* 617

037 *346–361:* 784; *383–395:* 1349

A.5

005 *346–361:* 812; *631–634:* 2646

012 *5th–early 6th century* (1)

019 *574–608:* 2406, 2438, 2499, 2501

020 *Procurator:* 269; *572–575:* 2420; *589/90:* 2468

021 *518–527:* 2219

023 *100 B.C.E.–256 C.E.:* 418; *383–392:* 1099

034 *534–591:* 2258, 2469; *602–640:* 2570, 2670

035 *Crusader* (1)

036 *383–395:* 1344; *428–533:* 1867

037 *214–215:* 82; *364–378:* 994

045 *351–361:* 713; *527–575:* 2357, 2421; *582–628:* 2480, 2486, 2538, 2681, 2682, 2689

048 *491–565:* 2189, 2374; *602–608:* 2506, 2524, 2567

048e *602–608:* 2551

052 *518–640:* 2396, 2721

080 *602–608:* 2574

104 *346–361:* 783

A.6

026 *Augustan:* 223

041 *378–383:* 928; *5th–early 6th century* (1)

052 *7th–8th century* (1)

083w *631–640:* 2669

096 *595/6:* 2482

102 *584/5:* 2465

115 *Tiberian:* 255

127 *100 B.C.E.–256 C.E.:* 408

128 *537–539:* 2365

B.1

016 *330–383:* 571, 1220; *518–618:* 2445, 2604, 2615, 2632, 2702

022 *330–333:* 563

023 *457–474:* 1612, *548–565:* 2321

038 *574/5:* 2422

047 *606/7:* 2496

048 *491–498:* 2190; *518–641:* 2394, 2640, 2649, 2712

053 *406–408:* 1143

067 *Islamic* (1)

080 *347–348:* 534

084 *425–533:* 1524, 1845; *498–565:* 2206, 2226; *534–565:* 2256; *602–608:* 2510

085 *527–528:* 2378

B.2

B.3

B.4

015 *353–363:* 729

016 *364–367:* 919; *428–533:* 1789; *518–630:* 2408, 2474, 2594, 2610; *7th–8th century* (1)

055 *614–616:* 2710

077 *388–394:* 1201; *568–618:* 2418, 2688

080 *541–549:* 1882; *602–610:* 2568, 2598

201 *Islamic* (1)

306 *7th–8th century* (1)

320 *602–608:* 2526

324 *355–363:* 677; *7th–8th century* (1)

331 *602–608:* 2520

337 *375–465:* 1255; *445–518:* 1747, 1764

501 *404–454:* 1486

B.5

031 *308:* 479; *570/1:* 2411

032 *7th–8th century* (1)

042 *527–565:* 2370; *Islamic* (1)

049 *383–395:* 1337

051 *630/1:* 2661

059 *7th–8th century* (1)

061 *625/6:* 2637

094 *602–608:* 2542

098 *330–335:* 522; *518–578:* 2429; *613–616:* 2663, 2709

110 *589–613:* 2447, 2625

112 *602–608:* 2532

113 *518–610:* 2591

118 *375–533:* 1267, 1858; *602–608:* 2581

120 *599/600:* 2487

134 *613–618:* 2685

135 *602–608:* 2523

139 *602–608:* 2590

166 *100 B.C.E.–256 C.E.:* 413

B.6

033 *Archelaus:* 216

041 *Islamic* (1)

052 *335–337:* 520

064 *7th–8th century* (1)

065 *Islamic* (1)

116 *596–608:* 2460, 2536

122 *613–618:* 2691

B.7

001 *582–608:* 2444, 2507

002 *534–565:* 2268

009 *294–305:* 509; *404–454:* 1488; *428–533:* 1786

B.8

006 *Severan:* 134

013 *351–361:* 770; *7th–8th century* (1)

016 *425–539:* 1441, 2366

022 *498–518:* 2201

025 *445–518:* 1726

028 *457–474:* 1592

043 *406–408:* 1498

044 *375–465:* 1260

045 *383–423:* 1168, 1197

053 *364–378:* 1013

067 *408–518:* 1511, 1658

B.9

002 *7th–8th century* (1)

003 *602–608:* 2584

019 *457–474:* 1621

C.1

103 *361–363:* 721

C.2

C.3

C.4

C.5

C.7

C.8

C.9

C.10

C.11

C.12

C.13

C.14

C.15

C.16

C.17

C.18

C.19

C.20

064 *383–395:* 1321; *445–518:* 1745; *5th–early 6th century* (1); *548–565:* 2319

C.21

004 *5th–early 6th century* (1)

012 *5th–early 6th century* (1)

016 *5th–early 6th century* (1)

023 *modern* (1)

036 *445–518:* 1678; *534–565:* 2301, 2333, 2350

049 *603/4:* 2503

055 *222–256:* 184

074 *518–527:* 2224; *5th–early 6th century* (1)

076 *5th–early 6th century* (1)

078* *347–392:* 560, 722, 775, 777, 808, 840, 854, 873, 874, 883, 885, 966, 1001, 1097, 1112, 1120, 1140, 1203, 1291; *4th century* (3); *375–465:* 1240, 1251, 1258, 1270, 1281, 1335, 1361, 1383, 1466, 1468, 1473, 1503, 1505; *425–457:* 375, 377, 1445, 1451, 1521, 1528, 1537, 1539, 1547, 1553, 1554, 1560, 1568; *457–474:* 1557, 1576, 1580, 1581, 1594, 1600, 1602, 1604, 1606, 1608, 1615, 1639; *445–518:* 1699, 1717, 1731, 1736, 1737, 1761, 1763, 1767, 2165, 2174; *5th–early 6th century* (22); *526–535:* 1885; *534–565:* 2293

079 *383–395:* 1399

080 *355–361:* 723

081 *378–392:* 1310; *428–455:* 1462

085 *383–392:* 1105

086 *351–392:* 648, 678, 867, 1133

097 *330–347:* 545

110 *383–395:* 1328

112 *408–423:* 1452

121 *538–610:* 2616

127 *498–518:* 2203

128 *378–383:* 926

137 *Procurators:* 284; *355–363:* 860, 862

138 *439–477:* 1784; *5th–early 6th century* (2)

141 *100 B.C.E.–256 C.E.:* 410

144 *450–457:* 1543

157 *364–465:* 1011, 1257, 1294, 1309; *428–533:* 1597, 1713, 1814; *5th–early 6th century* (6)

159 *355–474:* 380, 381, 871, 1271, 1282, 1296, 1436, 1450, 1514, 1579, 1587, 1588, 1601, 1609, 1611; *457–533:* 1579, 1626, 1641, 1653, 1681, 1719, 1773, 1787, 1875, 2153, 2166; *534–565:* 2295; *5th–early 6th century* (17)

161 *429–533:* 1798

C.22

133 *330–406:* 543, 1154, 1405, 1409; *425–455:* 1527

134 *4th century* (1); *425–455:* 1517

150 *594/5:* 2457

154 *445–518:* 1721

159 *Procurators:* 268

160 *612/3:* 2673

164 *347–348:* 558

C.23

035* *7th–8th century* (1)

042 *5th–early 6th century* (3)

045 *404–406:* 1187

060 *337–340:* 624

066 *4 B.C.E.–34 C.E.:* 72; *200–256:* 131, 183; *364–375:* 939; *5th–early 6th century* (1)

071 *404–406:* 1475

C.24

003 *571–608:* 2419, 2425, 2562

007 *Flavian:* 398

008 *350–392:* 634, 917, 1297; *518–538:* 2393

037 *631–640:* 2668

039 *603/4:* 2500

041 *518–640:* 2714

C.34

003 *8th century* (1)

C.41

015 *602–608:* 2564

C.42

003 *428–537:* 1824, 2202, 2361; *578–582:* 2440

006 *428–533:* 1832

010* *402–408:* 1427; *445–518:* 1765; *5th–early 6th century* (1)

032 *375–465:* 1234

037 *375–465:* 1229

E.1

023 *423–533:* 1782, 1830; *602–608:* 2577

026 *383–395:* 1354

027 *404–406:* 1477; *5th–early 6th century* (2)

035 *428–533:* 1820

046 *5th–early 6th century* (1)

049 *404–533:* 1455, 1573, 1803

076 *527–565:* 2372

080 *5th–early 6th century* (1)

E.3

047 *423–533:* 1781; *5th–early 6th century* (1)

048 *5th–early 6th century* (1)

054 *Procurators:* 311

055 *569/70:* 2409

061 *579/80:* 2434

074 *445–518:* 1744

E.4

033 *603/4:* 2502

043 *5th–early 6th century* (1); *548–565:* 2322

071 *347–361:* 638, 766, 845; *445–533:* 1572, 1702, 1722, 1794, 1834, 1841, 1850, 1855, 1874, 1883; *534–565:* 2269, 2275, 2298; *5th–early 6th century* (2)

E.5

031 *586–600:* 2446, 2494

037 *428–533:* 1860; *5th–early 6th century* (2)

041 *570/1:* 2410

043 *533–539:* 2281, 2362; *603?:* 2504

052 *428–533:* 1876, 2186; *5th–early 6th century* (1)

063 *375–465:* 1299; *518–610:* 2451, 2614

064 *428–533:* 1840, 2229; *518–640:* 2716

066 *534–539:* 2278

068 *383–395:* 1395

070 *548–565:* 2324; *5th–early 6th century* (1)

073 *428–453:* 1849

105 *491–539:* 2154, 2280

109* *375–465:* 1250, 1446; *491–498:* 2164, 2197

113 *445–565:* 1704, 1718, 2330

116 *257–300:* 511; *375–533:* 1280, 1622, 1691, 1748, 1766, 1833, 2167, 2187, 2192; *5th–early 6th century* (3); *534–565:* 2296; *602–608:* 2569

117 *5th–early 6th century* (1)

E.6

001 *375–465:* 1254, 1540, 1543, 1570; *4th century* (1), *445–533:* 1593, 1617, 1630, 1684, 1693, 1709, 1715, 1716, 1749, 1793, 1815, 1823, 2191, 2196; *518–565:* 1851, 1852, 1856, 1859, 1862, 1884, 2240, 2241, 2254, 2261, 2265, 2267, 2279, 2282, 2285, 2290, 2294, 2305, 2311, 2318, 2356; *5th–early 6th century* (10); *602–608:* 2545, 2583, 2587, 2589

G.2

G.3

G.4

G.5

G.6

G.7

090 *100 B.C.E.–256 C.E.:* 431

097 *7th century:* 2730

103 *Procurators:* 266

106 *268–187 B.C.E.:* 8, 12; *Herodian:* 198

110 *347–378:* 689, 998

116 *Herodian:* 201

122 *Herodian:* 206

126 *Herodian:* 193

128 *383–395:* 1327

G.8

003 *4th century* (1)

010 *Severan:* 127

011 *280–40 B.C.E.:* 397

023 *355–363:* 872

040 *Agrippa:* 308

041 *Herodian:* 208

046 *364–367:* 892

088 *1–300:* 66

100 *Procurators:* 312; *Jewish War:* 348; *100 B.C.E.–256 C.E.:* 174, 430

109 *Procurators:* 286

111 *Agrippa:* 287

112 *Hadrianic:* 367

118* *300–200 B.C.E.:* 384; *Seleucid:* 44

119* *280–40 B.C.E.:* 15, 19, 31, 34, 40, 48, 393

121* *Seleucid:* 13, 33, 49

123* *Seleucid:* 30

G.9

001* *314–361:* 501, 517, 562, 597, 824; *425–474:* 1433, 1628; *5th–early 6th century* (1); *565–578:* 2424; *614/15:* 2628

002 *7th–8th century* (1)

003 *337–340:* 621; *445–518:* 1760

004 *Trajan/Hadrian:* 98; *312–313:* 487; *383–395:* 1392; *445–518:* 1618, 1685

005* *Archelaus:* 212, 218; *1–24:* 5, 245, 254, 256, 260; *100 B.C.E.–256 C.E.:* 409; *250–300:* 510; *300–361:* 494, 531, 564, 583; *361–408:* 942, 951, 1059, 1079, 1188, 1204, 1287, 1499, 1506; *410–450:* 376, 1444, 1460; *428–533:* 1826, 2152; *5th–early 6th century* (1); *534–593:* 2292, 2304, 2399, 2428, 2478; *602–618:* 2512, 2556, 2573, 2679, 2700; *7th–8th century* (1)

012 *247–249:* 142

013 *457–474:* 1625

018 *236–238:* 440; *347–348:* 586; *375–465:* 1227; *428–533:* 1802

020 *Hasmonaean:* 191

034 *364–375:* 967

036 *518–527:* 2215

037* *364–408:* 959, 1492

045 *364–378:* 1009

049 *613–618:* 2703

053 *7th-8th century* (1)

056 *330–335:* 561

057 *Seleucid:* 42; *Herodian:* 199; *Procurators:* 247; *346–361:* 668, 758, 769, 814, 877; *361–375:* 734, 972: *375–465:* 1226, 1273, 1293: *5th–early 6th century* (2)

059 *630:* 2467

061 *4th century* (1); *5th–early 6th century* (1)

066 *346–361:* 793

067* *Archelaus:* 235; *347–378:* 700, 1008; *5th–early 6th century* (1)

068 *Procurators:* 278; *346–361:* 807

081 *Procurators:* 257

084* *Archelaus:* 211, 226; *Procurators:* 244

101 *Archelaus:* 231

109 *364–395:* 920, 1041, 1051, 1382

112 *Archelaus:* 219

G.10

G.11

G.12

G.13

G.14

H.5

H.6

H.7

K.1

K.2

K.3

K.4

L.1

N.1

Index

A

B

C

D

E

F

G

H

I

J

K

L

M

N

O

P

Biographical Information

Jane DeRose Evans (MA, PhD, University of Pennsylvania) is currently an Associate Professor of Art History at Temple University. Her numismatic work began at the American Numismatic Society Graduate Seminar, and she has received the American Numismatic Society Graduate Fellowship to complete her dissertation on propaganda and Republican coins. Her subsequent research has continued to focus heavily on coins, from her book *The Art of Persuasion: Political Propaganda from Aeneas to Brutus* (1992) to articles in *Numismatica e Antichitá Classiche Quaderni Ticinesi*, *Biblical Archaeologist*, the *American Journal of Numismatics*, *Opuscula Romana*, *Latomus*, the *American Numismatic Society Museum Notes*, and the *Transactions of the International Numismatic Congress*. She was named the Metcalf Lecturer for the American Institute of Archaeology in 2003.

Evans currently excavates in southern France, and she has excavated in England, Greece, Italy, and Israel. She also serves as a Fellow of the American Numismatic Society, and is a member of the Royal Numismatic Society, the American Institute of Archaeology, and the American Schools of Oriental Research.

Plates

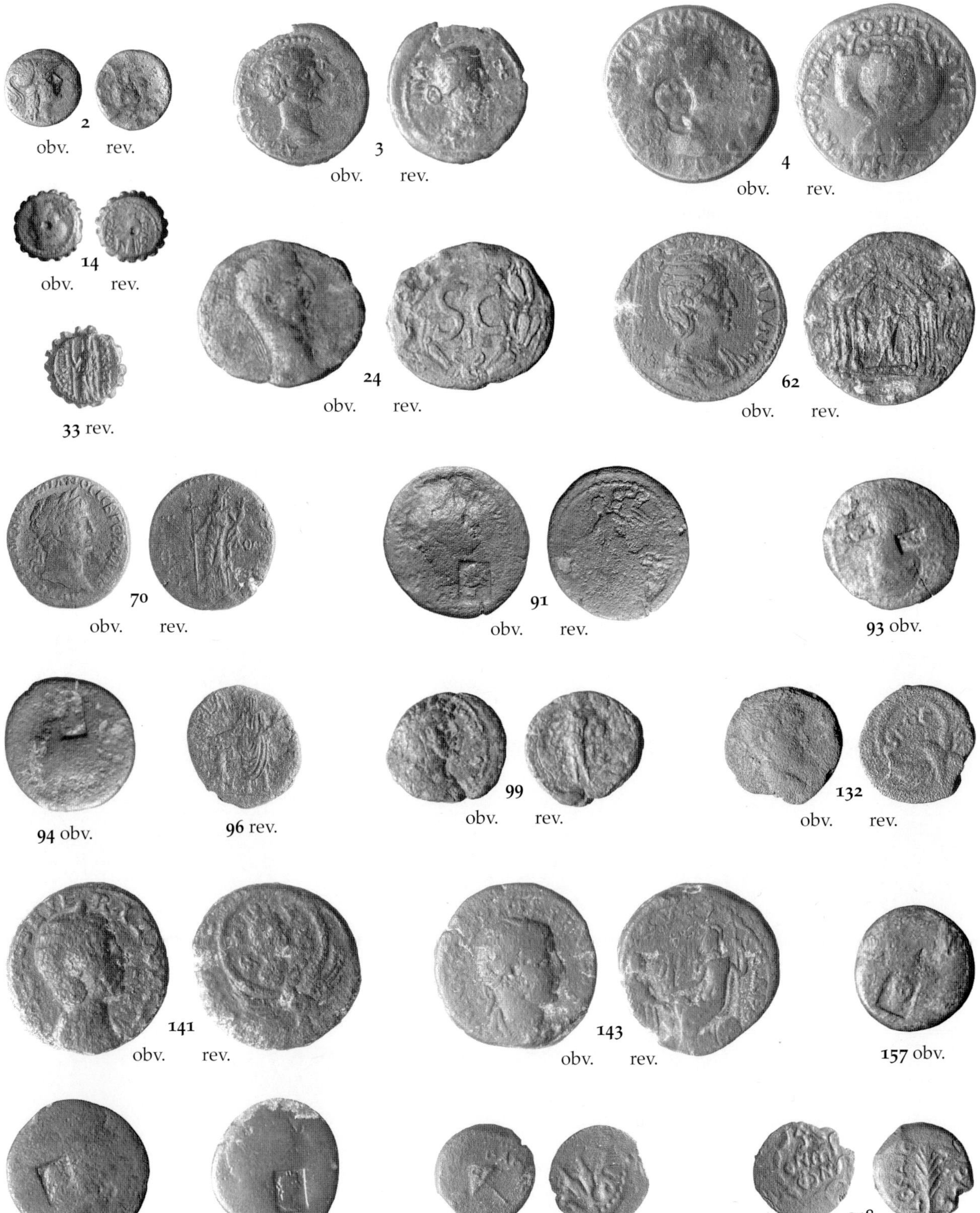

PLATE 1. *Caesarea Coins.*

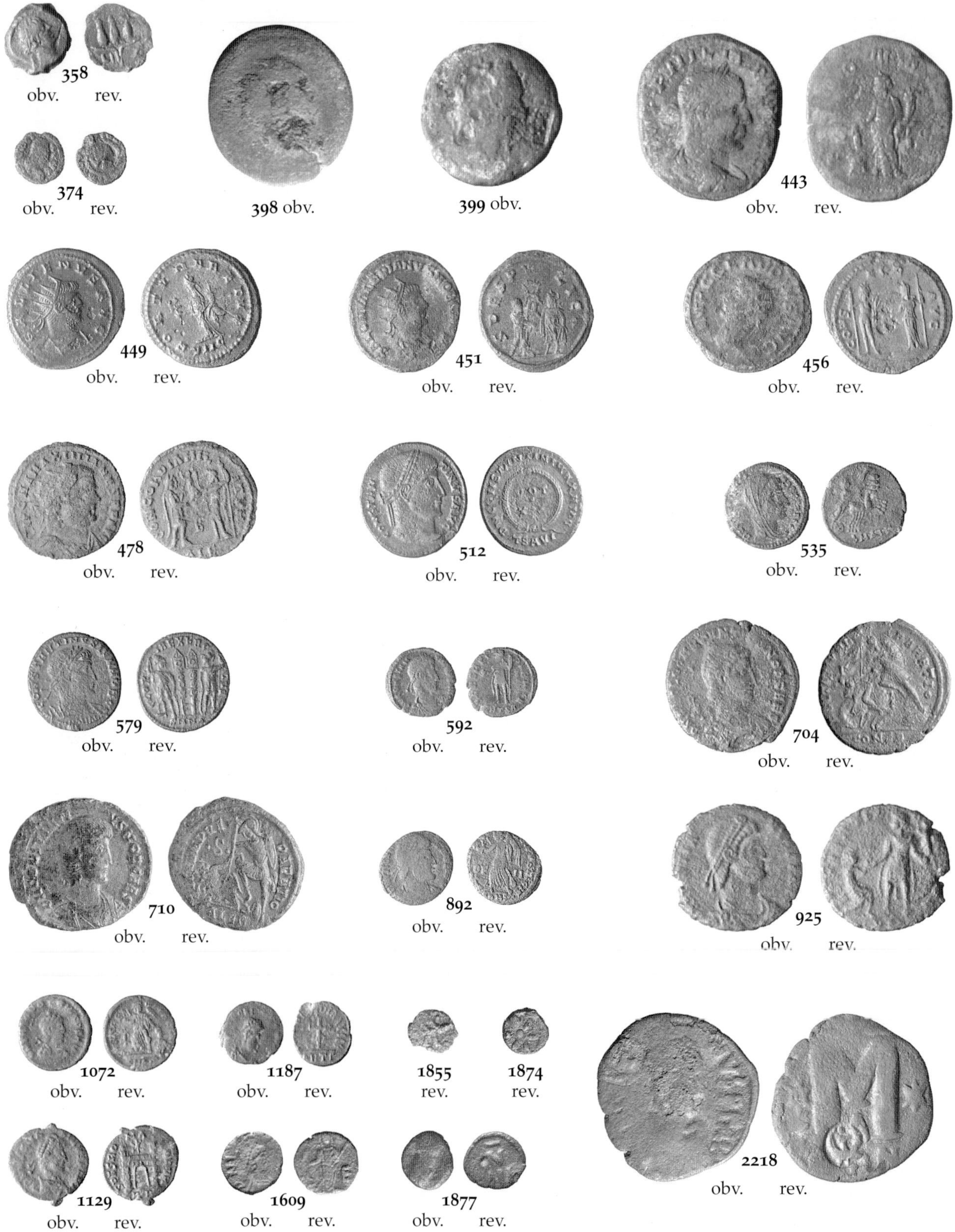

PLATE 2. *Caesarea Coins.*

2220
obv. rev.

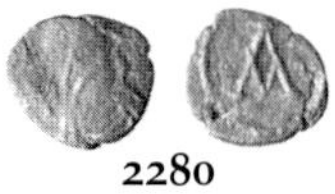

2280
obv. rev.

2326
obv. rev.

2363
obv. rev.

2394
obv. rev.

2453
obv. rev.

2455
obv. rev.

2456
obv. rev.

2461
obv. rev.

2467
obv. rev.

2462 rev.

2474 rev.

2503
obv. rev.

2505
obv. rev.

Plate 3. *Caesarea Coins.*

2620
obv. rev.

2627 rev.

2629 rev.

2645 rev.

2647 rev.

2651
obv. rev.

2654 rev.

2665 rev.

2672 obv.

2674
obv. rev.

2722 obv.

2727
obv. rev.

PLATE 4. *Caesarea Coins.*

Plate 5. *Caesarea Gold Hoard, nos. 1–24.*

PLATE 6. *Caesarea Gold Hoard, nos. 25–49.*

PLATE 7. *Caesarea Gold Hoard, nos. 50–74.*

Plate 8. *Caesarea Gold Hoard, nos. 75–99.*